Typography

Graphic
Design
in Context

Typography

Denise Gonzales Crisp

with primers by William F. Temple

Series Editor Meredith Davis

WITH 320 ILLUSTRATIONS, 264 IN COLOUR

Thames & Hudson

First published in the United Kingdom in 2012 by Thames & Hudson Ltd,
181A High Holborn, London WC1V 7QX

British Library Cataloguing-in-Publication Data
A catalogue record for this book is available from the British Library

ISBN 978-0-500-29050-7

Printed and bound in China by 1010 Printing International Ltd

To find out about all our publications, please visit **www.thamesandhudson.com**.
There you can subscribe to our e-newsletter, browse or download our current catalogue,
and buy any titles that are in print.

CONTENTS

foreword

MEREDITH DAVIS
Professor of Graphic Design, North Carolina State University

This book was written principally by Denise Gonzales Crisp, a highly respected educator with a distinguished history as a designer of inventive form. She brings that groundbreaking attitude to this discussion of typography, which represents a significant break in the tradition of how the subject is taught.

Most books on typography follow a familiar conceptual framework: a discussion of print-based form based on gradually increasing complexity, from the letter, to the word, to the paragraph, to the page, to the document. I believe this traditional structure is a residue from pre-digital times when the only way students could generate type was to draw letters and render facsimiles of set text by hand, yet it persists as an explanation of the medium and as an organizing principle for college-level typography courses.

Likewise, most typography books focus student attention on a few classical typefaces as representatives of historical classifications and a technological lineage that simply adds screen-based displays of text to the end of a print-based history.

The problem with these strategies is that current technology doesn't allow students to defer decisions about such issues as line spacing and page proportions. Software confronts students with simultaneous requests for specifications on these variables, and the only alternative to addressing them is to default to whatever settings the programmers have determined are optimal.

Further, we can question whether it is reasonable to deny students access to the expressive array of fonts that defines the digital communication environment, especially on the heels of post-modern challenges to notions of "good form." Given that technology now allows beginning students to design and set their own typefaces,

0.1 Packaging for Jamie Oliver Enterprises, 2009. Sarah Pidgeon and Natalie Chung, Pearlfisher.

0.2 House of Terror museum exterior, Budapest, Hungary, 2001–2. Attila F. Kovács.

0.3 "Typefaces of the World" poster, 2010. Shelby White.

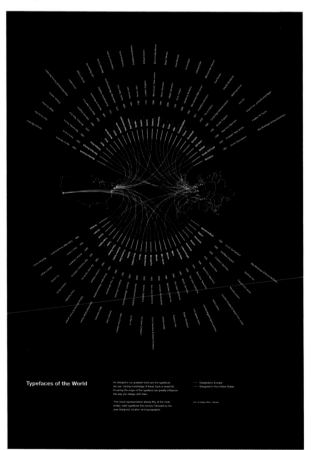

one might argue that designing a font and seeing it set in text is a powerful way of determining what does and doesn't constitute good typographic form. And for today's students, the reality is not that they will first design print applications and then move to screen-based contexts. Instead, it is likely that much of their work will live solely in digital environments, so it is important that their typographic education instills principles and predispositions that are based in screen-based contexts as well as print.

What is demanded by the contemporary design context is an understanding of systems: a recognition that design problems arise from and have consequences in the complex interactions between people, objects, and the settings in which they reside. In a typographic sense, this means that form, language, and technology interact in ways that are specific to particular physical, social, and historical contexts, as well as to the behaviors of readers. For this reason, typographic variables are always relational and situated: they defy hard-and-fast rules for "good form" and they are interpreted on the basis of particular circumstances.

Denise Gonzales Crisp has authored a text that acknowledges these conditions. Her engaging discussion presents students with a way of thinking about typography that resonates with their own experiences in a visual world. The text asks students to make critical judgments about typographic form, taking into consideration intention, context, and audience. Her narrative is bolstered by the primers, written by William F. Temple, that introduce each chapter. These primers offer concise definitions of key terms, and different historical and technical perspectives on the concepts discussed in the main text.

I believe a change in how we teach typography is long overdue: curricula need to catch up with the world outside of school. Denise provides a way of thinking about type that suggests a path for teachers and students that is both challenging and responsive to current conditions. I believe it will go a long way to shaping the future of typographic education in colleges and universities.

introduction

DENISE GONZALES CRISP

// THE PREMISE

Seasoned graphic designers usually have a firm grasp of typographic conventions and standards, the precedents against which "good" or "bad" typography is measured. Yet knowledge of them does not guarantee sensitivity to the subtlety or the variability of visual communication. This book addresses conventions and standards, certainly. At its heart, though, is the assertion that these precedents were founded in, and are perpetuated by, specific circumstances that must be understood as well. I maintain that teaching students how and why typography works, or does not work, at any given moment, helps equip them to expect, and to embrace, the ever-changing environment of contemporary typography. I place typographic practice at the intersection of the systems that influence it: vital social and cultural dynamics, written language systems, reader interpretation, material variability, changing technologies, and long-established design traditions. For instance, I present the "rules" of typography as components of larger systems—tastes, traditions, and reading practicality—rather than as the rules. Students introduced to these systems can learn to scrutinize and maneuver within new situations, new technologies, and new reading environments. Sensitizing students to contextual factors better prepares them to negotiate the varying contexts they will continue to confront. As their careers unfold, these future professionals will have the tools to respond imaginatively to any set of parameters, and to innovate—the life blood of any discipline.

0.4 Carved directional signs, Bass Lake, California, 2011.

Typographic practice is interconnected with cultural currents of all kinds. I offer *Typography* with the aim of encouraging students to become flexible in, and open to, a world that does and will include many varieties and uses of typography—a world where typography is not absolutely and always one fixed thing. I hope, also, to help new typographers see that their own moments are just as rich in creative potential as those of their honored predecessors.

0.5 Book spread from *Everyone is a Designer! Manifest for the Design Economy*, 2003. Mieke Gerritzen.

NOTES TO EDUCATORS ///////////////////////////////////

Typography is written to serve as a core textbook for typography course sequences, though the content would also suit graphic design and interdisciplinary studio courses where typography figures prominently.

I structured this book on a "need-to-know" basis. This organizational approach is consistent with the book's overarching premise: context is everything. I hold the related opinion that we humans learn languages, including visual and typographic languages, most effectively when we encounter that language in use. In other words, we learn language most concretely when we experience the parts in action. Whether we discover concepts and vocabulary through reading, making, or evaluating, understanding occurs *because* the terms are embedded in the context that creates their meaning.

PRIMERS

At the start of each chapter is a primer, written by William F. Temple, that defines typography terminology (serif, monospace), details technical and historical references (PostScript, lock up), and explains concepts (aesthetic, vernacular). The use of **bold text** in main chapters indicates that a definition of that word is in the primer. The underlining of a term in the main text refers to an extended discussion of this tangential topic in the margins of the page. Page numbers accompany each primer entry to refer students back to the main chapter content.

The decision to disperse fundamental terms throughout primers is informed by my many years of teaching studio courses. First, students more readily embrace and employ vocabulary, or understand the significance of, say, historical technologies, when they apply these otherwise abstract terms and histories to current typographic practice. Second, spreading the delivery of specialized terms over a longer span of time aids retention. If students learn a few new terms at one time, they are more able to grasp and use each one immediately.

0.6   Locked-up metal type.

An additional impetus is that some design students are less inclined to appreciate the exacting nature of the discipline, or are intimidated by typography in the early stages. I have found that measured dissemination of "the boring stuff" helps students warm to typography. They soon find themselves pursuing the subject with interest.

The relationship between primer and main chapter content, then, characterizes the principle of contextualized language learning. The concept of "type weight," for example, is not introduced within an explanation of font attributes but within a specific context—a discussion about relational form. Students do not learn the term in isolation: they are immediately taught *how* the term is meaningful.

I am aware that current curricular planning often calls for typography course sequences to begin with such concepts as the anatomy of letterforms, Vox typeface classification, and typesetting terminology. While the primers do cover all this material, their chief function is to serve students as they work through the main chapter content. Nonetheless, *Typography* can accommodate this kind of curriculum. Related terminology frequently appears in the same primer because the terms are relevant to one discussion. If not, the index, where all basic vocabulary is highlighted in boldface, will be useful. Suggestions on how to use the primers can be found under "Notes to Students" below.

CHAPTERS

Although chapters, sections, and subsections can be read independently, in any sequence, I do have reasons for presenting the material in the order you find it. All six chapter topics are of equal concern, but the sequence anticipates students' developing understanding and sophistication. It will help to know, too, that Chapters 1 through 5 share a similar conceptual framework. They open with discussions of the relevant systems in play, then move to formal issues, and conclude with matters of communication. System, form, message. It would be fruitless to interpret these ordering schemes as representing progressive complexity. The "relational" perspective is complicated from the get-go.

The first chapter, "Relational Systems," provides an overview and initiation into typographic systems, formal attributes, and message communication. "Reading Systems" follows directly because typography usually implies reading and the reader, even if that reader is only the typographer. This topic precedes the third chapter, "Formal Systems," because one might need to understand the nature of reading systems in order to learn how grids work, for instance, or how composition and reader navigation are interrelated. "Formal Systems" further addresses aesthetic and practical aspects of form-making (including a few important rules), which is discussed in terms of visual phenomena and cultural dynamics. "Materiality" follows on logically, describing a variety of possible manifestations. The fifth chapter, "Language Systems," gets into the cultural underpinnings of, and extensive options for, a full range of typographic expression and, ultimately, communication. The last chapter, "The Disorder of Things," explores the rather messy dictates of, for instance, production (i.e. measuring systems) and professional semantics (i.e. classification)—systems that influence what is likely to be produced.

In many instances the main chapters reveal essential concepts through several lenses. The first chapter initiates a discussion of hierarchy, focusing on its relational aspects. Later chapters present the significance of hierarchy to reading (in the chapter "Reading Systems"); how color and contrast affect hierarchy (in "Formal Systems"); and hierarchy as a means of exploiting visual syntax (in "Language Systems").

USING THIS BOOK

As mentioned above, the topics and concepts that make up *Typography* can be assigned in the order published, over several semesters. An introductory course might require all six primers, plus Chapters 1 and 2. Chapters 3 and 4 might provide a blueprint for an intermediate course, and the last two chapters for an advanced course. Following this sequence may ask you to rethink your curriculum slightly, or design a new set of projects that reflect the concepts introduced. I hope the book's premise will prompt educators to do so.

Because sections can be read out of sequence, however, this book easily adapts to any typography curriculum. A first semester might pair the "Formal Systems" section in Chapter 1 with the "pattern, variation, and contrast" discussion found in Chapter 3, followed by sections on materiality in Chapter 4, and measuring and classification systems in Chapter 6. The second semester might include reading and language discussions, particularly Chapters 2 and 5, but also related topics scattered throughout the book. The third semester would then focus on hierarchy and grids, on style, voice, and typographic expression, all found in Chapters 1, 3, and 4.

I advise against assigning the entire book in a single semester, although I realize not all graphic design curricula include three, or even two, discrete typography courses. Grasping the complexity of the concepts requires that students apply them through making, and reflect on them through discussion and writing. Students also need time to identify and observe the principles functioning in the world around them; and time to create typography that demonstrates comprehension and successful negotiation of the many factors that influence typographic production.

In the case of curricula limited to a single typography course, I suggest assigning sections that you consider to be the "basics" of typography. Other graphic design studio courses might then assign the remaining sections where they serve the relevant course objectives. Of course, only you can determine which sections are pertinent to your course. If it helps, here are my recommendations: "Dynamic Relationships" (Chapter 1); "Traditions and Tastes," "Typography Takes the Lead," and "Reading Contexts" (Chapter 2); "Mediating Formal Systems" and "Pattern, Variation, and Contrast" (Chapter 3); "The Four Typesetting Revolutions," "The Hot-to-Cold, Stone-to-Pixel Life of Trajan," "Tool and Medium," "Typographic Craft," and "The Means and the Ends" (Chapter 4); and "Measurement Systems" and "More Fuzzy Categories" (Chapter 6).

0.7 *Big Type Says More*, installation at Museum Boijmans van Beuningen, Rotterdam, 2007. Ryan Pescatore Frisk and Catelijne van Middelkoop, Strange Attractors Design.

NOTES TO STUDENTS ///////////////////////////////////////

I cannot predict what you, a student fairly new to typography, expect from a typography textbook. As you embark on what will be a long and thrilling (well, sort of) adventure, I can offer a little insight into how and why this book might be useful.

It will help to read through the content listings found at the beginning of the six chapters before you embark. You probably noticed that words like "relational" and "relationship" show up quite a bit, especially in the first chapter. That's because typography—the making of it, the physicality of it, the reading of it—is shaped by a host of parts that intersect all at once. You will negotiate their relationship to each other every time you design. This book discusses how and why the parts work (or don't work) by focusing on the contexts within which they work (or don't). The goal is to help you foresee and maneuver within these contexts as you design. In fact, if the book has a motto, it's this: context is everything.

Neither you nor I can know what your future contexts will be. But we do know that you will find yourself in many different circumstances; that you will encounter new technologies, unfamiliar languages, and new collaborators over the course of your design education, and beyond. One thing I can promise you: forces beyond your control will always be at play. Your work will be conceived, produced, distributed, interpreted, and possibly preserved within the confines of various systems. This book will help you prepare to maneuver within them.

The first chapter provides an overview of these two broad but essential concepts: "relational" and "system." It also introduces such key typographic principles as hierarchy, typeface design logic, and style. The subsequent five chapters describe how systems prevail on typographic practice. The five you will study are: reading systems—all that pertains to readers, including their needs and expectations; formal systems—the realm of color across media, for instance, or of typographic structures; material systems—forces that affect both actual and virtual physical aspects of typography; language systems—specifically, the language of visual communication as it relates to typography; and finally, descriptive systems—the somewhat inconsistent terms by which designers describe and define typography.

PRIMERS, MARGINS, AND INDEX

As you read this book, you will encounter words set in **bold**, which indicates that additional information awaits you in the chapter primer. The primers offer definitions of typographic and technological terminology, historical details, and general design terms. I recommend that you complete the assigned reading first, rather than jump back and forth as you read. If you do not understand the full implications of a term, don't worry. In time you will. Jot down highlighted words as you read them. When you have finished reading a section or sections, take the list to the primer to read the definitions all at once. Alternatively, without keeping a list, revisit the sections that you just read, locate the highlighted terms again, and, one by one, refer back to the primer. Or devise your own method.

Factoids and tidbits occasionally appear in the margins alongside the main text. They are not crucial to comprehending the content of the chapter, but do provide a little background on the fly. The brief remarks might sketch out the origins of a typeface referred to in the text, or define a term or idiom that is otherwise unrelated to typographic practice. These remarks are cued by underlined text in the main discussion.

With so many things to learn, and so much reference material at hand, the index will be a useful tool, particularly for locating typographic terms that are defined in the primers. Imagine the moment in the future when you cannot for the life of you remember what a "finial" is. Why would you? It's been an eon since you first read about it. You could do an online search, or you could use the index. The latter option has an important advantage. The index leads you to primer entries, which include page numbers that refer you back to the main discussion. Remember: context is everything. Of course, the index is also generally useful when you need to revisit or cross-reference certain topics.

BEYOND THIS BOOK

I have described what this book is about, and have recommended how to use it. Now I will speculate (since I'm no fortune teller) on the skills and knowledge you could gain from reading the book, should you grasp and practice its principles. Mighty typographic powers are in store, to be sure.

You will be fearless and agile, embracing all kinds of typographic form. Yet you will not tolerate mediocrity. You will be flexible, responsive to any means of production and to all reading circumstances. The typography that you and your collaborators will fashion keenly reflects the needs and wants of people (including you), and communicates the intricacies of the message. You will be a trusty friend to readers, sensitive to their situations and tolerances. Your command of visual rhetoric (look it up in the index) will engage readers. Your typography will motivate people! You will be a faithful guardian of typographic traditions, but also a fair-minded assessor of new practices. In fact, you will instigate new practices. You will think in two, three, and four dimensions. The realms of current media will be your playgrounds; emerging technologies your new frontiers. I believe you will be unstoppable. Actually, I think you will become a Supreme Dominator of Typography. And who doesn't want to be that? Let's get going.

0.8   Opening titles for *Typophile Film Festival 5*, 2009. Studio DVA (Brigham Young University students taught by Brent Barson and Wynn Burton).

relational

systems 1

Chapter 1 introduces the interconnectedness of systems, with a particular focus on what those systems are, and how their influence makes typographic practice "relational," a concept that is described here. The discussion presents concepts and principles that permeate the subsequent chapters: why understanding the contexts within which we work is crucial to design and typography; how contexts affect the production and interpretation of typographic messages; how meaning is constructed within the visual language of typography; and aspects of hierarchy. Specifically, this chapter addresses the logic of letterform and typeface design, the difference between typographic roles and expression, and the ways in which typographic form, style, and voice combine with words and readers to enable the communication of messages.

primer

AESTHETIC

The term "aesthetics" means the study of beauty and its effect on human experience, but in common usage it also means an arrangement of sensory attributes that create a particular visual style or feel of something. Typographically, a "biker" aesthetic might refer to capital letters circling patches sewn into a leather jacket, blackletter tattoos with scripted flourishes, and "Harley Davidson" engraved in chrome. On the other hand, "runner" typography might recall the digital numerals on stopwatches or the bold names of Nike or Converse molded in the soles of shoes or screen-printed on active wear. Typographers achieve an "aesthetic" through sensitive use of formal and material references that evoke a cultural context or social group. **> PAGE 26**

ALTERNATES

Formal variations in characters supplied as glyphs within a typeface or as a completely separate variation of the typeface. Alternates often add decorative flourishes and calligraphic details to individual characters, join more than one character in a ligature, and offer variations that are easier to read at small sizes. **ILL. 01 > PAGE 42**

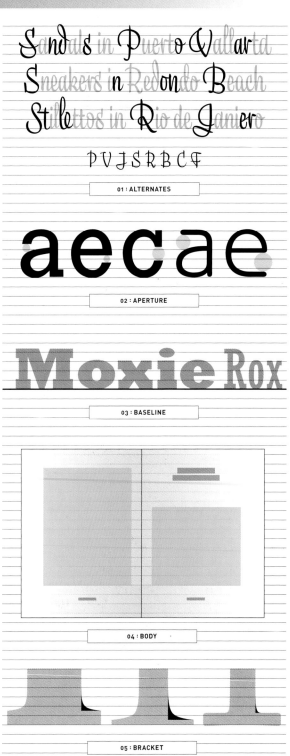

01 : ALTERNATES

02 : APERTURE

03 : BASELINE

04 : BODY

05 : BRACKET

APERTURE

The opening between strokes that makes a counter (see opposite) only partially closed. In such letters as a, c, and e the aperture is typically proportional to the x-height of the typeface. Typefaces with small x-heights frequently have large apertures so the counter appears open at small sizes. **ILL. 02 > PAGE 42**

ASCENDER

The vertical stroke of a lowercase letter that extends above the meanline. The letters b, d, h, and k have ascenders. Some ascenders are taller than the capital letters, others stop at the capline. **ILL. 08 > PAGE 45**

BASELINE

The invisible shared line on which capital and lowercase letters sit. Curved or pointed letters, such as o and v, often fall slightly below the baseline to adjust optically for their diminished points of contact with the line. **ILL. 03 > PAGE 46**

BODY

Related paragraphs of text in a typographic composition. "Body" typically refers to the primary copy set at text point sizes and supported by headlines, captions, raised quotations, and folios with different typographic qualities. **ILL. 04 > PAGE 51**

BRACKET

The transitional wedge-shaped form through which a serif joins a stroke. A "bracketed-serif" typeface, or "adnate" typeface, graduates from thin to thick as it nears the stroke. In typefaces without brackets, such as "slab serifs," the perpendicular serif meets the vertical stroke without any transition. Typefaces without brackets are called "unbracketed" or "abrupt." **ILL. 05 > PAGE 47**

CAP-HEIGHT

The height of capital or uppercase letters measured as the distance between the baseline and capline. Curved letters, such as C, O, and S, often extend above the capline to compensate optically for their diminished points of contact with the line. **ILL. 06 > PAGE 43**

CHARACTER

A single member of a typeface. Typefaces also include alphabetic and non-alphabetic characters (including numerals, punctuation, and any other forms that can be set within text). **> PAGE 42**

COLUMN

A rectangular setting of body copy, defined by line length, margins, and the number of lines of text. Columns may be set flush left/rag right, flush right/rag left, centered, or justified (in which all lines begin and end at the edges of the column). **> PAGE 26**

COMPOSITION

The arrangement of elements within a visual field or page. Composition is also a term that refers to typesetting. **> PAGE 51**

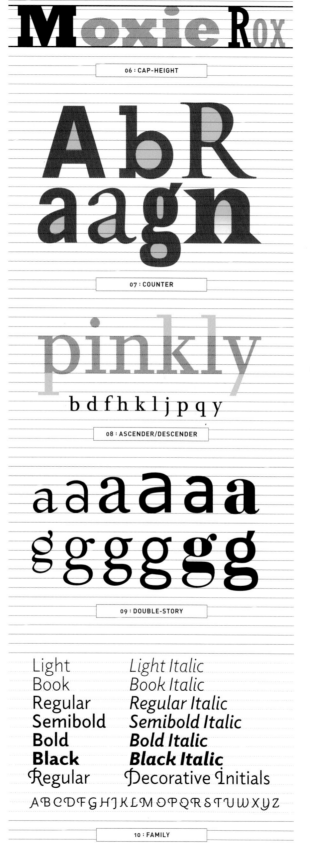

06 : CAP-HEIGHT

07 : COUNTER

08 : ASCENDER/DESCENDER

09 : DOUBLE-STORY

Light	Light Italic
Book	Book Italic
Regular	Regular Italic
Semibold	Semibold Italic
Bold	**Bold Italic**
Black	**Black Italic**
Regular	Decorative Initials

ABCDFGHJKLMOPQRSTUWXYZ

10 : FAMILY

COUNTER

The partially or fully enclosed space within a letterform. The visual impression of a typeface is influenced by how open its counters appear in relation to character strokes. **ILL. 07 > PAGE 41**

DESCENDER

The vertical stroke of a lowercase letter that falls below the baseline. The letters g, p, q, and y have descenders. **ILL. 08 > PAGE 45**

DOUBLE-STORY

The stacked features of the lowercase a and g in some typefaces. The bowl and finial of the a and the bowl and lower loop of the g represent two "stories." **ILL. 09 > PAGE 46**

ELEMENT

A distinct part of a visual composition, such as a photograph, word, or graphic shape. **> PAGE 26**

ENCODE/DECODE

To transfer meaning from producers of objects to consumers of objects. The sociologist Stuart Hall describes encoding and decoding as the production and interpretation of culture. Filmmakers, photographers, and automobile designers, for example, imbue films, magazines, and sports cars with material qualities that consumers use in constructing meaning. Type designers also encode meaning in form that goes beyond the literal meaning of words. **> PAGE 28**

FAMILY

All the variations, including different variations in weight, proportion, and posture, of a single typeface. The full collection of the font Hoefler Text, designed by Jonathan Hoefler in 1991, has twenty-seven different variations, including Roman, Italic, Black Swash Small Caps, and Fleurons & Arabesques. Hoefler Text is a typeface family and Hoefler Text Black Italic Alternate is one variation within that family. The illustration shows the family Elido. **ILL. 10 > PAGE 36**

FIGURE–GROUND

The relationship between an element (figure) and the visual field on which it sits (ground)—sometimes called "positive and negative space." There is an implied hierarchy in the figure–ground relationship: a figure advances and ground recedes. In some compositions, however, equal amounts of figure and ground cause the eye to perceive the same elements as simultaneously advancing and receding. **ILL. 11 > PAGE 40**

FIGURES (NUMERALS)

The set of characters standing for the arabic numerals from zero through nine. Typefaces sometimes have both lining figures, which share a baseline and cap-height, and old-style figures, which are of different heights and dip below the baseline or extend above the x-height. **ILL. 12 > PAGE 56**

FOLIO

A page number, from the Latin for "leaf." **> PAGE 51**

11 : FIGURE–GROUND

1234567890

NON-LINING FIGURES (OLD-STYLE)

1234567890

LINING FIGURES

12 : FIGURES (NUMERALS)

13 : GLYPH

Sam & Tony's
Charming Oddities
Vigorous

14 : GROTESQUE

FONT

A digital typeface sold singly or with other weight, proportion, or posture variations within the same family. Before digital typography, "font" referred to all the characters of a single typeface at a single point size. Metal type was sorted by point size, with all letters of the same typeface and point size stored in a single drawer; a "font" consisted of all the letters in the drawer. **> PAGE 32**

FOUNDRY

An organization that designs, produces, licenses, and distributes typefaces. The term refers to a time when type was cast in metal. Today's digital typefaces are downloaded from the web, yet the name persists. **> PAGE 32**

GLYPH

Any single character in a typeface. Letters of the alphabet, numerals, graphic symbols, and punctuation marks are glyphs. Some fonts are made up of glyphs that are ornamental, such as dingbats. **ILL. 13 > PAGE 30**

GROTESQUE

An early descriptor for sans-serif typefaces. The term today refers to sans-serif typefaces that harbor attributes of traditional fonts. **ILL. 14 > PAGE 43**

HIERARCHY

An organization of elements in a composition that assigns greater importance to some elements than to others. Hierarchy in typography uses visual properties to distinguish and create emphasis among kinds of information. Scale, making one element larger than another, is one commonly used property, as is value, making one element darker than another. A common hierarchical convention, using the principle of value, is to set the title of a document in bold and the main text in roman. **> PAGE 49**

ITALIC

One of three possible variations within a typeface family designating posture. Italics have a slanted posture, a calligraphic quality, and usually a narrower set-width compared with other variations in a family. Italics were invented in Venice at the end of the fifteenth century to use paper more efficiently by having the smallest set-width possible without a marked decrease in legibility. **> PAGE 46**

LANGUAGE

A system of communication through which members of a cultural group interact with each other and exchange meaning. Language involves the arrangement of written or spoken words into syntactical patterns controlled by a set of rules called "grammar." By extension, music, architecture, and dance are also languages. Typographic language, as distinct from the literal meaning of text, refers to any visual system in which letterforms are included and can speak with a particular "dialect"; the typographic language of graffiti, for example, is clearly differentiated from language systems found in classical book typography. **ILL. 15 > PAGE 28**

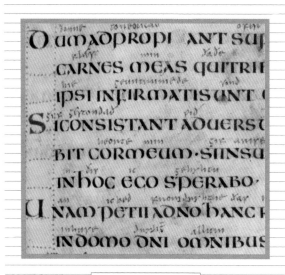

15 : LANGUAGE

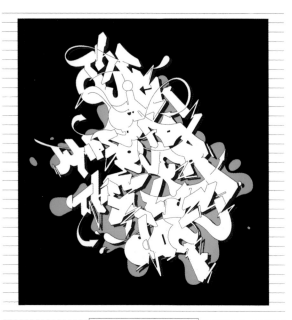

16 : LETTERFORM

THE VASTNESS OF SEAS
The Solidity of Earth
The Trickle of Time

17 : LETTERSPACING

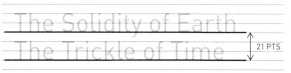

The Solidity of Earth
The Trickle of Time

21 PTS

18 : LINE SPACING

LETTERFORM

The design of individual letters and their parts, including the relationships among strokes, counters, and serifs. While all typography involves considerations of letterform, the term also encompasses the various calligraphic traditions, such as the uncial, which preceded the invention of movable type and have contributed to type design ever since. **ILL. 16 > PAGE 26**

LETTERSPACING

The uniform alteration of the spaces between three or more consecutive letters in a word. Alteration of the single space between two letters is called kerning. **ILL. 17 > PAGE 44**

LINE SPACING

The distance from baseline to baseline in a paragraph of text. This measurement was originally called "leading" as a reference to thin strips of lead added between lines of handset metal type to increase the vertical distance between lines of type. **ILL. 18 > PAGE 56**

LOWERCASE

The smaller letters in a typeface that sit between the baseline and meanline or possess an ascender or descender. The distinction between minuscule (smaller letters) and majuscule (capital) letters in a typeface dates to the tenth century. The term also refers to the location of metal type in drawers used by typesetters; the smaller letters were positioned in the type case below the larger ones. **ILL. 19 > PAGE 32**

MARGIN

The space around the edge of a page and that surrounds columns of text. "Gutters" are the spaces between columns. When setting up a digital document, software frequently asks for the size of margins and gutters, thus determining the size of columns by the space that is left over. **> PAGE 26**

MEANLINE

The implied horizontal line that delimits the height of such lowercase letters as a, r, and n. The curves of lowercase letters with ascenders, such as b, are also drawn to the meanline. The term implies a "midline" between baseline and cap-height, but in fact the meanline position depends upon the designed height of the lowercase letters. **ILL. 20 > PAGE 45**

MESSAGE

A communication recorded for reception. By sending messages through visual and spatial cues, typography enlivens our experience of information in the absence of direct communication. The term can also refer to meanings received by a reader or intended by a typographer, or both. These different messages may not always correspond. For example, the intended message of "masculine" might be delivered by the use of a "sophisticated" and "urbane" serif typeface, but when set next to an image of a galloping mustang it might color the message as "aggressive" or "athletic" instead. In this case the typographer intended, and the reader received, the message "masculine," but each with very different senses in mind. **> PAGE 26**

19 : LOWERCASE

Moxie Rox

20 : MEANLINE

Neither parallel
nor *perpendicular*

21 : OBLIQUE

1 INCH

72 POINTS = 6 PICAS = 1 INCH

1 POINT   12 PTS = 1 PICA

22 : POINT AND PICA

53 PT. TYPE

Exquisite

23 : POINT SIZE

Olive *Olive*
oleander

24 : POSTURE

OBLIQUE

The slanted version of a roman typeface, usually associated with geometric sans-serif typefaces. Italic typefaces also slant to the right but retain the more calligraphic qualities of humanist typefaces and scripts. **ILL. 21 > PAGE 46**

POINT AND PICA

The traditional units of typographic measurement. A point (or pt) is roughly $1/72$ of an inch. There are twelve points in a pica. The baseline-to-baseline vertical measurement of lines of type in a column is usually expressed in points, while the horizontal length of a line of type is expressed in picas. **ILL. 22 > PAGE 40**

POINT SIZE

The measurement used to designate the size of a letterform. Originally, point size referred to the vertical measurement of the body, a piece of lead or wood that held a raised letterform for printing (which allowed lines of type to be set one on top of the other without the letters touching), rather than to the actual size of the letterform itself. Today, digital point size refers to the height of an invisible "bounding box" in which the letterform sits. **ILL. 23 > PAGE 40**

POSTURE

The angle of a typeface that distinguishes the upright roman variation from the slanted italic or oblique. **ILL. 24 > PAGE 42**

SANS SERIF

A typeface without serifs. The terminals (ends of strokes) have no perpendicular lines. Sans-serif faces were used on signs and buildings in England as early as 1816 but did not become popular until 100 years later, when they were used by the European avant-garde to reflect its fascination with machine forms and geometry, as well its rejection of nostalgic references to the past.

ILL. 25 > PAGE 32

SCRIPT

A typeface that mimics handwriting. Like cursive writing, script typefaces have connecting strokes that join letters to one another. **> PAGE 32**

SERIF

Short perpendicular shapes at the ends of strokes in a letterform. It is thought that serifs originated with stone carvers as they tapped the end of each stroke with a chisel to emphasize the alignment of letters. Some serifs are bracketed, graduating in width from where they join the stroke to their end. "Adnate" serifs flow continuously from the stroke, while "abrupt" serifs are noticeably angled.

ILLS. 25/26 > PAGE 27

SET-WIDTH

The width of a letter, including the spaces to the left and right that keep adjacent letters from touching. Set-width varies for each letter at each point size, but is calculated to create optically equal distances between most letter combinations. In photo and digital fonts, set-width is measured in units, a horizontal division of the em. Unlike letterspacing in metal type, the distance between digitally set letters can be reduced by removing units.

ILL. 27 > PAGE 43

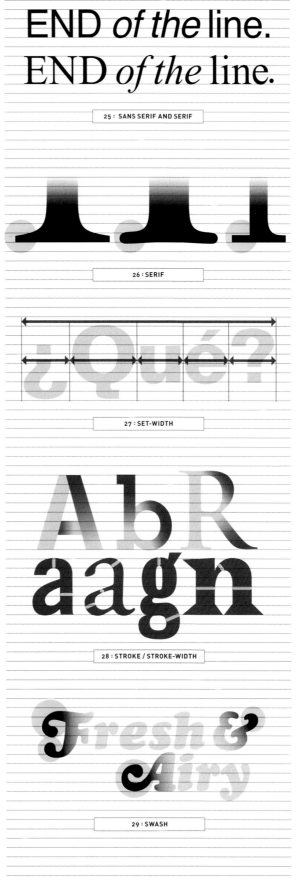

25 : SANS SERIF AND SERIF

26 : SERIF

27 : SET-WIDTH

28 : STROKE / STROKE-WIDTH

29 : SWASH

SLAB SERIF

A heavy, block-like, usually unbracketed serif. Slab serifs are often thicker than the strokes in the typeface. Typefaces with slab serifs are called "Egyptian" and emerged early in the nineteenth century as precursors to sans-serif or grotesque typefaces.
> PAGE 50

STROKE

Any continuous linear element in a letterform. The name refers to the hand gestures required to draw the letterform. **ILL. 28 > PAGE 41**

STROKE-WIDTH

The weight or thickness of strokes typical of each typeface. All typefaces, regardless of appearance, have some variation in stroke-width. Even the strokes of geometric sans-serif typefaces, which appear to have a uniform stroke-width, narrow at certain points in the letterform. For example, were strokes to maintain a uniform weight where they join in the letter k, there would be too much visual weight at the site of convergence. Therefore, these strokes taper slightly to maintain optical evenness. The difference in the thicks and thins of strokes is called "modeling" or "modulation." **ILL. 28 > PAGE 43**

SWASH

A decorative flourish that extends strokes and serifs. Swashed letters may be alternates for selected letterforms or the basis of a complete typeface, as in swash capitals. **ILL. 29 > PAGE 42**

SYMBOL

A type of graphic sign which, through some conventional use or cultural understanding, represents a person, place, thing, or idea. The alphabet is symbolic; "cow" and "vaca" both describe a farm animal, but in different languages, and it is only cultural agreement that allows speakers of each language to connect the letters to the animal. Other symbols bear some likeness to the things they stand for. The pictographic symbols for "barber shop" and "beauty salon" are understood, through context and social use, to signify gender-specific grooming services. **ILL. 30 > PAGE 30**

TEMPLATE

A preset layout used to make pages visually similar in a multi-page document. Templates determine the appearance of such recurring elements as margins, column widths, folios, captions, and headlines. They streamline the decision-making process and maintain graphic identity in publications that must be produced quickly or by many different designers. Templates also establish repeating patterns through which readers determine how to navigate content. **> PAGE 56**

30 : SYMBOL

31 : TEXT BLOCK

32 : TYPEFACE

TERMINAL

The end of a stroke in a letterform that does not connect to another stroke or a serif. Terminals can be flat, round, or tapered with finials and tails. **> PAGE 44**

TEXT BLOCK

Any unit of a layout containing a body of text. In digital layouts, "text block" also refers to an area through which text flows; three columns of type, for example, would represent three text blocks. **ILL. 31 > PAGE 48**

TYPEFACE

All letters, numerals, punctuation, and special characters that share specific visual characteristics. The look of a typeface is defined partially by the particular qualities of its strokes, counters, and proportions (x-height-to-cap-height and width-to-height relationships). A typeface is a subset of a type family. **ILL. 32 > PAGE 30**

TYPESETTING

The composition of text in finished, reproducible form. In earlier times, typesetters worked from a typewritten manuscript and retyped and coded text with specifications that determined a range of visual variables. Today, the designer applies these commands to text that is delivered digitally from the author or that the designer writes. **> PAGE 54**

TYPE SIZE

In metal type, the vertical height of a metal shaft containing a slightly smaller raised letterform. Today, type size refers to the height of the invisible bounding box containing a character. Printed type size is expressed in points, while screen-based type size is usually measured in pixels. **ILL. 33 > PAGE 45**

UNBRACKETED SERIFS

Serifs that meet the stroke at an abrupt, perpendicular angle. Also called "abrupt." **ILL. 34 > PAGE 44**

UPPERCASE

The larger, capital letters in a typeface, which touch both the baseline and capline. The term "capital" refers to Roman stone inscription. "Uppercase" refers to the location of metal type in drawers used by typesetters; the larger letters were positioned in the type case above the smaller ones. "Majuscule" is another term for uppercase letters. **ILL. 35 > PAGE 41**

WEIGHT

A typeface variation based on the relationship between stroke-width and the size of counters. Variations in type weight are typically described as thin, light, book, regular, medium, semi-bold, bold, extra bold, or ultra bold. The value of text (how dark or light a setting appears) is a reflection of type weight. **ILL. 36 > PAGE 39**

X-HEIGHT

The height of lowercase letters, measured from the baseline to the meanline (the top of the lowercase letter, minus ascenders). The visual appearance of a typeface is defined by x-height, as are its legibility and readability when subject to various spacing strategies. Generally, typefaces with large x-heights (Helvetica, for example) require more line spacing to be legible than do typefaces with small x-heights (Futura, for example). **ILL. 37 > PAGE 43**

53 PT. TYPE

Exquisite

33 : TYPE SIZE

UNBRACKETED SERIF   BRACKETED SERIF

34 : UNBRACKETED SERIFS

35 : UPPERCASE

REGULAR
BOLD
BLACK
ULTRA

36 : WEIGHT

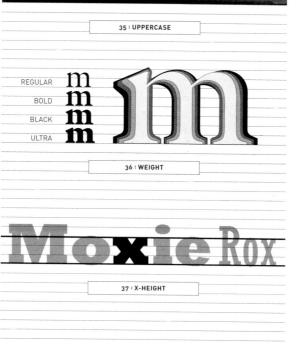

37 : X-HEIGHT

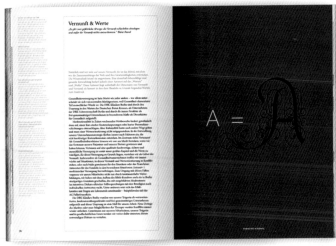

// INTERCONNECTION

Typography lands on our eyes complete, an amalgam of details subsumed by the whole like a settled landscape stretched out before us. As we approach the particular scene of this page, large-scaled elements command attention first.

Subsequent smaller-sized texts composed of individual marks called **letter-forms** collect into what we know to be paragraphs, contained within **margins**.

It may appear that all the visual **elements** here—from the smallest comma to the equal **columns**—have sprouted as naturally as leaves to limb. This landscape is, however, quite contrived, pointing indirectly to several interconnected social and physical systems. The typography here represents a slew of assumptions and prescriptions shared by the writer (me), the designer (me again), and the reader (you), all of which help translate the elements into **messages**. Already we see typography playing its basic roles: to give form to recognizable marks—what we call an alphabet; and to gather them into ordered words that ultimately compel a reader to begin deciphering. The more practiced the <u>typographer</u>, or the more familiar a reader is with the elements and arrangement, the more complete and natural the work appears [1.1]. Even so, regardless of any other creative skills, if a targeted reader is able to understand the words, then the typography will have accomplished its most fundamental job.

Typography might not be beautiful in a popular **aesthetic** sense, but if it gets an idea across, it works. Take, for instance, the temporary placards that people make to announce garage sales. The words might be handwritten with a fat marker on drawing paper, or constructed from <u>vinyl letters</u> stuck to cardboard. The result might be downright ugly by some standards, but it adequately announces the location and day of the event. Because the placard does not look professionally produced, it conveys the fact that a local resident is hosting a garage sale. Were the words somewhat difficult to make out, but colorful

Typographer

A person trained in graphic design with particular expertise in the subject of typography.

Vinyl letters

Alphabets (and other glyphs) cut from adhesive-backed vinyl often sold in small sheets at hardware and stationery stores. A typical typeface is Helvetica, but businesses that sell signs also cut vinyl letters to specification in nearly any typeface and configuration.

and bold, then the host's enthusiasm would be clearly expressed, which is another sort of message. Large, carefully drawn letters might emphasize the location of the garage sale, to be readable in a split second by someone speeding by on a bike. Glittering **serifs** would impress upon the cyclist that this is a very special garage sale indeed. If the aim is to zip people to the sale in eager anticipation, then this second placard works better than the previous one [1.2].

Say the event is an estate sale at a white-carpeted home where carved mahogany bed frames, antique china, and heritage silver are to be auctioned to the highest bidder. Would either of the previous posters work? Strictly from the standpoint of conveying basic information, absolutely. The location and time of the sale are clear enough. But do any of the placards effectively communicate "Estate Sale"? Heavens no! All manner of bargain hunters would show up at 6 a.m. looking for dollar deals, only to be asked kindly to remove their sneakers before crossing the threshold. Meanwhile, connoisseurs lounging at home would miss out on new treasures, and the sellers would miss out on profits.

Typography that works is acceptable for locals. You, on the other hand, will rather want to make typography *Work!* To do so requires an understanding of typographic principles, certainly. But you are also accountable to other systems within which typography functions—those that produce

1.1 *(opposite and above)* DRK Kliniken Triennial Report, 2009. Justus Oehler, Pentagram Berlin. *In a corporate report designed for the Hospital Group of the German Red Cross, typeface, columns, margins, color, and images combine to create a constrained system that unifies yet clearly separates varying kinds of content. The spreads all differ to some degree because the text is not the same from page to page.*

1.2 Garage sale stencils, 2010. Matthew Elium. *Although these spray-painted signs are well crafted, the materials and typographic attributes carry enough of a "handmade" quality to communicate that the garage sale is authentically local.*

typography, for instance, or establish conventions. Cultures, technologies, materials, languages, readers, and the design profession (to name but a few systems) all impose inescapable constraints and generate the contexts that trigger appropriate communication.

These interconnected systems add up to a knotty situation, one that I think warrants a <u>portmanteau</u>. I call it typogyroscopic. Imagine a series of dynamic rings of varying sizes, linked and nested. Together, they not only dictate orientation, but they also influence and inform every typographic decision you have made, and will make from this moment forward. Were you positioned at any one point inside this twisty-turvy world without a sense of the whole, ignorant of and unskilled in negotiating its forces, the only way to find balance would be to cling to a handful of details. But these fine particulars neither offer a perspective nor yield clues about how to make a decision within this realm of endless possibilities. So let us start out, gingerly, toward equilibrium.

Portmanteau

Literally, a large leather trunk with two hinged compartments. Figuratively, the term refers to a compound word built from two other words: in this case, "typography" and "gyroscopic."

RELATIONAL TYPOGRAPHY

As with all decisions that bring made things into being, the choices typographers make are influenced by certain circumstances: production, application, and intended function. To call typography relational, then, points up the fact that the systems at play set up particular conditions each time we design. We make one decision, and we make the next in relation to the previous one. The conditions of the screen will impel us to make choices in relation to that medium, which would differ from the conditions of print. Whether or not we acknowledge the relational nature of typographic production, as well as the conditions of interpretation, it is always present, and always active.

Our wayward estate-sale placard is a case in point. It does not *work* for its intended purpose because collectors of luxury items live within a cultural system, in this case a particular social class that has certain tastes and expectations, and whose members share a social **language** that each one comprehends. No doubt these people have received other notices in the mail in which the designer employed visual codes associated with the experience of "estate sales"—perhaps personally addressed invitations [1.3], handsomely typeset in <u>Bodoni</u> or <u>Snell Roundhand</u> and printed on cream-colored paper. In this instance, printed communication and reader expectation are two of the conjoining systems that establish the context within which the typographer **encodes** content and readers **decode** or interpret it—processes that we will discuss in greater detail in the next chapter. Content is the subject matter of the placards: event details, an indication that the location is an "estate" rather than a "garage," etc. Content is figured within yet other systems, most notably that of written language. These variables combine to form the complex activity sometimes referred to as message construction or communication.

Clearly, making typography *Work* is not that simple here in Typogyroscopic land. Let's revisit the garage-sale placard to gain a bit of perspective. Say the form consists of marker-drawn letters and arrows rendered on a piece of cardboard. The properties could change—the letters might be stenciled spray paint on plywood, for instance—but the handmade quality still falls within "garage-sale placard" conventions. The placard's form is familiar to people who have learned how such announcements look and function. Taped to lamp posts on the street—the physical context—the message is clearly directed at bargain hunters passing by in cars and on foot. Meanwhile, the coincidental collector driving past understands that the event will probably fail to offer him anything of value.

Imagine now a street not far from where the sale is taking place. Overhead the same text, in the same marker letters, is hand-rendered and scaled

Bodoni
A typeface family originally designed by the Italian engraver and publisher Giambattista Bodoni in 1798. Bodoni was the first in the Modern or Didone class of typeface, characterized by unbracketed serifs and highly contrasted stroke-widths.

Snell Roundhand
The English type designer Matthew Carter based this script typeface on the handwriting of the writing master Charles Snell, author of *The Penman's Treasury Open'd* (1694). Linotype originally released the font in 1966.

1.3 Wedding invitation, 2008. Jed Heuer and Jennifer Heuer.

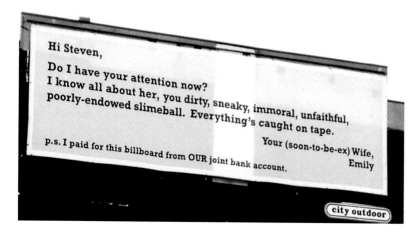

up to fill a billboard. Local people would be unlikely to attribute this notice to a fellow resident because billboards [1.4] work within a system

up to fill a billboard. Local people would be unlikely to attribute this notice to a fellow resident because billboards [1.4] work within a system of commercial advertising, which presumes a ready supply of cash and probably access to a very tall ladder. The more probable conclusion is that a clever adman appropriated the form of garage-sale placards to sell something. Yet the combination of <u>unschooled</u> form and garage-sale

1.4   Billboard promoting the truTV series *Parco P.I.*, 2006. © Turner Entertainment Networks, Inc., A Time Warner Company. All Rights Reserved. Advertising campaign creative courtesy of truTV. *An advertising campaign for a televion channel that airs courtroom dramas and reality shows cleverly capitalizes on context and reader expectations. The text and ordinary-looking typography differ from what the reader expects to see on a billboard, and thereby arrest the attention. Readers understand the humor, perhaps to the point of believing that an actual angry wife discovered a unique way to humiliate her spouse.*

announcement content, in the billboard context, results in a confusing message. The billboard names no seller, and no product or service is identified. There is just this strange text announcing a garage sale in the neighborhood. The two contexts, reader expectation and billboard advertising, have interfered with the intended message, even though the form changed only in scale and the content not at all.

Imagine that the form changes further. The text might be set in a beautiful <u>Fat Face</u>, the work professionally designed, printed, and neatly pasted. Now it is most definitely not publicizing a local garage sale, no matter what the text says. Why? Because, based on our experience with billboards, designed text signals advertising. Change the content to copy selling garages, and the pieces come together to make a little more sense.

Let's make one last alteration: print the same billboard-advertising content with the same type and design on a small flyer, then tack it to a lamp post just below another garage-sale notice. What will the neighbors conclude? The forms of both printed flyer and handmade placard still communicate commercial promotion and local announcement respectively—even though they occupy the same lamp post. Again, their readers understand that both types of communication are plausible, if not expected, within that particular context.

SYSTEMS IN GENERAL

Systems are numerous, and many are in constant flux. Our language system, for example, consists of interconnected, dynamic forces and governing principles that include grammar, vocabulary, and pronunciation. If spoken, the aspects of language are dictated by vocal and aural mechanics, another system. The success of both form and message is predicated on our understanding of the give and take of these dynamic systems, including production, reproduction, and distribution technologies; writing and reading conventions; material properties; and common cultural knowledge, to name some central ones.

Systems can be closed or open, to greater or lesser degrees. The system of on/off lights in two kinds of road-construction signs serves as a basic example [1.5]. The sign on the top accommodates only static or flashing arrows. The

1.5   LegiBrite arrows and message board.

Unschooled

An adjective that describes work accomplished by those who have not been trained in design practices and aesthetics. The opposite of "schooled."

Fat Face

An extreme version of a Modern typeface (see Bodoni, page 28), attributed to Robert Thorne, who introduced the font in England around 1803. With greatly exaggerated stroke contrast and "fat" serifs, this style is among the first designed for display and advertising rather than for book work.

system is quite closed, then, as compared to the more open system of the sign beneath it, which has a grid of multiple lights that can display unlimited **glyphs**. As the opening to this chapter indicated, systems combine to generate the underlying circumstances within which graphic design functions [1.6]. An invitation to an estate sale might seem to call for a <u>classic</u> **typeface**, printed on a small card tucked inside an envelope to be mailed, because these are simply the right choices. A no-brainer. In fact, they *work* because these details fit within a certain set of cultural expectations; because the postal system allows a small card to be mailed; and because these choices eliminate a multitude of other less elegant ones, such as letters typed out in an email. If the producer cannot afford postage, a consequence of some economic system, then the effectiveness of the invitation, for all its apparent appropriateness, is clearly compromised.

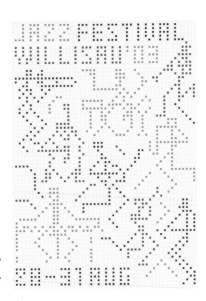

Classic

In the realm of typography, classic typefaces are those that have endured over many years, if not centuries. Favored classics include such serif families as Bodoni and Bembo, and the sans-serif families Univers and Gill Sans.

1.6 Jazz Festival Willisau poster, 2003. Niklaus Troxler. *A constrained formal system consisting of equal squares dictates the typographic and graphic form. The large-scale poster format supports the concept, in that the content is read from a distance.*

cultural systems in particular

The design scholar Malcolm Barnard describes culture as a reciprocal exchange of beliefs and values, including the ways in which these are communicated, reproduced, and contested among a group, or groups, of people:

The beliefs and values may concern any and all aspects of the world and its contents as they are experienced by the group in question: nature, children, material goods, gender, other people and so on. Graphic design is a cultural activity in that it is one of the signifying systems in which those beliefs and values are communicated . . . reproduced or challenged. Its products and process are examples of culture in so far as they reproduce or resist the social order.[1]

Simply put, a "signifying system" is any series of constructed **symbols** that refer to things and ideas for the purpose of communication: spoken words (signifying objects, people, and so on), written words (signifying the spoken word), and letterforms (signifying sounds). Because words in any form relate to the objects or concepts being called to mind (the signified), we cannot write or typeset "billboard" when we mean "garage" and expect anyone to understand what we mean. (Chapter 5 discusses this signifying system as it pertains to typography in greater detail.)

Back to Barnard's point. Design is a form of "cultural production" that signifies aspects of a society's belief and value systems. A catalog design for a Mercedes-Benz dealer might represent exclusivity and wealth, which reiterates and reinforces social values associated with prestige,

and beliefs related to capitalism. Barely readable text scratched onto film for a punk music video reiterates and reinforces counter-culture values. Our design products (catalog/video) and processes (distributing printed catalogs/uploading digital video) communicate to consumers and fans respectively, who in turn confirm beliefs and values by accepting the signifiers as true to them.

Cultural systems that affect perception and understanding involve economies, technologies, and aesthetics. Many societies in the global free market, for instance, accept and have an appetite for extreme typographic variety, in part because they have the means to produce it. Such technologies as digital media and and high-speed printing establish standards of information access and output quality, as well as possibilities for typographic form and delivery. Equally, aesthetic values play an important part in all subcultures, as is revealed by the fact that design professionals judge typographic choices as better or worse, tasteful or tacky, refined or amateurish. Designers tap into cultural histories as reference points that add meaning to words. And perhaps the most significant cultural system for typographers is language.

Language is often understood as being bound by the body: mouths make sounds; facial expressions, body stances, and gestures impart messages. In design we use the term "language" metaphorically. Designers and artists employ visual languages, just as musicians employ sound language, dancers use movement languages, and programmers work with code languages. The Hungarian designer and educator György Kepes introduced the notion of the "language of vision" in 1944, describing visual communication as a language that knows "no limits of tongue, vocabulary or grammar and can be perceived by the illiterate as well as by the literate."[2] It would be difficult to argue against the limitless potential for expressing visual form. Understanding what that form means as a language, at any given time and in any possible place, is, however, not at all simple. Everyone with eyes might be able to see form, but to construct an intended message "successfully" from visual form requires us to be familiar with that type of language.

Language systems are shared by people who have a need and desire to communicate with each other [1.7]. While language is elastic, it cannot be willfully or completely reshaped if it is to work as a communication tool, and so rules of language are relatively fixed, to offer some assurance that the ideas and feelings we want to express will be in sync with how the listener (or reader or viewer) will translate them. Like any

1.7 PaperGirl call for papers and exhibition poster, 2009. Florian Lamm and Lisa von Billerbeck, CtrlC. *PaperGirl is an ongoing Berlin-based art project, described as "a show, an urban action, a bicycle workshop, and a party." Brush-script headlines preside over an assortment of serif and sans-serif typefaces and combine with elements placed playfully and seemingly at random. The posters address subculture readers who are interested in art practices outside the mainstream. Both targeted and other readers would probably interpret that the posters represent the activities of an entity that is not a staid national museum, for instance.*

such human-constructed system, though, languages are open to innovation within the rules, and they evolve over time with usage. New words enter the culture constantly. The form and function of existing words might alter over time; "txt," for instance, is a term that distinguishes activity on mobile devices from other written "text." Words can also be adapted as they migrate across cultures or media—"rendezvous" and "portmanteau" are examples of French words now used as English, and today people working in white-collar businesses often "interface" with each other.

We learn words and understand their meaning when we encounter them repeatedly, and experience them in the context of their use. Today the term "9/11" resonates deeply for many people, whereas in 2000 it was simply a Catalan holiday, or maybe someone's birthday. Similarly, our interpretations of typography are informed by personal experience and the cultural norms to which we are exposed [1.8]. Suppose a person has encountered only text set in capital letters. Then imagine this person one day encounters text set in what we recognize as **lowercase** letters. The text would be so unfamiliar as to be absolutely illegible, essentially a foreign language. Say a person is accustomed to seeing street names typeset in a **sans-serif** gothic, and one day she stumbles into a part of town where all the street names are typeset in an elaborate **script**. What might she surmise about the neighborhood?

evolving systems

On the surface, systems seem immovable, but they are actually quite dynamic. Some, such as written language, change very slowly, while others, like technology, shift regularly and rapidly. The MP3 player and web browser that a person born after 1993 takes for granted were unknown to his parents in 1980. Neither did typography for tiny handheld and computer screens exist, yet today an entire industry of mini- and other low-resolution **font** production thrives.

These systems evolve, and as a result, any single movement within one will affect larger systems as well as others with which the system is in contact. Even a simple little typeface, existing within systems of form, style, and reading, can alter the landscape of each. Emigre, an early "alternative" **foundry** and creator of several unconventional fonts, released Template Gothic in 1993. Many designers viewed it as radical and unreadable, or just ugly. The resistance merely indicates that the detractors adhered to formal and reading systems that excluded such options. Similar typefaces that challenged conventions emerged throughout the 1990s, which further reveals that the cultural moment favored, if not generated, idiosyncrasy.

1.8 *I heart NY,* 1979, and *I heart NY More Than Ever,* 2001. Milton Glaser. *Milton Glaser built upon his iconic "I heart NY" logotype (top) for this poster commemorating the September 11, 2001, attacks on the World Trade Center in Manhattan. The State of New York commissioned the original logotype in the late 1970s to promote tourism for the entire state. The mark is, however, more typically associated with the city. Readers readily interpret the poster, then, as a statement about the 9/11 event in Manhattan.*

Template Gothic
This font was designed by the American Barry Deck and distributed by the Emigre foundry in the early 1990s. It was drawn in only two weights. During the same period Deck created similar wry fonts, such as Mutant Industry Roman.

1.9 (top) *Every Good Boy Live*, 1991. Rudy VanderLans and Elisabeth Charman, Emigre; type designed by Barry Deck.

1.10 (above) *New Modernism*, 2010. Anton Jeludkov. *This student designer used the "post-modern" font Template Gothic to express a written reflection on modernism's legacy, deliberately making one sensibility collide with the other and setting up a wry tension. In the context of a design school, his readers, primarily designers, would know something about the typeface's history.*

Still, few were as popular as Template Gothic, or as widely used [1.9, 1.10]. As the typeface was adopted, entire publications and advertising campaigns set in Template Gothic could be found. This once "illegible" and "ugly" typeface proved quite readable, if not attractive, once people became familiar with it; what had begun as a counter-culture blip ultimately altered what some societies considered viable. Did the typeface change? No—the cultural systems changed.

I should point out that the typeface was not the only star responsible for reconfiguring the constellations. I mentioned that other typefaces gained popularity, which strengthened Template Gothic's viability. Designers using Template Gothic also challenged reading conventions through their design of subculture publications, music packaging, and posters. Strange compositions added to the typeface's radical feel. Not coincidentally, 1993 is the same year the World Wide Web became freely available, which, by the late 1990s, had assisted in the wide distribution of the typeface.

I doubt that Barry Deck, the designer of Template Gothic, predicted the influence his work would have. One cannot throw quirky anomalies into society and just sit back and wait for them to catch on. Systems are not only mutable, they are also organic. They change through shared experience and shifting circumstances, over time. Template Gothic's eventual inclusion into mainstream culture indicates that the ground had been prepared to some degree. People in graphic design and other disciplines, notably architecture and fashion, had been exploring low-brow visual languages since the mid-1960s.

Recognizing that cultural systems affect typographic practice increases a typographer's ability to maneuver inventively, to harness these cultural contexts in a way that will allow readers to accept and interpret messages. To comprehend these phenomena more fully, we turn now to the concepts of connotation and denotation.

DENOTATION AND CONNOTATION

Spoken communication relies on word denotation and connotation, as does visual typographic language. Text elements always denote something—that is, have a literal meaning—and also always connote additional meanings by evoking associations. The English noun "neighborhood," for instance, might be denotatively defined as "a district forming a community within a town or city." This meaning describes "what it is" literally, based upon cultural use. The connotations of "neighborhood" might then additionally signify comfort, domesticity, or goodwill—established by the association of the word with lived experiences. Typographically speaking, words can never assume a quintessential denotative form free of connotation. Would "9/11" set in a typewriter font or heavy sans serif describe "what it is" more definitively than if it were handwritten or lettered in brush script? Let me offer a hint: no. Text elements are not reducible to pure denotation because the form itself biases word interpretation in one way or another. This fact becomes clear when nonsensical words are typeset in different typefaces:

Belngo Eioh *Jenoyc Rehi* **Qvpah Ceus**

Although these letter combinations are not from the English language, we try to construct meaning from them for a couple of reasons. First, strings of letters imply the formation of words. Letterforms, in the context of other letterforms, trigger understanding of language systems. More importantly, each typeface suggests forms we might have seen before: from left to right, American Typewriter reminds us of education; Bickham Script of elegance; and Cooper Black of a low-budget offer. These cultural meanings are reinforced when connotations of form agree with those implied in the word:

Teacher Day *Caravaggio* **Wheel'n'Lube**

The words and form suit each other here because we have seen the typefaces applied over and over again to communicate similar kinds of message. Others may read the combinations differently, though. It could be said that the closest typography gets to representing the literal, to being denotative, is when word meaning, form, and the experience of readers coalesce. Let's change the text to see if the typefaces yield different connotations:

The Weekly *Winter Sale* **Pumpernickel**

The connotations above are very similar to the previous ones. The difference is that now the typographic meanings are more particularized, more nuanced. The formerly generic connotation of American Typewriter is now honed, in its use for a masthead, to connote a local newsletter; Bickham Script alludes to the elegance of the holidays; and Cooper Black now connotes home-style baking. Form can also add a layer of connotation not necessarily denoted by the word. To see this in action, let's arbitrarily switch the typefaces:

The Weekly Winter Sale *Pumpernickel*

American Typewriter

Joel Kaden and Tony Stan based their typeface on the first Sholes and Glidden typewriter of the late nineteenth century. Released by International Typeface Corporation (ITC) in 1974, the font adapted the monospace font to a variable width.

Bickham Script

Richard Lipton designed this family for Adobe, taking inspiration from eighteenth-century writing masters, particularly the English engraver George Bickham. The family was released in 1997. It maximizes computational power by featuring hundreds of alternate capitals, ligatures, and swashed ascenders and descenders.

Cooper Black

Designed by the American Oswald Bruce Cooper in 1921, and released by the Barnhart Brothers & Spindler type foundry in 1922. The typeface was originally popular in advertising, and has since lost and gained popularity throughout the decades.

Masthead

A sailing metaphor for the top of the front page of a periodical, newspaper, or website that contains the name and date of the publication, along with other identifying information.

"The Weekly" set in Cooper Black now connotes a more official newsletter, or perhaps a community newspaper; "Winter Sale" now suggests just your average, everyday sale; and "Pumpernickel" looks as if it were baked with the finest ingredients. Another way to see the dynamic connotative relationship between form and content is by setting words in typefaces that have no obvious connection to, or are perhaps in conflict with, word meaning. To see that, let's change the text:

Jolly Belly *Garage Sale Deal* **Clown Toss**

"Garage Sale Deal" set in such an elegant script opposes the denotative meaning of garage sale ("a sale of miscellaneous household goods, often held in the garage or front yard of someone's house"), as well as the connotative meaning ("a sale of assorted oddments that could produce undervalued treasure"). Such a discrepancy has its function, though. Were the message painted on a car dealer's show window, it would clearly not refer to the familiar, domestic, community garage sale. The larger context (showroom window) particularizes the connotation with a clue that helps stabilize the meaning, in this case an allusion to one's own garage and the new car that might go in it. Imagine the rather ambiguous "Jolly Belly" stitched on the tag of a stuffed dog toy, and the same word and typeface silk-screened in white on a red T-shirt sold at Christmastime. "Jolly" and "belly" still denote "cheerfulness" and the "stomach area," respectively, yet the typeface and the context of their application yield wholly different connotations. I recommend taking the time to consider what those might be.

Clearly we have moved from connotation in typography to the contexts of application and use, with good reason. The contexts of application and use are major factors in communication. So, now would be the perfect moment to discover how contexts are formed.

CONTEXTS

Designers often say "context is everything." How can it be everything, given that systems (cultural, technological, cognitive, and so on) are so all-encompassing? Still, if I knew something about building, I would construct the word "CONTEXT" in ninety-eight-story wide letters to span an impressive stretch of desert, in neon pink so the word could be read from some distance on <u>Google Earth</u>. Huge.

As far as typography is concerned, context is the set of conditions and circumstances present at any given time, in any given place [1.11], including the motives and abilities of makers and readers, the material nature of the artifacts, and

1.11 *The circles in this Venn diagram represent a sample of the possible systems that influence design practice, and therefore typography. The solid shape in the center represents the overlap of these systems, which, at any given moment of typographic production and interpretation, determines the circumstances within which typographers work, and the terms by which that work is deemed successful.*

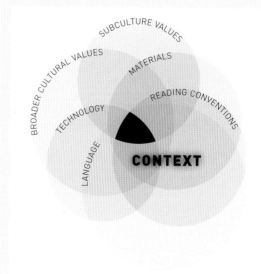

Google Earth

A virtual globe, map, and geographic information program that renders a map of the Earth on any sized screen using images obtained from satellites and aerial photography. The program was originally called EarthViewer 3D; Google changed the name when it acquired Keyhole, Inc., the inventors, in 2004.

the particulars of delivery. Context is produced by converging systems, among them the societal systems within which makers and readers exist, and the physical and technological systems that form and convey artifacts.

To get at the contexts that concern typographers, we need to ask six questions. Who initiates the work? Who are the readers? What is the artifact? How is the artifact manifested? Where does the delivery take place? When does the delivery take place? The answers to these questions begin to describe the context.

the initiator

Who is initiating or conceiving the work? Where does it originate? All sorts of people and enterprises commission design. And every person and enterprise is entrenched in a number of potent systems. At the risk of oversimplifying, imagine each individual's system as an orbit with considerable gravitational pull. A contemporary architect works within several orbits, one of which is the design system, where values shift regularly. Another is the societal system, where issues rise and fall in importance. The relevance of the architect's work to contemporary design tugs at him, as does the desire to respond to such social trends as the will to build environmentally friendly structures. The editor of a magazine is drawn by the publishing system. She feels the pull to release relevant articles and maintain or increase her readership. The art director at Big Cool Records is a member of a corporate system, of music production and distribution systems, and of the fashion system. Her concerns, then, are fierce competition, the demands of artists, attorneys, and agents, exorbitant costs, tight deadlines, and of course the fickle fans of musicians.

How on earth can these things matter to typographers? Whether we design with and for an architect, an editor, or an art director (or accounting firms, video-game producers, auto manufacturers, municipal managers, or hotel chains), our orbit (typography) intersects with theirs. Design decisions are constrained by the concerns of the people who initiate and sponsor the work. When staff of the UK daily newspaper the *Guardian* initiated a redesign, they commissioned a new typeface **family**, <u>Guardian Egyptian</u> [1.12]. The concerns of newspaper executives in this case were to maximize space and readability, which proposed certain possibilities for the <u>type designer</u>, and ruled out others.

Designers also produce work for themselves. They are then initiators. A type designer who produces typefaces of his own accord does so within the orbit of type design, rather than the orbit of a commissioner. Recall the initiator of Template Gothic. His orbit compelled him to be familiar with current design trends; to have some knowledge of the evolution of type design; and to follow his own interests. A type designer is free to explore letterforms motivated by his

Guardian Egyptian

An extended family designed by Paul Barnes and Christian Schwartz for a redesign in 2005 of British newspaper the *Guardian*. The font family, plus a companion sans-serif family, are used exclusively throughout the newspaper.

Type designer

A person who earns some part of his or her living by designing, drawing, and digitizing fonts. These designers fashion each and every serif, swash, and stroke that comprise fonts and families—from 26 basic upper- or lowercase letters, to the 256 glyphs of a complete font, to thousands of glyphs in an OpenType family.

1.12 Front page of the *Guardian*, September 12, 2005.

1.13 *Happy Days: A Guide to State Holidays,* 2009. Michael Newhouse. *This cheeky "infographic" surveying U.S. holidays resonated with readers, many of whom might have viewed the subject as charming but archaic.*

1.14 Poster for wine festival, 2009. Lopetz, Büro Destruct. *The reference to 1960s advertising styles would appeal to style-conscious wine aficionados.*

own inclinations. He might not be concerned with how many characters fit on a line, or how legible the typeface is. If this same type designer is asked to produce a typeface for a festival, his orbit suddenly interacts with those of industry executives.

the readers

Inasmuch as the goal of design is to facilitate access and comprehension for readers, type designers need to have a very clear idea of their readers, who are also referred to as the audience, or end users. They are those music fans, or the donors to the good cause, the voters, the scholars—in other words, the people to whom we hope our typography speaks. The numerous forces at play in any given reader's orbit include his or her experiences and education, values and beliefs, interests, and tastes. Where people have lived and traveled, their exposure to media, and their social practices, color how they interpret visual messages as well [1.13]. So, to have our typography understood, we must understand our readers. Although typographers often design for people much like themselves, it is unwise to assume that we know about others and their experiences without knowing something about their cultural values.

Some messages target a finite and definable range of readers, and therefore typographic features and character can match specifically [1.14]. In some cases, the intended readers are a finite and definable group, like the subcultures of surfers or classical musicians. If making typography *Work* is the typographer's aim, he needs to be versed in his readers' shared, and sometimes quirky, visual language. For example, classical music lovers are likely to be familiar with fine classical type and understand that it is consistent with their tastes. In other cases, the target audience is more general and less quantifiable. Readers of the *Guardian*, mentioned above, span varied economic, regional, and cultural circumstances. The redesign sparked enthusiasm, but also angry criticism of its new size, grid, and typefaces. The new typefaces, reduced size, and altered composition were alien to what readers understood, and knew they liked.

Another reader consideration is individual circumstance. An elderly person with diminished vision would have difficulty reading small type, for instance. A student trying to digest a biology lesson might appreciate a well-ordered textbook. Chapter 2 discusses the reader and reading systems thoroughly, so let's move on to the remaining four questions that address the form and delivery of messages.

the artifact and the delivery

What is the artifact? Is it a newspaper, a movie screen, or a telephone book? How is the artifact manifested? Is it printed, projected, or built? Where does the delivery take place? In the subway, in the living room [1.15]? When does the delivery take place? During a piano recital, during an emergency? So many questions! Although I have singled out these four components of context, they are not so easily separated. Typography exists in a confluence of all four: a distinct format (what), a certain medium (how), a singular place (where), and a span of time (when). Readers encounter animated text on scoreboards at the game while seated or jumping for joy in an arena. People read instructions in cookbooks while cooking in the kitchen. Readers pause amid the crowds to locate a store at a mall directory. Each situation is a unique combination of circumstances, and designers must anticipate all combinations at once.

A few scenarios should illustrate the point. The message of a printed one-sheet (how and what) posted above the overhead rack of a subway car (where) is directed to commuters (the reader). This situation may call for bold typography so that passengers will apprehend the message in the fleeting moments between stepping onto the train and settling in (when). On the other hand, if commuters ride that line every morning and evening, the typography could be more subtle and complex, with the fair expectation that people will read it in intervals over the course of several commutes. Say the commuter becomes absorbed in her iPad (how) that sits on her lap (where) reading a magazine (what). When seated, she is able to engage with an interactive essay about some faraway place. This situation affords greater typographic

1.15 Achievement First Endeavor Middle School, Brooklyn, NY. Graphics by Paula Scher, Pentagram, 2010.

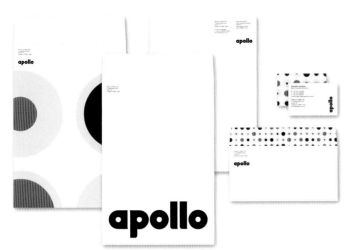

1.16 Apollo Tyres brand identity, 2008. Mike Abbink, Joshua Distler, and Judie Gatlin, Saffron Brand Consultants. *The typography and logotype for the identity system of a tire manufacturer anticipates broad application: use at a wide range of scales; reproduction in a variety of materials, from paint on steel to molded rubber, ink on paper to pixels on screen; and orientation when applied to artifacts, from business cards to shipping crates.*

subtlety. At some point our commuter looks up and realizes she missed her transfer stop. At the next stop she rushes off the train to find typography illuminated (how) within well-positioned (where) signage (what). The type is large enough to read at some distance, and is free of clutter, and so immediately directs her to the opposite platform, where she hops back on a train, backtracks, catches her usual connection, and arrives home on time.

The "wheres" and "whens" in these scenarios point up an additional condition of situations: competing messages from other media in the environment—sometimes called interference. Whereas the space of a printed novel suffers little disruption, a novel delivered on an iPad potentially competes with other texts, videos, or websites calling from beyond the virtual margins. By contrast, a television ad lives and expires in seconds. Although the medium affords the benefit of repetition over a longer span of time, the messages must contend with rapid delivery, competing advertising, network programming, and, if the message fails to captivate, the channel changer.

Often the same message is delivered in a number of different situations. Commercial brands and products, for example, profit from their message being delivered across any number of formats and media. Readers might encounter a slogan or a logotype stitched on a clerk's shirt, printed in a newspaper advertisement, painted on the side of a truck, stamped on in-store packaging, and rendered on a website [1.16]. As always, several systems come into play, but I'll name only a few. Technological and physical systems govern the material nature of the typography: stitching, printing, painting, stamping, rendering. Reading systems constrain the size and placement of typographic elements. Static text that is read at arm's length requires a different **type size**, for instance, from text read twenty feet away, speeding by on the highway.

Other chapters delve more deeply into the systems introduced here, as well as the contexts they produce. We now set out to discover the interrelated aspects of typographic form.

FORMAL SYSTEMS ///

The logic that governs proportions among font glyphs, gradual **weights** across a family of fonts, or page organization, is what I call a "formal system." Such human-devised rational systems have evolved over time, and employ parts of other systems. Technological systems, mentioned above, include the tools, machines, and software we use to give form to, and to deliver, typography. Because typography is visible, and exists in a tangible way on real surfaces, it is physical, so physical systems must be acknowledged as a major driver in typographic production. Perceptual systems, informed by human physiology and psychology, affect how humans perceive and interpret the visual world.

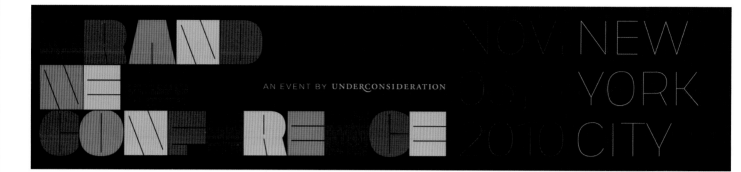

AN EVENT BY UNDERCONSIDERATION

NOV. NEW
YORK
2010 CITY

the alphabet, as are vertical, horizontal, angular, and curved strokes. If strokes terminate in serifs, the serif shape repeats throughout, whether abrupt and angular, as in slab serifs, or gradual and curvilinear, as in bracketed serifs. Strokes that terminate without serifs, or with partial serifs, do so across the alphabet. Whether the type designer's goal is overall visual evenness in a sans-serif typeface or a highly embellished display face, formal systems work to unify the parts [1.22].

Proportion is one such system. Each **character** within a proportional typeface is constructed relative to other characters, following certain traditions. For instance, the lowercase a and e are typically similar in width, and narrower than other characters, such as the capital B, P, and R, which are also proportionally consistent in comparison to, say, the wideness of the M or the narrowness of the I. This is not to say that all typefaces adhere to this particular logic. Some typefaces turn the whole idea upside down: the M might be super-narrow and I super-wide. Still, the characters submit to a formal system.

Once the designer has devised a set of overarching rules that apply to each glyph, variation might be added to the system. Modifying stroke thickness creates lighter or bolder fonts, and modifying **posture** constructs slanted versions of the typeface, or italics. **Alternate** letters might also be added, such as capitals with showy **swashes**. Each addition is submitted to the overall logic of the formal system to maintain visual affinity. Swashes tacked onto a display face that is not designed to support them can result in visual conflict [1.23]. Whether the disharmony communicates oddness, or suggests a designer's unsophisticated eye, the result is certainly not a unifying system.

The alphabet is filled with shape anomaly. Every letter is different because we need to be able to distinguish between an e and an h. The type designer's challenge is to balance character individuality with formal unity. Although no one letter or number is allowed to stand out defiantly from the others in a lineup, each still has a singular job: to stand resolutely as the letter or number it symbolizes. If the **aperture** of a c is too small, it may take on the appearance of an o, which not only compromises o's job, but also leads to mutual resentment. If the <u>tittle</u> sits over the vertical stroke too

Tittle
The common term for the superscript dot above the lowercase i and j in German and Latin languages. The dot was added to the letter ı in medieval manuscripts to distinguish it from adjacent vertical strokes in such letters as u, m, and n.

1.22 Identity for "Brand New" conference, 2010. Armin Vit, UnderConsideration.

Freshly

Freshly

Freshly

1.23 *Looping swashes that look natural to the typeface Giddyup are incongruous when applied to the upright DIN.*

abecedaria

Abecedaria

Abecedaria

1.24 Ferox, Luvbug, and Frank typeface designs. Miles Newlyn.

closely, it may be mistaken for an l. Dismissing such details as minor can have unwelcome consequences. The word "illusion" might read as "llluslon." Not good.

ratios

When more than 250 distinguishable Latin-based glyphs come together as words, lines of text, and paragraphs, the details add up to typeface "personality" [1.24]. The reasons for this are many, but a primary one is that the ratios of parts to parts within the typeface, and among the family, are consistent. The **x-height** and **cap-height** of the four Bembo members shown below are the same. Only the thickness, or weight, of each varies: the **stroke-width** increases relative to a constant height. In other words, the stroke-to-height ratio shifts, causing a thickening of the characters. Additionally, the **set-width** of each font expands, which changes the height-to-width ratio. Increasingly thick-to-thin

Bembo x embraces REGULAR
Bembo x embraces SEMIBOLD
Bembo x embraces BOLD
Bembo x embraces EXTRABOLD

ratios in the strokes of the Bembo family create heavier and heavier weights in relation to the Regular version. Compare the stroke of the B in the Regular and Extrabold. The horizontal strokes expand in smaller increments than do the vertical strokes.

Bureau Grotesque Book
Bureau Grotesque Compressed Book
Bureau Grotesque Condensed Bold
Bureau Grotesque Bold

Bureau Grotesque Book has a stroke-to-height ratio similar to its family member Bureau **Grotesque** Compressed Book, so the weights of both typefaces are technically the same, as are the cap-height to x-height ratio. The set-widths, however, differ dramatically. The compressed does look more uptight and crowded and visually more active, but not much heavier. It is also denser, because the space within and surrounding each character is much smaller.

The thick-to-thin ratios of the horizontal and vertical strokes vary across the Bureau Grotesque family, in part to accommodate the extreme set-width range, from quite narrow to very wide. Compare the lowercase e of the Book weight to that of Compressed Book, for instance. Still, within each weight the

Bembo

A twentieth-century revival of the classic roman typeface Bembo, originally cut by Francesco Griffo in 1495. Designed under the direction of Stanley Morison and released in 1929 by the Monotype Corporation, this "Old Style" typeface is distinguished by minimal variation in thick and thin stroke weights, a relatively small x-height, and angled top serifs on lowercase letters.

Bureau Grotesque

Based on "Grotesque" nineteenth-century typefaces, the original family was completed in 1989 by David Berlow for the Tribune Companies and the magazine *Newsweek*. It was issued by Font Bureau, and additional styles were drawn by Jill Pichotta, Christian Schwartz, and Richard Lipton.

stroke-width ratios aren't as appreciable as are the counter-to-stroke ratios, as in the o of the Bold and Condensed Bold. Unity is produced through the consistent application of these fine differences across the alphabet, within any given typeface.

The difficulty or ease with which a typeface can be read is determined in part by **point size** in relation to the x-height of a given font. A serif typeface designed for long-term reading might be quite legible at 9 pt because its x-height is demonstrably larger than, say, a script. The latter might be illegible set at the same size, owing to its typically small x-height. Berthold City is characterized by a rectilinear shape in traditionally round letters, such as the lowercase o, e, and c. This one idea is central to the logic of the typeface and permeates the alphabet, as do slab serifs and a relatively uniform thick-to-thin stroke ratio of the vertical and horizontal strokes. These and other minutiae not only distinguish City from other faces, but also help to consolidate the family. When contrasts are introduced—such as thinner or thicker stroke-widths to fashion light and bold weights—the rectilinearity, slab serifs, and stroke ratios maintain the resemblance.

Berthold City

Designed by Georg Trump, this font family was released in 1930 by the H. Berthold AG type foundry in Berlin, Germany. This slab serif features a strong geometric structure, with frequent right angles and quarter-round corners.

City Medium
City Bold

Vegeburger
Vegeburger

The o, e, and c are slightly squared in Cholla Sans Bold as well, although not as pronouncedly as in City Medium. Additionally, x-height-to-cap-height ratios and weights are similar. The formal logic holding Cholla together as a system, compared to City, is most evident in Cholla's lack of serifs (hence the descriptor "sans"). Whereas the strokes in City terminate with stark **unbracketed serifs**, Cholla letterforms end in subtly rounded **terminals**. Additionally, Cholla sports characteristic notches throughout the character set, as seen in the lowercase a and n, and the uppercase B.

Cholla

A family designed by Sibylle Hagmann in 1998–99 for the Art Center College of Design in Pasadena, California, and later released by the Emigre foundry. The typeface is named after a cactus species indigenous to the Mojave desert.

City Medium
Cholla Sans Bold

Burger buns
Burger buns

The differences between City Medium and Cholla Slab Bold, a member of the Cholla family, are less obvious. The width-to-x-height ratios differ, as demonstrated by the fact that City sets narrower. The equally square unbracketed serifs of Cholla Slab Bold are longer, and the **letter-spacing** is consistently more open, which together creates a wider set-width. Cholla's counters, too, are more open than those of City Medium. Compared to Cholla, City is strongly horizontal and looks like a row of mortared bricks. Cholla is softer and bumpy, like smooth stones loosely bound together. Next to Bureau Grotesque Book, though, Cholla looks sturdier, more architectural.

Baconburger
Baconburger

Baconburger
Baconburger

aggregate effects

The example below combines similar weights of Cholla, Bureau Grotesque, and City, though the **type sizes** have been adjusted to create consistent x-heights. What originally appeared to be minor differences end up being fairly significant. The words now look wonky and uneasy.

Cheezy Chili and fries

Similar typefaces set in paragraphs compared next to one another further demonstrate how the details add up. Cholla Slab Bold occupies more space than City Medium for the same amount of text; in typographic terms it yields fewer characters per line. The differences between the two typefaces in set-width and letterspace—less observable details at larger sizes—are exaggerated when the respective characteristics amass. Cholla Sans Bold turns out to have a narrower set-width than City Medium, and overall it looks both slightly lighter and softer.

The last time we were in the city we discovered a diner that had been in business since 1947. We ate the most delicious cheeseburgers, with a side of fries smothered in the diner's special chili and cheese.

The last time we were in the city we discovered a diner that had been in business since 1947. We ate the most delicious cheeseburgers, with a side of fries smothered in the diner's special chili and cheese.

The last time we were in the city we discovered a diner that had been in business since 1947. We ate the most delicious cheeseburgers, with a side of fries smothered in the diner's special chili and cheese.

The last time we were in the city we discovered a diner that had been in business since 1947. We ate the most delicious cheeseburgers, with a side of fries smothered in the diner's special chili and cheese.

The paragraphs at left are set at the same type size, yet Bureau Grotesque Book is noticeably bigger. Chapters 3 and 6 examine why typefaces that share the same point size are not always visually equal. Without knowing why at this moment, we can still conclude that while the width-to-height ratio of Bureau Grotesque is similar and its vertical stroke-width about the same, its x-height-to-cap-height ratio and **meanline** differ substantially. Take note, too, of the short **ascenders** and **descenders** in the h, t, y, and p, compared to the other typefaces.

The Adobe cut of Caslon Regular shown below is proportionally average for old-style serif romans, with an x-height-to-cap-height ratio slightly

Caslon

Various serif typefaces originating in the typeface of the same name designed by English type cutter and founder William Caslon I. Adobe Caslon is a variant designed by Carol Twombly, based on original Caslon specimen pages printed between 1734 and 1770.

Univers

A sans-serif typeface designed by Adrian Frutiger and released by the French Deberny & Peignot foundry in 1954. The typeface was the first to use a numbering system to name its members. More than twenty-five digital variations of the Univers family exist today.

Verdana

The American software giant Microsoft commissioned the type designers Matthew Carter and Tom Rickner of Monotype Imaging to design an very readable typeface for the screen. The result, Verdana, exaggerates glyph distinctions, for instance between the number 1 and lower case l. The typeface became a Microsoft system font in 1996.

Caslon **Univers Verdana**

greater than 1:2, not unusual for a classic book face originating in the eighteenth century. By contrast, Univers 55 clocks in at about a 2:3 ratio. Verdana, the most recent arrival of the three, has nearly a 5:6 ratio. Are typefaces perhaps expanding over time like the universe? Actually, no. Ratios change as technologies and tastes suggest or encourage variation. Verdana was designed in response to the increasingly popular and problematic reading space of the monitor—to improve type legibility on screen. With the bright open counters and relative hugeness of the lowercase, Verdana functions brilliantly at very small scales, utilizing every pixel efficiently. Different circumstances inspired the older two fonts, but the same proportional logic was in force.

VARIATIONS ON THEMES

So far we have discussed roman and regular letterforms exclusively. But type-faces also take the form of **italics** and **obliques.** These letterforms lean to the right slightly, between five and eight degrees. Each glyph of a "true" italic is designed as a separate typeface consistent with its serif. An oblique of a sans serif such as Univers essentially mimics the character of the regular version, but at a slant.

Didot

A group of Modern, or Didone, typefaces named for the Parisian Didot family. Firmin Didot cut the letters and his brother Pierre used the types in printing. Several revivals of Didot have since been designed and issued.

The classic Didot and its italic sister shown on the first line at right demonstrate how the shapes of the letters change: the lowercase a, for instance—a **double-story** letterform that becomes a single-story—and the f. Such variety, which is useful for distinguishing one kind of text from another, could easily sacrifice family unity. Here again, the formal system plays a role. A skilled type designer applies typeface attributes, such as thick-to-thin and x-height-to-cap-height ratios, to all family members.

Frothy affairs *Frothy affairs*
Frothy affairs
Frothy affairs *Frothy affairs*

The second line above shows a "faux" italic, created by imposing a ten degree slant onto the Didot regular font. Compared to the regular italic just above it, the degree of slant in the "faux" italic looks forced (because it is), and causes the letterforms to look as though they might tumble forward off the **baseline.** Each letter also looks to be impinging on its neighbor's space. The true italic letters, by comparison, flow gracefully one to the other, and are balanced securely on the baseline. Today most software programs automatically insert true italics if the typeface family includes them, but some programs still force upright fonts into a rigid slant.

Today true italics typically accompany serif typeface families, and sans-serif families include obliques, such as the italic version of DIN Light shown in the third line above. Type designers are certainly free to vary these traditions, and they do so often.

Fluffiest Pies *Fluffiest Pies*
Fluffiest Pies Fluffiest Pies

Odile

Sibylle Hagmann designed this family in 2004. It is a "vertical italic" inspired by Charter, a typeface designed by William Addison Dwiggins around 1936, and includes complete alphabets, ligatures, and decorative sorts.

Cholla (shown in the top line at right) is a sans-serif typeface, yet the type designer Sibylle Hagmann chose to design the italic in the tradition of a true roman italic. She also designed a vertical italic for her serif typeface Odile (in the bottom line above right). Hagmann had first to recognize the characteristics of italic letters in relation to roman letters in order to design an italic with an upright posture that is italic enough to differentiate it from Odile Regular.

dimpled   dimpled

dimpled   dimpled

1.25 Liza Pro typeface design, 2009. Bas Jacobs, Akiem Helmling, and Sami Kortemäki, Underware. *As one types letters using this "live script," the OpenType software selects versions of each letter from over 4,000 alternate letterforms. The designers drew every calligraphic stroke, swash, and ligature to simulate the variation of hand lettering, yet each letterform coordinates with the rest.*

In other words, altered details change overall appearances. The text above is set in <u>Bookman</u> Old Style Bold. The same letters on the right were altered in very minor ways. The original design, set at a reduced scale, appears to have a shorter x-height than the altered one on the right, but the x-height was not touched. Ascenders and descenders were shortened, serif widths were reduced, horizontal **brackets** were changed to angled brackets, and all the characters were slightly extended. Therefore, the right-hand version is slightly heavier and wider. The negative-to-positive-space ratio is slightly less uniform, causing the letters to look clumped.

Our personal appearance is the sum of many small details, and the same is true of typefaces. Carefully observing individual parts in relation to those of others within and outside a given typeface family clarifies how the details accumulate into a unique visual presence, even when typefaces share common features. The possible nuances are limited only by the alphabet itself, the context within which it functions, and of course the imagination of the designer [1.25].

Bookman

Bookman is based on a Scottish Old Style Antique that has been copied and revived since its introduction in the mid-nineteenth century. Popular variants have included American Type Foundry's Bookman Oldstyle, with added swashes, and ITC Bookman, by the

HIERARCHY AND STRUCTURE: PART I ///

STRUCTURE

Structure is not dissimilar to a skeletal system in that it holds together and helps govern the relationships among parts. Take, for example, our own bodies. Our pelvic bone is fused to a spine bound to our rib cage stacked below our clavicle. Our structure supports verticality, unlike, say, a snake's. Structures, therefore, delimit where and how elements behave [1.26]. And if nature is any indicator, structures can take just about any form.

100 Pages
714 Million Net Tu...
3 on the Board
8,304 Professiona...
22.9 Million Share...
62.1 Million Opera...
1 World
44.8 Million Net Pr...
32 Countries
2,500 Clients
0.80 EUR Dividenc...
1 Brand, 1 Vision
16.9 Million Tax

...nover Annual ...s Report ...ing Profit 2008 ...ofit

Brunel

1.26 Brunel Annual Report 2008, 2009. Matthijs van Leeuwen, G2K Designers. *A simple but strong structure helps anchor the dramatic scale shifts in this annual report. The typographic architecture is reinforced with consistent left-oriented vertical alignment.*

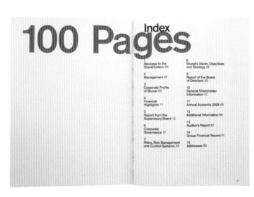

The most rudimentary typographical structure is orientation in relation to the top, bottom, and sides of any given two-dimensional space, or front and back, left and right in a three-dimensional space. If text is above or in front of an entrance to a shop, it will probably be read first, unless something more compelling in the window draws our attention away. If all elements are to be read, they cannot sit in the same place—say, piled up at the topmost edge of a screen. As soon as more than two elements are placed in some relationship to one another, structure comes into play. The elements might be loosely figured and appear to float autonomously, but they are tentatively tethered in relation to each other, as well as to the bounding framework. More complex structures help organize greater numbers of elements, supplying an underlying logic through a system of guides, such as regimented, intersecting lines in printed books, or a loosely defined path in dynamic media that guides elements as they move and intersect [1.27].

Type can be placed anywhere within a given space, especially in the digital environment, where space is virtually limitless. Say we have a 500,000-word text that we want to publish on a website. Do we start at the upper left-hand corner and pour the text into one continuous string? Well, that is one structure: a single line stretching from here to eternity. A delimiting right margin that forces line breaks results in lines following lines of text, which is another kind of structure—and better for reading. But if the browser window supports dynamic text reflow, line lengths could stretch as wide as the monitor screen—not so good. Given the length of the essay, an even better structure might be similar to ones we currently find in newspapers. These structures distribute lengthy texts over columns. Much better for reading, but still a little daunting. How about linked **text blocks**, where a click leads readers to the next or previous bit of text. This structure configures typography in smaller chunks, over a series of connected screens. Better still. Clearly, structure is necessary if we want to corral large amounts of text.

1.27 *Dividing space into grids in web-based typography is a common way of organizing extensive and varying kinds of text. Consistent spatial relationships and text placement across web screens help readers to navigate and identify different kinds of information.*

1.28 *Icons: Magnets of Meaning*, 1997. Bob Aufuldish, Aufuldish & Warinner. Exhibition catalog.

Text reflow

In web-based applications, expanding or narrowing a browser window often alters word and sentence placement relative to the visible area. As line length shortens, text "reflows" down the depth of the text area. In word-processing software, deleted or added text alters the placement of all text that follows.

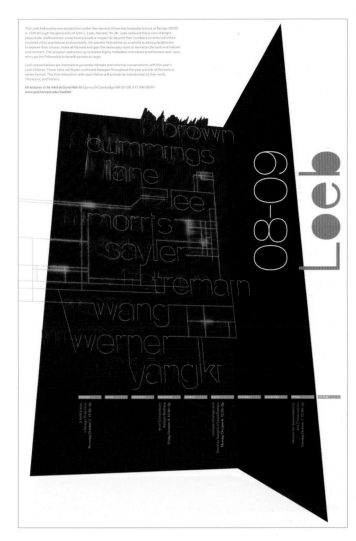

Invisible paths moving in time across a screen might guide letterforms as they move and intersect. The same path might be used for all letterforms that animate on screen, a structure that holds elements together over time. Animated typography employs another kind of structure: the linear timeline that creates a beginning, middle, and end. Within that framework, key points of action—for instance, the number of moments a rotating word pauses—structure motion sequences. These moments bring rhythmic structure to the action.

RELATIONAL HIERARCHY

Hierarchy, aided by such structures as columns and margins, is the set of relationships among elements that cause some to be seen first, and others to be seen in some descending order. With hierarchy, typographic elements gain primary, secondary, and tertiary (or lower) status—descending emphases that lead readers through reading spaces [1.28]. Hierarchy employs contrasts of all sorts, most notably of typeface, size, and weight. The relative position of elements, figure and ground relationships, and—in dynamic environments—duration, speed, and movement each contribute to hierarchy. Typographic hierarchy employed on a two-dimensional plane enlists our three-dimensional experience of space and time. It mimics the planes and depths that we encounter every day [1.29].

1.29 Poster for Harvard Graduate School of Design's Loeb Fellowships, 2008. Rick Valicenti and John Pobojewski, Thirst. *This complex hierarchy employs typographic scale, color, weight, and orientation within an implied third dimension. Are the paragraphs that are situated in the upper left-hand corner of the poster sitting in front of or behind the planes of text below it?*

Standing in the middle of a vast desert, we notice a giant boulder in front of us first, because it is close, and it is big. So we see it before we notice all of the other things we could look at. In hierarchy, this is called the first, or primary, hierarchical level.

Then we notice the yucca field a little farther away. It is smaller and fainter in relation to the boulder, but still large and distinct enough to have drawn our attention next, once our eyes wandered away from the boulder. This shift is equivalent to a reader moving from the primary level to a secondary hierarchical level.

Over time, we notice the silhouette of mesas spanning the horizon far behind the yucca field. Their distance and smallness kept us from paying much attention to them when we first arrived (and then there was that boulder). We have now moved from the secondary hierarchical level to the tertiary level. We might just as readily have noticed the tiny flowers on the ground to the right of the boulder. Their diminutive details, as compared to the boulder and the yucca field, were not visually strong enough to pull our eyes then, but now we notice them.

Degrees of visual prominence establish the order in which we see things. We can translate this to the two-dimensional plane common in typography: we comprehend the meaning of progressively smaller or fainter elements in the same way we understand objects in space. Larger, bolder elements seem nearer, and attract us more strongly, than smaller, more timid elements. Elements in motion tend to command greater attention than static elements, especially if the moving elements are in proximity to static elements. If a jack rabbit suddenly hopped out from behind that boulder, its skittish movement, compared to the lifeless lump of rock, would draw our attention immediately.

Hierarchy in motion-based media is a little more complex. Typography that moves is made of similar formal attributes to typography that remains stationary, but it has the added attributes of motion, obviously, and of time [1.30]. Say two lines of text sit idly on a screen. The one on top is bold and red, and the line below is smaller and gray. The hierarchy is clear: the topmost line of text constitutes the first level, the line beneath the second (it helps that we read in this order too). But if the second line is shimmying and the first line is static, the bottom line takes on the first hierarchical level because it draws attention first. If all elements are in motion, then the order in which they enter the scene establishes hierarchy, or the speed at which each element moves in relation to other elements.

Spatial (distance-based) and temporal (time-based) relationships among typographic elements also influence the order in which we see things. In two dimensions, readers are likely to jump from the first hierarchical level to the second if the two elements are spatially closer than any of the other elements. Formal parity can assist the leap as well. Readers naturally associate similar-looking things, so elements that share common visual attributes are likely to be seen in quick succession. For instance, if the first hierarchical level is a bright green, **slab-serif** 60 pt italic, and an element across the page is the same bright green, slab-serif italic but smaller, the second element will readily attract readers directly after the first.

Typographers put hierarchy to use in many more ways than I have presented here, and structures can be quite complex. Whereas this brief introduction has focused on the relational components of hierarchy and structures, the discussions in Chapters 2, 3, and 5 add more dimension to both. For now, understand that hierarchy is a system of relationships among elements, and structure helps control those relationships.

1.30 *Appetite Engineers Philosophy*, 2011. Martin Venezky, Appetite Engineers. *Presented within the limits of a web browser window, this "page" reveals its lengthy and continuous content as a reader scrolls. Scale shifts create visual rhythm and emphasis, and establish relationships among related texts from one screen to the next.*

RELATIONAL SYSTEMS

ANATOMY OF THE MESSAGE

content and function

Designed artifacts are visual stories: pronouncements and narratives, transmitted through a synergy of content and form, that include image, motion, **composition**, sound, and color. The meanings associated with both form and content invite people (readers), who share visual and written languages, to construct messages almost instantly.

We need a disclaimer here. As typographers, we have little control over the written content at our disposal, unless of course we write it ourselves. Likewise, we are rarely in charge of production budgets and distribution means, unless, again, we ourselves are the producers. The aspects over which we do have a modicum of control, though, are typographic roles and forms of expression, which are embodied in style to establish a voice, discussed later. These aspects interact with content and linguistic systems to generate entertaining, instructive, convincing, promising, surprising messages (and every other kind!) that are interpreted by the reader. Typography's chief function is to give form to content. When form joins content, the two together impart messages.

Many practitioners see typography as principally pragmatic, arguing that letterforms, including beautiful letterforms, serve reading first and foremost. Certainly web catalogs, news magazines, and pharmaceutical labels need to be read. The functional and messaging possibilities of typography, however, are rich beyond practical beauty.

role and expression

We ascribe two main functions to typographic content: roles, such as a **folio** or the **body** on a page; and expressions [1.31]: for instance surprise, authority, repulsion, loudness, playfulness, scariness, lightness. According to our earlier definitions, roles have a denotative function, whereas expressions are connotative. If the folio of a magazine set in 9 pt Caslon simply locates pages within *Ladies' Home Journal*, the typographer will thereby have given more weight to its role than to a form of expression. Fulfilling its role, the folio leads readers to articles, its utility no different than if it were working for any other magazine—*National Geographic* or *Boy's Life*. By contrast, folios in a book entitled *The Tao of Way Finding* set at 72 pt Johnston might assume the role of page identifiers as well. Designed at such a large scale, the folios express the subject matter by additionally referring to an historical moment in public signage, in 1916, when the London Underground commissioned the typeface and applied it to its new signage.

Periodicals feature all manner of subject matter, from political events to celebrity gossip to academic essays. Their content changes routinely: hourly in the case of blogs; daily in newspapers; weekly or monthly for journals.

1.31 *The 1% User's Manual.* Jeremy Mende, Mende Design. *The roles set up in this booklet are delineated by typeface, by the relative scale of each kind of text, and by placement. The design separates two sets of content—one written for architects, the other for non-profit organizations—transversely across the booklet. The cover typography announces each title in the same typeface, size, and place. Likewise, statements share spatial and formal attributes, as do lists.*

Johnston

The English designer Edward Johnston designed uppercase letters, numbers, and a few symbols for the London Underground signage system, introduced in 1916. This sans-serif "Humanist" font was further developed by Eric Gill in the family Gill Sans, between 1928 and 1932.

Metropolis, for instance, publishes diverse but related articles on design within each issue and across volumes. The typography, then, must assume various roles—pull quotes, bylines, captions—that will embody a range of content from issue to issue. The magazine also wants to express its unique identity, as distinct from its news-stand rivals *Architectural Record* and *Architect*. For this task we call on style. Akzidenz Grotesk will suit the magazine, owing to its stylistic affiliation with architecture. By the same token, a new periodical on the stand might prudently be launched under a different sans-serif masthead, or the designer might opt for something else entirely, to create and express a unique identity for the magazine.

style

Styles are connotative. They rely on generalizations about periods, movements, and places, all of which are open to interpretation and variation. Styles arrive by way of a designer's subjectivity—one of the most volatile of cultural systems—and add meaning to message(s). At base, they reflect designer intent. More frequently, they reflect cultural trends and tolerances, reading conventions, and changing technologies [1.32]. A designer working in a particular style draws on historical conventions yet interprets them afresh, so the style's meaning shifts as times change, which heaps layers of complexity onto typographic form.

Typefaces and treatments carry formal baggage. Their style might harken to a time as far back as ancient Rome, or to Art Deco design in the 1920s and 1930s [1.33], or a movement as recent as grunge in the 1990s. The period in which typefaces were used, and the purposes they were used for, influence their meaning now. The region and historical moment of origin sometimes give typefaces their

1.32 Jan van Eyck Academy program brochure, 2007. Matthijs van Leeuwen. *Styles can take an anti-style stance. This typography echoes styles that deliberately underplay or oppose commercial stylistic conventions.*

1.33 Public market signage using a version of Broadway, and the typeface redrawn for contemporary use (Pineapple typeface design, 2009, by Travis Stearns).

1.34 *Harper's Bazaar* front cover.

stylistic character, depending on how strongly they are associated with a visually distinctive period. And every period is visually distinctive. In the 1940s, *Vogue's* art director Alexei Brodovitch used an extreme version of Didot for the magazine's masthead and headlines. Its success and ultimate ubiquity helped to establish a lasting association of extreme thick-to-thin unbracketed serif typefaces with high fashion. As late as 1991 Hoefler/Frere-Jones crafted a new cut of Didot for the redesign of fashion-oriented *Harper's Bazaar* [1.34].

Readers interpret codified styles depending on their exposure to visual tropes, which will be discussed in Chapter 5. For instance, the typeface Broadway, designed and used pervasively in the 1920s and 1930s, conjures the jazz age for those who are aware of its origins. People ignorant of that history have, however, used Broadway for all sorts of non-jazz-age content, the reference be hanged. Since the 1930s, the font has become a popular option available from quick print shops. For decades business owners, shopkeepers, and real-estate brokers far and wide have chosen the face simply because it is the boldest option, or because it looks snazzy [1.33].

Commercial websites selling furniture inspired by the mid-twentieth century will, nine times out of ten, sport clean, sans-serif typefaces of the same period because they connote "modern" to those who know. Meanwhile, Barack Obama's presidential campaign used the modern-inspired typeface Gotham [1.35], in glaring opposition to a stylistic convention that dominated American campaign graphics at the time: the use of traditional, serif typefaces. In a discussion about the typography, creative director Brian Collins noted that to set Obama's slogan words "Change" and "Hope" in Comic Sans would have made the concept feel "lightweight and silly," or, in Times Roman, "self-important." Gotham, by contrast, makes the words feel "inspiring, not threatening." He concludes that "typography makes a real difference when it delivers words and ideas that are relevant to people. And for many, that seems to be the case here."[3]

Style is powerful when it melds with content in ways that resonate with cultures and subcultures, highlighting the interests and issues of the moment. The first Obama presidential election campaign will influence future American political graphics not because the typeface chosen for the campaign was powerful, but because the style of his message, applied somewhat contrarily in the context of campaign norms, is now associated with a certain set of values:

In the campaign the message is communicated through both content and form equally because of an implicit understanding of how form can also be content. The designed materials exude the campaign message from every tiny detail, making an impression that reaches far beyond vote getting. The tangibility of this campaign has inspired many thousands of new voters to register but more importantly has raised awareness about the democratic process itself.[4]

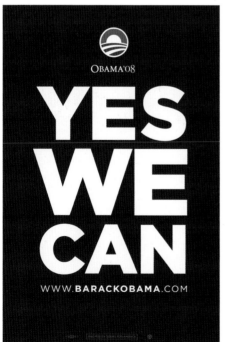

1.35 Barack Obama 2008 election campaign poster.

Codify

To organize aspects or establish rules into a system or code. In the case of style, any set of visual codes can become codified through exposure and usage, such as the use of blackletter in "Goth" style, or cut-out letters to signify "ransom notes."

Broadway

Designed by the American Morris Fuller Benton and released by ATF in 1928, Broadway, and its variant Broadway Engraved, grew to be synonymous with jazz age and Moderne styles. Many versions have been drawn and distributed since its introduction.

Gotham

An extensive family of sans-serif typefaces issued by the New York Hoefler/Frere-Jones foundry, Gotham began as a small family inspired by mid-twentieth-century signage found at the Port Authority Bus Terminal. Designed by Tobias Frere-Jones, Jesse Ragan, and Jonathan Hoefler.

Comic Sans

Vincent Connare based this design on comic-book speech bubble handlettering by John Costanza (*Batman: The Dark Knight Returns*) and Dave Gibbons (*Watchmen*). Since its inclusion in Microsoft's system software in 1995, the "friendly" font has become ubiquitous and is, by some accounts, overused.

The designer Lorraine Wild proposes a tongue-in-cheek theory as to how style inevitably cycles through a "great wheel." First there is good design: that's at the top, naturally. In time good design devolves to mass-market style and eventually turns to cliché, the third stage. Cliché becomes an embarrassment (stage four), which leads to the "it's over" fifth stage, in which the style becomes stultified and obscure. The style nevertheless cycles through stages six, seven, and eight: it is resurrected by a few as a fetish; consequently, hipsters turn the style into a revival; and ultimately a critical mass finds the style "interesting" again. The ninth stage returns the style full circle to the first stage, good design. Predicting how and when styles will shift is almost impossible, unless one has the influence and resources to shape the future. It depends on how the catalysts that fuel the cycle—those systems—interact.

Lest anyone think he is immune, I should point out that typography is style as soon as we choose one approach to the exclusion of others. Each and every decision situates us somewhere on the style train. If we cultivate a unique style, we are the conductor. We may ride along with others, accepting some version of a style, or grumble from the caboose declaring style to be irrelevant or superfluous. No matter. When we settle on a typeface, we step onto the train. Enjoy the ride.

1.36 Dunlap Broadside, 1776. John Dunlap. Beinecke Rare Book and Manuscript Library, Yale University.

voice

Think of typographic style as the dress of the producers. Information issued by a government office will be "dressed" in a different style than materials produced by a toy manufacturer. Style establishes voice, the underlying attitude and position that readers interpret, based on their experience of what the style means. Signage in an airport typically speaks with level-headed confidence, offering assurances of safe travel. The hipness of a retail logotype can convince a passerby of a company's "street cred," even if it happens to reside on the thirtieth floor of a downtown high-rise. A protest poster's "homemade" typography bespeaks an attitude of grassroots urgency.

In 1776 the authors of the American Declaration of Independence had the original document typeset in a traditional roman face. Copies, known as the Dunlap Broadsides, were distributed and posted across the thirteen states [1.36]. But who would understand such a quotidian form as "official"? A month later a single "engrossed" copy of the Declaration was penned by hand on a rather large sheet of parchment and signed by the Congress. Although common **typesetting** and printing arguably represented the more democratic voice, the authors opted for a voice similar

Nutrition Facts

Serving Size 3/4 cup (30g)
Servings Per Container about 12

Amount Per Serving		
Calories 120		Fat cal 10

	% Daily Value*
Total Fat 1g	1%
Saturated Fat 0	0%
Sodium 130 mg	5%
Total Carb 24 g	8%
Dietary Fiber 5 g	20%
Sugars 4g	
Protein 4g	

Vitamin A 0%	•	Vitamin C	0%
Calcium 0%	•	Iron 8%	

Not a significant source of *trans* fat or cholesterol.
*Percent Daily Values are based on a 2,000 calorie diet.

1.37 *(top)* Stenciled graffiti, 2009.

1.38 *(above) Food labels and similarly regulated typographic treatments embody the voice of standardization and control, once readers become acquainted with such labels through use.*

to that of authority, one shared by their former sovereign. Strangely, the engrossed copy that is proudly displayed in Washington, D.C. has come to be understood as the voice of democracy and independence rather than that of monarchy.

A different voice is found in spray-painted messages, stenciled onto public walls. This form of graffiti can embody the voice of the dispossessed, or of youths (usually) claiming alliegiance to them. But the visual form can also be put to rhetorical use for other ends [1.37]. A recent campaign advertising the latest sequel in an already protracted movie series employed stencil and spray-painted type in its promotions. Now, the previous movies made millions of dollars, and the new one took millions more to make. Surely the producers could afford the typesetting costs. But the cost could not be further from the point. I paused at first, wondering what new tagger had been let loose around Los Angeles. Once I realized the "tags" were sprayed onto otherwise pristine billboards and bus-stop one-sheets, I knew the promoters were assuming a familiar voice, one associated with the street. Annoying? A little. Misleading? Not really. The tactic is simply an effective application of style to ensure that the advertising speaks in a particular voice.

Voice is sometimes revealed in the form of typographic constraint. For instance, contemporary mail-scanners require that the type size and its placement on a flyer, for example, be recognizable to the machines. Consequently, some mail has an "official" voice. Legislation might dictate type treatment based on issues of possible liability. The U.S. Food and Drug Administration regulates nutrition labels printed on most food packaging: the typography must not only meet readability averages but also establish the voice of a fair-minded watchdog [1.38].

DEFAULTS, PRESETS, AND TEMPLATES

If any aspect of the typographic future is certain, it is that smarter and more automatic software will be available—turnkey programs that are primarily designed to anticipate production needs, but that also observe basic visual conventions. For instance, current software automatically designs nutrition labels using FDA specifications. Digital typefaces are quite impressive as well. A font renders accurately at nearly any scale on screen, adapting its appearance to utilize available pixels, through a process called "hinting." Such fonts also make typography reproducible in any medium, as refined as the medium will allow. It won't be long before digital images, vector graphics, and letterforms automatically scale to a specified area: simply type content into a designated space and watch it snap to fit the given parameter.

How did software get so smart? Programming wizardry, of course. More importantly for typographers, though, the smartness that programmers build in to software often represents baseline standards—common writing traditions, reading conventions, and a few professional typesetting standards. Imagine if our clothing options were reduced to comparable averages. We set out, let's say, to the College Student section of the department store (other sections might include Business Executive, Professor, or Landscape Architect).

Turnkey

A product or service ready for immediate use, generally referring to such goods as an accounting or manufacturing system.

It turns out the preset choices are either men's or women's boot-cut five-pocket denim jeans, size medium; white or black T-shirts, also in medium; and black, white, or lime-green trainers in women's size medium. Now, I happen to prefer extra-extra-large T-shirts and khaki shorts, and wear a smaller-than-average sneaker. My personal style also calls for a duck-patterned hoodie lined in yellow fleece. These anomalies are not included in the prescription for "college-student attire." Nor are such special options automatic in typography production software. Particularization is quite possible, and is intelligently facilitated by smart software. One just needs to know where to look, or, at the very least, to know that options beyond <u>defaults</u> abound [1.39].

Typographic defaults in most software typically include a prescribed typeface, like 12 pt <u>Myriad</u> set on 120% point **line spacing** (14.40 pt), and several other average <u>presets</u>, like non-lining **figures (numerals)**. These standards are transferable to any context, yet they cannot possibly suit every content or intention. For instance, margins typically default to a uniform half-inch, even if we change a default page size from 8.5 × 11 inches to 2 inches square. Other standards are Times Roman or Arial set at 12 pt, no matter the column width, with equally average line spacing [1.40].

Thankfully, smart software helps minimize the tedious details and decisions of some production processes. It saves rebuilding that which has been built millions of times before; or applies parameters—built specially by the typographer—to files universally. <u>Master pages</u> in many programs replicate and place elements perfectly and instantly—to the micromillimeter, from page 1 to 300 or frame 1 to 300,000. Print-production software registers the total page count minute by minute and automatically numbers pages in their correct sequence, even when we reorder entire sections. A single command to a style sheet adjusts line spacing or type size across any number of web or print pages. And complicated but manageable code, such as Cascading Style Sheets for a web browser or Action Script for <u>Flash</u>, works ingeniously behind seemingly magical buttons in dynamic design applications, assigning characteristics and behaviors to screen assets on the fly.

Less charming are the standardized layout **templates** offered in most word-processing, print, web, and image-production software. Everything from business cards to magazines can be set up in each program with typefaces, sizes, compositions, and colors built in [1.41]. Chapter 4 delves further into these typographic compilations. In terms of the current discussion, these

Default

The base specifications of attributes and tools that are designed into software.

Myriad

A contemporary "Humanist" sans serif designed by Robert Slimbach and Carol Twombly for Adobe Systems. Issued originally in 1992, the family has since been adapted for various technologies, including the version Myriad Web, which is optimized for the screen.

Preset

Measures, colors, margins, and other attributes that open in production software and are set up by the manufacturer as the base properties.

Master pages

A feature in web- and print-production software that defines and stores common margins and grids, plus such repeating elements as folios, running heads, and navigation bars. Like style sheets, master pages eliminate redundant setup of identical elements during production.

Flash

A software platform initially developed by Macromedia, Inc., but developed and distributed by Adobe. The software is used to design interactive and animated vector-oriented graphics.

1.39 (above) Poster, 2002. Stefan Chinof. *This typography is anything but default, and was not achieved using presets. Its visual intricacy was created through knowledgeable manipulation of software.*

1.40 (below) *2 in x 2 in page with word-processing software defaults.*

1.41 (opposite) *This simulated template presents clichés of newsletter design: rectilinear masthead; large, bold headline; medium-sized subheads; two columns; a drop cap (or other element signifying the beginning of an article); and images sized to the column width.*

Default margins and 12 pt Minion on 14.4 pt line spacing.

Cus Eosanita Expellab

Apienisqui Bere Di Revel

Opsame quo cus quos nullaut aut doluptam, sumet ese qui nonet officium ducid ut lique labor rate cus, abor accusam et, corate volore, as erumque delestiatur? Ximagnam que cum as dolorit, sequunt et aper ferio magnis etur re ped mo es dolupta tusanti strunt quistemo essinumquis dem et officias ma doluptior ate vit et erecus as eum, sandit occuptatur, tes del explisq uissecaeped maio tet quia comnis cum lis corem lacest dolupta quam, amet et earum nos et, nim aut aut ut magnatet ius a nem repremporem ullaut abo. Imo qui ut quam harum, quatius tiatum quos unt doluptatemo int voluptatus et ea dolore liqui nus velia sit magnihil il expla consed quunt ma eum et moluptam nem faccuptas sam, et audaesciur, voluptat odi ditassita vel mos entur antiis archil idi occae iligeni hiliquatur, aut aut adit omniscita qui am et andusam volendi pitiis quia et es que quo ipsunt pa cus aut in porepelit officie ndiam, occusam dolorit molores elest, cuptaquatiam expeliquidus quo bero mod minventur amet aspicil istem expligni dentor re moluptur?

Unt velecte niet eum qui

molorem ipitas cus et ipide corum fuga. Undundi ut untissit earchicil maiost et, tescide llique sintios si nulparciti coribus dolorum qui officimintur simodit atemqui busandis con cum endit et reicid quam hariaturis es nost ut et

Raecus, non pres eiur? Et maio. Tem exenti untur, voluptundit ent, volecumqua et liquam, aut offici ibor simodit ius dolorisit incita venditibus, ipenst aut peribus dolest eossequ iaecusdam, quod milt autemqu issequi atatur aut omnolupt dolor.

orum quis quodi rempereri officiae pel ipsum nullatur sin nobis conseque vendamusae solor aut eatibusdant et volorrovid endel eos excersperio mosti quis res mincto dolum re est, cus venis nonsers pisquuntis raectem pelicium abo. Lis apiciuntium sam harum, eniaspi deliate nis minctur res magni aut apicium estet aut odis aut rehenihit qui doleceserem quissin itionserum qui od eserum, vendae volende viderest praturibusam experro quas doluptas aliqui corum et qui ut plis aut occum venimpost alicte nis aut aboresto occatiae poritatus nobis exerspit auda quo diam la suntior re voluptatis utati aut res voluptatet inullentias et enetur sumquatum quo ducidebitate volecti rectasit optatiore, conest molore con nes anihic tem dolorit eserferae vellori oribusam.

"newsletter" or "menu" designs will not suit any and all textual information, for the simple reason that not all newsletters and menus contain the same content. As to style, if we're looking for something generic, then templates deliver [1.41]. Like defaults and presets, their uses are limited. They are handy for users who lack typographic skills and for people who just want to produce standard documents. For a typographer looking to make typography *Work*, though, the most that templates offer is evidence of commonly accepted averages.

Software programs today are so much more sophisticated than the pre- and proto-digital practices of the past that we often wonder how designers accomplished anything before such brilliant developments came to our aid. But we also know that the proficient typographer possesses skills and experience, not just tools. Mastery is the ability to adapt to the conditions and contexts of every detail, resulting in nuanced decisions—a capacity that neither software nor templates can match, at least not yet.

PROMPTS

/// **Next time you go** to your favorite coffee shop or cafe, locate the typography (and design) in use: on signage, menus, paper goods, and uniforms. Observe the patrons and the baristas. How do the cafe's graphic design and typography reflect the values of the people who frequent the place? *(See "Cultural Systems in Particular," page 30.)*

/// **Select any current** typographically rich periodical, website, sign, or video, and imagine the contexts of its production and distribution (including the context of your experience with the thing). Describe who you think the readers are, and the what/how/when/where of the artifact. What attributes of the typography, composition, material, etc. led you to your conclusions? *(See "Contexts," page 35.)*

/// **Many type foundries** and distributors provide downloadable PDFs showing the character sets of the typefaces they sell. Select two different type families, then download and print the PDFs. Identify and compare the ratios you find. *(See "Micro Relationships," page 41.)*

/// **Find a video** of title credits from a movie, or a typographic motion piece on the Internet. Study the structure, or skeleton, that positions typography on screen over the duration of the clip. Does the structure change over time? Is there an observable system? Is it a fluid or a static structure? Draw the underlying structure as you understand it functioning throughout the clip. *(See "Structure," page 47.)*

/// **Next time you visit** a shopping center, take pictures of storefront signage. Take note of the kind of store each one is for, and who you think the clientele might be. Select a few very different stores, and describe how their styles differ. Based on your knowledge of what the different stores offer, and to whom, identify the "voice" expressed in the typography. *(See "Style," page 52, and "Voice," page 54.)*

reading

Collect

Heavenly Father,
who didst send thine apostle Paul t‹
and gavest him Timothy and Titus
   to be his companions in the fait
grant that our fellowship in the Hol
may bear witness to the name of Je
who liveth and reigneth with thee,
in the unity of the Holy Spirit,
one God, now and for ever.

Post Communion

The Post Communion of Missionaries

28 January
        Priest, Philosopher, Te‹

Collect

Everlasting God,
who didst enrich thy Church with t‹
   of thy servant Thomas Aquinas
grant to all who seek thee
a humble mind and a pure heart
that they may know thy Son Jesus C
   to be the way, the truth and the
who liveth and reigneth with thee,
in the unity of the Holy Spirit,
one God, now and for ever.

Post Communion

The Post Communion of Teachers of t

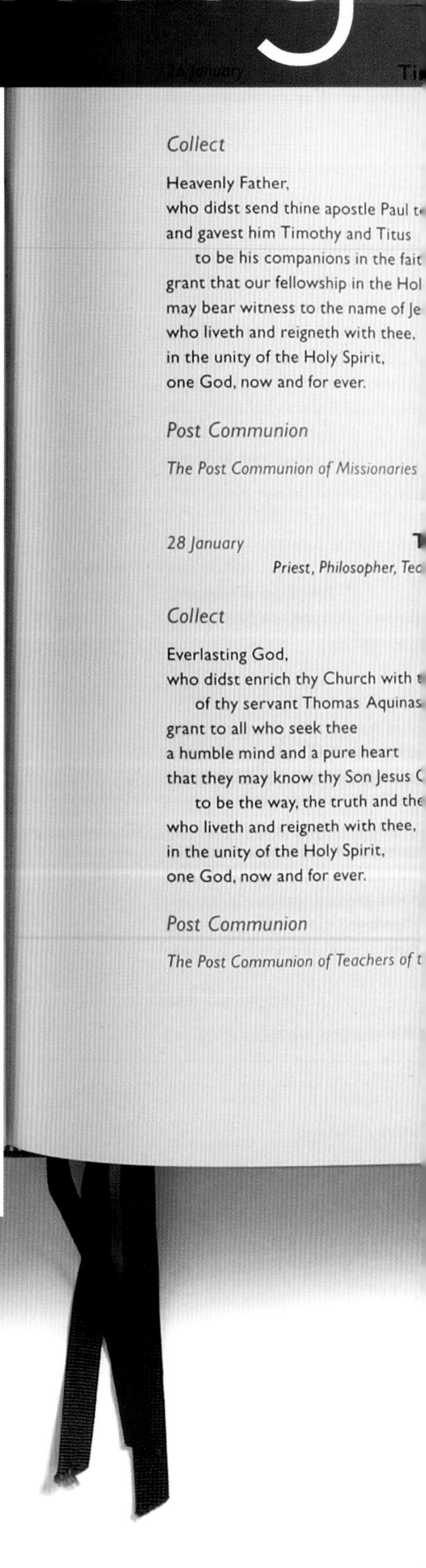

systems 2

Chapter 2 presents the myriad conditions and circumstances that make up the contexts of reading and readers. A range of scenarios is used to illustrate the systems at work when readers encounter, read, and interpret the messages that typography embodies. You will be reminded of the basic principles of writing and language that drive typographic function and reading (many of which you already know, because you are able to read this paragraph). Formal systems come into play through discussion of the expectations and experiences of readers, things that typographers need to anticipate. The chapter also covers the many ways in which typography delivers content to readers. I offer a few typographic rules in relation to underlying traditions, and to the preferences of the readers and typographers who perpetuate them. The chapter concludes with a look at why and how typographers adapt traditions for their own purposes, which of course affects how readers read.

primer

ASYMMETRY

The appearance of balance in the arrangement of form, achieved through an irregular distribution of elements around an implied center. In contrast to symmetry, in which one side of the composition mirrors the other, asymmetrical compositions are typically more dynamic and preferred by the modern eye. **ILL. 01 > PAGE 86**

BRAND

The recognizable identity of a company, product, or service that distinguishes it from other brands and that is expressed through its name, symbol, typeface, colors, or some other visual representation. Branding, however, involves more than the "look" of a company's graphic system. It is also reflected in the full consumer experience, which also results from choices about what products to make and the quality of service. **> PAGE 76**

CENTERED

A column style in which the center point of each line of type aligns with the vertical axis of the column, leaving both the left and right edges of the column ragged. **ILL. 02 > PAGE 86**

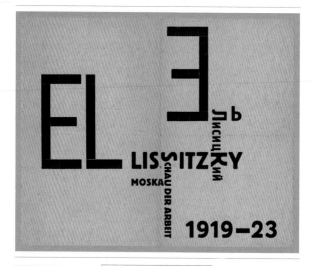

01 : ASYMMETRY

She sprang across to the booth
and picked up the directory hanging
beside the telephone.
Then a queer, bewildered look
came into her eyes and she stood still
with the book hanging uncertainly
from her fingers.

02 : CENTERED

03 : DIACRITICAL MARKS

She had forgotten
Nyoda's name! She
twisted her brows into
a pucker and made a
frantic effort to recall it.
No use; it was a
fruitless endeavor.

Where that name used
to be in her mind
there was now a blank
space, empty and
echoless as the original
void. Katherine gave a
little stamp of vexation.

04 : FLUSH LEFT/RIGHT

DIACRITICAL MARKS

Non-alphabetical marks used in combination with letters to indicate pronunciation in a variety of languages. Common diacritical marks include the acute (é), the umlaut (ö), and the tilde (ñ). Diacritical marks may be attached to specific letters in the design of the typeface or added to letters through keystrokes in a variety of software programs. **ILL. 03 > PAGE 66**

DYNAMIC TYPOGRAPHY

Screen-based or filmic typography that changes its state of being across time or through interaction with the user. Typography in these media may blink, fade, move, or change size or color. The opening title sequence of the *Harry Potter* movies, where viewers are made to feel as if they are passing though floating letters, is an example of dynamic typography. **> PAGE 78**

FLUSH LEFT/RIGHT

A column style in which all lines of type are aligned either to the left or right edge of the column, with the opposite side being ragged because lines of type contain different numbers of characters. **ILL. 04 > PAGE 87**

GRAMMAR

The set of structural rules governing the use of words within a particular language. Typography can reinforce these conventions, as in the application of capitalization at the start of a sentence or in line breaks in a headline, or cause readers to see some syntactical (reading order) relationship other than the one that naturally occurs in the linguistic ordering of the sentence. **> PAGE 67**

JUSTIFICATION

A column style in which all lines of type align with both the left and right sides of the column. To achieve this alignment, space is added between words to compensate for the variations in the number of characters per line. **ILL. 05** **>PAGE 86**

LINE LENGTH

The length of a line of body copy, measured in picas, inches, or pixels and containing an average number of characters and spaces in the selected typeface and point size. The number of characters and spaces per line influences ease of reading: too many and the reader has problems finding the start of each line at the left edge of the column; too few and eye movement is choppy. **ILL. 06 > PAGE 71**

LOGOTYPE

A specific typographic treatment of a company or organization name that is recognizable and consistent with its identity. A "monogram" or "word mark" includes only initials. **ILL. 07 > PAGE 76**

MEANS OF DELIVERY

The ways in which typographic messages reach readers. Books, television news tickers, and websites are means of delivery. **> PAGE 79**

It was not the first time a name had popped out of her mind at a critical moment. Was there ever anything so utterly absurd as the plight in which she now found herself? She knew Nyoda's name as well as her own. M. M. It certainly began with an M. After nearly an hour she gave it up in disgust and stalked out of the station.

> **05 : JUSTIFICATION**

17 PICAS

The next step forward is the development of the ideogram into the phonogram, or sound sign. When this step is taken, the ideogram, besides representing an idea in a general way, represents a sound, usually the name of the object represented by the ideogram or by

12 PICAS

one of its components. A succession of these phonograms then represents a series of sounds, or syllables, and we have a real, though somewhat primitive and cumbrous, written language.

> **06 : LINE LENGTH**

> **07 : LOGOTYPE**

> **08 : MONOSPACE (FIXED-WIDTH)**

> **09 : PILCROW**

MONOSPACE (FIXED-WIDTH)

Typefaces in which every glyph is the same width, regardless of its formal complexity. Text typed on manual typewriters was monospaced so that the carriage could move in uniform increments. Courier, a digital typeface that recalls this older technology, is monospaced, unlike Baskerville, which adjusts the spacing to reflect the differences in the set-width of a capital M and lowercase i. **ILL. 08 > PAGE 72**

PILCROW

A symbol used to denote the start of a paragraph. The pilcrow was used in the Middle Ages to mark a change in the train of thought. Eric Gill used pilcrows in his book *An Essay on Typography* (1930) to demarcate the paragraphs in continuous copy. **ILL. 09 > PAGE 72**

PRIME MARKS

Typographic characters referring to feet and inches. The single prime mark (') designates feet, and the double prime mark (") designates inches. Prime marks are often confused with the apostrophe and quotation marks, which are angled or curved. **> PAGE 72**

PUSH AND PULL TECHNOLOGIES

A category of network technology defined by who is responsible for initiating the flow of information. In push technologies, such as email, RSS feeds, and instant messaging, web servers direct information to users. In pull technologies, such as search engines, the user directs the flow of information from a personal device to a web server. **> PAGES 81/82**

READING PATH

The probable track a reader's eyes will take in moving through typography. While readers of English tend to move through a page of text from the upper left to lower right, variations in typographic emphasis can subvert this normal reading pattern and draw readers' attention to other areas of the composition. **ILL. 10 > PAGE 82**

ROLLOVER

An area on the screen of a digital device that is designed to be sensitive to touch or activation by a mouse or track-pad interaction. **ILL. 11 > PAGE 85**

SEMIOTICS

The study of signs. A sign is something that stands for something else to someone. Written language, for instance, is a system in which individual letters stand for sounds and groupings stand for spoken words and sentences. The Swiss linguist Ferdinand de Saussure (1857–1913) and American philosopher Charles Sanders Peirce (1839–1914) are credited with the development of semiotics. According to Saussure, the sign has two parts: a signifier (the physical entity, such as a typographic letter) and a signified (the mental concept brought forth by the signifier). The relationship between these two is arbitrary and only a matter of cultural agreement. The word "ketchup," for example, has no essential or analogous relationship to the condiment; we have simply agreed that in English the word stands for a tomato sauce. Peirce was famous for grouping signs in triads by performance. Iconic signs resemble the things they stand for (the icons on the bathroom door look like men and women); indexical signs point to a causal relationship (footprints in the sand are a sign that people walked there); and symbolic signs communicate only through cultural agreement (two raised fingers mean "peace" and L-O-V-E describes a deep emotion). The work of these men reminds us that typography is always bound up with context and experience. **> PAGE 90**

10 : READING PATH

11 : ROLLOVER

Thereby, THE INSTITUTE is right.
Thereby, THE INSTITUTE is wrong.

12 : SMALL CAPS

SMALL CAPS

Capital letters designed to be slightly taller than the x-height of lowercase letters but shorter than other capital letters. Small caps are designed to be used within text without disrupting reading flow as words set in all capitals might. When a type family does not include small caps, software can reduce capitals to match the x-height of lowercase letters but the proportions will not be adjusted optically to address the new size. **ILL. 12 > PAGE 71**

SMART QUOTES

The automatic setting of apostrophes and quotation marks. Earlier typesetting substituted prime marks for this punctuation, requiring deliberate keystrokes to make the corrections. **> PAGE 72**

STATIC TYPOGRAPHY

Typography that maintains a fixed position within the composition or visual field. While the reader may change his or her position with respect to the artifact, the typography in books, posters, and painted signage maintains its character and location within the format. Not all typography that is read on computer screens is dynamic; e-books are frequently digital versions of static media. **> PAGE 96**

STYLE SHEETS / CASCADING STYLE SHEETS

A web- or document-design feature that defines and stores typographic attributes for repeated application. Style sheets separate the content of information from the way it looks. Typographic decisions about various elements (the placement, color, and typeface choices related to headlines, subheads, and paragraphs, for example) can be assigned to a "style." Changes and additions can be made in the content of the document while maintaining the appearance of the page. **> PAGE 81**

SYMMETRY

A visual arrangement of elements in which balance is achieved by mirroring. Symmetrical compositions, often associated with classical form, are stable and formal. For this reason, symmetry is often used in such documents as diplomas, memorials, and wedding invitations. **ILLS. 13/14 > PAGE 97**

SYNTAX

The ordering of elements or words within a composition or sentence. In written language, syntax responds to the rules of grammar and determines the horizontal position of words in a sentence. Although the rules governing the reading of visual language are less clear, readers do attach meaning to the position of elements within space and in relation to each other. **> PAGE 67**

VARIABLE-WIDTH

A characteristic of a typeface in which the width of each glyph is determined by its formal complexity. **ILL. 15 > PAGE 72**

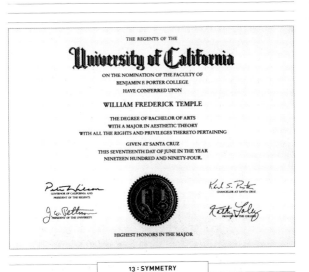

13 : SYMMETRY

14 : SYMMETRY

illumination
illumination
illumination illumination

15 : VARIABLE-WIDTH

16 : WORD SHAPE

WORD SHAPE

The shape of a typeset word. This shape is defined by the negative space surrounding the word and by the degree of difference in the shapes of individual letters. Words set in all capital letters, therefore, show little differentiation at the tops and bottoms. Words set in lowercase letters, on the other hand, are more distinctive because of the presence of unique combinations of ascenders and descenders. For this reason, highway signage is usually set in caps and lowercase. **ILL. 16 > PAGE 72**

Typographers always face a reader, albeit indirectly. It may seem that we face only written text on a screen or some other production tool when crafting work, but just on the other side of these tools, and of the artifacts they help us make, are the people to whom we direct our typography, and to whom we hope our work communicates [2.1].

The words we give form to are usually written by authors or other initiators who also want to communicate ideas, or mark ownership [2.2]. Even abstract typographic forms—letterforms that do not relate to particular words—are "read" by people capable of distinguishing between A and Z. Typographers, then, must be mindful, and preferably in control, of those attributes that favor readability—appropriate structure, character sizes, contrasts, line spacing, and margins. Additionally, typographers might design typography in ways that anticipate the reader's expectations and knowledge, but that also introduce surprising ambiguity.

2.1 *Hate*, 2008. Vaughn Hockey.

Typographic traditions are rooted in writing. Like the forms of writing, these traditions include a range of possibilities that encompass established conventions. This text, for instance, is not typeset in the same way poetry would be. The paragraphic form signals to the readers that the text is not a sonnet or an ode, and so do the words. Neither the visual character of this paragraph, nor the writing style, fit within codified poetic styles. Consequently, your expectation of what you are about to read no doubt differs from the expectations you would have facing traditional lines of verse. And the words corroborate your expectations.

Say I had written, instead: *The hearts, the eyes of men became filled with letters, messages, words, and the passing or permanent wind raised mad or sacred books. Beneath the newly written pyramids the letter was alive, the alphabet burning, the vowels, the*

We will publish emotions, feelings, suggestions — through poetry&photography illustrations&short stories, served with exquiste typography & layouts.

Appendix™

www.appendix-mag.com

Perhaps it's easier to start off what Appendix™ won't be. Appendix™ will not be a source of reviews discussing which face cream is better than another, Appendix™ will not go into length decadent gossip interviews with celebrities. Appendix™ will not be your source of daily news about the war on terror, or about how you should dress yourself for the next season.

But rather, Appendix™ is a collection of lifestyle details that updates on the main human collective. Like the appendix for a book, which fills the details missing from a main body of work, Appendix™ Magazine will act as a supplement to the main discussions covered by other mainstream sources and publications, thus, offering missing details and ideas that have been overlooked.

2.2   Manifesto for *Appendix* magazine, 2009. Paul J. Cheng.

The hearts, the eyes
of men
became filled with letters,
messages,
words,
and the passing or permanent
wind
raised mad
or sacred
books

2.3   Excerpt from "Ode to Typography," 1964. Pablo Neruda.

consonants like curved flowers. And say that we presented the sentences in a paragraph, just like this. You would not immediately interpret the text as poetry (even though an "alphabet burning" is vividly poetic), but you might be a tad perplexed. Say these words are those of the Chilean poet Pablo Neruda, which they are (translated from his native Spanish). His original version assembled the words into terse, incisive lines of text. In this form, you would instantly perceive that the text is a poem [2.3].

Neruda's complete "Ode to Typography" adds up to a mere 960 words. In one published version, the typography disperses those words across twenty pages. If the text had been typeset in a bookish typeface and contained by margins within one continuous paragraph, the poem would have occupied a scant two or three pages; fewer, had the pages been oversized. Would the "Ode" then still be an ode? Yes. And no. The written form would imply "ode-ness," certainly. But the typographic form would be dramatically inconsistent with the traditions of "ode-ness." Therefore, the "Ode" would not be as ode-like as it could be.[1]

The point here is that the form in which writing appears both shapes and is shaped by traditions. Exposure to these writing traditions determines reader expectations. Traditions of typographic form evolve from both—writing traditions and reader expectations.

Of course, not that much typography produced for reading fits within the category of sonnets or haikus. The form of any text conveys conventions of writing and reading to readers. Think of to-do lists, blog entries, and party invitations. We meet each of these familiar conventions with our own set of assumptions. If a typographer ignores them, she does so at the expense of both the writing and the reading. The ideas expressed in writing could end up a scrambled, unintelligible mess, or, worse, the words might never be read.

Conventions underpin the so-called rules of typography, whether applied to a book, a broadsheet, or a building. Unfortunately, the existing typographic rules do not suit all writing and reading situations. It is better to know that there is a set of traditions out there—long-held conventions that reflect a host of reader, and writer, expectations. We will now venture into those traditions by examining writing and reading, active systems that are inextricably linked with typography.

Broadsheet

A large vertical newspaper format, printed on both sides. Also refers to inexpensively produced prints (posters) that have been used since the seventeenth century to distribute information publicly, including public meeting announcements, political satire, and popular ballads.

WRITING, READING, AND VISUAL SYNTAX

writing

Meaningful marks made for the purposes of accounting and communication first emerged around 3200 BCE in Mesopotamia (the region we know today as Iraq) and spread throughout the ancient Near East: Turkey, Syria, Egypt, Palestine, Lebanon, and Israel. Anthropologists trace the genesis of the modern-day Roman alphabet, though, to the Phoenician civilization that occupied what is now Syria, Lebanon, and Palestine. Their scripts date from 2000 BCE, which means that the English alphabetic written form has been evolving and migrating for at least 4000 years. Modified variously by Etruscans, Greeks, Romans, Visigoths, Celts, the Dutch and English, Venetians, French, Germans, and Swiss, the system has survived perhaps because of its flexibility. These alphabets consist of only around thirty letters, plus **diacritical marks**, so the capacity of the Roman alphabet to be adapted by new cultures, and to represent complexity adequately, has helped secure its longevity [2.4].

Conquering empires, merchant cultures, and world exploration partially account for the migration and variation of forms of writing throughout history. Because written form can be studied, copied, and taught, the circumstances of its transference have helped both writing and reading practices to develop. If the <u>substrate</u> upon which text is written is portable—say, papyrus or slate, rather than a marble column—the written word is able to travel to remote places where it can be imitated and altered to suit its adopters.

What once took years to spread around the world now happens at unprecedented speed via cellphones, the Internet, and faxes, technologies which are used around the globe. Circumstances today differ significantly from those as recently as fifty years ago, when the first digital read-out technologies appeared. Our predecessors did not have the same text-generating machines we have today. Neither did they have information super-highways, nor multi-device, multi-channel, input–output feedback loops. New means and tools of distribution affect writing systems, to some degree reading systems, and, with them, acceptable typographic standards. Consider the impact of mobile "texting" and online "chatting" on writing and reading. Today, "TTYL" and "CYL" say "farewell." And yet, writing and reading practices change slowly. People

Substrate
Any underlying material surface—paper, wood, stone, metal, cloth, glass—upon which other materials, such as ink, paint, veneer, or gilt, are printed, painted, or layered.

2.4 *A Constructed Roman Alphabet*, 1979. David Lance Goines.

2.5 The *Guardian*, February 22, 2012. *Like most newspaper design, the typography for the print version of the* Guardian *supports reading in the order that stories appear, page by page. The typography for the web version supports reading in the order that a reader chooses.*

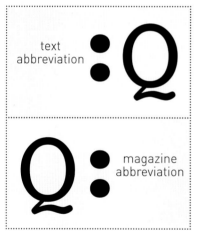

2.6 "Letter syntax."

can still only read a few words at any given moment. And while specialized languages can leak into mainstream habits, they do so incrementally.

Typographers' conscious manipulation of conventions can alter the ways we write. For example, most printed newspapers present articles as continuous, flowing stories, which may include only one jump. Compare this convention with online news sites that introduce articles in bite-sized portions. The full articles are then often broken up into several "pages" (or clicks). The two formats call for different forms of writing. The website format requires that the first sentences of each article capture the character of the story, sometimes in as few as thirty words. The formats also prompt us to read differently. Our next focus, then, is on reading.

reading

Although we are in the habit of jumping from article to article in a printed newspaper, we often begin on the front page and continue reading page after page in the order presented. Online news sites, by contrast, prompt us to scan dozens of short texts (including videos). When we select one, we find links to other articles and videos embedded in and around the text, constantly encouraging us to jump elsewhere. The format changes the order in which we read the news, as well as challenging our powers of concentration [2.5].

Luckily for us, typographers come to the rescue (sometimes). A later section in this chapter (see page 77) discusses how we do that. But we first need to address a fundamental constituent of reading, upon which leading the reader, and reading itself, depend: **syntax**.

Syntax, an aspect of **grammar**, is the order in which words appear as we read a sentence; by analogy, we might also refer to the order of letters within a word as "letter syntax." Syntactical arrangements drive the construction of meaning—so we need to be clear. Here is a simplified example. A colon following a Q in a magazine interview signifies a question [Q:]. Switch the order of the Q and colon, and meaning changes. In the case of a magazine interview, the colon placed before the Q is probably just a typo. In the case of the chat format, switching glyphs [:Q] introduces the emoticon symbol for the question "What?" Syntax, then, establishes meaningful sequences [2.6]. When I write "I love jam," word order makes it clear that it is I who

Jump

In journalism, a term used to describe the point at which readers "jump" from an article begun on one page to its continuation on another page located elsewhere in the publication.

Typo

In the early nineteenth century, a "typo" was the person who composed metal type for printing. Today the term refers to text typeset incorrectly, such as improper capitalization or punctuation, but also often means a misspelling.

Emoticon

A portmanteau ("emotion" plus "icon") that describes a graphic language comprised of punctuation and other glyphs. In certain configurations, the glyphs suggest images, which have come to express happiness, surprise, fright, teasing, and so on.

love jam, not jam that loves me. The distinction is critical in that it means the difference between sounding sensible and completely nutty.

visual syntax

The written order of words affects how readers construct meaning. For its part, typography gives form to the written word; typographic arrangement, therefore, will also affect how readers create meaning. The range of possible written forms—stories, scripts, plays, essays, poems, advertising copy, slogans—enables a variety of typographic expressions within the norms of writing and reading. Moreover, because linguistic systems originate with humans, they are adaptable to human needs and imagination. But were typographic expression to end there, we would be proven a bunch of automatons blinking on command, in thrall to the dictates of writing (and reading).

Designers create typographic sequences using spatial order, or visual syntax. This order might correspond with the writing sequence (top to bottom, left to right). Not all text, however, needs to be delivered in a particular way to be understood. We can disperse text within any defined space [2.7]—featuring at the top of a poster, for instance, the last text to be read, and at the bottom the first text to be read.

But what is wrong with correlating written syntax to visual syntax? Well, nothing. In fact, the strategy is useful for certain texts, such as software manuals and tables of contents. Communication based solely on known writing and reading conventions may be useful, but it does not always capture the breadth and depth of human ideas and emotions. Perhaps a better question would be: typographically, what is so exciting about following the customs of written syntax?

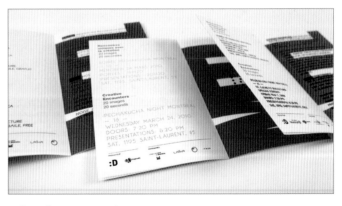

2.7 Poster for Pecha Kucha Night, Montreal, 2010. Anouk Pennel, Raphael Daudelin, and Leon Lo, Feed. *This large-format work serves as both poster and folded announcement for a "Pecha Kucha" event—an evening of brief presentations at which speakers are each limited to a talk accompanied by twenty slides, each shown on screen for twenty seconds. In this poster, various texts become readable as the work is turned. By contrast, typography for the event programs submits to written syntax.*

READING CONVENTION AND TYPE TRADITION

Typographic traditions tend to support common reading habits. Two common habits are active reading, such as skimming through or quickly rereading text on a website or <u>capabilities brochure</u>, and sustained reading (what we do when we absorb a novel).

Trained typographers uphold their traditions in tacit agreement with readers, producers, and fellow typographers. Tastes, too, are passed on from master to novice, generation to generation. Most traditions and tastes are

Capabilities brochure

A printed document that describes and promotes the services and products offered by a business or corporation.

2.8 *Common Worship: Services and Prayers for the Church of England, 2000–2011. Derek Birdsall and John Morgan. Understated but clear distinction among navigational texts and differences between kinds of content lend a respectful air and facilitate reading in the context of worship.*

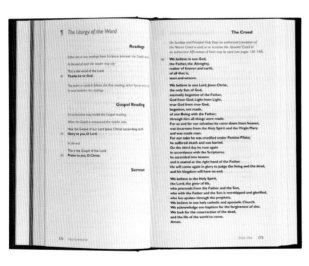

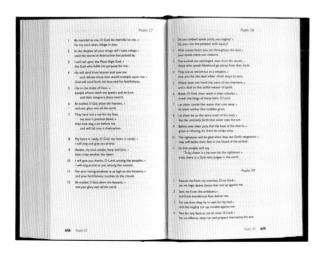

little more than statements of values by which we judge work to be good, bad, or mediocre. But adhering to them connects us to contemporary beliefs and historical precedent. When we abide by the traditions that are preserved as rules, and if the reader apprehends those qualities, our typography looks more "professional" or "correct" [2.8]. Imaginatively tampering with tradition (within taste and the limits of reading convention) can make typography appear fresh and innovative. Rejecting typographic traditions wholesale annoys people who know and abide by the rules, mostly because such effrontery indicates bad manners, also known as a lack of taste. Readers might suffer the repercussions of such deviation, though, when what they want to read is unreadable, or what they need to read is misleading.

Not all experts subscribe to the same typographic traditions, and if they do, it is not necessarily for the same reasons. *S book* 3, an anthology of interviews with twenty-three typographers published in 2006, reveals just how wide is the range of viewpoints among contemporary practitioners. Responding to the question "What are your views on the rules of typography?", the British designer Alan Kitching says, "There is a move away from the laws of real typography . . . but I have a feeling that a lot of poor reading text, that is being put down to perversity, is in fact the result of a lack of real knowledge about typography." Robbie Mahoney, of the design studio Graphic Thought Facility, states that people confuse rules with principles: "Typographic principles are very important to know, they are not some old typographers' opinions, they are fundamental rights and wrongs that need to be known."[2]

If that is the case, among those we can thank for laying out many influential rights and wrongs is the Swiss typographer Emil Ruder. In his book *Typographie* (1967), he writes that "typography has one plain duty before it and that is to convey information in writing. No argument or consideration can absolve typography from this duty. A . . . work which cannot be read becomes a product without purpose."Wolfgang Weingart, a former student of Ruder at the <u>Basel School of Design</u>, strongly disagrees. He claims freedom from "dogma and the constraints of mere legibility," believing that a poster that cannot be read does have a place within typographic practice.[3] The "dogma and the constraints" to which Weingart refers are typographic traditions and tastes that have evolved out of two concerns: pragmatic, such as reading and efficient production methods; and aesthetic, the sense of beauty and style that presides at any given moment in history. Rather than check off a list of typographic rules, let's evaluate a few traditions through pragmatic and aesthetic lenses to understand the underlying forces that established these traditions.

PRAGMATIC AND AESTHETIC RULES: PART I

When experts speak of typographic rules, they typically refer to those that serve the pragmatic goal of clarity and unfettered reader access to the written word. We might think of these constraints as the "rules of play." Just how the game is played, though, falls under the rubric of aesthetics, the internal logic and formal beauty of typography, which varies from society to society, era to era. Neither pragmatic nor aesthetic concerns are categorical until a majority of readers and connoisseurs use and claim allegiance to them over a period of time. For example, the Nazis reintroduced <u>Fraktur</u> in the 1930s as part of their attempt to express a sense of German nationalism in printed books and official announcements, despite the long-held typographic wisdom that roman typefaces are ideal for continuous reading. As the Nazi regime began occupying multilingual Europe from 1938, the typeface was rejected in favor of traditional romans and sans serifs. Not only were these letterforms more suited to translation into a variety of languages, but Fraktur had also by now been discredited as a "Jewish invention" and was therefore unacceptable to the anti-Semitic Nazis. Since the mid-twentieth century, Fraktur and other unfamiliar (to contemporary eyes) typographic inventions, both historic and newly minted, have met with renewed appreciation for their aesthetic value, craft, and rich legacy [2.9].

2.9 Pages from *Fraktur Mon Amour*, 2008. Judith Schalansky.

The need for economic expediency inspired the sixteenth-century printer Aldus Manutius to commission Francesco Griffo to design a font with a narrow set-width so that books could be produced on smaller, and in fewer, pages.

Wuthering Heights is the name of Mr. Heathcliff's dwelling. 'Wuthering' being a significant provincial adjective, descriptive of the atmospheric tumult to which its station is exposed in stormy weather. Pure, bracing ventilation they must have up there at all times, indeed: one may guess the power of the north wind blowing over the edge, by the excessive slant of a few stunted firs at the end of the house; and by a range of gaunt thorns all stretching their limbs one way, as if craving alms of the sun. Happily, the architect had foresight to build it strong: the narrow windows are deeply set in the wall, and the corners defended with large jutting stones. Before passing the threshold, I paused to admire a quantity of grotesque

Wuthering Heights is the name of Mr. Heathcliff's dwelling. 'Wuthering' being a significant provincial adjective, descriptive of the atmospheric tumult to which its station is exposed in stormy weather. Pure, bracing ventilation they must have up there at all times, indeed: one may guess the power of the north wind blowing over the edge, by the excessive slant of a few stunted firs at the end of the house; and by a range of gaunt thorns all stretching their limbs one way,

2.10 Paragraphs set in italics. *Adobe Jenson Italic is based on Venetian old-style italics cut by Ludovico Vicentino degli Arrighi in the late fifteenth century. Long texts set in the typeface, with normal line spacing, might prove challenging to read. ITC Berkeley, based on a typeface designed by Frederic Goudy, would be more readable, especially if submitted to shorter line lengths and greater spacing.*

Bearing in mind that pain or stiffness is the result of want of *supplesse*, the first desideratum is to acquire this most desirable elasticity. To accomplish this, three months before the pupil is put on horseback she should begin a course of training. No amount of dancing will do what is required. Even the professional *danseuse*, with her constant exercise of the *ronde de jambe*, never possesses that mobile action of the waist and play of the joints of the upper part of the figure.

Drill SHOULD BE PRACTISED DAILY. The course of instruction should begin with very short lessons, lasting not more than twenty minutes at first; but these, given in the presence of mamma, should be MOST RIGIDLY CARRIED OUT, otherwise they are useless. They should gradually be increased in length, according to the strength of the pupil, until she can stand an hour's drilling without fatigue.

2.11 Proper use of true italics and small caps.

Hence the first notable italic typeface was devised. As the number of low-cost, portable books typeset in italics increased in the decades that followed, the practice became a standard. Today we would rarely, if ever, typeset an entire book in italics, lest we appear ignorant of the unspoken rule "never typeset an entire book in italics." The reasoning behind the rule is that reading italics over a sustained period supposedly taxes the eye. In fact, some books with extensive text are set in italics, but the choice might be made in relation to many other choices: the type size might be larger, the line spacing greater, the line length shorter, the page size and margins more generous [2.10].

Rules are useful only when they can be applied to the same or similar circumstances that were present when the rules were established. Let's look at a few other rules and their motivations to get a clearer picture of what I mean by this.

The rule "always use true italics" addresses readability (the pragmatic) to some extent. When we want to emphasize a word, phrase, or sentence within a paragraph of text set in a roman typeface, a true italic accomplishes the job more adequately than a faux italic because the true italic is specially designed to maximize differentiation and minimize visual disruption. But the same rule also favors elegance (aesthetics) by fulfilling standards of classic typographic beauty, standards that are learned through considerable study by people who have cared and continue to care about such things. The italics rule to which today's typographer adheres did not exist before phototypesetting, a technology that easily distorted typefaces photographically. Later, desktop publishing software developed in the 1980s featured an "auto-italics" button that forced roman typefaces into an uncomfortable slant—a more economical use of memory and code. Today, true italics are available, if not standard, in most software, and using them carries forward the tradition of italic fonts designed to complement the roman of each weight in a family.

Typesetting that ignores the rule "always use true small caps" may annoy the expert typographer, but the effect on readability is usually negligible. Like italics, specially designed small-cap character sets harmonize optically with the weight and size of their equivalent roman characters [2.11] (this level of detailing separates a well-designed and complete text family from lesser specimens). By comparison, regular caps, when typeset at a reduced size to feign small caps, look anemic and cramped, to the trained eye. The average reader would not see their use as offensive, though.

A current slap in the face to typographers is the common use of **prime marks** instead of apostrophes and quotation marks, crimes perpetrated against the rule "always use quotation marks (for quotes) and apostrophes" [2.12]. Such technologies as vinyl sign-making apparatuses and video software were not originally designed to produce proper marks, so the use of prime marks proliferated. Whatever the impetus, most publication software now comes with factory defaults called **smart quotes** to deter such an outrageous act against typography. In website production, "quote-educator" software automatically reforms ASCII quotes into typographic respectability, an example of contemporary technologies bending to the will of tradition.

Most pragmatic traditions make good sense in that they help direct readers through the text. For instance, the spaces and punctuation that separate words and sentences—writing conventions to which readers are accustomed—alert readers to pauses, progressions, and shifts in the action. Today a dominant rule strongly recommends that typographers differentiate the beginning of a paragraph with space, whether an indent or added space between paragraphs. Contrast this with ancient manuscripts, where the **pilcrow**, rather than spaces, signaled a new paragraph. The rule "never follow a period with a double space" reveals more about the aesthetics of publishing and typesetting than the needs of the reader. Inserting two spaces between sentences originated with typewriter technology, in which the evenness of **monospace**, or fixed-width, characters required more pronounced spacing to announce the end of one sentence and the beginning of the next. Double spaces in **variable-width** fonts look odd to someone used to reading text typeset in the tradition of publishing.

The rule "never letterspace lowercase" acknowledges that typefaces are designed to join any combination of lowercase letters smoothly, forming easily recognizable **word shapes** while maintaining the uniqueness of each character. To letterspace words set in lowercase, then, would be to interfere with word shapes, and, so the assumption goes, the speed of access to words. Although recent research indicates that we do not read words as shapes, the advice persists because, to the schooled eye of some experienced typographers, open letterspaced lowercase letters just look wimpy [2.13].

This same tradition makes less pragmatic sense in screen-based typography. Letters printed in ink can tolerate closeness, whereas letters made up

ASCII

The American Standard Code for Information Interchange, a code employed initially to print on teleprinters, and then adapted for computer displays. It consists of 128 characters. Today ASCII can refer to "keyboard art"—images created from a limited number of "old-school" computer characters.

Manuscript

Before the invention of woodblock printing in China, and metal type in Europe, documents were produced and reproduced by hand. Letters, diagrams, and illustrations were hand-inked and painted on vellum and other parchments, on papyrus, and later on paper, in the form of scrolls or codices (books).

2.12 Quotation marks (correct) and prime marks (incorrect).

2.13 Open-spaced uppercase and lowercase.

2.14 Tightly spaced letters and interlocking words.

of light need more room to compensate for light emanation. Experts who insist on observing the rule under any condition are probably acquainted with the famous warning, "those who would letterspace lowercase would steal sheep." They would not want that on their conscience. While Frederic Goudy's actual words were "those who would letterspace blackletter would steal sheep," the adaptation of the concept into a rule ensures readily identifiable words for those used to reading lowercase letters set closely together. By contrast, few typographers bristle at letterspaced capitals. On the face of it, the same principle should apply, but because open letterspaced capitals have reached acceptance, the treatment is acceptable. In fact, the historical practice and associations it triggers often signal typographic sophistication.

One of the maddening things about typographic rules is that the pragmatic needs of reading do not always trump aesthetic traditions and tastes. Super-tight letterspacing, a 1960s trend that regained favor in the early twenty-first century, earned popularity when phototypesetting allowed letters to be set extremely close together, even to overlap—something metal typesetting could not do [2.14]. The technology not only ushered in a taste for different letterspacing, it also proved that readers can and do decipher overlapping, touching, and near-touching letterforms without much difficulty, depending on the context, of course.

Typographic rules are less fixed than writing and reading rules. We observe them as long as they remain relevant to the application, the time, the place, and the powers that be. Typographers attach great importance to traditions, primarily because they respect the written word and the readers of those words. They might cherish taste as an inheritance from their great predecessors, and see themselves as the custodians of a rich past that continues to resonate. They might regard their history highly because they take pride in the legacies and, ultimately, want to preserve and perpetuate them. Or they might choose to resist their typographic legacy. Given the sometimes arcane nature of typographic rules, the one it would be most prudent to observe is "always recognize rules as traditions and tastes, motivated by pragmatic and aesthetic concerns."

LEGIBILITY AND READABILITY

Typography corresponds to an array of tolerances that varies from reader to reader. Bitmap fonts designed in the mid-1980s made a comeback around 2001, despite their original reputation for being illegible and unreadable [2.15]. Zuzana Licko, who designed the first bitmap fonts for the foundry Emigre, offers some insight into their revival. She speculates that a generation of designers, people who grew up playing video games and "surfing the web" in the early days of the Internet, became quite comfortable reading low-resolution typefaces. The typefaces of the "crude computer phenomenon"—typefaces that previous generations considered difficult to

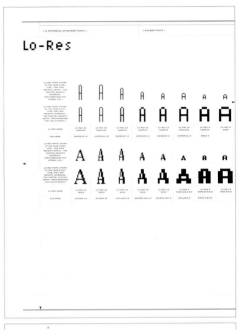

2.15 *Lo-Res*, 2001. Rudy VanderLans, Emigre. Pages from *Emigre* issue no. 59.

read—were perfectly normal to the readers who encountered them. Most, in fact, grew up with them. Licko's observation implies that the dynamic between readers and their cultural environment affects the legibility and/or readability of typefaces and typography.[4]

We tend to describe legibility as the readiness of the type to be apprehended: unambiguous form that renders culturally familiar alphabetic shapes. Allan Haley, Creative Director at <u>Monotype</u>, suggests that the most legible typefaces are "transparent," which means they do not "call undue attention" to their form. Additionally, "big features"—such as large and open counters, ample x-heights, and obvious character shapes—improve legibility. His view is that excessively light or bold typefaces, and those with dramatic weight changes among character strokes, tend to make letterforms less legible. Likewise, exag-gerated serifs or terminal shapes can command attention at the expense of alphabetic shapes. It could be argued that those features yield greater leg-ibility because they are consistent with reader experience. I should point out that the ongoing debate—that is, which typefaces are more or less legible—usually involves typefaces designed for sustained reading.

Readability is a more slippery concept than legibility. Sometimes read-ability is described as word recognition, and sometimes as the degree to which typography is comfortable, or desirable, to read—again, reader tolerance. Readability concerns the compound effects of how typefaces are used more than it does any given typeface. Dosages and warnings on drug packaging, for instance, are often typeset in quite legible typefaces, but in such minuscule sizes as to be unreadable, unless one takes the time to fetch a magnifying glass. Letterspacing, kerning, and other circumstances that place letters and words in proximity to each other also affect readability. A more or less legible typeface, then, is considered to be readable in relation to the circumstances and conditions in which it appears [2.16, 2.17]. A perfectly clear typeface, such as Verdana with its open counters and high x-height, could

Monotype
Today a part of Monotype Imaging, the Monotype Foundry began as the Lanston Monotype Machine Company, which, along with Merganthaler's Linotype, ushered in automated typesetting in the late nineteenth century.

2.16 Signage for Cité Internationale Universitaire de Paris, 2004. Ruedi Baur. *This typographic system invites readers to engage with the text in a variety of ways, over intervals of time. A person walking past the signs or sitting on the benches might read parts of the text in one stop, and other parts in subsequent stops. Some text is emphasized, to be read quickly and from a distance, while other text is set along wide spans to be read slowly.*

2.17 *(above and opposite)* Anamorphic typography (installation), 2010. Joseph Egan and Hunter Thomson.

2.18 Book cover using Andika typeface, 2008. Annie Opitz Olsen.

be unreadable under adverse conditions—say, where there is insufficient contrast between letterform and background. Then again, such low contrast may be preferred to communicate an idea.

Line length in relation to typeface affects readability, because set-width prefigures the number of characters that fit on a line. Characters set in a narrower typeface yield more characters per line (CPL) than wider set-width typefaces. A 3-inch line might hold 110 characters of a narrow typeface and 70 characters of a wider one. This means that the same number of characters set in different typefaces yield varying line lengths. Following the logic, paragraphs set in a very narrow typeface at a very long line length will fit more words on a page, certainly, but such a treatment would hardly be easy on the reader.

A common CPL recommendation is around 70 characters per line. This standard, however, does not take into account the circumstances of the reader, the artifact (the media, the material), or the delivery. Meanwhile, printed newspaper-column line lengths are set at around 35 CPL, yet are read daily without complaint (at least not about the typography). Why? Because readers have adapted to the newspaper format. Were small mobile-device screens to stick to the 70-character guideline, the glyphs would be 2 pixels high—in other words, illegible. Similarly, 70 characters filling the width of a 20-foot wall projection would be asking people to walk back and forth and back again as they read. Very tedious indeed, unless the intention is to tire readers out.

Some research suggests that excessively short or long lines interrupt normal patterns of eye movement. Good to know; but common sense, and sensitivity to the conditions of reading, are more useful guides. For example, when readers try to follow the meaning of text along lengthy lines that span a wide screen, they might get to the end of a line and struggle to find their way back across the screen to land on the beginning of the next line. Even if they are lucky enough not to get lost, by the time they finally get to the next line, they may have forgotten what they just read.

There are two aims to 70 CPL set in a standard typeface designed for sustained reading, combined with reasonable line lengths: to make reading comfortable and to make reading faster. The letter shapes of typefaces can also increase or limit eye strain, as well as decrease or increase reading speed. If a person cannot read well, or at all, then neither comfort nor speed matters. In such cases, letterform recognizability becomes the more significant typographic attribute. SIL International, located in Texas, helps "ethnolinguistic minority communities" to learn, build, and sustain their own languages. The institution employed Annie Opitz Olsen in 2006 to research and design a font that would maximize glyph recognizability in order to teach literacy. Taking into account the needs of beginning readers, she developed Andika [2.18], focusing on "clear, easy-to-perceive letterforms that will not be easily confused with one another." Before she designed the font, her research showed that the typefaces many experts deem most legible, including Arial and <u>Times New Roman</u>, did not fare well with novice readers. In fact, the much-maligned Comic Sans, considered

Times New Roman

Legal action between Linotype and Monotype foundries in the 1980s resulted in a new name for Times Roman. Linotype licenses the typeface as Times Roman, and Monotype as Times New Roman, with slight differences between the two.

silly and tasteless by some, proved to have more consistently legible letterforms for the purpose.

Other conditions, such as reader orientation and perception, can affect the legibility and readability of type. Two students at Chelsea College of Art & Design, London, created the message "It's more than just print" to be read from a single perspective [2.17]. Seen from other vantage points, though, the forms appear to be abstract graphics and fragments of letters.

Manhattanites read the abstract shapes on a banner outside the Museum of Modern Art as a **logotype** because they are well acquainted with the museum **brand**. Outsiders might puzzle over what the letters, if they are letters, signify [2.19]. Experience changes perception, which in turn increases or decreases legibility and readability.

Type designers might create a wide spectrum of letterforms, from utterly legible under the most favorable conditions, to nearly illegible and barely readable under any condition. As existing technologies improve and new ones are introduced, counters, strokes, and serifs are refigured and adapted. For example, eighteenth-century foundries developed more refined type-faces when printing techniques advanced.

2.19 Museum of Modern Art (MOMA) sign, 2009. Paula Scher (Pentagram) and Julia Hoffmann (Museum of Modern Art).

Twentieth-century program developers devised letterforms for early <u>CRTs</u> that optimized legibility in an "imperfect" medium, but were still quite coarse. Even the good old legible roman letterforms, designed as digital revivals for today's refined print reproduction, don't always hold up on low-resolution screens. More recent technologies, including high-definition screens and electronic readers, indicate that these problems will soon be as rare as typewriters.

If not applied with readability in mind, typography in digital environments can be offputting to readers. A 57-inch plasma television is probably not the most pleasant medium for reading, say, seven volumes of *Harry Potter*. Animation, too, sets up conditions that can interfere with readability. If the time on screen is too brief, or speeds are too fast, words are lost. The good news is that, if the type is unreadable in one moment as it zips and flips, it can be quite clear in the very next instant.

Cathode ray tube (CRT)

A cathode ray tube is a vacuum tube used in twentieth-century televisions and computer monitors. An image is produced on a glass surface by controlling the intensity of red, green, and blue electron beams. Resolution is very coarse compared to the light-emitting diode (LED) screens in use today.

2.20 Poster for Net Label festival, 2006. Fabian Leuenberger, Europatype.

2.21 App for *Weekendavisen* (Danish newspaper), 2011. Marcus Fuchs. *Typography designed to be read on e-readers and digital tablets utilizes flexible space to order content, and delivers information by way of reader interaction. Unlike web browser windows that readers size at their discretion, the screen space of these devices is constant.*

No matter what the medium, legible typography is readable by definition, in that alphabetic and word shapes are readily identifiable. Typography that is somewhat illegible can still be quite readable, depending on the context [2.20]. And while completely illegible typography is not readable as text, it might still be readable as an image or symbol. We'll get to that issue in the next chapter. We now turn to leading the reader through the reading space.

LEADING THE READER /////////////////////////////////////

TYPOGRAPHY TAKES THE LEAD

It may seem that syntax limits the expressive possibilities of language, but in fact it assists more free-wheeling typography. In certain circumstances, elements need not be composed in strict correspondence to typical writing sequences. If readers are reasonably familiar with the words in use, and if the typography provides sufficient directions as to how to proceed, they will search for connections to construct meaning, taking cues from the visual order to make linguistic sense.

Typography guides readers who are conditioned to decipher the written word, often through recognizable steps. A habituated reader, for instance, knows by heart the moves to access the text of a novel: open front cover. Read first word, the next and the next. Turn page. Words and pages end. Done. Experience with book conventions bears out the rightness of these actions, time and time again. The same holds true for any established reading space, although expectations differ because conventions are specific to each medium. We now anticipate that blogs will present the most recent content at the top of the browser window, so the entry we read the previous week is somewhere below—a very different convention from returning to the place where one last left off in a printed book. Comments run beneath posts from first to last sequentially, at least for now. Readers scan newspapers and magazines, and choose which articles to pursue, spurred by headlines, images, and captions [2.21].

Blogs
Short for weblogs, websites that collect personal observations, excerpts from other online sources, images, and hyperlinks on every topic imaginable. The genre was introduced in 1997 and has since been adopted by corporations, institutions, and governments worldwide.

Comments
Responses to blog posts, written by readers, listed and linked directly to posts.

Posts
Text or image entries written and "posted" to blogs, typically by the host author or blog editors.

The first web browsers imitated the reading order of the material page or poster. Perhaps the first interface programmers anticipated that the screen space would flummox users who were accustomed to reading static material. More likely, print-based text was the most expedient reading model and so was adopted for the computer screen. Despite other models in existence at the time, such as **dynamic typography** in film, print-based reading conventions and spaces momentarily arrested investigations into reading order that exploited the time-based aspects of the mutable screen.

The scroll bar was an alien concept as well. Many readers did not understand scrolling as a variation on the page turn. Others did, but industry wisdom warned that if a complete text did not appear within the first bounding frame, users would not venture beyond what was visible on screen to retrieve the rest. Computer users have since developed new habits as web developers have invented ever more surprising means of loading content onto the screen.

I have suggested that to compose type unconventionally has its place. In fact, many societies operate under unwritten ideals that value such variety. Some cultures reward originality or embrace peculiarity, if for no other reason than that always starting at the upper left (or right) and reading through to bottom right (or left) can get boring. Typographers have been known to experiment with the limits of readability for the sheer joy of visual play. Commercial and professional competition, too, inspires designers to distinguish their work from that of so many others. In the end, we might safely conclude that people want neither to see nor to read the same thing repeatedly. To assist and delight the reader facing less familiar territory, typography serves as a guide [2.22].

Leading readers means anticipating what they know, what they can know with adequate visual cues, and what they want to know: in short, planning for reader tolerance. Typography designed within conventional standards, in

2.22 *(above and opposite)* Stills from opening title sequence of *Stranger than Fiction*, 2006. Directed by Marc Forster.

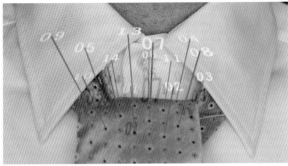

concert with reader experience and expectations, tends to meet with acceptance. Designing against these expectations simply demands that the typography manifest enough familiarity to lead readers, in less routine ways, through surprising new paths.

THE READING SPACE

Typographers anticipate short- or long-term reading needs, and make typographic choices that balance the amount of text, the kind of content, the effort required from the reader, and the **means of delivery**. The latter defines the reading space—the artifact within which the typography will appear. One reading space might be a 5 × 7-inch printed menu, read at arm's length, and another, a wall-sized silk-screened menu board read from 8 feet away. Placing 36 pt type printed within the confines of the small menu would make the words unavoidable. The same-sized type silk-screened on the menu board, however, would be an insignificant blip. The limits of the means of delivery, and how readers interact with it, necessarily sway typographic choices. Both of these means of delivery are examples of the simultaneous reading space. Two other kinds are the sequential reading space, and the reader-ordered space.

2.23 Program for "4 Hours Solid," event at Art Center College of Design, 2010. Juliette Bellocq, Handbuilt.

simultaneous reading space

Finite text contained within a defined area presents all content simultaneously in static space: menus (as we saw), newspaper pages, book spreads, billboards, storefronts, and web pages. The reader is left to navigate through the text at will, but cannot alter the fixed relationships among the elements [2.23]. For example, a movie poster features the title, the names of starring and supporting players, the director and producers, legal details (the ultra-condensed unreadable type positioned at the bottom), awards won, and critical kudos—all in one rectangle, typically shared with a commanding image. From a typographic perspective, the reading order, hierarchy, and structure lead readers through a morass of information, beginning with the title and image and moving to all the rest of the material, in some preset, descending order. This well-considered logic, however, does not hogtie a reader to the typographer's intentions.

The documentary *No Direction Home* by Martin Scorsese (2005) captures Bob Dylan reading two signs flanking the door of a pet store in a conventional reading order, the order that the proprietor probably intended. Dylan then proceeds to read the words out of order, stringing together unexpected sequences that sometimes make sense, and at other times make no sense at all. He even adds words as he plays with the ones before him. Pure pleasure. This playful response illustrates how readers are, in a way, "writers" of content because, in simultaneous reading spaces, they are free to choose what text to read and when to read it. The sign painter probably thought only about how the type would announce the pet merchandise inside. Passersby read the simple, direct information accordingly, the occasional poet notwithstanding. In this instance, reading order is not critical to understanding the messages. Content that does rely on a particular sequence to communicate a message, though, obliges the typographer to visualize that order quite emphatically.

sequential reading space

Like the simultaneous space, sequential reading spaces again fix typographic elements in stable relationships to each other. This time, though, the words are delivered over time, and in space [2.24]. Typography in motion spans frames in a predetermined order. The contents of a book span pages. And signage extends throughout a corridor. The freedom Dylan had to reorder the store-front text would be limited in a movie sequence for the simple reason that, in the latter, words appear on screen in a prescribed, linear order. Dylan could not read something that had yet to cross his vision.

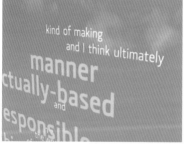

We might imagine that sequential spaces yield the greatest control over reading. It is true that some means of delivery lock readers into preordained sequences—animated website banners or film titles and credits, for example (providing that fast-forwarding and rewinding is not part of the reading experience). Nothing, though, prevents a reader from entering the sequential reading space of the book right in the middle, writer and designer be hanged. Compared to simultaneous reading spaces, though, sequential spaces allow the typographer to predict reading order, over a specified space, more accurately. We can also presume that readers approach these spaces intending to read text in the order and time presented.

Sequential reading spaces sometimes limit how detailed or layered content can be, if, that is, the words are to be apprehended. Animated typography might grab a reader in dazzling Technicolor, but cannot deliver more information than the human eye and brain can absorb moment by moment. Imagine type scrolling up a screen, and a reader following along dutifully. That works. Now imagine the text is the Sunday *New York Times* in its entirety. Designing the multi-leveled content, in sequence, over time, would require meticulous calculations, interminable labor, and a diligent reader who, if I may say so, needs to find a hobby.

Television news and sports programs seem to test the outer limits of sequential reading space, combining individual story graphics, layers of up-to-the-minute news flashes and assorted daily headlines, each entering, occupying, and exiting the stage statically or dynamically. Some texts are delivered sequentially, while others attach like labels. Digital sophistication and the competition in TV programming for audience share have turned what was once a strictly sequential reading space into a simultaneous reading space, where readers jump about at will.

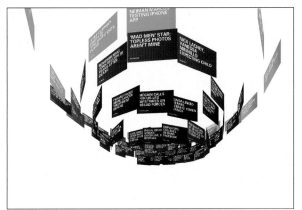

2.24 *(opposite) Create What's Next, 2007–10.* Baker Brand Communications. *The sequential reading space of motion typography allows text to appear within the screen space in ways that do not necessarily match written word and sentence order. The text in these stills reads in reverse order, from the top of each screen to the bottom. Each new set of words, however, appears at the top, while the previous set moves lower.*

2.25 *(above)* MSNBC Spectra Visual Newsreader, 2010. Remon Tijssen (Fluid), Matt Ferrin (SS+K), Sam Mazur (SS+K). *Readers select from headlines that swirl within this newsreader application. The typography gives the illusion of spatial perspective. Once a user selects a headline, it moves to the center at the bottom and becomes static.*

reader-ordered space

Complex, multi-tiered volumes of information, such as encyclopedias, are designed to allow readers to access content according to their needs and interests. Browsers pulling data from the bottomless Internet let readers determine the order in which the text they retrieve will be read. So much for leading the reader. This "random-access" behavior is conceivable in both simultaneous and sequential spaces, as news graphics prove, but in these cases typographers prompt reading order through hierarchies and time-based delivery.

Interactive and <u>hyperlink</u> environments, such as web browsers, allow readers the freedom to read any number of sources in any order [2.25]. Start with an op-ed piece, jump to a shoe catalog, pop over to a sports blog. In addition to having control over what they read, people can choose how they read it, which limits the typographer's jurisdiction. Consider such sites as Google and MySpace, or blogs and <u>newsfeeds</u>. While the content is automatically changeable and expandable (good for users), the typography is not prescribed (bad for typographers and other control freaks). **Pull technologies** that download formattable data, user preferences, and programming adaptability free readers to select type size, style, and sometimes the position of text. But what if the typeface is hideous? What if hierarchy is confused? Whatever shall a typographer do? Well, we have three options. Join the Type Anti-Defamation League. Educate non-typographers about pitfalls. Or just deal with it. Should a person choose 20 pt <u>Braggadocio</u> for screen text over the arguably more legible 12 pt Verdana, so be it.

Designers of such reader-ordered spaces as blog and <u>aggregator</u> frameworks are concerned with context-driven typography more than traditional content-driven type. Like systems engineers, these professionals anticipate best-case scenarios, as well as worst. These designers are less attentive to typographic details; they think in terms of relational delivery, or "if/then" scenarios. Say body text is specified in a **cascading style sheet** as 100 percent, and headlines are coded to set at 120 percent of the body text size, captions at 60 percent, and so on. No matter what size a reader chooses, the code adjusts the remaining text accordingly. So if the body text is set at 16 pixels by the user, then headlines and captions are set proportionally to 19.2 and to 9.6 pixels, respectively [2.26]. Compare this way of thinking to that of a traditional

Hyperlink

An on-screen link within a document, which, when selected, causes another related file or program to be displayed or activated.

Newsfeed

An Internet service that delivers news and other frequently updated information, regularly or continuously, to readers through online browsers. RSS (Really Simple Syndication) is one format that facilitates feeds.

Braggadocio

This brassy and bold 1930s typeface, designed by W. A. Woolley, features both modern and sans-serif characteristics, as do other jazz age hybrids, such as Broadway.

Aggregator

A personalized website that automatically scans for and retrieves user-determined data available on the Internet, such as news and blog posts. Readers access ongoing updates, as an aggregator "pulls" data from any number of specified sites, compiled into lists of articles and links.

typographer. Instead of setting up relative percentages, the designer establishes that the body text will be 16 pixels and the headlines 20 pixels, with no programmed if/then relationship. If the reader changes the body size to 30 pixels and leaves the headlines at 20, that is to say, significantly smaller than the body text, then hierarchy goes awry, and the typographer goes berserk. Meanwhile, the programmer is flushed with pride.

Push technology, on the other hand, does maintain typographer control. The typography and layout of weather- and stock-report widgets adhere to a prescribed plan as they display changing data. Flash sites offer the best of all worlds: typographers retain their dominion over typographic style and relationships; programmers install mighty actions; and readers determine the order in which they access content. As bitrates grow faster and bandwidths wider, typographers will probably have the means to get even pushier.

Planning and managing the delivery of complex information in any reading space can be hair-raising, especially if a lot of content needs to be read in a particular order. To assist us, and to keep our visual life a little more interesting, several principles come to our aid.

FLOW, DISRUPTION, GRAVITY

We read words over time. Words add up to sentences; and then a text line affiliates with subsequent ones to form paragraphs; and then paragraphs lead to other paragraphs. These perceptible steps seamlessly connect one piece of text to another, directed in part by reading norms. Texts that share visual attributes—typeface, proximity, scale, alignment—reinforce smooth linkage among components, and result in a **reading path**, that is, how readers move from element to element. Continuity over space and/or time is called flow, and is deliberately designed to draw readers through compositions and across pages.

Paragraphs of a book are basic examples of creating uninterrupted flow. Arbitrary breaks or exaggerated line lengths disrupt reading flow (which argues for comfortable line lengths—particularly for content requiring deep concentration). Disruption, though, is useful. An indent warns the reader to prepare for a conceptual transition. A bottom margin momentarily arrests smooth flow, sending the reader to the next page.

As the discussion of legibility and readability in the previous section pointed out, line lengths can make or break the reading experience. They also affect flow and reading speed, depending on the kind of medium and content, and, unsurprisingly, reader exposure to both. A study examining line length in relation to online reading found that longer lengths, a full 25 more characters than the proposed 70 CPL standard, generated the fastest reading speed:

Those that liked the 35 CPL indicated that the short line length facilitated "faster" reading and was easier because it required less eye movement. Those that liked the 95 CPL stated that they liked having more information on a page at one time. Although some participants reported that they felt like they were reading faster at 35 CPL, this condition actually resulted in the slowest reading speed.[5]

Bitrate

The rate at which digital bits (eight bits equal one byte) are transmitted or processed per unit of time: 1 mbps, for instance, refers to one million bits conveyed per second.

Bandwidth

Average rate of successful data transfer through modem, cable, fiber, and wireless technologies.

120%	Headline
100% =16 px	Body
60%	Caption

120%	Headline
100% =12 px	Body
60%	Caption

2.26 Relative sizing in Cascading Style Sheets.

Note that quantifiable efficiency is less important to readers than comfort or perceived reading speed.

Formal shifts, spatial and temporal distances, and the presence of other elements, such as images or <u>color breaks</u>, redirect reading paths, and therefore disrupt flow. Enter, the dance: type springing over empty space while we follow, bottom left to upper right; type popping up here and there as we make connections on the fly, like Dylan reading storefront signage. These discordances are exactly the attributes that can punctuate a point and infuse variety in a visual composition [2.27].

For this type of work, we enlist typographic roles and graphic encoding (to be discussed later in this chapter), as well as known grammatical sequences, to tug readers in specific directions. These visual and verbal cues help them see and follow the recommended reading paths, often installing the subtlest little rhythms within a steadily paced flow.

As the "Role and Expression" section in Chapter 1 explains (see page 51), roles are the jobs given to typography: titles, pull-quotes, navigational menus, marginalia, and any other formation familiar to seasoned readers. Graphic encoding establishes clear-cut formal distinctions that separate one kind of text from others: bold quotes in relation to paragraphs, 30 pt headlines in relation to 12 pt bylines, et cetera. Graphic encoding also sets up connections between portions of text by "chunking" and "clustering" them, drawing pieces of content into proximity to confirm their association, and suggesting the next place to

Color break

The shift from one solid color area to another adjacent color.

2.27 *More*, 1998. Adam McIsaac, The Felt Hat. *Pages from a corporate capabilities brochure for a regional investment bank. The placement of text and graphic elements introduces disruptions that assist reader navigation, establish hierarchy, and create variety among elements. Juxtaposition of sequential texts supports flow.*

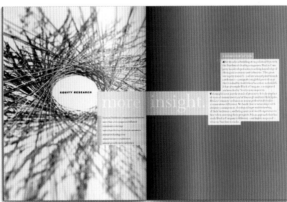

look [2.28, 2.29]. Grammatical sequences assist the reader in drawing connections as well, even if texts are spatially far apart. Given the many options of where to move next in a simultaneous reading space, readers will search for connections through grammar. Say a text line on one page stops suddenly, and continues a few pages later in the same location and with identical typographic treatment: grammatical logic will link the two pieces of text, despite their distance from each other.

Flow and disruption are governed in part by typographic gravity. The topmost elements within a simultaneous reading space, such as a poster, tend to be seen and read first because reading conventions dictate that we start there. European languages are read left to right, top to bottom, so the top-leftmost corner emits the strongest gravitational pull. Likewise, the gravity of Arabic and Japanese draws from the top, but reading from right to left. Dynamic typography is linear because the sequence of elements over time dictates what will be read when. Therefore, gravity pulls in the direction from which elements appear.

Typographers may choose to fulfill the reader's expectations within a given environment, or defy them, forgoing the conventional geography of the page or screen. An experienced reader needs little if any orientation to understand typography that utilizes visual gravity and facilitates flow. If, in a composition, the elements submit to grammatical reading order, the composition and lack of interruption might create a satisfying sense of repose. By contrast, a strange reading order may bring deliberate tension, and with it, a learning curve on the part of the reader.

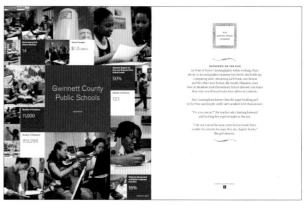

2.28 Broad Prize brochure, 2010. Monica Schlang, AdamsMorioka. Creative directors: Sean Adams and Noreen Morioka. *The opening pages of this brochure (top) introduce the content, but also introduce aspects of the brochure's graphic encoding. In subsequent spreads (middle and bottom), centered blue texts placed opposite similar image compositions signal that the information is related. Readers will make a connection between the two spreads, despite the fact that they are separated by several pages.*

A READING SCENARIO

Recall (from the subsection "Typography Takes the Lead," above) that to lead readers, typographers must anticipate what readers know, what they can know with familiar and irresistible visual cues, and what they want to know.

For example, a website designer produces a campaign site in the typographic style and voice of political campaigns, imbuing it with formal qualities that most voting citizens would recognize (what readers know). The site uses simultaneous, sequential, and reader-ordered reading spaces, and the intended audience has considerable experience with each. As the designer developed the website, he proposed to introduce at random huge

2.29 Broad Prize brochure, 2010. Monica Schlang, AdamsMorioka. Creative directors: Sean Adams and Noreen Morioka. *The pages shown above follow those shown opposite. All share such attributes as margin widths, typefaces, and folio style. This content is clearly of a different kind, evident in the related but distinct structure, colors, and amount of text. Within these sections of the brochure, the red lines of text cluster to indicate affiliation, in this case functioning as quotations from the text. The quotations serve to punctuate the flow.*

2.30 Catalog for Tobias Frere-Jones exhibition, 2009. Abi Huynh.

animated excerpts from the candidate's speeches. Unusual for campaign websites, but the campaign manager agreed.

Now one of those citizens is reading a page from the website, and suddenly one of the animated texts enters from the bottom of the browser and proceeds to march up the page, disrupting her reading and obscuring the text. Surprised and amused, our citizen reads the statement. Unsure of what to do next, she hovers over the text, causing the color to change, much as standard, less insistent hyperlinks behave. The designer opted to include this detail in part because he understood that the delivery was unconventional, but he also understood that his readers would be familiar with this particular visual cue. The designer also added a little wiggle to the text with the **rollover**. Again, unusual for a campaign site, but enticing. In short, the designer used a familiar attribute of screen-based typography to prompt readers toward what they can know, and threw in a little entertainment to boot. Our citizen surmises quickly enough that if she clicks the text, she will be taken elsewhere. Although she does not know where the link will lead, the politician's statement engages her, as does the peculiar delivery. Intrigued, she opts to click, and lands on the campaign speech from which the quotation was taken. Both the content and the typography met with this reader's desire and curiosity (and might not have piqued the interest of another's). This goes to show that what readers want to know influences how willing they are to respond to unusual typographic treatments.

HIERARCHY AND STRUCTURE: PART II //

"What you need is structure." We have all heard this advice more than once—we need a day planner, an exercise routine, a sock organizer. This advice definitely applies to type: it does not have the luxury to lie about; it has a job to do.

Letters aligned on a baseline to form text lines are the most elemental of typographic structures [2.30]. As we have seen, such elements can also be trusted to ensure smooth flow. Next to that we find the list—fragments of text stacked

COLIN BEATTY
KAREN LEWIS
GARY NICKARD
CRAIG SMITH
BEN VAN DYKE
GAYLE YOUNG

DEPT OF **VISUAL STUDIES**

College of Arts and Sciences
University at Buffalo The State University of New York

FEB 12

A CONFERENCE ON FAILURE IN THE ARTS

University at Buffalo Center for the Arts
The CFA 112 (Screening Room)

10:30a   Panel Discussion
12:00p   Lunch Break
1:30p   Keynote Presentation

along a vertical margin guided by a paper edge, for example. We read each new line as a discrete thought with minimum visual differentiation. Taking this basic structure a step further, outlines also separate fragments in stacked lines, but added indents align subcategories to create levels in descending order. Scanning an outline, we are able to isolate and read nested secondary and tertiary elements within the larger list because they are visually positioned along shared vertical alignments, which signals that they are related.

2.31 Poster for "Failure: A Conference on Failure in the Arts," 2010. Ben Van Dyke and Mike Phillips.

Left-oriented vertical alignment is a structural scheme called left **justification**. Full justification creates strong, straight edges at both the left and right edges of text blocks, supported by margins. We could ask whether the lines created by the text block precipitated the margins, or vice versa: a chicken-and-egg question. Whichever way you look at it, the rudimentary structure, alignment, is in play [2.31].

Symmetrical alignment on a central axis, asymmetrical alignment along a common axis, and right alignment (an opposite of left-to-right-oriented languages) are each structural schemes that serve different reading functions. **Centered** type is common in posters, invitations, scrolling film credits, and signage, for instance [2.32].

Centering schemes are as old as mark-making itself. They dominated typography until twentieth-century European modern movements controversially rejected the practice in favor of **asymmetry**. The proponents of modernist typography believed that asym-

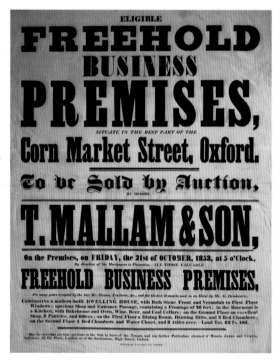

2.32 Auction poster, 1853.

metrical, or left/right, alignments were more responsive to and representative of modern reading demands. As one might guess, the mainstream was slow to adopt the practice, though today our reading habits readily embrace asymmetry.

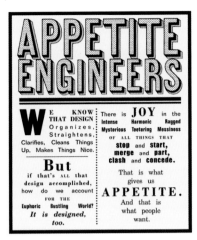

2.33 Appetite Engineers Philosophy, 2008–11. Martin Venezky. *The composition in these screen-based displays creates a compelling tension between centered and justified alignments, which are further complicated by shifts of scale and weight. The best and worst possibilities of old and new technologies combine in this design.*

2.34 Croatian Insurance Bureau (HUO) Annual Report 2008, 2009. Nedjeljko Spoljar and Kristina Spoljar, Sensus Design Factory.

Text balanced asymmetrically on an axis might not appear to be aligned at all, but text lines are in fact working with each other along an invisible vertical fulcrum [2.33]. This structure easily underpins a series of brief fragments, such as ad copy or poetry. Right justification (right alignment) is more troublesome because, as the theory goes, readers find it difficult to locate the beginning of lines, and so tend to read more slowly. There is nothing inherently problematic in right-aligned text unless readers are accustomed to reading the opposite, which left-to-right-language readers are. Given this inclination, readers of English or other left-to-right languages tolerate right alignment in small doses and short line lengths, but might decline to read a text-heavy news site designed under that scheme.

Diagonal and circular alignments have, on occasion, proved popular. Historically, text set on a circle or arc was problematic because the technological means—metal sorts—were designed to be used on perpendicular structures. Consequently, for centuries such novel structures were rarely used. As photographic and then digital tools afforded greater flexibility, structures became more varied.

Simple alignments reinforce correspondences among elements. Text lines aligned on the left (**flush left**) or right (**flush right**) help to affiliate the lines with each other. Text can certainly float about without being anchored or connected, but imagine a menu board that scatters entrees and beverages and prices across the wall, with no discernible alignment. This structure might make for a fabulous mural, but probably would not be so useful for a diner wanting to decide what to order. Menus provide information, and would not be nearly as efficient in serving up data without a set of alignments that logically connect related parts, and that differentiate those parts from others.

Alignments assist hierarchical relationships, too. Well-ordered elements fixed consistently to a structure supply a kind of map: a guide that helps readers navigate the content of a lengthy book, for instance, or a signage system on campus. The hierarchy of chapter title, text block, and folio (first, second, and third levels) is stronger when the relationship among the levels is uniformly fastened to specific points on a page, whether the parts are found on page 1 or page 218. Readers not only readily pick out chapter beginnings and distinguish folios from text blocks, but they also comprehend that each chapter title, text block, and folio is part of a navigable whole.

In cases of extensive, related content spanning pages or dispersed over distances, typographers establish consistent alignments using a network of guides called a grid [2.34]. Chapters 3 and 5 cover grids extensively. For now, think of grids as a set of alignments that construct the place where each hierarchical level will live. Applied to a campus signage system, the grid might set up consistent hierarchical relationships among tiered identifiers. The first level might be the university name, the second level a building name, a third the name of the college, and the fourth level a list of the departments housed inside. Every building entrance presents the same hierarchical and structural relationships. Readers notice the system as they walk through campus because they want to know where they are. Aware that they are located within the university, they can bypass the first hierarchical level and quickly locate the second, third, or fourth level of information, guided by the unvarying structure.

Leading the reader is clearly a complicated business, but it is part of the typographer's challenge. And it's fun, because no set of circumstances is ever exactly the same. The content, media, delivery, and reader are as unique to a given set of circumstances as the days in our lives. If we want fully to engage the reader in the dance, though, we must consider how the steps we take are interpreted. We also need to understand the principles that lead producers and readers to construct meaning.

/// INTERPRETATION

ENCODING AND DECODING

Chapter 1 introduced the concepts of roles and expression in typographic form, of both style and voice. These aspects of typography are codes that typographers use to corroborate or add meaning to words, and which readers interpret [2.35]. This equation has been true throughout the history of written communication: Dutch merchants advertised goods and recorded sales for business; Roman inscriptions set forth decrees to citizens; French oaths declared loyalty to the king. Similar communiqués exist today in the form of corporate annual reports, municipal signage, and political propaganda. Each form is typographically encoded according to convention.

As typographers encode content to assert meaning, though, readers may or may not decode the message as intended. Reader interpretation is colored by individual experiences, cultural beliefs, and values. The good news is that typographers employ codes with which their intended readers are reasonably familiar, and so the messages produced are likely to be not terribly distant from reader expectations. As straightforward as this process sounds, the path of message encoding and decoding is not direct, nor always predictable. The more particular the expression, the more refined the encoding and exclusive the language [2.36]. As the terms of communication in such a case are specialized, the promise of mutually understood messages among those who share the language will be greater, and the less likely they are to be decipherable by outsiders. Written and typographic forms evolve just as languages and dialects do.

Approximately 6,500 spoken languages exist around the world. Linguists and ethnologists estimate that half are threatened with extinction because so few speakers share the language, and younger generations have not continued using them. Of these languages, those with written counterparts are more likely to be preserved. Several indigenous peoples of the Americas, for instance, have developed alphabets that represent the sounds and grammatical structure of the language. The resulting letterforms are as mysterious to, say, readers of English, as English

2.35 Human Being T-shirt, 2010. Matt McKinney and Harry Garnham, Origin 68. *This T-shirt design employs the graphic codes of product boxes, aiming to communicate human vulnerability and the need for careful handling.*

2.36 Boats on the canals of Xochimilco, Mexico.

ʔ	tiʔaʔ diʔaʔ ʔaciɬtalbixʷ ʔal tiʔiɬ
a	tuhaʔkʷ dʼixʷbid čaɬ. gʷəl tusʔasɬaɬlils
b ƀ	ʔal tudiʔ sq̓xʷabac. d(i)ɬax̌ʷ tuʔux̌ʷ.
c ċ	tuɬaɬlil. gʷəl x̌uxʷʔiʔxʷʔiʔ. gʷəl diɬ
č čʼ	tudax̌ʷʔux̌ʷs algʷaʔ. gʷəl tuɬaɬlil algʷaʔ.
d dᶻ	gʷəl absbədbədaʔ algʷaʔ? absbədbədaʔ
ə	algʷaʔ? gʷəl tiʔiɬ ʔiɬlux̌ bədaʔs algʷaʔ
g gʷ	gʷəl ʔasq̓ʷupq̓ʷup. ʔasq̓ʷupq̓ʷup. xʷiʔ
h	gʷəjəsəds gʷədəxʷuʔibəšs. gʷəl daẙ
i	tiʔaʔ čalʼčaləss.
ǰ	ɬ(u)asɬaɬlil tiʔaʔ yəlʼyaləbs ʔal tudiʔ
k k̓	q̓ix̌ʷ sq̓xʷabac ʔal tiʔaʔ pədhədəb gʷəl
kʷ k̓ʷ	laťsil. gʷəl ʔalil tiʔiɬ x̌usq̓il ʔə
l	tiʔaʔ diʔaʔ sʔuladx̌ʷ. tiʔaʔ diʔaʔ x̌x̌ʷayʔ.
ƚ ɬ	tulʼʔal gʷəl ləšabalik̓ʷalgʷaʔ? ʔə tiʔiɬ
x̌	baləsʔuladx̌ʷ ʔi tə biacs suxʷʔiʔxʷʔiʔs
m ṁ	algʷaʔ. *Lushootseed Sulad*
n ṅ	gʷəl ʔalilax̌ʷ ti səčitils dxʷʔal kʷi səťsils.
p ṗ	gʷəl ɬuʔəx̌ax̌ algʷaʔ? ɬubəbəlk̓ʷax̌ʷ
q q̓	algʷaʔ? dxʷʔal tiʔaʔ diʔaʔ čit ɬq̓ucid ʔə
qʷ q̓ʷ	tiʔaʔ diʔaʔ sʔilucid ʔə dxʷqəlb. ʔal
w ẇ	k̓ʷədiʔ tusʔasɬaɬlils algʷaʔ. tulʼʔal gʷəl,
s š	gʷəl ʔəx̌tx̌ʷax̌ʷ algʷaʔ? tiʔaʔ stəbs
ɬ ťʼ	algʷaʔ? ʔal tiʔaʔ dadatu. gʷəl
u	ʔuʔabgʷasəxʷ algʷaʔ? ʔal tiʔaʔ q̓xʷabac
w ẇ	ʔal tiʔaʔ stk̓ʷab. *Lushootseed School*
xʷ x̌ x̌ʷ	
y ẙ	Excerpt from "The Legend of the Boy Who Could Not Walk," as narrated by Emma Conrad (Sauk-Suiattle).

2.37 Lushootseed School and Lushootseed Sulad typeface samples, 2009. Juliet Shen.

2.38 Flatbush Junction Chop Suey. Graffiti and Chinese food sign on Nostrand and Glenwood Avenues, Flatbush, Brooklyn, NY.

letterforms are to a pre-schooler [2.37]. Graffiti letterforms and structure, too, encode messages that include people who know the code and, by extension, exclude those who do not.

Conversely, the broadest of audiences is able to decode very generic typographic languages. Take for instance "Chop Suey," a <u>simulation typeface</u> [2.38]. Most towns in Europe and North America have at least one Chinese restaurant. Odds are good that the sign out front, the menu, or the take-out boxes use a typeface that mimics the calligraphic strokes found in traditional <u>kanji</u>. Although this stereotype has nothing to do with Chinese cultures, and is quite disrespectful to them, the typographic code yields its simplistic message to most people who have lived in the West.

Designers' work routinely crosses cultural boundaries, which makes typography susceptible to miscommunication, or what many presume to be "failed" communication. This perceived problem stems from the assumption that designers actively "send" messages and that readers passively "receive" them. The design theorist Malcolm Barnard challenges this notion:

Where one "receiver" interprets a typestyle as conservative and another sees it as a little racy . . . and where a "receiver" objects to the depiction of women in an advertisement as "degrading" but another sees it as "a bit of fun," these theories would see only "breakdown" or "failure" in communication. The idea that different people, from differing social and cultural backgrounds, can actively interpret graphic designs in different ways cannot be accounted for except as failure.[6]

The sender-to-receiver theory does not account for the confluence of multiple interpretations. Barnard's point is that some kind of communication always occurs. Readers may interpret the message differently from how the writer or typographer intended, or they may decode only a fraction of the message. Still, some communication is achieved, informed in part the context. A reader unfamiliar with the specific meanings of graffiti letterforms may not be able to decipher a message painted on a wall, but his experience with the visual code, seen in the context of the street, might at least convey "street culture." In short, the producers of messages do not miscommunicate; rather, they communicate with varying degrees of success in relation to their intentions.

TYPOGRAPHIC COMMUNICATION

Writers, typographers, and readers construct messages together. Some linguistic theory uses the terms "encoding" and "decoding" to describe this process. "Coding," however, implies a one-to-one connection—a direct cause and effect between the intentions of writers or typographers and interpretation by readers. This definition resembles any we find in a dictionary that offers a precise but generalized

Simulation Typeface

Also called "faux fonts." These typefaces are designed to evoke other alphabets and writing systems. "Herculanum," designed by Adrian Frutiger, imitates ancient Greek letterforms.

Kanji

Chinese characters used in the modern Japanese logographic writing system, along with hiragana, katakana, arabic numerals, and the occasional use of the Latin alphabet.

definition, as compared to a thesaurus, which lays out ranges of meaning. The terms "encoding" and "decoding," then, do not adequately represent the nature of language exchange and communication.

The **semiotics** scholar and novelist Umberto Eco posits that this way of thinking suggests that there is some ideal reader; one who is able to interpret expressions in the same way we are able to generate them. Individuals, however, also carry around perspectives and experiences that trigger unshared and unexpected meanings. Decoding might be better described, then, as a linguistic system whereby readers interpret codes under the influence of private association. Eco equates this dynamic with an encyclopedia, where readers draw from any number of possible associations to establish meaning, some of which are unique to the reader, and therefore unpredictable.

2.39 *(above and opposite)* Newsmap website, 2004. Marcos Weskamp.

Eco further theorizes that communication hinges on what people already know. If this is true, communication is an ongoing exchange of words, ideas, and forms that any given group has already encountered and understand. Let's try this concept out in the typogyroscopic sphere. We enter a news site to discover content we already knew would be there: news about current events, weather, sports, and lifestyle trends. We also know the typographic form and configurations: section titles, front-page headlines, and captions set in suitable, familiar typefaces. The hierarchies among headlines, stories, and images, coupled with the structure, also communicate that we are confronting a news site, because we have seen similar ones many times before. We easily comprehend that this website is, indeed, one that will deliver the news. Communication accomplished.

Eco compares communication with information—the occasions on which people encounter that which they do not know. Consider the news site Newsmap, where a miscellany of headlines seems to collide on the screen, each one displayed at different type sizes and crammed into a host of variously sized and colored rectangles. What does it mean? We are confronted with an alien form, and communication is arrested [2.39].

If we spend more than a few minutes exploring the site, though, we quickly learn that it is a news aggregator. We learn that the size of each rectangle and its orientation to others are generated from data culled from the Internet. The largest rectangle represents world events that are getting the most online news coverage at the moment we enter the site. A closer look reveals that the type size is determined by the size of the rectangle in relation to the number of words in the headline (which means, unfortunately, that very long headlines for events that do not get much coverage are illegible). If we reload the page later in the day, we see that the rectangles, their orientation to each other, and the type sizes have all changed.

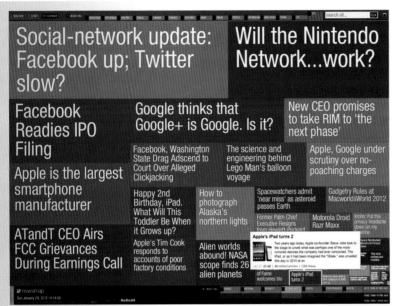

Once we become familiar with this visual "information," communication can start. We read a headline in a familiar language, which communicates the content. And we comprehend that the size of the rectangle in which it sits corresponds to the story's importance in the world.

The relational and dynamic system of Newsmap leads us to the conditions and circumstances that make up the contexts of reading. Recognizing the systems and contexts that underpin communication enables us to design with a degree of confidence that at least some part of what we mean to say will be understood.

As I hope this chapter has revealed so far, reading systems employ a few principles over and over again. In a nutshell: people are able to read because they have experience with cultural and linguistic conventions. If order is not immediately evident, or even "wrong" by grammatical standards, readers attempt to make sense of what they see because the very presence of letterforms presumes intended communication. Additionally, reading typography is an act of seeing and of interpreting, of absorbing and grasping.

READING CONTEXTS ///

The section "Context" in Chapter 1 introduced the importance of considering the "who," "what," "where," "when," and "how" of contexts. Here I look at these contexts as they concern readers. Whether our typography takes wing across the seas or just across the street, it always exists beyond the reach of our hands once we release it into those of readers. The eyes and minds of others—from one, to a roomful, to multitudes—interpret our messages within conditions over which we have limited control. We can, however, reasonably predict the context of readers and the physical conditions within which the typography is to be read, and make decisions according to what we learn about them.

2.40 Times Square, New York.

READERS

the public context

Although reading is often seen as a private act, typographic production for reading is typically aimed at a "public." Think of the thousands of New Yorkers and tourists who pass each day through Times Square [2.40], where messages are directed at a mass of "individuals." Readers who know the visual codes absorb the spectacle as if it were constructed and delivered exclusively for them. I hate to break the news, but typography—whether delivered on a home computer screen or on a theater billboard—does not care about the details of a reader's background and personality. Typography addresses readers as participants and as members of groups within larger cultures, not as individuals.

the personal context

Readers personalize public messages by sorting through content that coincidentally enters their view, then filtering it according to preference and their concurrent preoccupations. Someone standing in Times Square cannot anticipate each and every message blaring down (coincidence), but they will settle on some messages and ignore others (preference). Each member of a family watching CNN will be drawn to different elements according to their individual interest. While one has an eye on breaking news running through the news ticker, another has his eye trained on the stock report. Readers tend to perceive the presence of those messages to which they are predisposed. A person might pay attention to street signs, preferring not to get lost, or someone craving ice cream might pause at every magazine ad that promotes sweets. Most readers aren't conscious of their culturally bound and self-referential response to the visual world until they visit a region where the codes and conventions are strange—where the person is neither part nor a product of the society.

News ticker
A portion of television screen space on news programs reserved for up-to-the-minute reports and headlines; also called a "crawler." Ticker can refer to LED displays installed in or on public buildings.

the global context

Typographers who design artifacts that reach across linguistic and cultural borders—a common request in today's worldwide communications—need to seek the insights and experiences of people who understand the targeted reader. If the work originates in one language, translators deal with the content. But as any one of them will testify, the nuances of meaning can be almost impossible to translate. Even when translation is accomplished adequately, those "others" interpret meanings through their own layers of cultural and personal experience. Typographic translation can be just as difficult. The basic act of choosing a typeface for text written in one's native language, directed at some segment of one's own society, is already fraught with potential for failure. How, then, does a typographer decide on a typeface that communicates effectively to readers who speak the languages of far-flung countries [2.41]? Understanding typographic and graphic codes is impossible without sufficient research and deference to people who know something about the intended readers and their culture at first hand. While international

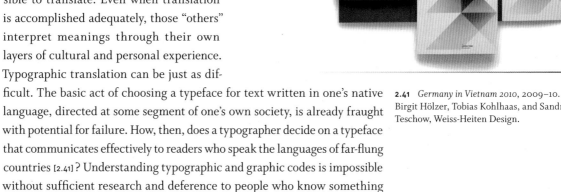

2.41 *Germany in Vietnam 2010*, 2009–10. Birgit Hölzer, Tobias Kohlhaas, and Sandra Teschow, Weiss-Heiten Design.

exchange today appears to be training global readers primarily in the visual languages of commerce, these codes are but one facet of visual culture. Fortunately, as public access to global media increases, the spread of non-commercial visual languages will increase as well.

THE PHYSICAL CONTEXT

Anticipating the immediate physical contexts in which typography is to function can improve reader access and comprehension. We cannot anticipate every physical condition in advance, of course. A future massive snowfall could easily obscure even the most carefully considered typographic treatment. Still, being mindful of where and how readers will encounter typography increases the chance of delivering a successful message. Here are a few conditions to consider.

2.42 *(above and below)* Exhibition graphics for Established & Sons. MadeThought.

visual competition

Magazine mastheads crowded together on news-stands, for example, vie for attention, whereas explanatory text at the entrance of an exhibition suffers less visual competition, save the draw of the exhibit itself [2.42]. Visual competition is a constant concern in packaging and book cover design, but of less concern in instructional booklet design. Under favorable circumstances, visual competition can actually augment an experience. For instance, the Latin names on signs in a botanical garden might be obscured by plants, a condition that might invite readers to move closer and peer through leaves, which heightens the sense of discovery.

reader orientation

It is tempting to presume that the optimal way to present text is parallel to the reader's view. But in reality, we see type from many angles [2.43, 2.44]. If the Department of Transportation wants drivers to yield at a small intersection, they paint the word on the street, taking into account the orientation of the reader positioned behind the wheel. Consequently, text that appears perfectly normal to an approaching driver, the targeted reader, looks absurdly exaggerated to pedestrians. Google Earth has made typographic messages readily available that would remain unseen were we to stay planted on the ground. The producers of these texts obviously had in mind a reader oriented high above.

2.43 Satellite view of Luecke, Texas.

2.44 Museo Italiano Cultural Center, Melbourne, 2010. David Pidgeon and Marilyn de Castro, Pidgeon. *This signage design anticipates that readers will encounter the sign from distances down the street, as well as from just below the sign. The design also fully exploits the dimensionality of the material.*

the point of delivery

The point of delivery involves what, where, when, and how readers see typography. Such conditions as available light and reading distances have a bearing on type size and compositional complexity, for instance. A typeface for a cookbook needs to be readable when you stand at ladle's length under good light conditions, whereas a trail marker needs to be readable under poor light conditions, say by flashlight from 50 yards.

How much time readers have or are given to read the text is another condition. The cook has plenty of time to pore over a recipe in his kitchen, so directions can be detailed in content, complex in hierarchy, and small in scale. In a movie theater, viewers have less time to read lots of film credits, so the amount and size of text, and complexity of composition, will be wholly different than that of the cookbook. The less time readers have to access content, the faster the speed of delivery. The speed of delivery in a cookbook is very slow—readers have all the time in the world. But what if the cook is charging past in a car and sees a recipe plastered across a retaining wall? One might question the wisdom of a recipe displayed thus, which would be my point. Retaining walls are singularly inefficient points of delivery for recipes.

The means of delivery, also known as the artifact, compounds the conditions that typographers have to consider. If the artifact is a cellphone screen where brightness causes letterforms to lose definition, we design a typeface to accommodate the condition. If the artifact is a trail marker made of wood, the typography needs to be sturdy enough to be carved and large enough to be seen from a distance.

We will spend more time looking at the physical and material aspects of artifacts in Chapters 3 and 4, as they influence designing with typography. The previous sections have focused on the existing conditions and circumstances

2.45 Laika dynamic typeface design, 2009. Michael Flückiger and Nicolas Kunz, Berne University of the Arts. *The typographic attributes of the word "time" mutate smoothly and proportionally as users adjust knobs on the control console. The Laika project includes other experimentation, such as typography that mutates in response to pressure and body movement.*

of reader interpretation and context. But things change, all the time. A look at new reading technologies and contexts might lend some insight into our future reading habits and expectations.

READING FRONTIERS

All means of delivery—whether printed, constructed of dimensional materials, or screen-based—present the typographer both with specific advantages and with constraints relating to reproducibility and readability. In 2001, the Internet pioneer Joe Gillespie noted that "the luminous nature of a computer screen throws some print typography taboos on their head." Controlling excessive contrast and glare is more important in screen-based media, for instance. "Black text on a white background, to which print has accustomed us, no longer makes sense . . . . Some diehards expect their type to be black on white and complain bitterly if it is not, and also want their electric heaters to look like log fires."[7]

Explorations in the last twenty years have challenged how typography behaves in two, three, and four dimensions, which challenges how text is read. We have discussed letterforms that are revealed only when a targeted viewer is oriented properly. This, and similar work, firmly establishes typography as something that readers move around and through, and can manipulate. A set of wood blocks, called Toypography, cleverly deconstruct Japanese—for example, the symbol for "bird"—into pieces that can be reconfigured as the English word, or as a graphic representation of a bird. The <u>applet</u> Caligraft allows users to type and manipulate words as the program animates the letterforms in real time. The applet not only introduces a different kind of reading, it also calls into question the definition of "font." The Swiss Laika project carries such experiments into an entirely new dimension [2.45]. Its designers and programmers describe the apparatus in terms that are as radical as the project:

Laika is neither bold nor thin, but swings between these two extremes. Its form is no longer defined statically, but alters dynamically . . . . The font's weight, the stroke contrast, serif lengths and italic angles . . . all behave dynamically . . . [and] parameters can be driven and influenced by a range of inputs . . . . Why should a typeface be rigidly set, if it is not going to be printed? In a dynamic medium, why shouldn't the form and the character of the typeface be understood dynamically as well? Why shouldn't its forms change, transform, and respond to circumstances?[8]

Rendering type on screen and in the environment as it reacts to user input, as if by magic, presents possibilities for alternate reading experiences, with attendant concerns. MIT graduate Ben Fry develops such projects as "Tendril," a <u>web crawler</u> that turns text culled from websites into volumetric form [2.46]. The program builds the first structure as a slowly rotating, organic funnel. Links within the text are highlighted in a color and, when selected, the linked page sprouts from the cursor location in a tuber-like mass. Over time, guided by reader choices, an enormous branching structure is constructed from retrieved data. We do not necessarily need such a <u>web crawler</u>, and skeptics doubt that people could ever learn to read in such a format. But

Applet

A small application program (hence "app") that performs a discrete function within larger software applications, such as an operating system. StickyKeys, for instance, allows users with physical disabilities to type two or more command keystrokes in sequence rather than simultaneously.

Web crawler

A general term for a computer program, or script, that "crawls" the Internet looking for data, then gathers it into usable indices. Also called a web spider, web robot, or automatic indexer. The original software was written by the computer science student Brian Pinkerton in the early 1990s.

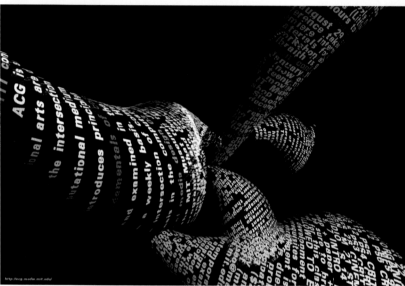

Fry is a researcher in information visualization. He and others are striving to discover ways of representing the massive, continuously changing amount of content we deal with today. Other experimental projects also play with existing reading habits, however tentatively.

Despite the fact that reading limits have been tested extensively in print and film, typographic innovation in these media continues to be as provocative and investigative as their sophisticated digital counterparts. Since the late 1990s, the artists of Young-Hae Chang Heavy Industries have been writing typographic stories that exploit reading conventions in real time. Pacing and quick cutting synchronize **static typography** to music, often original scores, uncannily capturing in a textual medium the subtleties and cadences of the spoken word. Two-dimensional media are perennial playgrounds for typographic experimentation as well. Designers test the limits of reader tolerance with labyrinthine letterforms silk-screened on T-shirts, type drawn by hand on skin and photographed, and typeface design that might make a purist desperate to return to the sanctuary of Legibility Island, never to venture forth again. Ah, well. The frontier is sometimes unsavory.

2.46 *Tendril*, 2000. Ben Fry, Aesthetics and Computation Group, MIT.

This chapter has emphasized readers in order to focus on how typographic practice is influenced by them. In reality, it is impossible to separate any aspect of typography from the motives of producers and typographers. We are, after all, still in Typogyroscopic land. To conclude this chapter, let's look briefly into a few forces that involve the needs and expectations of readers, but that originate with the producers and makers of typography.

CHALLENGES TO READING CONVENTIONS:
A FEW PRECEDENTS

Early twentieth-century typographic work of the Dada and futurist movements intentionally disrupted normal reading for philosophical reasons. Dadaists made an exemplar of nonsensical words and randomly ordered compositions to comment on bourgeois values. Futurists clamored for mechanized progress through typography designed to clang and roar visually. In the late twentieth century, post-modern typographers set out to epitomize what they perceived as the active construction of language, and the instability of meaning. Unlike the viewpoints of traditionalists steeped in proper form, these artists and designers flaunted visual disruption and distraction in order to express their respective political and theoretical agendas. The importance and impact of these experiments we can leave to the historians. The point here is that the act of reading has cultural and political dimensions, and that typographic experimentation is one way in which society expresses its evolving cultural and political ideas.

One challenge to reading conventions originated with the early modernists, whose theories were summarized and refined in an influential book by Jan Tschichold, *Die Neue Typographie*, published in 1928. Proponents of the "new typography" decried **symmetry**, as the subsection on structure in this chapter explained. The early modernists also denounced undifferentiated text blocks and visual clutter that were common at the time, and familiar to readers. Asymmetrical composition was the antidote to what these typographers viewed as the escalating demands being made on readers. Text arranged and styled according to multiple hierarchical levels promised quicker access. Reading conventions that formerly required typographers merely to make text legible, and sometimes beautiful, eventually gave way to a new order in which the typographer became a self-conscious information "engineer" as well as a fabricator of aesthetics—a perspective that continues to this day.

Some approaches to typography do not challenge so much as play with reading conventions [2.47]. Concrete poetry in the first half of the twentieth century exploited form to illustrate a poem's meaning and to enrich the reading/seeing experience. The typographers of *Raw*, *Wet*, and *Octavo* magazines, among several others, designed with type in ways that rendered

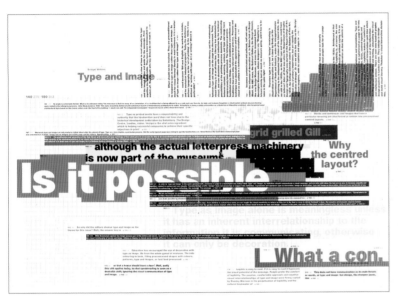

2.47 *Is it Possible*, 1990. Mark Holt and Hamish Muir, 8vo. *Although this large-format magazine spread challenged reading conventions, the multi-tiered but controlled hierarchy still provided readers with visual clues that assisted reading and navigation. Interestingly, the design and production were not accomplished on a computer, though the complexity appears to predict the capabilities of digital software.*

Raw
Comics anthology edited by Art Spiegelman and Françoise Mouly, published from 1980 to 1991.

Wet
Los Angeles-based culture and graphic arts magazine, published (under the wry banner "gourmet bathing") from 1976 to 1981 by Leonard Koren.

Octavo
The British studio 8vo produced eight issues of this magazine from 1986 to 1992, with a strong focus on modernist graphic design sensibilities. Two members of the team had studied with Wolfgang Weingart in Basel.

the content ambiguous, and sometimes more visible than readable by conventional standards. Naturally, this work tested the limits of reading tolerance. More importantly, these approaches are evidence of insatiable curiosity about the written word, perpetual fascination with typographic form, and ongoing enquiry into how the two combine to explore reading and meaning.

NEEDS AND WANTS

According to many typographers past and present, the function of typography is to aid reading. Typographic form, then, primarily serves the mechanics of reading: how efficiently letterforms collect into decipherable words; how readily the typography pulls the eye across text lines and through paragraphs. The argument centers on reader "needs," and calls for typography to make words as visually clear as possible, free of any impediments that might stall reader access to the content. Formal beauty and legibility are the practical objectives. Other objectives, however—such as the message a typographer might want to impart—also inform typographic choices. Note the word "want," not "need."

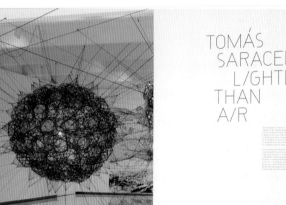

Bus riders "need" to be able to read timetables readily, which typography "needs" to facilitate. Readers need to navigate e-books. Not far removed from so-called needs, though, are "wants." Commuters want the convenience of accessible information, and bus-company managers want complaint-free work shifts. Readers want to be caught up in the latest thriller, authors want their stories read, and publishers want their books sold. Insofar as pleasures and livelihoods are at stake, wants are as much a part of typographic function as needs. If in business, a designer wants to meet the demands of those who commission him (the initiators described in Chapter 1) because

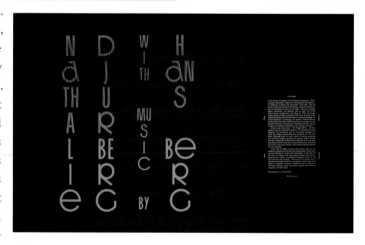

he wants (and needs) to be paid, and to build his design practice. He might want to produce stylistically unconventional work that challenges readers, but that inspires them to read nonetheless. "Functional" typography amounts to more than letterform clarity. Typography functions to engage readers intellectually and emotionally, to maintain commercial and societal viability, and to provide an outlet for creative expression. Importantly, none of these functions is mutually exclusive.

Let's design a wall with information (a "<u>didactic</u>") for a public exhibition [2.48]. The curator wants her thesis to be displayed prominently so that visitors

Didactic
Museum jargon for information walls, panels, and labels installed within gallery spaces to help inform and educate visitors about the exhibited artifacts.

2.48 Exhibition graphics: *(top) Tomás Saraceno: Lighter than Air*, 2009. Mylinh Trieu Nguyen, Walker Art Center Design Studio; *(bottom) The Parade*, 2011. Dante Carlos, Walker Art Center Design Studio. *Typography for these two descriptive panels captures the character of the work it represents. Top: adjusting the capital I in the light and airy title is subtle, inventive, and appropriate to the sculpture on display. Bottom: likewise, this title's uncomfortable word arrangement and coloration reflect the work—animations described by the artist as "fairy tales gone mad."*

will be aware of her intent. She wants the text to be legible and readable. The typography's primary function, then, is to express the exhibition's character and to be legible to readers entering the galleries. But we also want the curatorial perspective to be influenced by our own views. It turns out that the typographic approach we propose not only sacrifices readability but is also incongruous with the curator's intent. Even if we prove to the curator that our proposal would enlighten and engage visitors, our wants have deviated so far from hers that a most unpleasant confrontation awaits us in her office.

On the other hand, suppose the curator agrees that the point of the exhibition is well served by our proposal. Perhaps the more challenging treatment represents the exhibition's perspective in a way she had not considered. She thinks the typography will educate, surprise, and delight visitors, even though they will need to invest more energy to read her thesis. On opening day, visitors are, in fact, surprised and delighted as they read the information. Our design perspective has contributed to a successful show and the curator pays the invoice. Happy outcomes abound.

The needs and wants of designers and those who commission them stimulate invention. The researcher who wants to investigate typeface legibility on screen might be funded by the wants of a software company, but the work is not driven by market demands. Speculative typographic investigations, on the other hand, do not need to serve specific ends, as the work of Ben Fry [2.46] demonstrates. His kind of typography manifests ideas that aim to jolt others into thinking differently. Similarly, designing an uncommissioned typeface foregrounds the creative wants and needs of the type designer. Reader needs and wants might ultimately inform researchers and speculators; in fact, they can be a major factor in determining whether or not the work is viable. During the process of research and speculation, however, readers may end up being a secondary concern.

2.49 *Bottle*, 2012.

2.50 Screen grabs from Amaztype (http://amaztype.tha.jp). *A rather obvious example of typographic novelty.*

NOVELTY AND WONDER

Commercial competition often leads designers to seek ways of distinguishing their work from other people's. The design system within which typographers work also compels some designers to make "original" work. Whatever the impetus, designers try to imbue their work with something special. They might introduce a more efficient way to navigate a website, or attract readers with unexpected form [2.49].

Typographic novelty is one typical strategy. Novelty deliberately pushes against convention and reader expectations to get a reaction from the reader. A more difficult strategy, and therefore a less common one, is to create wonder.

Wonder works with convention and reader expectation to make familiar things unfamiliar, so that readers experience them anew.

Typography can illustrate the denotative meaning of content (to readers familiar with both). The typography that opens a video tribute to heavy-metal music, for instance, will be, predictably, a thick, angular typeface that drops into view with an aggressive thud. If the subject is anorexia, however, the type might shrink to a painful thinness. No novelty, no wonder. Just business as usual. Suppose the words "heavy metal" are set in peach-colored ribbon script—similar to the type treatments we might see in a lingerie catalogue—and the letters slither into shape salaciously. How novel! Layering form that is opposite to how we expect the words to look adds an uncomfortable irony. The contrast is slightly jarring, but the effect is not wondrous. It is business as unusual.

Typography created by the online app Amaztype is novel [2.50]. Enter a word in the dialog box, and miniature images of book titles associated with the word begin to appear. As we watch, book covers pile one on top of the other to shape the letters of the word we typed. Tiny book covers continue to pop up inside the letters, even after our word is completely formed. The animation entices users to click, and they are directed to Amazon.com, the online bookstore. This piece of brand innovation and programming prowess promotes the company. But there is more to Amaztype than novelty. The design embodies the vast array and variety of books available on the subject in a fresh way—a definite leap from your standard list. The novelty of letterforms made from book covers is surprising, but the dynamic assembly of book covers into a visual form that demonstrates variety is what lends wonder.

Wonder is more subtle than novelty. Wonder reforms the reading experience of readers, whereas novelty makes them snap to attention. Toyota's campaign "The Car that Reads the Road" uses animated, dimensional typography as the backdrop to a real car traveling through both country and city [2.51]. The typography takes on the shape and character of inanimate and animate things: the words "clouds," "rain," "sheep," and "birds" respectively float, pour, graze, and fly. The motion-graphics studio

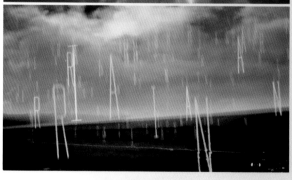

2.51 *The Car that Reads the Road*, 2006. Jonathan Notaro and Jens Gelhar, Brand New School. *Ad campaign for Toyota Camry.*

READING SYSTEMS

Brand New School rendered every element in exacting detail—a bridge, a park, a bus, a bank building, an art museum, a diner, and more. We cannot possibly see or read every word over the brief duration of the ad, yet the delivery compels us to do so. It engages our understanding of what we know typography "is," what exists in the world, and, conversely, what is impossible. The work then meshes our understanding with the interplay of word and image, reality and fantasy. The work is wondrous.

So, why be concerned with the difference between novelty and wonder? As much as our motives drive us to make typography that stands out, we cannot overlook our desire to surprise and delight readers. Encyclopedias and news sites might not call for either novelty or wonder. The typography might instead enable quick and seamless access to information. Other contexts and content call for delightfulness and ingenuity, as well as readability.

PROMPTS

/// **Select a periodical** you find at the library, ideally one that you are completely unfamiliar with. Open it to a type-heavy spread. Notice the order in which you scan the page. Read through the page. Draw a map of the hierarchy, the flow, and disruptions to the flow. *(See "Visual Syntax," page 68, and "Flow, Disruption, Gravity," page 82.)*

/// **Do an online search** using the keywords "typography" and "rules," then look through a few of the results. Select a couple of rules that aren't covered in this chapter (don't worry, you'll find them in other chapters). Imagine the pragmatic and aesthetic reasons why these rules are in place. For instance, what motives are behind the rule "avoid beginning three consecutive lines with the same word"? *(See "Pragmatic and Aesthetic Rules: Part I," page 70.)*

/// **Find examples of typography** that you think are (1) very legible, (2) less legible but readable, (3) illegible. Identify and list the attributes of each that make the typography legible (or not). Show each list to different people: your friends, older and younger relatives, your teachers. How much does their view echo yours? *(See "Legibility and Readability," page 73.)*

/// **Stand back from a magazine stand** and you will notice that it is both a simultaneous and a reader-ordered reading space. Try closing your eyes for a second. Open them and consciously track where your eyes move. What factors influenced your jumps from one point to the next? Was it the proximity of elements? Color? Titles that interest you? *(See "Typography Takes the Lead," page 77 and "The Reading Space," page 79.)*

/// **As you work on your next project**, list the ways in which your typography addresses the reader. (It may be that the readers are your peers, or just your teacher.) Itemize the needs of the project in a second list, which could include the need to make something that scores a high mark. Make a third list of the kinds of "wants" you encounter. Make connections among the lists to pair the influential motives that affect your design. *(See "Needs and Wants," page 98.)*

formal

systems 3

Chapter 3 focuses on the visual and physical systems that exert particular force on typographic practice. We return to the practical (pragmatic) and taste (aesthetic) issues introduced in Chapter 2, and apply them now to formal typographic traditions. An overview of such visual phenomena as color systems and Gestalt relationships leads to key principles in visual composition: pattern, variation, and contrast—three central aspects of the formal systems that unify typefaces, connect typeface families, create useful differences, and set up meaningful associations among elements in reading spaces. A section on grids follows, which covers grid origins and uses, then describes the formal and functional considerations that are the contexts for making grid-design choices. The chapter ends with a brief look at the aesthetic concerns of typographers, and how such aesthetic options as "white space" communicate to readers.

primer

ANALOGOUS

Color relationships based on hues that are adjacent on the color wheel. Yellow, green, and blue, for example, are analogous colors. **ILL. 01 > PAGE 120**

BASELINE GRID

A set of parallel horizontal lines, spaced equally according to the desired vertical distance between lines of text. Baseline grids mimic the line spacing for large bodies of text, and the typographic units of measurement define proportional modules for the sizing and alignment of other elements on the page. The Swiss designers Karl Gerstner and Josef Müller-Brockmann were known for their use of baseline and modular grids. **> PAGE 147**

BEHAVIOR

The action of elements on the screen in time-based media or the actions required of the user to produce such outcomes in interactive media. Typography in these virtual worlds responds in ways that are both consistent and inconsistent with the laws of nature in the physical world. Type moves, fades, and morphs into new forms in a manner not possible in static media. Interactive media establish behavioral conventions to which users assign expectations; for example, the finger gesture used with touch-screen cellphones to expand the size of text is now applied across other media platforms. **ILL. 02 > PAGE 128**

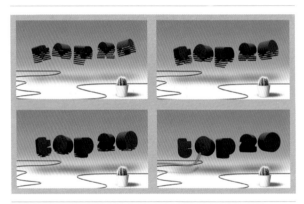

01 : ANALOGOUS

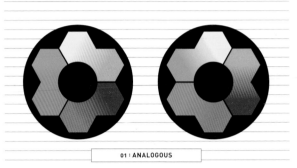

02 : BEHAVIOR

03 : BOWL

04 : CMYK

BINARY HEX

Short for binary hexadecimal color, a two-figure alphanumeric notational system for specifying color that will be projected or read only on computer screens (as opposed to printed). In screen displays, color settings are in RGB (referring to the red, green, and blue primary colors of light) and measured at 255 levels for each color. In determining a single color, the designer chooses settings of each of the three primaries; a blue hue, for example, may result from settings of red at 102, green at 204, and blue at 255. By contrast, binary hex abbreviates a traditional decimal expression of three numeric figures to a hexadecimal expression of only two alphanumeric figures. In binary hex, the blue hue described above would be expressed as 66 CC FF. **> PAGE 121**

BOWL

The curvilinear stroke of a letterform that completely encloses a counter. The enclosed descender of the lowercase g is called a "loop." **ILL. 03 > PAGE 130**

CMYK

Initials that refer to the inks used in four-color process printing: cyan, magenta, yellow, and black. Overlapping dots of the four colors produce the full spectrum of subtractive or reflective color found in photographs (as opposed to the additive color of RGB). New colors may also be "built" for type and graphic elements using these colors in varying percentages as tints; for example, a solid 100% yellow with an overlapping 50% tint of magenta will produce orange. **ILL. 04 > PAGE 118**

COLOPHON

A brief description in a book that includes facts related to its production and publication. In addition to the name and location of the publisher and date, a colophon may also include the paper and typeface used in the design of the book and the number of copies printed. Some colophons provide additional typographic details, such as the history of the typefaces and their designers. Traditionally, the colophon appears at the end of the book or on the back of the title page. ILL. 05 > PAGE 150

COMPLEMENTARY

Color relationships based on opposite hues on the color wheel. Red and green, orange and blue, and yellow and purple are complements. Complementary colors of equal intensity appear to vibrate when juxtaposed. For this reason, placing colored type on a background of its complement compromises legibility. ILL. 06 > PAGE 120

DURATION

The amount of time that elapses in dynamic media. Specific episodes of screen activity and the totality of the time-based experience have durations. Designers control these periods of time, unless interaction by a user is self-directed and self-paced. Duration has meaning. If the typography in the opening titles of a film moves across the screen at a particular pace or fades from the screen across time, we attach meaning to those durations. In some cases, the amount of time between actions can actually determine whether we see the typographic episodes as related or discrete. Motion typography, for example, involves the same letters being redrawn at different locations on the computer screen. If the duration between these images is too long, letters appear as individual elements rather than as one element in motion. > PAGE 129

Primers are typeset in varying weights of DIN, an extended family designed by Albert-Jan Pool and published by the German foundry Font Font in 1995 and 2009. Chapter text is typeset in Whitman, a text face designed by Kent Lew, released by the American foundry Font Bureau in 2003 – 2008.

05 : COLOPHON

YELLOW

GREEN

ORANGE

BLUE

RED

VIOLET

06 : COMPLEMENTARY

07 : EAR

EAR

A small stroke protruding from the top of a lowercase g. ILL. 07 > PAGE 132

FORM

The shape or visual appearance of an element or object. Designers determine typographic form in the same ways that writers select words and writing styles to convey particular meanings. Typographic form is defined by the visual qualities of typefaces; their size, spacing, placement, and orientation within a composition; and their similarity and contrast with other elements on the page. There are conventions for "good typographic form" that have been established over time. For example, hanging delicate punctuation outside the block of type to maintain a strong column edge, and removing widows (dangling words at the end of a paragraph), are generally seen as desirable. Across history, however, there have been times when designers have challenged prevailing conventions of typographic form for expressive purposes, creating new visual vocabularies against which future design is judged. > PAGE 111

FRAME

A means for subdividing a browser window using HTML code. Frames are designated in HTML by the <frameset> tag and enable the system to display multiple documents in the same browser window at the same time. Each HTML document is housed in its own frame, independent of the others, and can be changed or replaced without disrupting the remaining documents. Before the development of Cascading Style Sheets (CSS), frames were the typical means for developing complex presentations of information on the Web. > PAGE 123

GOLDEN RECTANGLE

A particular proportional relationship in which the side lengths of a rectangle are in the golden ratio, 1:1.618. Used across visual history and seen as "divine" because of its mathematical logic, the golden rectangle is one of several strategies for dividing space. The medieval draftsman Villard de Honnecourt developed a ratio based on the golden rectangle for the organization of the page and of the text and images placed on it. His goal was to convey the "truth" of geometry as opposed to the individuality of the artist's decision. **ILL. 08 > PAGE 135**

GRID

A division of space by horizontal and vertical lines that is used to structure content and form. The best-known locative grid was developed by the seventeenth-century philosopher René Descartes, though page designers had used grid structures well before Descartes. Grids guide the proportional division of the page and the size and alignment of elements in a composition. Modules—rectangles of a particular proportion—may be repeated or combined when determining how much space is occupied by text and image. Specific measurements within the grid are typically determined by the point size and line spacing of type. **> PAGE 132**

HUE

The fullest expression of any single color in the visual spectrum. Hue is sometimes called "chroma." The term "value" refers to the lightness or darkness of a hue (pink is a value of red) and "intensity" refers to brightness or dullness (slate is a dull version of blue). **> PAGE 118**

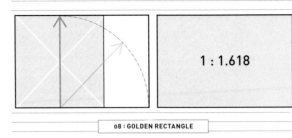

08 : GOLDEN RECTANGLE

SeventyTwo
UNEVEN KERNING

Seventy Two
EVEN KERNING

Seventy Two
KERNING PAIRS

09 : KERNING/KERNING PAIR

aBCDeFG HIjkLMNO PQrsTUV WXYZ 2468

10 : MONOCASE

Here lived Peter the goatherd, a boy eleven years old, who daily fetched the goats from the village and drove them up the mountain to the short and luscious grasses of the pastures. Peter raced down in the evening with the light-footed little goats. When he whistled sharply through his fingers, every owner would come and get his or her goat.
These owners were mostly small boys and girls and, as the goats were friendly, they did not fear them. That was the only time he spent with other children, the rest of the day the animals were his sole companions. At home lived his mother and an old blind grandmother, but he only spent enough time in the hut to swallow his bread and milk for breakfast and the same repast for supper. He left early in the morning and at night he came home late, so that he could be with his friends.

11 : ORPHAN

12 : PACING

KERNING

The selective adjustment of the space between two letters. Certain letter combinations represent problems for the optical uniformity of letterspacing in a word or sentence. The "Ty" combination in "Typography," for example, creates an awkward collision of white spaces, making the capital T appear to be distanced too far from the rest of the letters. Preset kerning in a software program may not recognize this combination as problematic in type sizes larger than 14 point, and therefore the designer is required to reduce the space between the letters. Conversely, such letter combinations as the "illi" in the word "filling" may require additional space to appear equivalent to other letter combinations within the word or sentence. **ILL. 09 > PAGE 113**

KERNING PAIR

Specific combinations of letters that require kerning. Kerning pairs are recognized by software as requiring spacing adjustments; the system automatically makes these reductions or additions of space. A single font can have more than a thousand kerning pairs, but most do not exceed five hundred. **ILL. 09 > PAGE 131**

MONOCASE

A typeface lacking any distinction between uppercase and lowercase letters. Monocase typefaces are made up solely of upper- or lowercase letters, or designed to integrate aspects of both in a single alphabet. Monocase typefaces are generally used for display purposes. **ILL. 10 > PAGE 130**

MONOCHROMATIC

Using only one color. Monochromatic color schemes achieve contrast through variations in value, using tints and shades. In one-color printing, such variations are achieved through screen tints and expand the expressive possibilities of a limited ink palette. **> PAGE 120**

MORPH

In computer-based media, a special effect that transforms one image seamlessly into another. **> PAGE 131**

ORPHAN

The first line of a new paragraph appearing as the last line of a column of text. As a general rule, it is best to have at least two lines of a new paragraph at the bottom of a column before it continues to the next page. **ILL. 11 > PAGE 117**

PACING

The visual rhythm or rate of presentation of elements in sequential print formats, such as books, and in time-based media. The patterned placement of contrasting elements across the sequential pages of books and magazines reinforces changes in content. The rhythm of magazines is different from the rhythm of books because the magazine pattern signals frequent changes in content and encourages scanning. The amount of time for which elements are present on the screen determines perceptions of pacing in time-based media. **ILL. 12 > PAGE 128**

PATTERN

A predictable ordering of recurring elements. Typeface designers seek a rhythmic pattern in the repeating strokes, counters, and angles of glyphs. In book design, page numbers and running heads recur in predictable styles and locations. **ILL. 13 > PAGE 124**

13 : PATTERN

From the demure breeze that marched behind us came far-flung sighs of spice trees and nutmeg flowers. The slow prodigious swells of the Pacific

14 : POOL

rose and fell beneath the planks, our hearts lifting and sinking with the sea's rhythm. We swayed as trees ourselves, in harmony and willing submission.

15 : RAG

VERSO   RECTO

16 : RECTO/VERSO

POOL

A wide, distracting white space created by the coincidental vertical stacking of word spaces among successive lines of text. Pools are frequently created when justifying type in a narrow column; too few words prevent an even distribution of the extra space necessary to make all lines of text the same length. **ILL. 14 > PAGE 114**

PROPORTIONAL SYSTEMS

A mathematical strategy for visually dividing a page. For example, the DIN 476 system of paper sizes is based on a single aspect ratio of the square root of 2; when the page is divided in half, the proportions of each half will be the same as those of the original whole. The DIN standard was adopted in Germany in 1992 and is now a standard in most of the world, except the United States. The DIN A4 letterhead has slightly taller proportion than the American 8½ × 11 inches. **> PAGE 135**

RAG

The uneven left or right edge of a typeset column. Flush left/rag right text, for example, describes paragraphs aligned on the left and ragged on the right (as here). In such settings, normal word spacing is maintained, producing different amounts of white space at the end of lines containing different numbers of characters. **ILL. 15 > PAGE 116**

RECTO/VERSO

The names applied to the two sides of an open book spread. In languages written from left to right, the recto page is on the right and the verso page is on the left. In a typical book, recto pages carry odd page numbers and verso pages carry even page numbers. **ILL. 16 > PAGE 147**

REFLECTIVE COLOR

Concerning surfaces that "throw back" the light cast upon them. In print-based typography, we see type as an effect of the sun's light or that of a light fixture. We would call this typography "reflective" because we experience it indirectly, as an effect of a detached light source. In reflective typography, figure and ground are distinguished by differently colored pigments in ink, toner, and paint, and colors found in the material that is printed upon. Reflective type is usually produced by a printing press or printer at the maximum number of printable dots per inch (DPI) possible with the device. It is output in grayscale for single-color printing and CMYK format for full-color printing. **> PAGE 118**

RGB

Initials that refer to the primary colors in light (red, green, and blue) and as seen in computer displays. **> PAGE 118**

RHYTHM

An ordered recurrent alteration of elements in a visual sequence. **> PAGE 128**

RIVER

A vertical or diagonal fissure of negative space in two or more successive lines of text. Rivers are frequently created when justifying type in a narrow column; too few words prevent an even distribution of the extra space necessary to make all lines of text the same length. They disrupt the horizontal flow of reading. **ILL. 17 > PAGE 114**

SATURATION

The purity of a color. Saturation is measured by the amount of gray in proportion to the hue. A fully saturated color has 0% gray and 100% hue. **> PAGE 118**

No one, seeing the tall, clever looking girl stepping briskly out of the station and turning up Main Street with a businesslike tread, would have guessed that she was a stranger in a strange town and hadn't any idea where she was going. There was such an air of confidence and capability about Katherine that people would have been more likely to ask her to help them out of their difficulties than to suspect that she needed help herself. Certainly, Nyoda's house wouldn't be hard to find. Oakwood lay in a valley, curled up among its sheltering hills like a kitten in a heap of leaves.

17 : RIVER

18 : SLOPE

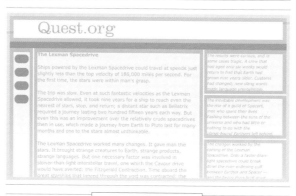

19 : STEM

20 : TABLE

SHADES AND TINTS

The adjustment of the value of color by the addition of black or white. Inks are made darker by mixing the hue with black pigment and lighter by mixing the hue with white pigment or a neutral base. Screen tints are made up of dots of the same size. The smaller the dots, the more white paper shows through, lightening the overall impact of the color. Screens of black dots printed on top of colors darken the value of the base color. **> PAGE 118**

SLOPE

The common angle of stems, ascenders, and descenders in a typeface. Many script faces have a diagonal slope, while most others have a vertical slope. **ILL. 18 > PAGE 114**

SPECTRAL COLOR

A color that is created by a single wavelength of light in the visible spectrum. Color on digital screen displays is spectral color created by pixels containing red, green, and blue phosphors. In typography produced by spectral color, letterform and light source are one and the same. **> PAGE 118**

STEM

The primary stroke of a letterform, minus serifs. Stems are usually vertical. **ILL. 19 > PAGE 130**

TABLE

A matrix built within HTML code that allows designers to arrange information in rows and columns. A table is defined by the <table> tag, and the designer can specify how text is to appear in one cell versus another. **ILL. 20 > PAGE 140**

TAIL

The stroke that extends below the bowl of the capital Q and R. **> PAGE 132**

TEMPERATURE

A metaphor applied to color. Warm colors (red, orange, and yellow) tend to advance, and cool colors (green, blue, and violet) tend to recede. When figure and ground are the same temperature, the figure will tend to recede into its background. **> PAGE 120**

TEXT TYPE AND DISPLAY TYPE

Any type set at a size below 14 pt is text type. It is typically used for body copy, folios, and captions. Display type is any type set at 14 pt and above. Display type is used for headlines, posters, and signage. **ILL. 21 > PAGES 127/129**

TIMELINE

A graphic representation of time. Timelines are among the authoring tools in software used for developing interactive applications. Designers use this tool to script the sequence and duration of movement in dynamic typography. **> PAGE 123**

TINT

A light value of a hue. In pigment, adding white to a color lightens it. In printing, creating a screen tint lightens color by converting a solid area of ink to a dot pattern, allowing white paper to show through. The percentage of tint is a factor of the size and spacing of the dots. **> PAGE 118**

TRACKING

An overall adjustment made in the spaces between letters in a block of type. Tracking uniformly reduces or increases spaces between all letters, while kerning adjusts spacing only between selective letter combinations. Tightening tracking uniformly reduces spaces between all letters and loosening tracking increases the spaces. **ILL. 22 > PAGE 113**

As already indicated, the writing materials in use in different places and at different times have varied greatly. Obviously anything capable of receiving an impression or bearing a mark of any kind may be used as

EXPRESSIVE

material for receiving records or bearing communications. The surface of a stone, a bone, or a shell, a flat piece of wood, bark or leaf of a tree, a plate of metal, the facet of a gem, any one of a thousand things can be used and has been used for this purpose.

21 : TEXT TYPE AND DISPLAY TYPE

MINUS TRACKING (-60)

The real impulse, however, to the construction of books as distinguished from rolls came with the use of sheets of vellum. These could not be attached easily to make long rolls as could be done with the papyrus sheets, while even the single sheets were large enough to be unwieldy when spread out.

NORMAL TRACKING (0)

The real impulse, however, to the construction of books as distinguished from rolls came with the use of sheets of vellum. These could not be attached easily to make long rolls as could be done with the papyrus sheets, while even the single sheets were large enough to be unwieldy when spread out.

PLUS TRACKING (+45)

The real impulse, however, to the construction of books as distinguished from rolls came with the use of sheets of vellum. These could not be at tached easily to make long rolls as could be done with the papyrus sheets, while even the single sheets were large enough to be unwieldy when spread out.

22 : TRACKING

Here lived Peter the goatherd, a boy eleven years old, who daily fetched the goats from the village and drove them up the mountain to the short and luscious grasses of the pastures. Peter raced down in the evening with the light-footed little goats. When he whistled sharply through his fingers, every owner would come and get his or her goat. These owners were mostly small boys and girls and, as the goats were friendly, they did **not fear them.** That was the only time he spent with other children, the rest of the day the animals were his sole companions. At home lived his mother and an old blind grandmother, but he only spent enough time in the hut to swallow his bread and milk for breakfast and the same repast for supper. He left early in the morning and at night he came home **late.**

23 : WIDOW

Here lived Peter the goatherd.
Here lived Peter the goatherd.

24 : WORD SPACING

VALUE

The lightness or darkness of a color, controlled by the addition of black or white. **> PAGE 118**

VARIATION

A deviation from or within a repeating pattern. Typography creates continuity within a typeface by maintaining a consistent x-height from lowercase letter to letter. The shapes of letters, however, offer meaningful variety in the appearance of the alphabet. Likewise, a block of text creates an even gray pattern but variation can be introduced for emphasis through the use of bold and italic type. At the scale of publications, page layouts can repeat compositional strategies from spread to spread but introduce surprising variations to connote a change in content. In time-based media, changes in point of view or pacing introduce dramatic variations that break the pattern of viewing. **> PAGE 124**

WIDOW

The last line of a paragraph that falls at the top of a new page, separated from other text in the paragraph. As a rule, it is best to have at least two lines of text in a continuing paragraph at the top of a column and more than two words in the last line of any paragraph. **ILL. 23 > PAGE 117**

WORD COUNT

The total number of words appearing in a single publication, including titles and captions. **> PAGE 142**

WORD SPACING

The space between words, produced by pressing the space bar on the keyboard. Word spacing is uniform unless a paragraph is justified, in which case spacing is reduced or increased to make all lines of text the same length, regardless of the number of characters in each line. **ILL. 24 > PAGE 116**

The formal systems within typography are closely allied to taste—or, more accurately, to good taste, a narrow range of the taste continuum. Despite the fact that all designers work toward it, taste is the proverbial elephant in the well-designed room.

This ever-present beast eludes our direct attention; yet were a person to proclaim out loud that "beauty is in the eye of the beholder," most designers within earshot would turn to him and say flat out, "You couldn't be more wrong." As with all good taste, typographic taste embodies a *je ne sais quoi*; that unnamable something that certain people recognize immediately but cannot seem to explain, or will not explain, because the matter needs no discussion. One just knows.

In truth, anyone possessing such discerning taste could explain why something is tasteful, but to do so would be a waste of time (they might huff). Just look at it! The typography is so very clearly timeless (they might say) and obviously immune to subjective judgment.

Taste is actually a constituent of social systems that are in constant flux: they can relegate a thing considered divine in one moment to the halls of hideousness in another. If typographic artifacts or typefaces (or all designed things) are met with acceptance and ultimately endure, it is not because of any intrinsic worth. Rather, these artifacts are beneficiaries of a tacit social agreement concerning the work's relevance, both at the time they emerge and in subsequent ages. I could, right at this moment, name some tasteful typefaces. I might say Baskerville

Baskerville

Originally designed in 1757 by the English printer John Baskerville, this typeface is considered "Transitional." Baskerville introduced greater stroke contrasts than were then common in Oldstyle types, which predated the high stroke contrasts of such later "Modern" typefaces as Bodoni.

Mrs. Eaves

Zuzana Licko named her revival of Baskerville, released by the Emigre foundry in 1996, after Sarah Eaves, John Baskerville's second wife, who continued his work after his death. The typeface and the name recognize the contributions made by women that have often been overlooked in typography and printing history.

is better than <u>Mrs. Eaves</u>, or claim that <u>VAG Rounded</u> is inferior to <u>Courier</u>. And I could take the necessary time to set out the reasons why. Then, a year from now, anyone revisiting this chapter could read my declaration and call me an uncultured Neanderthal.

Are people born with good taste? In a manner of speaking, yes. If they were brought up surrounded by a degree of aesthetic sophistication, then they may be able to claim at least a little. These people are at least likely to recognize tastefulness when they see it. If, however, an individual is not reared in an atmosphere of taste, the path to achieving a discriminating eye may be a bit bumpier. Using my own experience as an example, some of my environments growing up involved <u>Herculon</u> and paint-by-number renditions of *The Blue Boy* by Gainsborough and Leonardo's *Mona Lisa*. Consequently, I have had to work a little harder to acquire certain kinds of taste. The good news is, I definitely know tacky when I see it, which has proven to be equally valuable knowledge. Aspiring designers are educated in typographic taste as they develop sensitivity to typographic **form**. Even those who seem to have a natural eye continue to refine their judgments as they mature in their work. The bottom line is that good taste reflects social standards and is manifested in so-called "good" form [3.1, 3.2].

Historically, designers and producers worked within value systems that associated good design with fine art, a product of "high" culture once created mainly by the elite. Meanwhile, the visual stuff of everyday life, or of popular culture, took on "low-brow" status in comparison. Robert Venturi, Denise Scott Brown, and Steven Izenour famously conducted a study with architecture students, published in 1972 under the title *Learning from Las Vegas*. The book celebrates forms and tastes that spring from commercial necessity and ingenuity, including unremarkable architecture and gaudy graphic design. The treatise enlightened designers about the merits of popular visual languages [3.3].

Tastes gain and lose favor from generation to generation, vary from social class to social class, and change from decade to decade. To be safe, some designers restrict their font and form palettes to a handful of tasteful options they believe do and will withstand the test of time. It is a strategy that keeps designers from hurting themselves because, like running with scissors, a person can poke out an eye when flailing tasteless type about.

We must understand taste in relation to societies and subcultures. We are the producers and products of our environments, after all. As typographers, charting our own path within these domains requires a bit of exposure and considerable practice. Awareness of typographic history clues us in to tasteful (and tasteless) precedents. And because we tend to develop taste and form-making preferences that mirror those of the people with whom we associate, working with others who we believe make good form exposes us to existing perspectives. Even if we are inclined to design contrarily, to challenge dominant tastes, success favors those who know the opposition well.

AUSTIN ★ TEXAS

VAG Rounded

Designed for Volkswagen AG in 1979, this Rundschrift (round writing) typeface is a modified version of nineteenth-century grotesques, distinguishable by its rounded terminal and stroke ends.

Courier

A monospace slab serif that resembles types designed for early typewriters. IBM commissioned Howard Kettler in the 1950s to design the typeface for their typewriters, which other manufacturers quickly imitated. Kettler went on to produce several variations of his original design.

Herculon

The trade name of a durable, stain-resistant synthetic fabric made of Olefin, a polymer fiber invented in the late 1940s. The fabric was a popular, albeit hideous, option for upholstery in the 1960s and 1970s.

3.1 *(opposite, top, and this page, top)* Packaging for Jamie Oliver Enterprises, 2009. Sarah Pidgeon and Natalie Chung, Pearlfisher. *In a clever mix of "good" and "bad" taste, this typographic form plays with the expectations of "foodies," people acquainted with celebrity chef Jamie Oliver's reputation. Although the handmade quality suggests everyday ingredients, people who know the chef's work might expect the products to be better than average.*

3.2 *(opposite, bottom)* Lavender May identity and business stationery, 2010. Ceci Johnson and Erin McCue, Ceci New York.

3.3 *(this page, above)* Luther's logo, 2010. Andy Cruz, Ken Barber, and Chris Gardner, House Industries. *This logo—an example of "tacky" drawn well—accompanied an exhibition of work by House Industries that was on view at a store in Austin, Texas, called Luther's. House Industries' work consistently shines a positive light on the lettering and illustration styles that originated with twentieth-century commercial artists and other "low-brow" talents.*

///////////////////// **MEDIATING FORMAL SYSTEMS**

Form and word unite into one symbiotic entity: typography. We might imagine words (content) as liquid—wine, say—and form as the container, a wine glass, which shapes words into narratives and pronouncements. The typographic researcher Beatrice Warde used exactly that "fragrant metaphor" in her charming speech "The Crystal Goblet," which is worth quoting at length:

"The Crystal Goblet"

An oft-quoted speech written in 1930 by Beatrice Warde, assistant librarian at American Type Founders Company (ATF) and a typography researcher. Delivered to the British Typographers' Guild at the St. Bride Institute, the speech was later transcribed and published under Warde's pseudonym Paul Beaujon.

You will find that almost all the virtues of the perfect wineglass have a parallel in typography. There is the long, thin stem that obviates fingerprints on the bowl. Why? Because no cloud must come between your eyes and the fiery heart of the liquid. Are not the margins on book pages similarly meant to obviate the necessity of fingering the type-page? Again the glass is colourless or at the most only faintly tinged in the bowl, because the connoisseur judges wine partly by its colour and is impatient of anything that alters it. There are a thousand mannerisms in typography that are as impudent and arbitrary as putting port in tumblers of red or green glass! When a goblet has a base that looks too small for security, it does not matter how cleverly it is weighted; you feel nervous lest it should tip over. There are ways of setting lines of type which may work well enough, and yet keep the reader subconsciously worried by the fear of "doubling" lines, reading three words as one, and so forth.

Now the man who first chose glass instead of clay or metal to hold his wine was a "modernist" . . . . That is, the first thing he asked of his particular object was not "How should it look?" but "What must it do?" and to that extent all good typography is modernist.[1]

This essay registers good taste without being explicit (*je ne sais quoi*). In addition, it reveals that form communicates ideas as much as words do, which Warde makes crystal clear. But can visible or tactile form be literally transparent? With or without wine, to extend the metaphor, a glass goblet is a goblet made of glass—a vitreous, sparkly, delicate, reflective substance that embodies cultural significance, perhaps connoting connoisseurship and a high social class. A clay mug would interact with wine in its own thick, textured, earthy way, perhaps alluding to simple and common pleasures. Just as Warde consciously invokes the properties of a crystal goblet, typographers choose form to construct meanings. Words can be modestly jacketed or subtly bloused, poetically gowned or wittily costumed.

The essay rhetorically pits "how typography should look" against "what it must do." The fact is, typography does both. Chapter 1 describes these two aspects as connotative expressions and denotative roles. Now we look at the same principles through aesthetic and pragmatic lenses, the terms by which

King Arthur was at Caerlleon upon Usk; and one day he sat in his chamber; and with him were Owain the son of Urien, and Kynon the son of Clydno, and Kai the son of Kyner; and Gwenhwyvar and her hand-maidens at needlework by the window. And if it should be said that there was a porter at Arthur's palace, there was none. Glewlwyd Gavaelvawr was there, acting as porter, to welcome guests and strangers, and to receive them with honour, and to inform them of the manners and customs of the Court; and to direct those who came to the Hall or to the presence chamber, and those who came to take up their lodging.

King Arthur was at Caerlleon upon Usk; and one day he sat in his chamber; and with him were Owain the son of Urien, and Kynon the son of Clydno, and Kai the son of Kyner; and Gwenhwyvar and her hand-maidens at needlework by the window. And if it should be said that there was a porter at Arthur's palace, there was none. Glewlwyd Gavaelvawr was there, acting as porter, to welcome guests and strangers, and to receive them with honour, and to inform them of the manners and customs of the Court; and to direct those who came to the Hall or to the presence chamber, and those who came to take up their lodging.

King Arthur was at Caerlleon upon Usk; and one day he sat in his chamber; and with him were Owain the son of Urien, and Kynon the son of Clydno, and Kai the son of Kyner; and Gwenhwyvar and her hand-maidens at needlework by the window. And if it should be said that there was a porter at Arthur's palace, there was none. Glewlwyd Gavaelvawr was there, acting as porter, to welcome guests and strangers, and to receive them with honour, and to inform them of the manners and customs of the Court; and to direct those who came to the Hall or to the presence chamber, and those who came to take up their lodging.

3.4 Text texture.

Typeface is the primary contributor to color and texture variation. Faces with very open counters and thin strokes yield a lighter paragraph color, relatively speaking, than with smaller counters and thicker strokes, which darken color.

Typeface is the primary contributor to color and texture variation. Faces with very open counters and thin strokes yield a lighter paragraph color, relatively speaking, than with smaller counters and thicker strokes, which darken color.

Typeface is the primary contributor to color and texture variation. Faces with very open counters and thin strokes yield a lighter paragraph color, relatively speaking, than with smaller counters and thicker strokes, which darken color.

Typeface is the primary contributor to color and texture variation. Faces with very open counters and thin strokes yield a lighter paragraph color, relatively speaking, than with smaller counters and thicker strokes, which darken color.

Typeface is the primary contributor to color and texture variation. Faces with very open counters and thin strokes yield a lighter paragraph color, relatively speaking, than with smaller

Typeface is the primary contributor to color and texture variation. Faces with very open counters and thin strokes yield a lighter paragraph color, relatively speaking, than with smaller counters and thicker strokes, which darken color.

Typeface is the primary contributor to color and texture variation. Faces with very open counters and thin strokes yield a lighter paragraph color, relatively speaking, than with smaller counters and thicker strokes, which darken color.

Typeface is the primary contributor to color and texture variation. Faces with very open counters and thin strokes yield a lighter paragraph color, relatively speaking, than with smaller counters and thicker strokes, which darken color.

3.5 Text color.

we judge typography to be good, better, or best; and more to the point, the terms by which we determine whether or not typography *Works*.

PRAGMATIC AND AESTHETIC RULES: PART II

Recall from Chapter 2 that pragmatic values address the limits of readability or production, and aesthetic values address the presiding senses of beauty or style. Remember, too, that the typography we consider optimal is deemed so because the experiences of readers, within specific contexts, have helped to condition what seasoned typographers believe to be ideal. These same values inform how typographers make decisions within complex formal and perceptual systems, exemplified in the way typographers assess the formal attributes of paragraphs.

text color and texture variables

Text color refers to the relative darkness or lightness of paragraphs (text set en masse). Texture is a metaphor for the perceived surface quality of paragraphs, such as "rough" or "smooth" [3.4].

General wisdom says that long-term reading requires a uniform, mid-value text color so as not to tax the eye with excessive or uneven contrast between figure and ground. The question may arise: Just what is "mid-value"? If we run a spectrum of grays from white to black, mid-value sits right in the middle. Sounds simple enough. Note, though, that typeface, size, line spacing, **tracking**, and **kerning** can render this mid-value gray perfectly in one set of circumstances, but may make it appear darker or lighter in others [3.5].

Tradition also dictates that paragraphs should be free of disturbances that would distract a reader's fluid course as he moves from word to word, line to line. In typographic terms, paragraphs should not "snag" or "dazzle," for instance.

Typeface is the primary contributor to color and texture variation. Typefaces with very open counters and thin strokes yield a lighter paragraph color, relatively speaking, than those with smaller counters and thicker strokes, which darken color. Typefaces with extreme thick-to-thin ratios, such as Didot, bring more lively texture to a paragraph than evenly stroked typefaces, such as Goudy, and other typefaces designed for sustained reading. Even diminutive serifs or terminals accumulate over many letters and lines, modifying overall color and texture. The posture of a typeface, such as the **slope** of an italic or the uprightness of a geometric sans serif, can transform a somber texture into a vivacious one.

The assembly of typeface details facilitates or impedes reading to greater or lesser degrees. Also, line length will establish the horizontal measure of surface area within which the typeface and size can fit. Longer line lengths clearly accommodate larger point sizes, whereas shorter lengths suit smaller point sizes, particularly in fully justified texts. To illustrate: a small surface area, say a 6-inch square pillow, cannot display large patterns as fully as a 7-foot sofa can. Better to choose a thin stripe or petite floral for smaller surfaces. This is not to say that a large point size packed artfully into short lines cannot work. The choice does, however, radically affect text color and texture.

A font of any size, typeset within a justified line length that is too narrow to contain it, produces **rivers** and **pools**, the result of a point size ill fitted to the line-length ratio. Not only do these holes resemble bodies of water large enough to drown in, they also create spotty texture and uneven color, which can interrupt reading flow. Avoiding these blemishes serves aesthetics, to be sure, as well as the pragmatics of reading. Should too many rivers or pools collect in paragraphs, take steps to drain them. Adjust the line length, decrease the point size, change the typeface. If desperate, try all three.

Talking to each other is both one of the most simple and one of the most complex things that we can do. It is effortless and enjoyable; it is part of being a human being and a participating member of society. As a species we are compulsive communicators, using language to convey our deepest

Talking to each other is both one of the most simple and one of the most complex things that we can do. It is effortless and enjoyable; it is part of being a human being and a participating member of society. As a species we are compulsive communicators,

Talking to each other is both one of the most simple and one of the most complex things that we can do. It is effortless and enjoyable; it is part of being a human being and a participating member of society. As a species we are compulsive communicators, using language to convey our deepest

Talking to each other is both one of the most simple and one of the most complex things that we can do. It is effortless and enjoyable; it is part of being a human being and a participating member of society. As a species we are compulsive communicators, using language to convey our deepest

3.6 Line spacing and letterspacing.

We can lighten or darken text color by adjusting letter space, word space, and line space between and around letterforms. Imagine letters and lines as dark pigment (figure) intermixing with contrasting bits of light (ground). Just as black and white pigment blend to achieve shades or tints, so spaces and accumulated strokes combine to create text color. Altering paragraph tracking of black text on a white ground, for instance, modulates lightness or darkness, as well as paragraph texture. Increased line spacing within the same paragraph works similarly, except that it emphasizes lines rather

3.7 Page color and texture.

3.8 *Written languages yield different textures: English, Spanish, Finnish, and Czech.*

Talking to each other is both one of the most simple and one of the most complex things that we can do. It is effortless and enjoyable; it is part of being a human being and a participating member of society. As a species we are compulsive communicators, using language to convey our deepest feelings, our advances in knowledge and understanding, and—often—the trivia of our everyday lives.

Hablar unos con otros es una de las cosas más simples y más complejas que podemos hacer. No nos representa ningún esfuerzo y resulta agradable; es intrínseco en un ser humano que forma parte de una sociedad. Como especie, somos comunicativos de forma compulsiva, utilizamos el lenguaje para expresar nuestros sentimientos más profundos, nuestros progresos en el conocimiento y la comprensión, y (a menudo) las trivialidades de la vida diari.

Toisten kanssa keskusteleminen on sekä yksi kaikkein yksinkertaisimmista että kaikkein monimutkaisimmista asioista, joihin kykenemme. Se on vaivatonta ja miellyttävää; se on osa ihmisenä ja yhteisön osallistuvana jäsenenä olemista. Lajina olemme pakkomielteisiä tiedonvälittäjiä; käytämme kieltä välittämään muille syvimpiä tunteitamme, tiedollista ja ymmärryksellistä edistymistämme ja – usein myös   jokapäiväisen elämämme vähäpätöisyyksiä.

Řečová komunikace je jednou z nejjednodušších a zároveň jednou z nejsložitějších věcí, které umíme. Je snadná a příjemná; je součástí bytí člověka a jeho zapojení do společnosti. U našeho druhu se projevuje nutkavá potřeba komunikace, používáme řeč k vyjádření nejhlubších pocitů, pokroků ve vědění a chápání a často k hovoru o běžných denních záležitostech.

than overall color. Decreasing line spacing creates darker and denser text. Be aware, though, that the more open the tracking or line spacing, the more the words or text lines struggle to stay connected [3.6]. As words and lines lose a sense of proximity to each other, at some point the words, or indeed the whole paragraph, will snap apart to form a fabric of dissociated letters, or a pattern of separate lines. Note that variation of these same attributes—tracking and line spacing—also applies to white text on black ground, or lighter-hued text on darker grounds.

Following this principle of mixing dark and light, the amount of text determines paragraph depth, which affects the color and texture of the overall page or screen [3.7]. Short paragraphs in a long text mean more paragraph indents or spaces between paragraphs than we would see in longer paragraphs. There will be frequent, forced line breaks at the end of paragraphs, too. These factors will create a lighter page of text than will those of longer paragraphs, where the high density of text in relation to intermittent spaces increases. Choices of typeface, point size, and line spacing also affect paragraph depth. A typeface with a narrow set-width allows more characters per line, and will therefore shorten paragraph depth. More line spacing increases paragraph depth, but the additional space could also lighten density. What a balancing act!

Another variable, language, affects texture and color. The frequency of certain letters, word sequence, and sentence structures in different languages adds up to visibly distinctive patterns. German, for example, uses more capital letters than English, and collects words into long strings. Languages that include diacritical marks, such as Czech, are visually more complex than those without, and so yield different kinds of texture than languages without them. Languages such as Swedish and Finnish have glyphs not used in any other language, and Japanese and Arabic look wholly distinct from Romance and Germanic languages. As global exchange becomes the norm, we are practically guaranteed to make design decisions in languages other than our own, which itself introduces typographic challenges well beyond questions of color and texture [3.8].

Long words and sentences should cause us to consider their treatment differently than when we work with advertising copy, which tends to use fewer and shorter words, simpler sentences, and briefer paragraphs. Specialized vocabulary and complex sentence structures are characteristic of scientific, philosophical, and academic writing. Newspaper articles include many capitalized names of people and places, and a heap of numerical data compared to most standard expository text. A typeface and structure that work for one writing convention will not necessarily work for another.

We put text color and texture to work to distinguish levels and types of content. By varying densities through a book—say, "dark and rough" for quotation paragraphs peppered throughout "medium and smooth" paragraphs for the body—we highlight quotations while separating them from the main text.

rags, breaks, and other cruelties

Although they sound perfectly ghastly, rags and breaks are important players in paragraph aesthetics, and can be useful to the pragmatic aspects of reading.

A handsomely ragged (pronounced "rag'd" not "rag-ged") paragraph varies line lengths, one line after the next, averaging longer and shorter lines into optical vertical evenness. Good **rags** keep obvious shapes, such as arcs and strong diagonals, from forming in both the paragraph and the space around it. Of course, if the design calls for a strong diagonal, then work that rag! Another benefit to ragged lines is that letter and **word spacing** set naturally to the spacing designed into the font, rather than dividing and spreading those spaces across a specified line length, as in fully justified text. Ragged text also makes good reading sense. Line and paragraph breaks can correspond to snippets of thought and phrasing in the writing.

The aesthetics of tasteful rags and readable line lengths change according to the kind of media and reading. We make typography *Work* only when we consider these circumstances in conjunction with variables in paragraph aesthetics [3.9]. How disheartening to see text color, texture, and line length, which rendered so beautifully on screen, turn dark and murky in the final output, as ink on heavily textured paper.

Adjusting any one variable means stepping back routinely during the design process to judge pragmatic and aesthetic qualities as we fine-tune. Negotiating so many details at once requires visual and contextual sensitivity as well as a willingness to attend to the minutiae, to say nothing of spending time at the task. I once congratulated a colleague on his work designing a book. "Nice rags!" I noted in the email. "Thanks for noticing!" he replied, adding, "I was up until 3 a.m. for days getting them right." Not the most healthy strategy, to be sure. But if aesthetic nuances matter, then we find ways to accomplish them according to need.

Publication software offers some help. When prompted, Adobe InDesign will push words up or down to settle on algorithmically balanced rags. Some programs also allow preferences that watch for widows and orphans, two atrocious idioms for additional concerns that have both aesthetic and pragmatic

MRS. POPOV	Day after tomorrow you will receive the money.
SMIRNOV	I don't need the money day after tomorrow; I need it today.
MRS. POPOV	I'm sorry I can't pay you today.
SMIRNOV	And I can't wait until day after tomorrow.
MRS. POPOV	But what can I do if I haven't it?
SMIRNOV	So you can't pay?

MRS. POPOV	Day after tomorrow you will receive the money.
SMIRNOV	I don't need the money day after tomorrow; I need it today.
MRS. POPOV	I'm sorry I can't pay you today.
SMIRNOV	And I can't wait until day after tomorrow.
MRS. POPOV	But what can I do if I haven't it?
SMIRNOV	So you can't pay?

Mrs. Popov	Day after tomorrow you will receive the money.
Smirnov	I don't need the money day after tomorrow; I need it today.
Mrs. Popov	I'm sorry I can't pay you today.
Smirnov	And I can't wait until day after tomorrow.
Mrs. Popov	But what can I do if I haven't it?
Smirnov	So you can't pay?

3.9 *Line breaks are affected by the choice of typeface, size, and weight.*

3.10 Poster for *One Act Plays*, 2007. Adrian Newell.

3.11 *The countless colors used in digital typography displayed on screens are built from varying combinations of just three colors—red, green, and blue.*

implications. When the first line of a paragraph sits all alone at the bottom of one page, separated from the paragraph it belongs to that sits on the next page, that line of text is an **orphan**. The odd last line of a paragraph languishing at the top of a page, uncoupled, as it were, from its preceding lines, is one instance of a **widow**. Disaffiliation in both instances creates fragments that can disrupt reading flow, but they are also unsightly to the seasoned typographer. A word dangling at the end of a paragraph like an unwanted appendage, also called a widow, looks sadly anemic under the text block and adds unnecessary, unused space. I cannot imagine who would choose such awful metaphors; but whatever the case, widows and orphans in typography are disturbing in more ways than one.

COLOR SYSTEMS

Color, like every other physical phenomenon that humans perceive, is almost always seen in relation to another color. There is no such thing as an absolute "pure" red without a surrounding color helping it to be so [3.10, 3.11]. No single color stands on its own. Here is a simple demonstration of the principle. Turn on the lights in a room and put on some fabulous red shoes. Now walk on over and turn off the light. The shoes are neither as red nor as fabulous. Every color in the room has been affected similarly, in relation to the lack of light bouncing onto the retina.

Many theories and systems have been devised for understanding, producing, and controlling color. Color phenomenology, for instance, is the study of the physical properties of color and light in relation to human perception, laws theorized early in the nineteenth century by Johann Wolfgang von Goethe and published in his *Theory of Color*. Early in the twentieth century, the painter, designer, and Bauhaus tutor Johannes Itten investigated color phenomena as they function in composition and materials, and captured his findings in his seminal book *The Art of Color*. Josef Albers joined Itten at the Bauhaus, and later experimented with the phenomenon of color interaction through an extensive series of abstract paintings and prints up to the mid-1970s.

Disciplines other than the visual arts put forward other kinds of theories relating to color. Color symbolism, which is typically studied within the discipline of anthropology, attempts to categorize the connotations of color as understood within specific social groups. Several musicians have drawn theoretical parallels between color and sound, for instance equating major and minor keys with particular colors. Then there are the somewhat dubious color theories rooted in psychology that link color with emotional and behavioral responses.

No matter which theory we subscribe to, the fact is that color is always an attribute of letterforms, even though we tend to think of them as black figures on a white ground. So we focus next on color phenomenology and mixing as they pertain to typography in print and screen media.

color anatomy

In the **spectral color** system, black and white are not technically colors. They are the absence of light (darkness) and the presence of all shades of visible light (lightness). **Reflective color** systems—ink and paint, for example—simulate darkness and lightness with black and white pigments made from such materials as carbon and titanium. In reflective terms, black and white are most assuredly colors.

Three- and four-color process printing is a reflective color system that overlaps percentages of cyan, magenta, and yellow inks (CMY), or the triad plus black (**CMYK**). This system achieves a finite range of **hue**, **saturation**, and **value**. In three-color process printing, black is simulated when the three pure colors are printed solid, one on top of the other. White, in this system, is the absence of ink (if printed on white paper stock)—essentially no printed color. As color adds up in the reflective system, light decreases, which is why reflective color systems are referred to as subtractive. Conversely, spectral color systems—red, green, and blue light (**RGB**) on a video display—are called additive because as color lays over color, the amount of light increases. When all three colors are present at full strength, all the lights are on, so to speak, and bright whiteness ensues.

Color has three relational attributes [3.12]. The most basic and observable is hue, as in primary red, secondary orange, tertiary red-orange. Full saturation, such as cadmium red straight out of the tube (reflective color) or blue light at full strength on screen (spectral color), are as intense or as "bright" as a given

3.12 Saturated and desaturated hues, and shades and tints.

3.13 Figure–ground contrasts: saturated, tinted, and shaded color on high- and low-contrast color backgrounds.

material and technology will allow. When a saturated color, say yellow, mixes with violet, its opposite color on the spectrum, it dulls yellow's intensity. The color is then a desaturated yellow. The third attribute, value, refers to relative darkness or lightness. Adding white or black pigment creates **tints** or **shades** of hues in reflective systems. Combining or subtracting light in a spectral system lightens or darkens hues.

A major principle comes into play here: how the color properties of the type interact with those of the surrounding space: the figure–ground relationship discussed in Chapter 1. We perceive the hue, saturation, and value of any given

HUES
shades
DESATURATED
TINTS
& tinted

color in relation to the hue, saturation, and value of the encompassing color. These three variables supply astounding range, depending on the medium and a reader's capacity to perceive it [3.13].

The most basic figure–ground color combination in typography is fully saturated, dark-value, black letters set against a fully saturated, light-value, white ground. Text in books designed for continuous reading is commonly printed in black ink on off-white or ivory-colored stock to maximize legibility. Undue contrast is said to fatigue the eye over the long haul. Not coincidentally, production costs are also lower, because black ink in printing technologies is standard. Although it costs no more to produce millions of colors on screen than it does to produce black and white, web browsers and other reading software specify dark type on light ground, imitating print-based conventions. Meanwhile, some software offers the reverse—light text on dark ground—because it is said to lessen eye strain while reading on screen. I should point out here that the effects of color contrast rendered on a backlit screen are quite different from those rendered in print, on a reflective surface, something we shall get to momentarily.

Typographers rely on their own eyes and those of their readers to make color decisions. It would be a rare person who could memorize every possible combination that the properties of color afford. Some basic formal criteria for a designer to make decisions would include the degree to which she intends the letterforms to be read in relation to each other, in what order, and at what speed.

color in hierarchy

The principal consideration when using color to establish hierarchy and guide reading order is contrast. Readers achieve quick access to text by a contrast that sufficiently separates figure from ground to make visible words. If the contrast between figure and ground is less noticeable, then the text will be read less immediately, just as the brightest stars call attention first and lesser ones enter our vision later [3.14].

BOLD and LIGHT   BOLD and DARK
BOLD & BRIGHT   BOLD & MURKY
LIGHT AND LIGHT   LIGHT AND CLEAR

3.14 Color contrast and typeface weights.

Fully saturated yellow type on a dark, desaturated ground screams "look at me first!" The same yellow set against a ground similar to it in value and saturation—bright white for instance—squawks, but not loudly. Color contrast is also negotiated through typeface, size, and spacing. In this example, when the typeface is heavy enough to hold more hue than the white within and around the letters, the text will call attention to itself, although less assertively than text of more dramatic contrast. Dial down the contrast further by setting a thin typeface with more space between the letters, effectively more white than yellow, and the text retreats to the point of disappearing. Note that stroke-width contributes to its weakness.

The reading order begins where the greatest contrast is found, and predictably the reading order is reconfigured as contrasts between figure and ground are modified [3.15]. Color at varying saturations and values visually recedes or advances naturally to assist hierarchical relationships. Fully saturated magenta, for instance, has a particularly fiery personality and so advances first against a white ground, at least in relation to a comparatively decorous medium brown. Additionally, colors advance and recede by **temperature**. Cool colors, such as blues and greens, tend to recede. By contrast, warm colors, such as reds and yellows, tend to advance. Figure–ground relationships work to heighten or reduce all this advancing and receding. The same magenta advances with gusto when surrounded by a gray ground that is close to it in value and desaturated, whereas an advancing, equally intense orange ground nearly swallows magenta up, and simultaneously yields a very "hot" visual effect because both are warm colors. Shy pink is a muted blush against aggressive orange, yet set against a gray ground it advances like a happy piglet.

We begin to see in these combinations useful color phenomena that afford flexible reading order in addition to connotative expressions. The gray ground activates the magenta type, so much so, that the color seems to vibrate fiercely and compels our eyes to linger. As exciting as the vibration is, the text's visual properties also impede reading. We might jump quickly to the less difficult type, say the soft and higher contrasting pink, before we are drawn back to the jittery magenta so as finally to read the words.

3.15 Color and hierarchy.

color systems and production

Current software and websites include sophisticated tools for discovering **monochromatic, analogous**, and **complementary** color schemes. Software also offers sets of colors in the form of palettes ("Spring" or "Corporate" or "Mexican"), plus tools that systematically adjust or alter color distribution

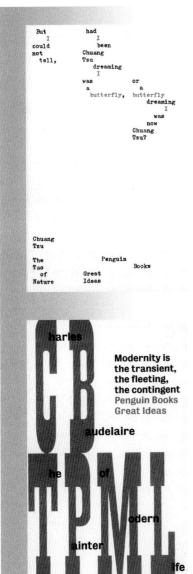

But I had I could been not Chuang tell, Tzu dreaming I was or a a butterfly, butterfly dreaming I was now Chuang Tzu?

Chuang Tzu

The Penguin Tao Books of Great Nature Ideas

Charles CB Baudelaire TPML The of Modern Painter Life

Modernity is the transient, the fleeting, the contingent
Penguin Books
Great Ideas

3.16 Covers from Penguin Books' *Great Ideas* series, 2010. Phil Baines *(top)* and David Pearson *(above)*. *The Gestalt principles are at work in these book covers. Top: texts seem haphazardly placed, but in fact the proximity of certain texts establishes sensible sequences. Above: owing to formal similarity, dispersed words in the author name and title appear as a visual layer floating above the initial caps.*

on the fly. These useful tools allow designers to try dozens of possible color configurations before settling on one. Not so long ago typographers drew or painted type, letter by letter, to judge the effectiveness of their choices. The sheer tediousness of the task tended to limit color palettes either to tried-and-true combinations, or to choices based on learned rules and production capabilities. Luckily, our digital tools are much more powerful and agile, to say nothing of fast, so we can easily explore complex color schemes. Such websites as Adobe Kuler and Colourlovers archive color combinations created by designers, artists, and whoever else might discover the perfect "Fuzzy Sweater" or "Vintage Christmas" palette.

What if we find the ideal "Obfuscated Gray," calculated in **binary hex** for the backlit screen, but cannot match it in the reflective realm? This becomes an issue when related typographic messages need to cross media. Web colors may not translate easily to ink for offset lithography, or dyes for polystyrene plastic—and vice versa. Compare the output of an inexpensive color printer to the color rendered on the computer monitor. Which one is correct?

Color can be studied and learned only through visual trials, and color in typography is no different. It takes experimentation and time to observe color systems in action: in light and on paper; in <u>Pantone</u> and silk-screen inks; in dry and wet pigments; on paper, cloth, wood, and stone. Physical properties also need attention: shadow, texture, orientation, and transparency interact with color and alter its effect. And typefaces of every shape and complexity hold color in ways nobody can fully predict. Take heart, though. Discovering the exponential variety afforded by all these factors is half the fun.

GESTALT: GROPING AND SEEKING

Chapter 1 introduced figure–ground relationships, the dynamic interplay between positive and negative space. Now we look at Gestalt principles of perception that describe how we interpret these form relationships: why we see one part as a figure, separate from a ground; and why ambiguous figure–ground relationships trigger back-and-forth perception.

Gestalt means "configuration" in German, and posits that humans innately seek pattern from which they configure and navigate the visual world. In his book *The Sense of Order*, the art historian E. H. Gombrich describes the phenomenon as capitalizing upon our bias for "simple configurations, straight lines, circles and other simple orders," and for "regularities rather than random shapes in our encounter with the chaotic world." Gestalt theorizes

Pantone
The Pantone Color Matching System (PMS) is a color-reproduction system developed in the 1950s, and used largely to standardize printing inks, thereby minimizing color differences from manufacturer to manufacturer, print run to print run.

A P CTURE IS W RTH A THO SAND WO DS

3.17 United Stencil typeface design. Tal Leming, House Industries.

how seeable things stimulate human perceptual responses. Gombrich adds that humans actively reach out to their environment, "not blindly and at random, but guided by an inbuilt sense of order." We are constantly engaged with external, visual stimuli, and we attempt to order them by way of groping or seeking, which we do before we grasp, or actually see [3.16, 3.17].

The theory reveals that we never perceive elements in isolation, but always in relation to a whole visual field. And because these ways of seeing are common among our fellow humans, we can assume that the formal relationships we create will be seen by others similarly. At first glance the line of letters below looks like type-related jottings [3.18]. Recognizing the string of shapes as a series of roman letters, we quickly seek to form words. If we know the adage "a picture is worth a thousand words," then the sentence surfaces in a short time. People unacquainted with the maxim would see the forms either as abstract shapes or an odd mix of letters. Or maybe they would fill

ΛΙϽ CTURE IϨ VV RTH Λ THϽ ϨΛΝΙϽWϽ ϽϨ

ΛΙϽ C;ͳϋRϵ_IϨͰWͰ ϽΤΙͰΛͰΙ ΙϽϨΛΝΙϽWϽ|ϽϨ

3.18 United Stencil typeface design. Tal Leming, House Industries.

in letters thus: alpacturedisewarthyanthorsandiwoods. I can't imagine why, but then people never fail to surprise us.

Readers know that letters strung together often make words, which is not so much perceptual as cultural and cognitive. Meanwhile, readers register these particular shapes as letters, despite breaks in the letterforms. The principle of *closure* prompts readers to leap over lesser gaps to complete a shape, in this case to connect the shapes separated by thin gaps to construct complete letterforms. We see that the forms we understand as letters are sitting in close *proximity* to other letterforms. For instance, at first glance we connect "RTH" and "DS," even though they do not make linguistic sense. We perceive each elemental component to be of a system because they share *similarity* of form: they are all black, are built of similar shapes, and have the same general profile. Each letter also appears to follow the next in a linear fashion, along the same baseline, which reveals *continuity*. Break that continuity, confuse the proximity and closure, and multiply similarities, and we get a very different picture.

The exaggerated spaces between strokes and letterforms refigure proximity, and they therefore alter closure, which makes it more difficult to pick out words. As the serif

3.19 Cover for Penguin Classics edition of *Little Women* by Louisa May Alcott, 2010. Barrie Tullett and Philippa Wood, Caseroom Press. *The spaces within the X and Y appear to be arrows. The nearness of the slab serifs causes them to enclose the interior space. We see them as a form from which the arrows emerge.*

3.20 Cover for Penguin Classics edition of *Dracula* by Bram Stoker, 2010. Non-Format. *Readability is of less concern in this typographic illustration than is capturing aspects of the story. Gestalt principles, however, help the patient reader to piece together the excerpt from the novel.*

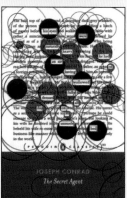

3.23 Spread from *Books on Modernism*, 2005. Rick Valicenti and John Pobojewski, Thirst. *Pattern and variation work to assist navigation while creating a dynamic composition.*

3.21 Cover for Penguin Classics edition of *The Turn of the Screw* by Henry James, 2010. Studio Frith. *Text set in a dimensional typeface, typeset larger than any other typographic element and placed along a center axis, visually unites these letterforms to each other rather than to others. The two vertical text lines to the left and right also imply a rectangle by way of the Gestalt principle of closure.*

3.22 Cover for Penguin Classics edition of *The Secret Agent* by Joseph Conrad, 2010. Coralie Bickford-Smith, Penguin. *We read the text in the background as a whole because the implied lines clearly continue across the cover, despite overwhelming interruption. Similarity of words set off in rectangles and circles impels us to see them as another whole.*

features are pulled away from the strokes, we perceive their shared similarity in comparison to the vertical shapes that correspond to and connect them. When continuity is disrupted, the words disintegrate altogether and we perceive the overall form as a dynamic abstraction.

Were the same shapes animated, Gestalt would continue to be in effect. When a letter appears to be moving across the screen, it is really a series of letters situated on a **timeline** of frames, placed in progressive locations and logical sequence one frame after the last. Too much delay, or time between each frame, breaks our perception of motion and we see letters sitting on the screen. This Gestalt notion is known as the phi phenomenon, where intervals of time between stimuli, in this case elements in frames, appear fluidly in motion as long as the intervals between the frames are not too long.

Closure, proximity, similarity, and continuity can work to connect and separate elements, both subtly and dramatically, to infuse compelling tensions and harmonies of form and connotation [3.19–3.23]. These principles reveal how we interpret form. Now we look at how controlling pattern, variation, and contrast can further enliven (or weaken) typographic composition.

PATTERN, VARIATION, AND CONTRAST //////////

Humans are predisposed to put two and two together, as the Gestalt principles reveal. We seek pattern to minimize the imminent threat of chaos, and possible risk to life and limb (bear grazes for berries every morning, ergo, avoid berry patch in the mornings). Our highly developed capacity to connect the dots, as it were, naturally extends to the things we make. The perceptual and reasoning skills we use to avert peril also come in handy for farming, manufacturing, and, yes, typography. Typographic form capitalizes on our innate capacities to see repetition by exploiting similarity (**pattern**) in relation to difference (**variation**) [3.24].

Say every element on a surface or screen is equally dissimilar. The result would be uniform dissimilarity, like music in which every note of every octave strikes simultaneously at the same decibel to produce one cacophonous thrum. In the same way, overall low-contrasting elements create a featureless field of monotony reminiscent of a speaker who drones on, never altering pitch or cadence or gesture.

3.24 Spread from *Books on Modernism*, 2005. Rick Valicenti and John Pobojewski, Thirst. *Space and typeface repetition establish pattern. The variety of content, in this case different text lengths and depths, coupled with interspersed images, breaks the pattern and adds variation.*

CONTRAST AND HIERARCHY

Typographic form works in accordance with our abilities to see pattern by emphasizing contrasts, or gradients of difference. In fact, designers are fond of saying "contrast is everything." Well, how can contrast be everything when hierarchy and context are everything too? All three rank highly in graphic design, though, so let me put it this way: if I knew anything about building I would sprawl the word "contrast" in huge neon letters across the tops of "context" and "hierarchy."

We use variation to accentuate and distinguish elements (high contrast). We use similarity to draw out pattern (low contrast). High contrast emphasizes the differences between elements to produce variation. Low contrast makes use of similarities to unify elements and establish pattern.

A rule of thumb in typography is that substantial contrast among elements is generally better, more aesthetically appealing, than wimpy contrast. But what elicits pleasure in one decade may be distasteful in the next. Were we to focus solely on what makes one artifact more pleasing than another, as relates to contrast, we would debate for ever without reaching a conclusion. Let's focus instead on contrast as it serves hierarchical order.

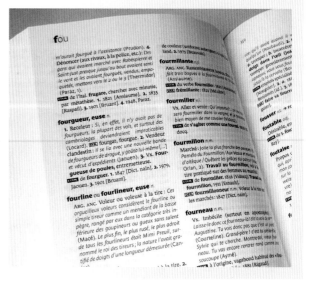

3.25 Page from monolingual French dictionary published by Larousse.

The formal contrasts of typographic size and weight figure prominently in hierarchy. The larger or weightier the element, the more power it has to attract the eye in relation to less assertive elements within both static and dynamic compositions. Experience teaches us that big and bold text usually indicates importance: the largest-scaled words, which often demand attention first (barring the presence of imposing images), initiate the message. Decreased type size and/or weight in proximity may indicate that secondary content completes the message or gives more detailed information. The differences between larger and smaller suggest that content has moved from the general idea to something more specific. So the relative sizes and weights of text in a composition begin to suggest levels of information and kinds of content—for example, the main body and footnotes in a book demarcate two kinds of subject matter, a main topic and detailed asides or references.

Applying the same typeface, point size, and weight to multiple texts signals their connection, whether in a single composition or dispersed throughout a website or book. By reading and seeing, readers learn the categories of text established by the typographer. Standard dictionaries are prime examples [3.25]. Their typography treats each entry in exactly the same way—same point size and weight, often in boldface. We can call this level the first reading level within the main body. A less heavy weight—a medium, say—separates a second level, the definition. Depending on the degree of contrast between the bold and the medium, a typographer may set the definition in the same point size as the word entry, or she may increase or decrease the size by a point or half-point to adjust contrast ever so slightly.

In the typography of dictionaries, not only does a bold weight stand out next to medium, but we can also correctly assume that the bold at its size will always denote "a word entry" and the medium at its size will always denote "a definition." Additionally, their differences command two reading behaviors. The bold text invites the eye to scan and single out a desired word amid what would otherwise be a sea of text. The medium weight, meanwhile, facilitates horizontal reading across lines. Once readers understand the system, reading behavior becomes automatic and the system of order is complete. A different typeface, say a medium italic of the same size from the same family, might be used to denote an additional level, for example a listing of word usage following the definition. Here another denotative level is aided by typefaces that are different enough.

Contrasting shapes, typefaces, sizes, weights, textures, and text color help lead the eye to and through texts [3.26]. Directed scanning, landing upon, and reading text generates movement as a reader shifts focus from point to point. This movement relates to the subjects of flow and disruption discussed in Chapter 2: text typeset in paragraphs of the same typeface and size

3.26 Poster for discussion series at Rhode Island School of Design, 2009. Nancy Skolos, Skolos-Wedell. *Several contrasting attributes add up to powerful hierarchy in this poster designed for the Department of Teaching and Learning in Art and Design at Rhode Island School of Design. The highest contrast, the rectilinear glyphs T+LA+D set against a yellow ground, is read first. Although contrasts are less extreme in subsequent levels, sufficient differences in color, size, placement, and structure clearly announce each, and help guide the reader into the information.*

encourages steady movement, owing to low contrast; higher contrast arrests steady movement by disruption. Movement implies continuity of or abrupt shifts in the direction that movement takes. Compositional hierarchy might compel readers to begin at the center, then go left, cross diagonally up and to the right, and pop back down to the bottom: a rather lively reading path.

mixing contrast

Typographers make use of a range of contrasts when they combine typefaces [3.27]. Conventional wisdom argues for creating multiple-level hierarchies using one type family because, as the theory goes, homogeneity predisposes family members to harmonize. Though they are diverse enough to allow for individual identity, family members still look and act like kin. One might be skinnier than its fat cousin, or loopier than an upright uncle, but because each share some formal features, they are likely to be more compatible. Typefaces outside families are less guaranteed to agree, so inserting non-familial typefaces into the mix can be a bit trickier, like bringing one's girlfriend—lead vocalist of her band the Screamers—home to meet the classical-music-loving parents.

We choose typefaces from the thousands that are published (plus from those we might design for our own use) in order to find surprising combinations that suit our intentions. With such extensive options, infinite expressive possibilities await us, as well as infinite complications. A typographer designing a dictionary could decide, of course, to set each hierarchical level in typefaces that are barely discernible to the average reader. The result could look oddly fussy, or just confused. Wildly different typefaces might create a high-spirited spectacle. The choice depends upon one's stylistic and functional aims. If a project calls for multiple levels of function, many typographers would recommend choosing typefaces with extensive families. Alternatively, mix certain serif typefaces with certain other sans serifs (many designers have their canon of mixable typefaces, their fail-safe combinations). Both are reasonable guidelines, especially for those learning to control hierarchy.

While the advice is sound enough, the practice of using one family, or tried-and-true serif/sans-serif combinations, is often merely a way to prevent so-called bad design. Better to understand *why* the formal properties of typefaces are compatible (or not), according to certain tastes. This gives us much more flexibility to make fresh, appropriate decisions while designing.

Members of typeface families relate to each other because they share visual attributes. An appreciably heavier weight within a family will offer

sufficient similarity
favors
compatibility
among **family**
MEMBERS

• • •

{ insufficient }
difference

• • •

SUFFICIENT DIFFERENCE
among typefaces
and assigned functions
IN RELATION TO EACH OTHER
favors compatibility

3.27 Typeface compatibility. *The shared curves and letter shapes of two related families shown at the top, Odile and Elido (Odile spelled backwards), ensure compatibility. Two neo-grotesques, Univers and Helvetica (middle) are too much alike to be compatible. Juxtaposed, the set looks a bit off. Specific weights, postures, and glyphs within typefaces might be compatible, even when the entire range of characters might not. At the bottom, the heavy, erect capitals of Legato combine well with the light, lyrical lowercase of Dolly.*

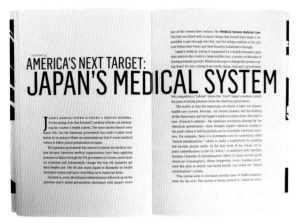

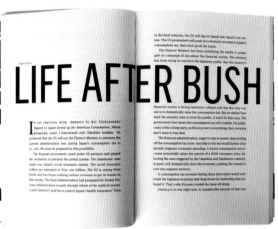

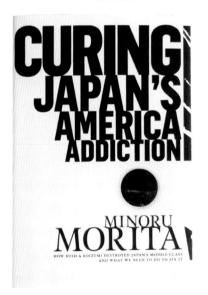

3.28 Spreads and cover from *Curing Japan's America Addiction* by Minoru Morita, 2008. Craig Mod. *Combining sans-serif with serif typefaces in the same composition is a common strategy. However, differences in scale and weight, as well as relative placement, also contribute to compatibility.*

sufficient contrast while other details remain constant enough to promise harmony. The members are, in effect, frictionless, elegantly agreeing among themselves as they each go about their business. Variation increases when serif faces are mixed with sans serifs; their clear differences maximize contrast without creating conflict.

Many serif typefaces are similar, as are many sans serifs, so it should follow that all are on the whole quite compatible. Different typefaces of the same sort can share nearly identical details: similar stroke-width ratios, bracketed serifs, or terminal shapes. In combination, however, not-quite-alike-ness and not-quite-different-ness can muddle things up. The typefaces neither smoothly agree nor firmly agree to disagree. In other words, putting two or more not-quite-alike typefaces to work in the same hierarchical system can weaken contrast.

Let's not forget that contrast is also affected by the relative size and weight of each typeface. Scale changes the visibility of typographic attributes: text set quite large emphasizes details that are barely noticeable at smaller sizes . We might choose a typeface based solely on how the details work at 400 pt, but would not then need to use the same typeface for **text type** set at 14 pt [3.28]. Short lines, or a paragraph, set at 10 pt on 13 pt line spacing, leave typeface pattern to dominate, and the minute details to work behind the scenes.

Radical scale shifts or different typefaces are a fraction of the variables one can adjust to lessen or heighten contrast. Paragraph color and texture might subtly separate texts, for instance. Varying the density of a paragraph (lighter or darker paragraph color) can be achieved by simply increasing or decreasing line spacing. Selecting a slightly heavier weight within the family can distinguish one kind of text—say, mid-value, roughly textured paragraphs of primary text—from secondary texts.

contrast and time

Elements in a static composition do not physically move about, but we do use the terms "movement" and "direction" to describe how the eye tracks around a two-dimensional surface. The screen is a compositional space as well, and screen-based typography shares a concern for contrast with static typography. Designers working in screen-based media also produce motion or animation typography, which moves over time.

Allow me to clarify, lest we confuse direction, movement, and animation. Movement refers to the fact that eyes move about on a static screen or page, drawn by this or that element. And they do so in a particular direction. On screen, when one element at the top blinks out and another situated at the bottom bounces in, the difference causes the eye to move. Animation, by contrast, is the literal action: type blinking and bouncing, fading in and out, morphing, enlarging, rotating—what is often called **behavior.** If type tracks across the screen, our eyes will follow its direction.

The pattern and variation that animation affords is, of course, quite different from what is possible in print or signage. When typography wriggles back and forth or glides smoothly down the screen, it contrasts with any static typography in its proximity. For instance, animated banners on most websites today insist we settle on them first, hierarchically speaking, because the animation seizes our attention, sometimes with annoying efficiency. When the performance is complete or loses its draw, we move to the remaining elements of the composition: first a photograph; then a bold headline; then perhaps the main text.

Pattern, variation, and contrast are implicit in motion- and time-based media through the **pacing** and **rhythm** of animated elements across frame sequences [3.29], or of static elements across page sequences. Pacing establishes the overall speed of the animation. Regular visual beats or marks within pacing introduce patterned emphases, or rhythms. Elements constantly jumping up and down on screen, fast as a jackhammer, are rhythmically regular and very quickly paced. Elements sputtering sluggishly like an old Volkswagen Beetle are rhythmically erratic and paced relatively slowly. Static typography employs pacing and rhythm across physical rather than implied space: pages instead of frames. A typical novel, for instance, is visually uniform, and therefore proceeds at a steady pace, compared to a retail catalog designed to arrest the eye strategically as it pitches merchandise page after page.

An active design, whether in a static book or on a dynamic screen, has a fast pace coupled with complex rhythms. Dial up the pace and rhythm, and

3.29 *HBO Dreams.* Trollbäck and Company. *It is nearly impossible to demonstrate in print how typography in motion introduces contrast (or any other time-based attribute). Here, though, contrasting scales and changes over time are evident. Letters swirl onto the screen rapidly, then snap together to form readable text, which pauses momentarily. The contrast between the two behaviors, and the duration of each, constitute pattern and rhythm.*

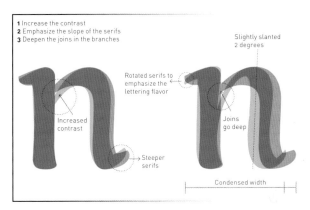

1 Increase the contrast
2 Emphasize the slope of the serifs
3 Deepen the joins in the branches

Rotated serifs to emphasize the lettering flavor

Increased contrast

Steeper serifs

Slightly slanted 2 degrees

Joins go deep

Condensed width

typography becomes the tiger that runs so fast in a circle his contrasting stripes blur into a single color. Conversely, the slower the pace and subtler the rhythms, the more subdued the result, and, in the hands of those insensitive to delicately balanced contrasts, the more monotonous.

We modulate **duration** of action to control hierarchy and readability as animated typography moves about. Duration is the length of time that elements are animated in relation to how long they remain still. Type may burst onto the screen in an instant, then stop motionless to allow just enough time to be read, then be flicked off the screen by another piece of careening text. Readers cannot see the text for the duration of its entrance and exit, but they can read it during slower moments.

LETTERFORM VARIATION

An obvious example of variation in letterforms is the one we find in the alphabet. Each letter and glyph of any written language has its own shape. If the letter d assumed the shape of an m, then we would sound out m. . .ate rather than d. . .ate, a rather provocative mistake. Then again, variation can be quite subtle. The lowercase i in the Latin alphabet is very similar in shape to a lowercase l, and the n and u are virtually identical except for orientation. Yet we do not confuse one for the other, because they are different enough. Pattern emerges in the form of letters—the typeface. Uniform strokes and curves visually connect the range of glyph shapes.

Typeface designers apply formal systems to sets of alphabetic and numerical glyphs. Common stroke-width ratios, proportions, serif details, curves, posture, and so on, collect into themes adapted to each character. More accurately, as the parts and shapes of characters blend with the designer's ideas about form, commonalities emerge and are exploited by the designer to establish patterns.

The formal system not only responds to the demands of individual characters and components, it often also encompasses family members. Type-family variation might include a range of weights, from light to super heavy; a variety of set-widths, from narrow to extra wide; and changes in posture. For example, the Rumba family (Small, Large, and Extra) maintains relative weight and set-widths, but the attitudes that each member strikes are quite different [3.30]. Rumba Extra, designed for use at **display type** sizes, is much jauntier than Rumba Large, whereas Rumba Small, designed to be used at smaller, text type sizes, is more sedate than Large. Consistent and incremental shifts change the overall construction of the three fonts, while each reflects aspects of the other two. Enough commonality unites them, and enough uniqueness distinguishes them.

Type designers sometimes test the bounds of letter shapes to the extreme. The e of a typeface might look very similar to the c. In the context of typeset words, however, the two will be reasonably distinguishable. Typographers

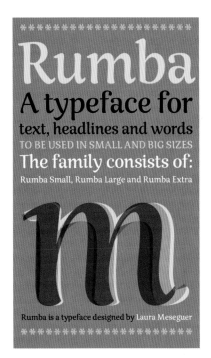

Rumba
A typeface for
text, headlines and words
TO BE USED IN SMALL AND BIG SIZES
The family consists of:
Rumba Small, Rumba Large and Rumba Extra

m

Rumba is a typeface designed by Laura Meseguer

3.30 Rumba typeface design, 2006. Laura Messeguer.

combine the shapes of letters with other formal attributes—typeface details, scale, color—utilizing the human capacity to distinguish variation and pattern to subtle or dramatic ends.

theme casting

Classic themes in more traditional fonts use an inventory of curves and counters, serifs and strokes, with delicate adjustments made for each glyph. One such typeface, Houston—a family of fonts designed for use in headlines, bylines, captions, and text—alludes to Hearst newspaper typography of the 1920s, as well as Venetian Oldstyle types. Subtle quirks echo throughout the typeface, creating an overall, complex, and nuanced formal scheme. As the subtleties of letterform and shape variation decrease, more discernible visual themes emerge, and typefaces inch toward the fanatical. For instance, modern geometric sans typefaces, such as ITC Avant Garde and Bauhaus, draw some characteristics from tradition, but add and subtract details that constrain the system significantly. The upper **stems** of the n are greatly truncated, or removed altogether. The vertical stroke and stem of a and d smoothly transition into near-perfect circles to form the **bowls**. In the case of Bauhaus, curves loop back around, ending just shy of the vertical stroke to create a thin gap. Also, the letterforms have limited stroke range and angle switches. Compare the s curves, for instance: more and continuous in Avant Garde, fewer and straighter in Bauhaus [3.31].

As letterform variety decreases and pattern becomes more noticeable, the typeface becomes more forceful. In other words, more repetition and less variation adds up to quite an insistent font. The doodads and outlines of Circus Ornate submit all letter parts to such a constrained formal system that some letters struggle desperately to fit. The C and U seem quite comfortable with their counters. On the other hand, the counters of the R and S are pinched and squished [3.31].

Type Jockey is a complex system of interlocking thick and thin lines that can be assigned any color. Limited formal variation restricts the **monocase** letterforms to rectilinear shapes, not unlike typefaces that constrain letter shape by square pixels. The resulting obvious pattern creates a forceful, beautiful, and unconventional typeface.

Type Jockey uses modular shape systems to build letterforms, highly elaborate forms with an extensive set of variables [3.32]. Other systems might employ relatively

ITC Avant Garde

Tom Carnase, with Herb Lubalin, designed a full complement of interlocking letterforms built from a masthead design by Lubalin for his magazine *Avant Garde*. Its popularity prompted the formation of the ITC foundry.

ITC Bauhaus

A "Geometric" sans-serif font designed by the Americans Ed Benguiat and Victor Caruso based on Herbert Bayer's experimental typeface, Universal, designed at the Bauhaus in Dessau, Germany in 1925. It was released by ITC in 1975.

Circus Ornate

One of many typefaces based on nineteenth-century wood types of the kind frequently used on posters to announce traveling circuses and other events.

Type Jockey

Andrea Tinnes designed this font for the "Playground Project," started by the designer Rick Valicenti. Two different font sets—backgrounds and alphabetical structures—work in combination. Based on a 1000 × 1000 em grid divided by 40. All 14 fonts overlay precisely.

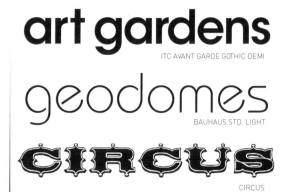

ITC AVANT GARDE GOTHIC DEMI

BAUHAUS STD. LIGHT

CIRCUS

3.31 *The formal themes in these typefaces are increasingly constrained (from top to bottom) to form-based systems.*

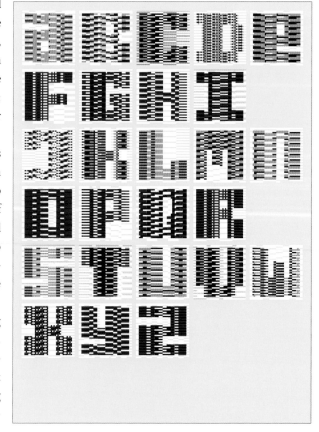

3.32 Type Jockey, 2005. Andrea Tinnes. *Five layers were designed for each letter of the alphabet. Each layer is engineered to interlock precisely. This system dictates the shape of the letters. Applying the system to a script-based letterform would be folly.*

simple forms with only a few parts. Alphabets, too, are modular in the sense that a p almost always serves as a p, no matter what the word. Type designers are mindful of this modularity, knowing that each letter will live next to or between nearly every other letter at some point, depending on the language. Letter juxtapositions create negative spaces of endless variety, which means that pattern and variation occurring between letters are as much a concern as they are across the letterforms themselves. A well-designed typeface includes relational calculations between pairings (called **kerning pairs**) to ensure unobtrusive pattern.

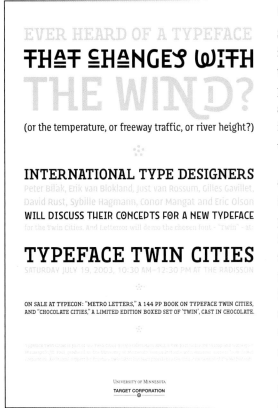

3.33 Laika dynamic typeface design, 2009. Michael Flückiger and Nicolas Kunz, Berne University of the Arts.

3.34 "Typeface Twin Cities" lecture announcement, 2003. Deb Littlejohn.

dynamic typefaces

Skilled type designers control the formal variables of the fonts they design to guarantee sufficient pattern and variation. What if, then, those variables are dynamic? Chapter 2 presented Laika, a "font" that **morphs** letter weight, stroke, serif, and slope instantaneously, dictated by code and user input [3.33]. In such contexts, how are typeface pattern and variation to be controlled?

Since the dawn of digital platforms, designers have explored letterforms that respond to user preference, or are influenced by code. The pioneering font FF Beowolf employs programming to draw letters randomly. PostScript technology, introduced in 1985, inspired the designers to write programs that modify typefaces "in the printer" so that each character is rendered uniquely. Rather than there being one fixed form for each letter, the shapes move and wobble. This and similar projects designed by early font innovators challenged the formal systems of type design, yet they did so by introducing alternative ones, namely, those that embrace variability without sacrificing pattern. Beowolf adds layers of variation onto a common frame, so letterforms are structurally uniform.

Letterror's typeface Twin Cities [3.34] echoes typeface design standards in that the letterforms share certain characteristics throughout the family. Meanwhile, software adds dynamic features: the typeface then responds to external data—such as ambient temperature—when used in browser software. A user assigns one of the ten designed fonts, each a complete character set, to an external condition. Let's say she chooses "Loopy" for cold, and "Weird" for warm. Text set in Twin Cities would then, on a chilly morning, display text in Loopy. The program randomly switches out glyphs as the thermometer goes up, one by one over time, until the temperature is warm enough to render the words in Weird.

Twin Cities software maintains font scale and position; it also controls glyph replacement to achieve relative unity over the course of dynamic display, similar to the Laika font. The system constraining Laika, although much more fluid, creates uniformity by applying alterations to the relative

FF Beowolf

The Dutch designers Erik van Blokland and Just Van Rossum developed this "randomized" typeface, released in 1988. The designers exploited programming and the then new capacities of PostScript printing, pointing up the symbiotic relationship between digitally produced typographic form and computational code.

Twin Cities

The winning submission in a competition to design a typeface for Minneapolis–St. Paul, sponsored by the University of Minnesota Design Institute in 2002. The designers, Erik van Blokland and Just Van Rossum, generated the font via their "Panchromatic Hybrid Style Alternator" software.

whole. Each "dial" corresponds to a continuum of shape possibilities applied to each typographic aspect, including bracket, posture, character width, letterspace, and stroke-width (one for vertical, another for horizontal, a third for diagonals). Therefore, each modification affects all letters on screen at the same time. Also, the code limits the range of options to be consistent with typographic norms. Each configuration, then, fits comfortably within known formal systems. Animated behaviors between transitions are also consistent, adding not only the dimension of time but also the aspect of motion to the list of characteristics that unify glyphs.

Typographic pattern and variation are fundamental to aesthetic and pragmatic aspects of hierarchy. Animated typography—in contrast to static type—attracts, or at least sustains, attention, whereas quiet uniformity brings a sustained hum. Disruption works with flow to punctuate text, or redirect the eye. With all this movement and direction, and varying paces, rhythms, and durations, typography is clearly anything but still. Which is why it often needs structure.

3.35 Irregular margins.

///////////////////////////// THE FORM OF THE GRID

ORGANIZATIONAL SYSTEMS

When we place text intuitively within a space, we are composing with type. This method is useful, but it does not constitute a system. Aligning elements along random invisible threads moves us a step closer to a system. But we really start to see a system emerge in **grid** construction. Here, vertical and horizontal lines, separated by uniform distances, set up shared attributes among paragraphs, such as line length, and establish consistent relationships among parts. While this very basic and functional structure helps manage greater amounts of text and other elements, this kind of grid still falls a little short of being a full-strength system.

What separates a grid system from a basic grid structure is modularity—where a base unit or units, of some size and measure, build(s) larger units. The larger whole is configured from the sum of the constituent parts: a screen and its assets over time, measured in pixels and frames; or a magazine, with its articles and ads in picas and pages. Grid systems help typographers assign active or supporting duty to every pica, pixel, or inch, and to order elements across space and time. Before we jump into complicated grid logic, let's first consider a rudimentary organizational idea, the margin.

the margin

Margins function in a number of ways. First, they help ensure that all the type that needs to be present and intact is indeed present and intact—every **tail** and **ear** safe from the page trimmer or webbrowser frame. Second, they prevent words from getting lost in the gutters of books and from being lopped off on street signs. Third, margins keep our eyes from inadvertently slipping off the page or bumping into competing

3.36 *Newspaper Translated into a Book*, 2011. Maurits Wouters. *This small book contains the entirety of an online newspaper edition. The student fitted the data to a small page without margins. The result is a very thick book.*

3.37 Poster for the film *Typeface*, 2008. Dennis Y. Ichiyama.

screen text as we read, which is annoying. The margin's primary function is to define the boundaries of text as a complete and comprehensible entity.

Margins on four sides within any format predetermine that the space they enclose is reserved for the content at hand. Despite how important margins are, then, they compel us to ignore them. They recede further as we replicate the exact same margins over a series of pages or screens. The total work shares a common, but quiet, structure. Why are margins destined for anonymity? Why can text not be enlarged or shrunk according to whim? Well, it can. We can devise and apply any structure imaginable, any combination of constraining frameworks [3.35. 3.36]. Such recklessness, though, has its costs.

Imagine typing a fifteen-page research paper in word-processing software that requires us to set new margins for each page. The tedious process would have us spending more time organizing text blocks than thoughts. Still, say we find the time and end up with different margins on every single page. Of course the professor notices the text moving about, not the margins. "Odd," she might think. Perhaps each page contains an independent idea? A quick scan proves that the paper covers just one thesis (good for us). Because the random organization looks strange according to the conventions of research papers, the professor questions its seriousness (bad for us). Our paper loses credibility, and we don't make the grade.

Our brief focus on the humble margin points out several core functions of organizational systems in general: production efficiency (the research paper is written in five days rather than eight), reading facility (the professor focuses on the writing, not the structure), and in this instance, corroboration of worth within certain literate communities (the professor recognizes the page composition as that of a research paper).

the armature

Chapter 2 used the metaphor of teaching readers the steps to a dance to describe leading readers through a reading space. Let's now compare typographic elements to the actors we direct on a stage—the page, screen, or space—to enact a "play." If elements are indeed like actors, then the armature is an assortment of connected stage marks that set up interactions among the players. Armatures are built through alignment [3.37]. The structural logic that underpins what I have named an armature emerged in the late nineteenth and early twentieth centuries with the Russian constructivist and Dutch de Stijl art and design movements. Artists invented "pure," flat abstraction, renouncing the affectation of three-dimensional perspective forced onto two-dimensional spaces. Some artists also designed public communications. Alexander Rodchenko in Russia and Theo van Doesburg in the Netherlands, for instance, both brought these new abstract visual languages to the design of posters, ephemera, and books. The seemingly freeform typographic and photographic compositions were built on a structural logic of relationships among elements. Graphic artists in Europe and the United States deployed similar strategies and structures in advertising and "layout" design. In the manual *Layout in Advertising* (1929), the graphic designer W. A. Dwiggins does not address structure per se. Rather, he identifies such aesthetic principles as "unity" and "balance" to justify compositional schemes:

I want to make my design so that it neither scatters itself aimlessly all over the field, nor rambles off into contiguous areas and attaches itself to matter owned by other proprietors . . . . I want to give the design unity. The simplest way . . . is to make a centered, symmetrical arrangement . . . drive a stake down the middle of the field and tie everything to it. Such symmetrical design achieves unity—at the expense of certain other valuable qualities . . . . There is a kind of unsymmetrical balance that . . . has been known for a long time as the "principle of the steelyard"—where a heavy weight near the fulcrum balances a light weight out on the end of the beam . . . . This principle applies to typographic layout.[3]

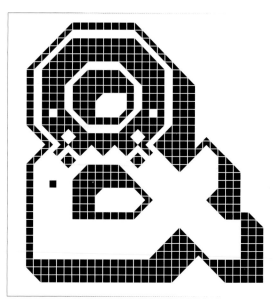

3.38 Teatral ampersand designed with Fontstruct, 2008. Tobias Sommer.

A basic armature is a vertical center line balancing horizontal text lines. Other schemes are the arc and curve. From spindly webs to radiating spokes, armatures are pliant, so they work brilliantly for straightforward content and one-off productions, such as advertisements and posters. For extensive text of greater complexity, distributed over a series of pages or spaces, we need the help of a grid.

the grid

Grids are brigades of intersecting, invisible lines that demarcate space; they are organizing schemes as basic to civilization as mark-making. We install them to marshal all manner of material things: groups of buildings, networks of roads, acres of crops, the bricks and mortar of architecture, the span of sports fields, and the elements of typography. Even the alphabet has been submitted to rationalized grids at various points in history. A contemporary example is Fontstruct, an online software tool that supplies glyphs to build letterforms based on gridded modules [3.38]. Grid logic reveals the human capacity to imagine ways of constructing perfection, and of perfecting construction. We will stay with typography and printed matter for the time being, where our deepest ties are to the faint rules that scribes drew on parchment to guide their hand.

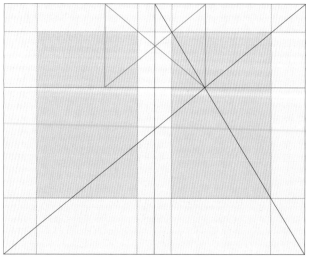

3.39 *Classical grid proportions based on the golden rectangle.*

CLASSICAL GRIDS

In Western civilizations, early book grids evolved from **proportional** relationships, particularly the golden mean, a ratio of 1:1.618, which ostensibly mimics a proportion found in many natural structures—conch shells, for example. This ratio is one that both nature and numbers have inspired, and that man has codified through use [3.39]. For instance, the "rational" 3:4 ratio of the quarto format is popular in book publishing, and was for a long time the standard aspect ratio on television screens; and the octavo format, a 2:3 ratio, is as common today as it was when Johannes Gutenberg used it back in 1454 for the forty-two-line Bible.

The **golden rectangle** was inherited and applied in various ways to medieval codices, precursors to the books we design and read today. By the thirteenth century, copyists were preparing codex pages for inscription using the Villard diagram, devised by French architect Villard de Honnecourt. Perpendicular and diagonal lines bisect the space, at intervals determined "by the compass and ruler instead of computations," as Jan Tschichold writes in *The Form of the Book*. The points found at intersections, when connected, establish margin widths and text areas that harmonize with the page. As Tschichold sees it, "if efforts are successful to combine page format and type area into an indissoluble unit, then the margin proportions become functions of page format and overall construction, and thus are inseparable from either."[4] A beautiful, relational notion. The classical grid also creates other features that we relate to the form of traditional books, including spacious margins and symmetrical facing pages.

Tschichold reinvigorated the classical grid in the mid-twentieth century through his work and writings, which continue to influence book design [3.40]. In principle, any page proportion can be divided by the relational methods he promoted. The results, however, do not automatically produce the revered classical proportions.

MODERN GRIDS

Tschichold returned to and refined the logic of the classical grid after disavowing the modernist principles he had practiced and defended earlier in his career. Another exemplar of modernist ideas is the Czech-born designer Ladislav Sutnar, particularly in his design for the Sweets Catalog Company after he emigrated to the United States in 1938. Sweets produced sales catalogs for manufacturers of machines, screws, and the like. In this work, Sutnar refined early modernist concepts by developing guidelines for organizing and arranging different kinds of information into levels [3.41]. His design visually sorted both text and image into primary, secondary,

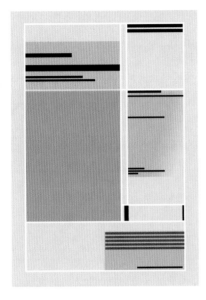

3.40 *These grid fields and alignments are replicated from an advertisement by Jan Tschichold (1928). Gray areas depict text blocks, and black bars depict lines of text (headlines) set in bold. The compositional logic moves strikingly away from then-dominant centering schemes.*

3.41 Redesign of *American Craft* magazine, 2007. Jeanette Abbink and Emily C. M. Anderson, Rational Beauty. *The relationships among elements and the structure of this magazine spread reveal the heritage of modern grids: distinguishable levels of information; useful supporting white space; and asymmetrical composition.*

the will to achieve architectural dominion over surface and space; the will to adopt a positive, forward-looking attitude; the recognition of the importance of education and the effect of work devised in a constructive and creative spirit.[5]

Grid systems signaled the emergence of "systems thinking" for typographers. Müller-Brockmann and others, including Emil Ruder (*Typographie*, 1967), Karl Gerstner (*Designing Programmes*, 1968), and Max Bill, advanced a rationale for page and spatial layout—ostensibly foolproof means for ordering any kind of information in any format contained within the system. Collectively, the insights of these designers introduced the principles that typographers continue to apply today.

Grid systems readily accept changing data. They are transferable and scalable to any space or medium. And they maintain uniformity, associating similar information across applications and artifacts. Grid systems manifest "the will to penetrate to the essentials" in that they are conceived from fundamental and intrinsic parts. Think of it as creating typographic life at the atomic level, where the master identifies essential units, and from them builds structures that refer back to the unit measure. The designer integrates "elements of color, form, and material" by designing a rule set for the players on the stage. I will leave you to decide whether or not this practice cultivates "objectivity," or affords "architectural dominion over surface and space."

The uninitiated typographer confronting a modular grid for the first time might experience anything but creative freedom. In unpracticed hands, any system can seem rigid and unforgiving at first. Yet the very nature of modularity

STEP 4:
PERCEPTUAL & DEPICTIVE SALIENCE
AND RATIONALISM IN SPACE
DEC. 8, 2006

An interest in mental imagery suggests an interest in both perception and depictive capability; the traditional argument holds that mental imagery doesn't truly exist, but is built linguistically; perhaps, though, it's reversed, and imagery can operate as language.

3.44 Page from *Reading is Situational, Reading is Experiential, Always*, 2007. Matthew Peterson. *The typefaces Avant Garde Monospace and FF Balance are fitted within the 4.7 × 3 (14.1 pt) grid.*

EPTUAL SALIENCE

Garde Monospace), the character widths equal their cap-heights. These cap-heights and character widths have been equalized with Times Ten's x-height, and lock solidly into the underlying grid.

There is a remarkable benefit to this rigorous typographic structure. Any illustrated book is a challenging production, and this kind of regularity makes the process manageable. But aside from expediting my work, what does all of this detail matter? Eleanor Rosch, studying the nature of cognitive categorization, saw fit to identify *perceptual salience*: "which things are most readily noticed by people." (*Lakoff 90, 42.*) What of all of this typographic detail can be readily noticed by the reader? I expect the answer is *none of the above.*

Specialized training will render some things noticeable that otherwise wouldn't have been. Designers *will* notice typographic details—at least those which are actually perceptible. And, essentially, some things will be perceptible to designers and nobody else. That means that perceptual salience isn't absolute, but mutable. A remarkable

DECEMBER 8, 2006

offers flexibility within a logical system, and allows us to specify the rules of organization that are quite particular to our intent and the needs of a given project. "The more exact and complete criteria are," Karl Gerstner writes, "the more creative the work becomes." His point is that working within systems, in this case grid systems, concentrates the creative process on acts of selection, rather than continuous decision making.

3.45 Pages from *Reading is Situational, Reading is Experiential, Always*, 2007. Matthew Peterson. *Body text and marginalia align on the baseline, set at 14.1 pt. Column, gutter, and margin widths are fixed to the grid as well. A range of typeface weights and scales introduces variety within the design, as do decisions about placement.*

A highly rationalized grid system devised by the designer and educator Matthew Peterson captures the essence of grid-system principles to the nth degree [3.44, 3.45]. He begins with a base unit from the x-height of 10 pt <u>Times Ten</u>, which equals 4.7 points. Line spacing is set at 14.1 points, or 4.7 points × 3 units, resulting in a three-by-three grid module. Every detail, from paragraph indents to line lengths, submits to the module. Larger fields are divisible by 14.1 points. Typefaces other than Times Ten, including Cooper Black Italic and <u>FF Balance</u>, are sized so that their x-heights also measure either 4.7 or 14.1 points. The character widths of ITC Avant Garde Monospace equal the font's cap-height. When sized to 14.1, the letters lock to the grid module both vertically and horizontally. Peterson calls this approach "bottom-up" because the system builds out from one detail. A "top-down" approach, by comparison, fits type into measures determined by format, or worse, by software defaults.

Whereas the modern grid designates a fixed regime of immutable blocks, and restricts text to standardized rules, the modular grid system grants the typographer more options for deciding the terms by which he designs. Of course, this approach asks more of typographers. Rather than adopting rules codified by history, we must invent our own. What this means is that we are in control of our work. The precedents and software work for us, not vice versa. If four unequal columns suit our aims, we can make them. If we want every last element to align precisely with every other element, we can easily do so once the system is in place. Ideally, the parameters we devise exactly meet the particular needs of the content, manifest the intended expressions, anticipate our readers' needs, and maximize functionality.

grids in space, and in real time

The rationale of grid systems is frequently applied to physical space, and to objects. Placing uniform signage on the floors of a building, for instance, lessens the effort for visitors as they try to locate an office on the sixteenth floor in the north wing of the main building. When layers of assorted text need to exist in both sequential and simultaneous reading spaces, such as signage distributed throughout an airport [3.46], a grid system helps travelers to recognize related information easily as they come across each sign within the system. The grid assists the reader by patterning the hierarchy of information, discussed in "Hierarchy and Structure: Part II" in Chapter 2.

Times Ten

Times Ten is a member of Stanley Morison's Times Roman family, developed by Linotype and added to the family in 1988. With wider character widths and thicker hairlines than Times (New) Roman, the font was designed for setting text sizes at 12 pt and smaller.

FF Balance

A family of sans-serif fonts designed by the Dutch type designer Evert Bloemsma. This innovative family is drawn entirely of curves.

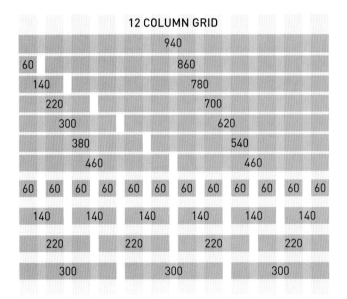

3.46 Airport signage in Toronto.

3.47 Column-width possibilities in the 960 Grid System.

Many web-page grids apply print-grid logic, evident in **tables** and **frames** (web-page layout norms) that imitate the text blocks of the printed page. Tables and frames are free to float just about anywhere, were it not for the exacting control of programming, specifically CSS code. The 960 Grid System, for instance, sets up code that structures grids—either 12 equal columns at 60 pixels wide, or 16 equal columns at 40 pixels wide—separated by 10-pixel margins at left and right, creating a 20-pixel gutter between columns [3.47]. Both schemes add up to 960 pixels, which also happens to be evenly divisible by 2, 3, 4, 5, 6, 8, 10, 12, 15, 16, 20, 24, 30, 32, 40, 48, 60, 64, 80, 96, 120, 160, 192, 240, 320, and 480 pixels. Isn't it nice when someone else does the math? That someone is Nathan Smith, the programmer who devised the system and wrote the code. About web-page design, he wrote that "as long as we're using right angles, we might as well make some logical sense of it all." Why 960? The web designer Cameron Moll proposed that 960 pixels is the optimal width for web pages. Smith then designed the grid framework accordingly and he freely distributes it for other web developers and designers to apply. This system allows the possibility of endless reconfiguration to meet the needs of specific content.

Smith's idea has motivated other screen-based grid systems. "Typogridphy"—designed by the then eighteen-year-old Harry Roberts—supplements the 960 system with code that forces horizontally adjacent text to align, creating a uniform "vertical rhythm." The alignment of text across space is a quality that trained typographers hold dear in paragraph aesthetics, and one not necessarily shared by web developers. Were Müller-Brockmann alive to witness Roberts's attention to typographic detail in the on-screen environment, he would be pleased indeed.

If Müller-Brockmann could lay eyes on the Fluid 960 Grid System, he might weep tears of joy, and of despair. The Fluid framework reconfigures the grid in real time, and reflows text within columns that change in relation to the width of the browser window [3.48]. These grids are truly relational systems (joy), but are blind to content (misery). Typeface and size remain constant (joy again), but as the browser window narrows, column widths follow suit, affecting optimum type-size-to-line-length relationships (more misery). A user can extend lines of text to the outer extremes of a screen, or reduce them to asphyxiating narrowness. Paragraph depth and gutter size change, too, as does the position of tables and elements. When the topmost elements reshape and occupy more vertical space, those positioned below are pushed farther down the page. Lively and versatile, yes; but from a typographer's perspective, the grid is frustratingly unstable.

Designing typography within fluid media is challenging, to be sure, but those who share Müller-Brockmann's tastes can take heart. Just as we account for the reading limits and design constraints of static media, so too we find ways of balancing typographic concerns and reader preferences with the capabilities of dynamic environments [3.49].

3.48 Text reflow in the 960 Grid System. *As the width of a browser window narrows, column widths narrow proportionately, and text flows farther down the column. The first sentence in the top configuration occupies eight lines, whereas the same sentence in the bottom configuration extends to eighteen lines. Were the headlines longer, they too would break into two or three lines. In this case, the color bars would also deepen, which would radically change the relationship between headline and text.*

FORMING AND USING GRIDS

As noted earlier, grids have been with us since humankind began its attempt to harness the world, have been adapted to every medium, and seem likely to live on in perpetuity. The all-pervasive nature of the grid surely raises many questions about making and working with grids at all. Why devise them? What are the advantages once a grid is settled on? How does one decide on grid divisions and spaces?

First, why devise grids? Well, because they work. A knowledge-able use of grids simplifies planning and standardizes production, so they are fundamental to design and typographic practices. Employing a grid can have economic benefits, such as maximizing resources and minimizing labor. The tools we use and our standard practices of production also sustain grid use. (All of our tools—rulers, paper cutters, printing presses, rectilinear screens—are designed around the logic of spatial division. Or did grids emerge from our tools?) Once a grid and its guiding rules for placement have been designed, they also streamline the task of managing a lot of text. And of course, grids work to facilitate reading if they are mindfully organized and populated with clear visual cues.

Using a grid also brings manifold advantages for the designer: for starters, frictionless production, tamed text, coordinated content, and happy readers. Grids also provide frameworks to establish visual pattern and hierarchy, which results in relationships among elements that serve both aesthetic and pragmatic ends. Orderliness, attractiveness, and expressiveness, on the aesthetic side, and on the pragmatic, reader access to content and content comprehension.

Finally, how does one decide on grid divisions and spaces? The answer to this question is a little more complicated. Several considerations come into play for each and every grid that is to be designed.

physical needs

Text needs room to breathe. It needs adequate space to function well in its physical environment. When content of varying kinds interacts in the same context, each part also needs to be supported by the whole, so that when called upon to "speak," every part is prepared to do its job. So, typographers always take stock of the kind of content, the amount of text, and the medium as they begin to settle on an appropriate and functional grid.

KIND OF CONTENT

A primary consideration in building a suitable grid is the kind of content to be contained within it. Specific grids are predisposed to manage specific content, and certain kinds of content inspire certain grids. Fluid grid systems (described in the previous section) are good for organizing unrelated blurbs or story lead-ins dispersed among many fields, accessible in any order. Similarly, books or signs or websites that contain simultaneous and

3.49 Black Estate vineyard website, 2008. Mathew Arnold and Tim Kelleher, Sons & Co. *This scrollable website is built from six columns. Horizontal structure is established by alignments and by texts that cross columns. Text is allowed to flow loosely because space is virtually unlimited.*

nested levels of information and images are typically structured using comprehensive grid systems. Finite grids, like those used for novels and newsletters, readily accommodate longer, continuous texts. Armatures in posters and advertisements anchor very brief texts. In each case, the grid anticipates access and use, including the nature of the reading space: simultaneous, sequential, or reader-ordered.

A standard book jacket contains a lot of information: title, author, and publisher on the front, back, spine, and flaps; promotional statements; a brief author biography; and images. Content on a book jacket clearly serves a different function from the content inside. The jacket, a simultaneous reading space, allows readers to scan and land on content at will. The book itself, a sequential reading space, supports reading in the order written by the author. Note, though, that the book might be a simultaneous reading space, as in the case of a dictionary [3.50] or travel guide. The general kind of content found in a travel guide is reducible to sub-kinds of content, too. And sub-kinds to sub-sub-kinds. Readers approach each kind of content with certain expectations, informed by the structure and hierarchies we assign. Consequently, the grids we build for any of the above will be, or should be, specific to the kind of content needing to take shape.

3.50 Page from the *Shorter Oxford English Dictionary*.

AMOUNT OF TEXT

The amount of text in a book substantially exceeds the amount on a book jacket, unless it is a picture book. Therefore, we must calculate the full **word count**, beginning on page one and ending with the index and bibliography. The grid accommodates word count, relative to page count, within the trim size. Typographers are duty-bound to include the total number of characters supplied by the author and producer. Had we done the writing or financed the production, we would certainly want every detail of our labor represented.

Say we are designing an anthology of essays, and we find that some of the texts are a little too long to fit our design plan. What do we do? Writers and editors believe that the final manuscript is exactly the length it needs to be, so we are stuck with the word count as given, unless we are collaborating with the author and publisher. What we can do is expand the grid or reduce the type size to increase the amount of text per page. Or we can select a typeface with a narrower set-width. Or decrease the line spacing. If the publisher can afford a higher material cost, we can increase page size or page count. Then again, we can also storm indignantly out of the publisher's office, refusing to alter our design. We do have choices.

It is conceivable that a book contains so many words, in relation to the maximum physical space and production budget, that the type is forced into an unreadable size. At least one such book exists: The *Oxford English Dictionary* Compact Edition. The full-sized edition of the OED is a twenty-volume publication with approximately 500,000 definitions, 290,000 main entries, 137,000 pronunciations, 249,300 etymologies, 577,000 cross-references, and 2.4

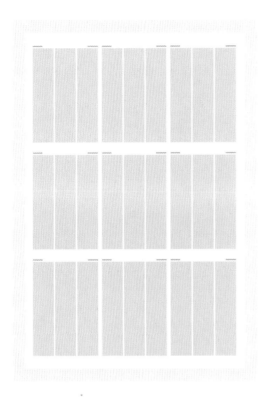

3.51 Page structure of the *Oxford English Dictionary Compact Edition*.

million illustrative quotations. The compact edition gathered this same text into two volumes; two very thick volumes, I might add. Each page is photographically reduced to one-third of its original size, and each reduction is positioned three by three to a page [3.51]. As one might guess, the text size went from readable to tiny enough to justify packaging the book with a magnifying glass.

The structure for the OED is less a calculated grid than it is the consequence of a commercial enterprise, plus the motive to make the content available to more people, and more affordable. The result, however, is not so easily accessed. The columns that are captured to scale in each image reveal the original scheme: a straightforward modern grid designed to disperse legible text across twenty volumes. Oxford University Press clearly avoided the laborious task of devising and applying a grid to accommodate the new format. What if the publisher had opted instead to design a grid suited to a massive amount of text fitted into two volumes? A better grid might have maximized the use of space so that the type size would be less dinky, although I doubt it could ever be read without some magnification: there are limits. What if a typeface were also designed to work especially with that grid, one that is readable at minute sizes (assuming that a reader does not need glasses)? Or a typeface that allows more characters per line? Any of these options would boost readability, if not sales. Another alternative is to change medium. The amount of text would be less of an issue in the digital realm where data know no bounds.

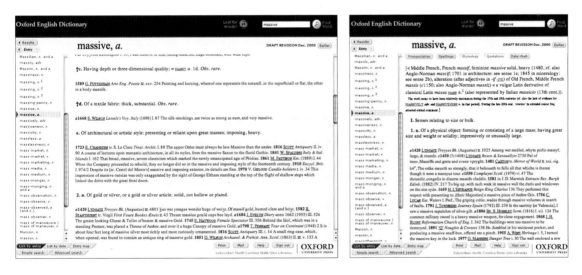

3.52 Pages from the *Oxford English Dictionary* website, 2006.

CLASS OF MEDIUM

It happens that the OED content does also reside on a website [3.52]. An older design of the screen version used a two-column grid, like the twenty-volume print-edition grid. Such a structure is common in reference books and in data-driven media where related information sits side by side. The online

structure, however, functions quite differently. Whereas the text is fixed and complete in the print version, the online version stores text in reserve, as data on a server, accessible with a click.

This online grid system collected entries down one narrow column on the left of the screen, separate from definitions displayed on the right. I looked up "massive." The system located the word—stationed in its rightful place amid an alphabetic list of other words—and highlighted it with a red arrow. I was then able to scroll through information related to my search in the adjacent, fluid column, while my word remained static.

Now imagine the printed OED organized in similar fashion: entries positioned in a column on the left of the page; definitions, etcetera, running down the right, on and on, probably spilling over into sequential pages. Entries stacked to the left, as they were in the screen version, would not work because each word would soon dissociate from its definition. How would readers know which word corresponds with which definition? Entries would instead need to be dispersed to align with respective definitions. Meanwhile, the left column sits empty as the information related to an entry concludes, and the next entry appears. The benefit of such a structure, we assume, is that each entry has plenty of breathing room. Unfortunately for the publisher, this organizational choice would waste whole pallets of paper. Twenty volumes would grow to forty or fifty or more. The buyer would be saddled with a higher price tag, to say nothing of the need for more shelf space.

The OED example demonstrates that, compared to the seemingly limitless storage and modal nature of screen-based media, physical artifacts in the three-dimensional world can store only as much readable text as their surfaces allow. In physical media, once typography is fixed within the space, the area is occupied. Finito. Two dimensions, determined by an "X" and a "Y" axis, can contain only so much (readable) stuff.

We can introduce the third dimension by simulating a "Z" axis, but the grid still only occupies two dimensions, so no real space is gained. Motion-oriented media also have the capacity to create the illusion of real space [3.53]. Elements can travel as if advancing or receding through an expanse, anchored to a "3D" grid. Such media can also add the fourth dimension by way of a timeline. Not a grid exactly, but an organizational structure nonetheless. The timeline plots when elements are to appear on screen.

Even though space and time are conceivably limitless in motion-oriented media, they are not ideal for the typographic presentation of extensive texts that argue complicated issues. Motion structures, then, tend toward alignments and armatures rather than grids. Similarly, billboards and other media, while static, are taken in by readers who are themselves in motion. The encounter is brief, and so the structures must be compact. Hybrids, such as screen-based, interactive media in which users control motion, are organized within complex spatial grids: readers fly through masses of content and, on demand, pause to read what they choose [3.54].

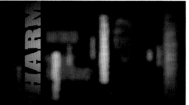

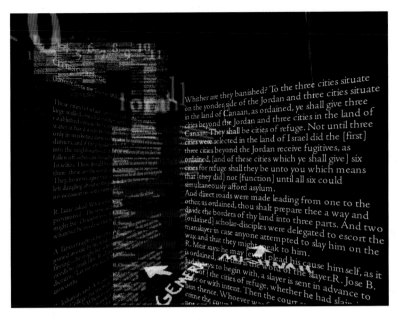

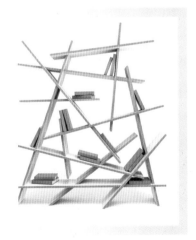

Some grids help to map out physical typographic structures—actual volumetric grids in real three-dimensional space, for instance. Likewise, the area of a cube divided into smaller segments might organize type anywhere within that space.

organizational and navigational needs

Given how most typographers fuss over grids, it can be disheartening to learn that readers hardly notice them, unless their interaction is hindered by the lack of one. Readers do tend to register curvilinear or interlocking structures, primarily because such schemes are less common. Still, a reader would probably not identify a grid as a grid, though she would readily benefit from the patterns and hierarchies that typographers design within grids. Recall the question: what are the advantages once a grid is settled on? To recap, grids are designed to set up relationships that serve two aims: aesthetic (a beautifully organized reading space) and pragmatic, including "findability" and comprehension of content.

To understand grids a little better, let's use the example of a bookcase [3.55]. Most bookcases are modular, whether a narrow box divided into equal sections by shelves, or an expansive structure where shelves and struts partition interior spaces, measured out in regular intervals. The shelves are analogous to grid lines that delineate fields (active zones), and the struts are not unlike vertical gutters. The top, bottom, and ends of the bookcase are the grid perimeter, and beyond those is the margin.

Each structure allows or precludes arrangement and usage: book placement, for instance, is limited to the available shelves. A perpendicular bookcase predicts that book orientation will be vertical, horizontal, or leaning at some angle in between. The quantity of books will be constrained by the size of fields; more thin books than fat ones will fit in a given shelf span, for instance. Structure also inclines us to sort books in certain ways. Extensive, rectilinear structures furnish enough space to arrange vast collections alphabetically by author or title. Think of the rows and stacks in any public library. More restrictive bookcases might favor subject categories or themes. A bookcase constructed of angled, intersecting shelves, or of dimensional letters (yes, such furnishings exist), prompts haphazard placement. These more chaotic structures also make retrieving books a higgledy-piggledy affair. It might be difficult to alphabetize books at intersecting angles, for instance. And it's likely that someone would browse randomly in order to locate one. Rectilinear shelving can favor more orderly searching and finding, in part because that is how humans have prescribed such structures to be useful, and how they have learned to interact with them.

3.53 (opposite) Trailer for *Who Killed the Music?*, 2010. Sebastian Lange. *The implied third dimension, added to the fourth dimension, time, adds structural complexity. In this promotional trailer, text appears in front of and behind Sam Goody.*

3.54 (above) *Talmud Project*, 1999. David Small. *This project organizes the Torah in virtual three-dimensional space. Readers maneuver through text on screen using dials on a connected console. The digital interface allows readers to follow ideas from one text to another and to read translations in the context of the larger corpus.*

3.55 (above) *Crash*, 2005. Rainer Mutsch. Bookshelf.

Books, like typographic elements, can be sorted within a given structure in a variety of ways, depending upon the organizer's aims and readers' needs. One might order books rationally by theme, author, or year of publication; visually by height, width, or color; or even by surprising conceptual criteria. Grid structures likewise promote order over chaos by inviting consistency and rhythm among elements—no matter what the logic of placement or the disparity among elements.

Getting back to typography, designers can similarly place elements at will within grids, as the arrangement suits organizational, navigational, and communication aims. The structural system grounds the array, while visual characteristics of elements and their arrangement direct readers through the assortment to access the content they seek [3.56]. Let's look at typographic roles, grid rules, and the hierarchical levels they produce to appreciate how and why elements function in relation to each other, which is sometimes a very complicated matter indeed.

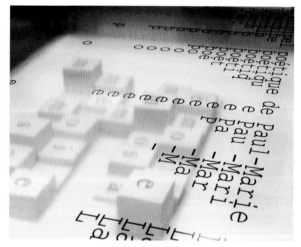

ROLES AND RULES WITHIN GRIDS

Several types of information need ordering so that readers are able not only to access the content, but also to understand the relationships between the levels. The design of this book, as an immediate example, manages primary, secondary, tertiary (and so on) hierarchical levels devised from several divisions of content. The chapter section, one such division, includes a variety of typographic levels, and each level has a role to play: headlines, subheads, body text, captions, and so on. The primer sections, another division, include other levels and roles. These levels are consistent across all members of the division, so each chapter employs the same typographic roles in the same way.

I assigned visual and spatial attributes to each typographic element, or role, in order to accommodate the kind of information and hierarchies required by each division and its respective texts. After many variations and testing, the final choices became my rules. Every instance of each role—say, the chapter main heading—is then typeset with the specifications of the corresponding rule: in this case, the typeface DIN Bold; the size, 13 pt; tracking is optical; line spacing is 14 pt to the next baseline, which is the first line of the paragraph. The type's position within the grid aligns to the second column grid line from the gutter. Other rules include "main headings occupy only one line." This rule is possible only because the written text and my design choices allow for it. Were the written main headings lengthier, or had I chosen attributes that made them occupy more space, such as a wider typeface, this rule would soon be broken. Another rule is "all main heads, subheads, and subsequent headings align to the spine."

The chapter body includes additional roles, such as the main text, plus figure, sidebar, and primer cross-references. Each is assigned rules, beginning with the body. The rules for the other three roles are more subtle in order to emphasize the reference without heightening hierarchy, which could interrupt reading flow. Add to these parts the sidebar headings and their definitions, running heads and folios situated around the margins, and other divisions, like the bibliography and index sections, with other kinds and amounts of text. All of these elements have their own levels, roles, and rules. With so many different but necessary roles, one can begin to comprehend the value of the grid that reduces placement options, and its rules that help readers recognize the various levels of information.

Placement rules for elements that serve particular roles are set out within the grid system. For instance, although the sidebar texts can appear anywhere vertically along the marginal column, the titles are set to align to the **baseline grid**. Additionally, titles are set flush right on the **verso**, and flush left on the **recto**. Placement rules apply to captions as well: position them in the column nearest the spine, and leave one clear baseline between caption and image edge. Sometimes breaking rules is unavoidable, but overall adherence to the system downplays the anomalies.

communication needs

In addition to the design choices that address the physical needs of text, organization of content, and navigation for the reader, designers make judgments as to how those choices might communicate. Ideally, all these decisions result in a grid that is both functional and expressive of the content. The need to juggle so many variables helps explain why designers commonly turn to the precedents, or grid genres. If the artifact is to be a newspaper, with dozens of information levels, sections, articles, and images, the structure that both contains and communicates "newspaper" to readers will seem self-evident, based upon thousands of existing and historical models. To both designer and reader, such genres are so ingrained in typography that it is difficult to see them as anything other than a natural phenomenon [3.57].

Not all projects are newspapers, of course. And even if they were, each set of conditions and intentions will inform and generate a unique grid within that genre. Coupled with rules for headlines, images, and text, each grid and the compositions it facilitates will communicate with lesser or greater specificity. For any book to be read, hallway to be navigated, or application form to be filled out, a detailed grid can be designed not only to fit the set of circumstances exactly but also to communicate what specifically the artifact is about.

Let's look at this book again as an example. On one hand it is just another college textbook: the grid and typographic rules bear that fact out. As such, it

3.56 *(top, above left, and above) Exposition l'archipel poétique de Paul-Marie Lapointe, 2009. Sebastian Bisson, Louis Gagnon, and Jean Doyon, Paprika. The roles assigned to typography in this exhibition function to identify parts of the exhibition and to reinforce word- and formal play.*

3.57 *(left) Telephone book listings.*

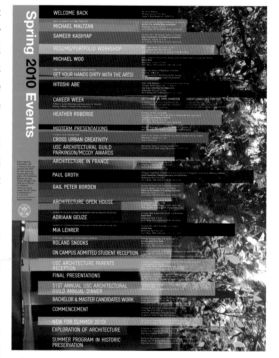

must accommodate all of the main text, plus headlines and subheads, captions, a glossary, the primers, table of contents, index, and bibliography. On the other hand, this is a textbook quite different from, say, a high-school geometry or chemistry textbook, which might include shorter snippets of information and lots of tables, charts, and formulas. The design conventions of such textbooks communicate that useful (and necessary) facts are at hand. This college-level typography textbook allows for lengthier discussions and good-sized images, presented in more "designerly" than "textbook" fashion.

Different circumstances, uses, communication requirements, and so on help typographers to make decisions about the attributes of the grid, and its rules. A <u>monograph</u> designed to communicate the subject of

Monograph
A book that contains a single body of work by a particular artist or presents scholarly research on a specialized subject.

modern architecture might understandably look quite different from one about a contemporary comic-book artist. The former might follow the strict rules of mid-century modern grids and display big, juicy photographs, whereas the latter might use a grid in which the page can be divided into playful compartments. Some of the decision over the final look of the grid will be based on the material needs of the text, and some on the meaning of that text. The grid function of a language textbook, for example, will certainly support pages of dialogue, vocabulary lists, and short essays, but it will also communicate the step-by-step process that learning a language from a textbook tends to be.

//////FORM AND CULTURAL MESSAGES

AESTHETIC

As the previous section showed, grids help establish relationships among modules of text, and the space that surrounds them. In addition to addressing functionality and reader concerns, typographers deal in aesthetics, which is understood as relating to beauty. When we call something unaesthetic, we usually mean it is not beautiful or pleasing. An aesthetic, however, is any aesthetic; any deliberate visual approach that intends to communicate in a particular way. Therefore, an aesthetic of "ugliness" communicates as validly as one of "beauty," depending upon a typographer's intention (which may be just to annoy those who adhere to the aesthetics of beauty).

As we have seen, the aesthetics of typography—of letterforms, lines, paragraphs, and whole compositions—is rooted in the long history of the craft. Grid aesthetics includes: the proportions of margins to text areas relative to

3.58 *Lunch Wall*, 2009. Eric Collins, Larry Pipitone, Joseph Ellis, Keiji Ando, and Phil Chang, Attack. *This wall, created for the New York office lunch room of the advertising agency Weiden+Kennedy, jams together restaurant names and food items. The aesthetic reflects signage seen on the streets of SoHo, as well as "low-brow" typography typical of neighborhood eateries.*

3.59 *(above and opposite)* Posters for University of Southern California School of Architecture events program, 2010. Michael Worthington, Counterspace. *These posters combine at least two aesthetics: that of high modernism (strict structure, neo-grotesque typefaces, bold color); and what might be called an "everyday" aesthetic (in this case, typography shown in situ, on book spines gathered on a window sill). The posters target architects, architecture students, and other design-oriented people whose tastes embrace this kind of aesthetic fusion.*

the page proportion; proportions of columns to the gutters that sit in between; text color and texture relative to the additional elements on the page or screen; and visual balance among elements, whether drifting in motion on a television screen or juxtaposed on a poster or wall [3.58, 3.59].

Recall from the opening of this chapter that "good taste" is implicit in "good typography." It is very unlikely that a person would be reading this book if he were not seeking the "acceptable" or "correct" way to design with typography. A formal aesthetic, however, might also tend toward styles that challenge good taste, or that explicitly abandon good taste in favor of more commonplace aesthetics. This work is no less effective as a means of communication. The fact that some typographers have adopted such an aesthetic—a deliberate demonstration of "poor" taste—indicates the fact that aesthetic values vary from person to person, society to society. Through a typogyroscopic lens, all have validity, and *Work* in relation to the contexts of their creation and reception.

The reality is that beauty is, as the saying goes, in the eye of the beholder. The other, more influential reality is that, of many beholders, some hold

more cultural clout than others. Typography has a long history throughout the world, generating many schools of thought and a variety of principles relating to aesthetic preferences. Additionally, artifacts and typefaces do not contain beauty in and of themselves. Rather, preferences that rise at the intersection of cultural, technological, and economic systems elevate certain tastes over others. So, a thing of beauty is not necessarily a joy forever, unless the dominant beholders nurture it, preserve it, and pass along its virtues as "good." A quintessential example is the high value that designers place on "white space."

WHITE SPACE

If typography had lungs to draw air, white space would be ether. It's the rarefied stuff that separates ordinary typography from the sublime. White space is not always white and not at all vacant, although the word "space" implies a void. White space is in fact extremely functional. Like any good compositional negative space, it contains forces that hold a composition in harmonious tension. Unless someone is sensitive to its role, both functionally and connotatively, white space can be perceived as a useless luxury. Designers often have to defend their white space to clients because the untutored eye (uncultured, according to some) may not see white space except as a nice spot to add more text, or a reason to enlarge everything else. Which ushers in another sort of tension—the kind that raises blood pressure.

Type and all its properties work to balance negative space, as with all visual figure–ground relationships. Some negative space, or ground, is inert blankness, unfortunately for the composition. Supportive spaces, such as margins, follow where typography leads, as sensible and dutiful companions. White space, while it is sometimes seen as deferential, stands as typography's peer.

The concept of white space can be traced to the early twentieth century, when typographers began to consider the demands placed upon modern readers. Addressing problems of too much information and competing messages, they applied art-based experiments using abstraction and arranged text differently than the more standard hierarchy based on reading conventions: top to bottom, left to right. Color fields, rectangles, triangles, and circles of color, and contrasting negative space, purportedly helped the modern reader's weary eye sort through content. As Jan Tschichold wrote in 1930, "the white surface is not regarded as a passive background but as an active element."

By the mid-twentieth century, the concept had been refined as part of a more extreme design economy, one that aimed to balance minimal form with maximum function, aided by the modular grid system. Eventually, graphic designers across Europe and North America saluted the flag "less is more." The work of proponents of the Swiss Typographic Style, among them those designers who devised modern grids, was characterized by modern sans-serif typefaces, a coherent grid, dramatic photography, and copious, well-considered space. These values ushered in a modern version of beauty. The use of white space came to signify not only information stripped of anything "nonessential," but also design that is tasteful, supremely functional, and often a product of the elite [3.60].

White space supports typographic composition and clarity—a humble but critical task—but has earned a reputation as an expression of high, or at least slightly elevated, culture. It's not unusual to find the **colophon** of a finely printed hardbound book sitting regally in a field of space on the last page, for instance. Certainly, to some, white space is a luxury. Printing surface areas are often referred to as "real estate" in commercial production, and as we know, only the affluent are willing to devote costly square footage to expansive lawns and sparsely furnished grand rooms. Additionally, white space running through a press costs as much to print as the typography itself, a detail that people funding the production notice.

Web pages, by contrast, cost next to nothing to reproduce, so the decision to include white space often means simply adding more depth or more pages. In fact, the more white space, the lighter the bits on any given page, and the faster each page loads. White space can be strictly functional as well.

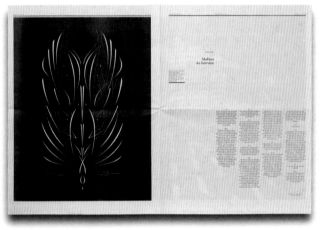

3.60 *Materiel* magazine, issue 1, 2009. Michael Freimuth and Kyle Poff.

For instance, it might add needed breathing room to online environments complicated by dozens of navigational elements and nested content lists. According to current web-design standards, however, too much white space can appear to be a coding error.

In the case of white space, the dominant beholders are designers and other visually sophisticated producers: those people who nurture, preserve, and pass it along. Today, many cultures continue to perceive the presence of white space as an indication of high-end goods. Look at nearly any expensive coffee-table book or juried competition annuals to find it hard at work. Similarly, pricey couture boutique racks are not stuffed with merchandise, nor do five-star restaurants offer row upon row of seating; and their clientele has grown accustomed to food plated like exotic islands dotting an expanse of white porcelain. Unused space helps to communicate specialness.

Try this at home: when preparing dinner, arrange the food in half portions in the middle of a plate, preferably white. Does it look high-end? No! Why not? Because "good taste" goes well beyond white space, or any other isolated detail. The aesthetics of artifacts, whether in good or mediocre or bad taste, are created by combinations of minuscule decisions, in which white space can play a part. In this way we assign formal attributes to an object and the space around it, and together they impart aesthetic value.

PROMPTS

/// **Meet up with classmates** at the library to collect and photocopy typeset paragraphs from any printed source. Trim headlines and surrounding text. As a group, arrange the swatches in a row first by text color, from lightest to darkest; and second by text texture, from smoothest to roughest. What attributes account for the differences? *(See "Text Color and Texture Variables," page 113.)*

/// **Find images of designed artifacts**—either online, or photograph ones you encounter—in which color figures prominently in the hierarchy. On a computer, open the images in a simple image viewer such as Preview, and adjust the color to full desaturation (black, white, grays). How does the hierarchy, or reading order, change? *(See "Color in Hierarchy," page 119.)*

/// **If you have access** to a bookcase filled with books and other things, photograph a few of the shelves straight on. Remove the articles and determine a set of rules for placing the things back on the shelves. Place items accordingly and take another photograph. Try it again with another set of rules, and photograph. Should people look at you askance, tell them you're studying grids. *(See "Organizational and Navigational Needs," page 145.)*

/// **Select a series** of related packaged goods—a brand of canned soups or of tube paints, for example. Take note of the various roles assigned to each element (brand identification, primary product name, secondary product information, ingredients, and so on), and the rules that dictate their relative placement, typeface, scale, and color. Analyze how the roles and rules establish a cohesive system across the package line. *(See "Roles and Rules within Grids," page 146.)*

materiality

4

Chapter 4 looks at the many physical forms of typographic production and reproduction, and how they carry meaning. To appreciate our contemporary material moment, the chapter opens with an overview of four typesetting revolutions, beginning with the invention of movable type and ending with the digitally produced OpenType used in software today. A look at the material life of the typeface Trajan exemplifies the transitions and advances that each shift introduced. This chapter also discusses the relationship between the tools typographers use (means) and the media within which they work, with an interlude introducing the importance of craft. Because materiality today is both physical and virtual, this chapter argues for the full spectrum of typographic expression and communication by distinguishing among various kinds of materiality, from tangible—"real" material—to digital typography that imitates other materials and media.

primer

ANTI-ALIASING

On-screen smoothing that minimizes the stair-step effect of curved and diagonal strokes in digital type design. The jagged edges result from letterforms being constructed from rectangular pixels on a grid. Anti-aliasing software reduces the tonal contrast between pixels at the edges of the letterform and the background, creating the perception of a smooth contour. **ILL. 01 > PAGE 168**

ASPECT RATIO

The ratio of image width to image height. In 1892, film became the first medium to adopt an aspect ratio, 4:3, that is now called "standard." Competing for viewers with television in the 1940s, film adopted additional ratios, including Panavision/cinemascope at 2.39:1. Since that time, different media have standardized their aspect ratios to guide content producers in design decisions. High-definition television uses 16:9; the iPhone uses 1.5:1; and the iPad uses 4:3.51. **ILL. 02 > PAGE 186**

BIT

A shortened term for "binary digit," the smallest recordable unit of information in computer memory. In screen display, assigning one bit per pixel produces only two choices: white and black achieved by on/off binary code. Continuous tone is accomplished by increasing the number of bits that the computer can process for each pixel by boosting its random access memory (RAM); the more bits, the greater the range of color. **> PAGE 163**

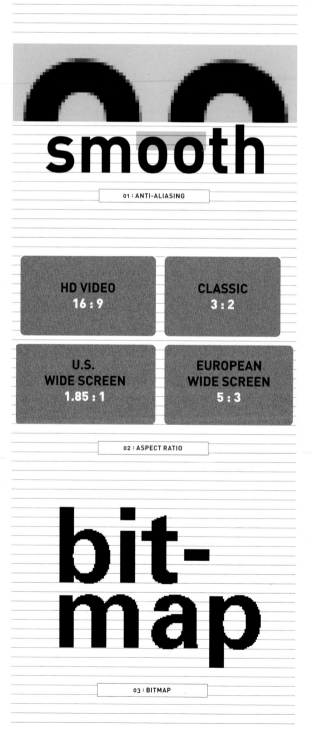

01 : ANTI-ALIASING

HD VIDEO 16 : 9	CLASSIC 3 : 2
U.S. WIDE SCREEN 1.85 : 1	EUROPEAN WIDE SCREEN 5 : 3

02 : ASPECT RATIO

03 : BITMAP

BITMAP

A digital format that converts an image, letterform, or shape to pixels, and then maps each pixel to a place on a grid. Although most formats are in essence bitmaps, the term is used today to describe images composed only of black and white pixels and lacking continuous tone. Bitmap fonts are characterized by stair-step or jagged edges in the curved or diagonal strokes of letterforms. **ILL. 03 > PAGE 166**

CALLIGRAPHY

The art of hand-lettering. Calligraphy has a history in many cultures across centuries. It reflects not only the tools of nib pens, brushes, and sponges, but also the gestures of the calligrapher. It is both language and image. Today calligraphy is a fine art practice that is distinguished from typography, but it played a role in the development of typographic form. The uncial (a script letterform used from the third through eighth centuries); the Carolingian minuscule (a script developed in the ninth century as a European writing standard); and Gothic Textura (blackletter used from the twelfth through eighteenth centuries) are styles of handwriting that influenced typeface design. **ILL. 04 > PAGE 164**

CHASE

In letterpress printing, the non-printing metal frame into which all type, leading, and furniture are placed and locked up. **ILL. 05 > PAGE 166**

COMPOSING STICK

A metal tool used by type composers to assemble metal sorts (type) into lines and paragraphs by hand. The tool is precisely machined, and is designed to contain metal sorts snugly within a given measure, in preparation for being locked up on a letterpress.
ILL. 06 > PAGE 165

DPI (DOTS PER INCH)

The standard measure of resolution for outputting a halftone image in printing. A halftone simulates continuous tones through dots that vary in size, shape, or spacing. The resolution of a halftone (how sharp or coarse the image) is determined by the number of dots in a one-inch line. DPI is often chosen for printed images on the basis of the paper quality. Eighty-five-line screens are typical for printing on newsprint on which ink bleeds, filling in some of the space between dots. One-hundred-and-fifty-line screens are more appropriate for printing on smooth coated papers that show little ink spread in the size of the dots. **ILL. 07 > PAGE 169**

DTP (DESKTOP PUBLISHING)

A popular term that describes the ease of printing and publishing documents from personal computers. Desktop publishing emerged in the 1980s when user-friendly software made it possible for people not trained in design to make finished-looking documents. Advances in screen simulation produced a work environment in which "what you see is what you get" (WYSIWYG). **> PAGE 166**

04 : CALLIGRAPHY

05 : CHASE

06 : COMPOSING STICK

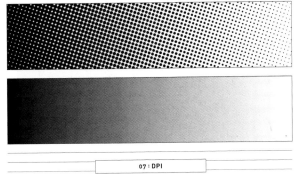

07 : DPI

E-INK

A digitally activated display technology used in some e-readers that simulates ink on paper. Electrostatic particles are negatively charged (for black) and positively charged (for white) by circuitry and displayed on a screen. Unlike backlit computer screens, which are constantly refreshing text and image, e-ink images are stable and reflect light. This makes them easier to read, especially in bright sunlight. **> PAGE 166**

ENGRAVING

A printing process in which letterforms and images are carved into metal and charged with ink, which is then transferred to paper. First used to print images, engraving became a popular eighteenth-century method for reproducing text in books as well. Wood engraving, perfected by Thomas Bewick in 1790, involved cutting away the non-printing areas and inking the raised surfaces (the reverse of metal engraving). Bewick was able to achieve prints of remarkable detail and to integrate word and image in a single medium. **> PAGE 180**

FILM (CINEMA)

A series of still images viewed in rapid succession (24 frames per second) when projected. Film is measured by width, with 35 mm being the commercial industry standard and 16 mm and 8 mm used for other purposes. The aspect ratio of 35 mm film (the ratio of width to height) is 4:3. Typography played a central role in early cinema as intertitles for silent movies. For decades, film titles have represented a rich field for typographic expression. Saul Bass and Kyle Cooper are among the well-known designers of main titles. **> PAGE 176**

FLARE

The tendency for screen-based typography to exhibit weaker contrast when viewed on light backgrounds. **> PAGE 170**

FORME

The chase with all type, leading, and furniture locked into place for letterpress printing. **> PAGE 165**

FURNITURE

Rectangular block used around a metal or wood type composition to hold the lines of type stable in the print bed. Traditionally made of oiled hardwood and cut to standard lengths, furniture may also be manufactured in metal. **ILL. 08 > PAGE 183**

HANGING QUOTES

Punctuation marks that fall outside the edges of a column of type. Because quotation marks sit atop relatively large areas of negative space, or pools, they break the otherwise even edge of text when aligned with the column. Hanging quotes solves this optical problem. **> PAGE 175**

INK SPREAD

The tendency for printed ink to bleed slightly at the edges of letterforms before drying. In text type, this spread significantly changes the appearance of the typeface by widening strokes and filling in counters, especially where strokes join. Typefaces are often designed to compensate for this problem. The type designer Matthew Carter addressed this issue in Bell Centennial (1974), which he designed for use in phonebooks (which are typically printed on newsprint in 6 pt type). Carter's design of counters compensated for the anticipated ink spread. **ILL. 09 > PAGE 170**

08 : FURNITURE

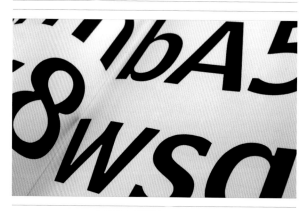

09 : INK SPREAD

10 : LETTERPRESS

KITSCH

Forms of creative work that appeal to or refer to popular or "lowbrow" tastes. Some free online typefaces attempt to replicate classical features but lack the refined form, craft, and consistency found in good type design. Other typefaces, which appear thoughtfully crafted in comparison, deliberately draw their inspiration from the vernacular forms of popular culture. In this case, designers create such typefaces to comment on taste— that is, interpretations informed by experiences related to social class, cultural background, or education. **> PAGE 185**

LETTERPRESS

Any printing process that uses a raised, ink-coated surface to transfer text and image to a pliant material, usually paper. **ILL. 10 > PAGE 180**

MEDIA

Modes or systems of communication. Media use different tools for their creation and reach audiences through different means of delivery. Photography, for example, is a medium delivered through posters, social networking websites, and email attachments. The method of delivery determines what is possible formally and how something is interpreted. The medium of typography as distributed through the Web looks different and carries different meanings than typography in a printed book or scrolling at the bottom of the evening news. **> PAGE 164**

MERGANTHALER LINOTYPE

A typesetting technology invented by Ottmar Merganthaler in 1886. The Linotype machine involved typing a letter key, causing a brass matrix to fall into place in a growing line of letters and spaces. Once the line was complete, molten lead would pour over the matrix to produce a "slug" corresponding to the line of text. The slug was assembled with other slugs for printing. Once the slug was cast, the letter matrices were returned to storage for use in other settings. After printing, the slug was melted down and the lead recycled in the next setting. The Linotype machine reduced the labor in typesetting and eliminated the need for re-sorting and storing a large inventory of metal type. These advantages over handset type composition were useful to a newspaper industry that demanded quick production. **> PAGE 165**

MONITOR

A screen-based display device that produces images by translating electrical signals into pixels. Monitors vary in physical size but rarely exceed 96 pixels per inch. **> PAGE 169**

MOVABLE TYPE

A system of typesetting for relief printing that binds multiple metal or wood characters together and prints them simultaneously as text. Characters are then re-sorted and reused, making type composition more efficient. Movable type was used in China as early as the eleventh century and Korea in the thirteenth, but is most frequently associated with Johannes Gutenberg's printing of the Bible in the 1450s—the first major book printed on the printing press. This technology encouraged the spread of literacy by making books faster, cheaper, and easier to produce. **ILL. 11** **> PAGE 164**

11 : MOVABLE TYPE

11.
CHŒUR DE TOKYO
CINÉ-CONCERT

12 : OPACITY

O P E N T Y P E
O P E N T Y P E
Γ Δ Θ Λ Ξ Π Σ Φ
Б Д Ж З И К Л У
ħ ḱ ÿ Ђ ɵ ν ґ ə
À À Á Á Â Â Ã Ã
Ţh Ţ ţ ŉ Ŋ ŋ ŋ Ŋ
⅓ ⅔ ⅛ ⅜ ⅝ ⅞
1 2 3 4 5 6 7 8
1 2 3 4 5 6 7 8
√ ∫ ≈ ≠ ϐ ϑ
₣ ₤ ₱ € ¥ ¿ ¡

13 : OPENTYPE

OFFSET

A printing technology in which ink is transferred (offset) to a rubber blanket, then to the printing surface of the paper. Unlike letterpress, in which paper is in direct contact with the inked raised surfaces of letters, offset printing uses an intermediate step that keeps the plate from touching the paper. Type and image are transferred onto a plate. Oil-based inks stick to the image areas and water keeps the ink from collecting on the smooth, non-image areas. The image is transferred to the blanket roller and then to the paper. This keeps the plate from breaking down and its fine lines and dots from clogging with debris from the pulpy paper surface, thereby producing cleaner images and more copies per plate. In four-color printing, there is a set of rollers (plate and blanket) for each of the four process colors (CMYK). **> PAGE 181**

OPACITY

The degree to which the passage of light is inhibited by a material. Opacity has three applications in print design: in image production, printing ink selection, and paper choices. Images (and type) can be assigned varying levels of transparency (from 1 to 100%) through software settings. Making an image transparent allows whatever is beneath it (paper or other images and text) to show through. Printing ink can be opaque or semi-transparent (thinned to a lesser or greater extent by the amount of clear base used in its composition). One color printed on top of another in semi-transparent ink will be an optical mixture of the two colors. And paper quality is graded based partially on its opacity—that is, the degree to which images and text printed on one side of the sheet show through on the other side. **ILL. 12** **> PAGE 169**

OPENTYPE

A digital font-file format developed by Microsoft and Adobe as an improvement upon the TrueType format. It is a scalable format that defines the shape of each character but not its size. Unlike other formats, OpenType places no practical limit (65,536) to the number of glyphs in a typeface and allows the full type family to be combined in the same font file. OpenType works across platforms, performing equally well in Mac, Windows, and Unix environments. Since the late 1990s, OpenType has been the preferred font-file format among digital typographers worldwide. **ILL. 13 > PAGE 166**

PANTOGRAPH

A mechanical duplicating device made from an assemblage of moving metal bars. In type production, where wood types were individually hand-carved for centuries, the introduction of the pantograph in 1834 helped to mechanize wood type production. The inventor of the wood type pantograph, William Leavenworth, combined the pantograph apparatus with a lateral router, which since 1927 had been used to cut wood types quickly and precisely. **> PAGE 165**

PHOTO-POLYMER PLATE

A printing plate made by a photomechanical process. A light-sensitive coating is hardened or "cured" in areas not blocked by a film negative, and exposed to UV light. Unexposed areas wash away, leaving a raised surface for inking. Although these plates are not as durable as metal, they eliminate the need for hand composition in letterpress printing and allow greater variety in typographic form. **ILL. 14 > PAGE 174**

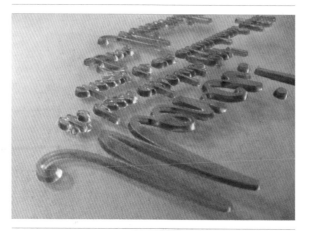

14 : PHOTO-POLYMER PLATE

15 : PHOTOTYPSETTING

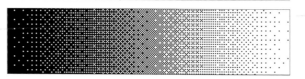

16 : PPI

PHOTOTYPESETTING

A mid-twentieth-century technology in which fonts were stored as film negatives (on long strips or on circular disks). Light was projected through the negative, one letter at a time, striking photographic paper. Once letters were exposed, the photographic paper was developed and pasted into a layout on illustration board. These paste-ups, or "mechanicals," were then photographed to make negatives for the production of plates for offset printing. Because a magnifying lens determined phototype point sizes, and text-sized letters were exposed through a spinning disk, some fonts exhibited soft or blurred edges. **ILL. 15 > PAGE 166**

PIXEL

The smallest visible unit of information in a digital display. Every digital display has a fixed number of pixels per inch (PPI), with 72 pixels per inch for most LCD or plasma screens and more than 100 for high-definition displays. Image or type resolution influences file size; the more pixels per inch (PPI), the higher the resolution and the larger the file. **> PAGE 163**

POSTSCRIPT FONT

A digital font built from the PostScript computer language. PostScript was developed by Adobe to translate vector-based digital information to a bitmap-based format for printing. This technology is hardware-independent and prints fonts well at different printer resolutions and point sizes. **> PAGE 166**

PPI (PIXELS PER INCH)

The standard measure of image resolution for both screen display and printed output. In screen-based typography, resolution is measured in picture elements, or "pixels," and pixels per inch (PPI). The pixel resolution one sees on screen is the number of pixels built into the screen. **ILL. 16 > PAGE 169**

PROJECTION

The use of a lens and directed light to cast an image onto a screen or other surface. **ILL. 17 > PAGE 169**

RESOLUTION

The detail an image or type holds, typically described by the number of dots or pixels within a given space. The quality of images produced by digital cameras, screen displays, and printers is determined by resolution. Anti-aliasing and the PostScript printing language are ways of producing better resolution in viewing and printing type. **> PAGE 169**

SIDE BEARING

The non-printing space at each side of a typeset character that keeps it from touching the next letter. Originally, the side bearing was the physical distance between a raised character and the edge of the metal sort; the space between letters was established by adjacent side bearings and could be expanded but not reduced. Today, the side bearing refers to the distance between the letter and its bounding box. This distance, always the default measure when typing, is preset during the font design process and saved in the code of digital fonts. While the side bearing is a permanent value of a font's code, its visual appearance can be altered using kerning and tracking adjustments. **ILL. 18 > PAGE 166**

17 : PROJECTION

18 : SIDE BEARING

19 : SORT

20 : SPREAD

SOFTWARE

A collection of code-based programs that tell a computer what to do and how to do it. Software drives the central processing unit of a computer and allows it to talk to peripherals, such as screens, cameras, scanners, printers, and projectors. **> PAGE 164**

SORT

A single unit of metal type in letterpress printing. Sorts result from the typecasting process and are arranged by character into type drawers. **ILL. 19 > PAGE 176**

SPINE

The spine is where the pages of a book are fastened to one another and to the cover. **> PAGE 162**

SPREAD

The left (verso) and right (recto) pages of an open book or magazine, which together represent a single visual field for typography and image. For this reason, publication designers compose spreads rather than single pages. **ILL. 20 > PAGE 162**

STAT CAMERA

A large-format stationary camera once used to photograph layouts and expose film for platemaking in offset printing. Type and graphic elements were pasted on a board and called "camera ready" for pre-press operations. Stat cameras were also used to enlarge and reduce black-and-white artwork created in another medium. With the invention of digital processes that allow printers to go directly from an electronic file to a plate, stat cameras have become obsolete. **> PAGE 166**

STEREOTYPING

Duplicating a forme for use on more than one printing press at a time. Papier mâché, plaster, or some other pliable material is pressed onto the raised characters of metal type, forming a "matrix." Once dry, it is filled with molten metal, creating a sturdy duplicate or "stereo" of the original handset composition that can be inked and printed. This process, invented in the nineteenth century, supported high-volume, low-quality printing, such as newspapers.
> PAGE 165

STOCK

The paper or other material on which type and images are printed. Paper stock is either coated (covered with a compound to make it smooth and reduce how much ink is absorbed) or uncoated. Color and image quality will be affected by these characteristics.
ILL. 21 > PAGE 169

SURFACE

An area with breadth and length but no thickness. Our perception of typography is shaped by the surface on which it sits. Motion typography viewed on an LCD display, books printed on thick soft paper, and signage on the side of a building, for example, gain meaning through the qualities of their surfaces. The level of contrast between typography and its surface can also determine legibility. **ILL. 22 > PAGE 164**

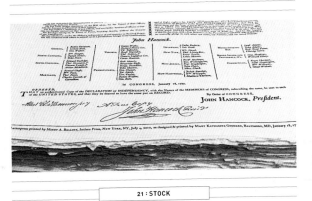

21 : STOCK

22 : SURFACE

23 : TRANSPARENCY

TECHNOLOGY

The making or use of tools, techniques, or systems for doing something. Typographic technology can be mechanical, digital, or both. Typography can be mechanically precise, show traces of the technology used to produce it, and mimic other technologies. Typography is also a reflection of the technology available in the time in which it was produced, and therefore carries historical references as part of its meaning.
> PAGE 165

TELEVISION

A device for receiving and decoding broadcast signals. Televisions convert signals into scan lines at a rate of 30 frames per second. Digital video, which was introduced in 1996, developed independently of television, and is recorded in the widescreen aspect ratio of 16:9 at a resolution of 720 × 480 pixels. High-definition televisions use the same ratio but have a higher resolution of 1920 × 1080 pixels. In 2009, the United States replaced older formats with digital television, of which HDTV is one format. **> PAGE 164**

TOOL

An instrument for performing mechanical or digital operations. Tools are typically associated with a medium. For example, a stylus is a tool for mark-making in soft clay and a press is a tool for printing multiple copies of the same text. Mechanical tools often leave traces of their use in the forms they produce. Digital tools are frequently represented by icons of mechanical tools to reinforce a metaphor for their functions and behaviors (a pair of scissors for clipping a line into sections and a magnifying glass for enlarging something). **> PAGE 167**

MATERIALITY

TRANSPARENCY

The physical property of a material that allows light to pass through it. Printing inks are composed of pigment and a transparent base, so overprinting one color on top of another allows the first color to show through the second. Digital files can be made transparent, so one image overlaps another, allowing the first to show as it might in the double exposure of a photograph.
ILL. 23 > PAGE 169

TYPECASTING

The process of casting metal type, or sorts, by pouring molten metal into molds called "matrices." The matrix is placed at the bottom of a hollow shaft (type mold) and an alloy of lead, antinomy, and tin is poured in, filling both the matrix and the mold. After cooling, the shaft and raised character are joined into a single metal sort of one character. **> PAGE 164**

TYPEWRITER

A largely obsolete mechanical device with lettered keys that are struck individually to print on paper. The organization of today's computer keyboards (QWERTY) mirrors the arrangement of keys on the typewriter and reflects the most comfortable hand positions for the most frequently used letters. The typewriter carriage moved paper from right to left and could do so only in uniform units of space. Typewriting, therefore, was monospaced and is the basis of such contemporary typefaces as Courier. The typewriter was replaced by personal computers in the 1980s, which allowed easier editing and storage of documents. **ILL. 24 > PAGE 165**

24 : TYPEWRITER

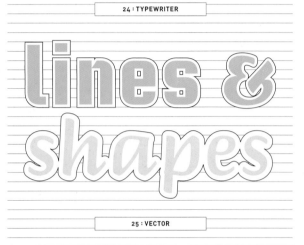

25 : VECTOR

26 : WOOD TYPE

VECTOR

A digital file format that specifies how a computer will draw geometrical points, lines, curves, and shapes for on-screen display. Vectors are expressed on screen using "paths," "strokes," and "control points" as designated within a digital file's code. The file size of a vector image depends on the number of elements it contains.
ILL. 25 > PAGE 166

WOOD TYPE

A form of letterpress printing in which type sorts are carved from wood rather than cast from metal. The American printer Darius Wells, using a lateral router, was the first to mechanize wood type production in 1827. Seven years later, William Leavenworth added a pantograph, a mechanical duplicating device made from an assemblage of moving metal bars. The pantograph operator traces the letterform and the router cuts the exact same shape in wood. This invention allowed printers to set larger type than was possible in metal, producing bolder design opportunities. For a time, wood type posters played an important role in early consumer society, but their use declined after 1879 with advances in lithography.
ILL. 26 > PAGE 174

XEROGRAPHY

A photomechanical copying process that converts varying tones of light into toner on paper through electrostatic charges. The Haloid/Xerox Company introduced the first plain-paper copier in 1960. Most laser printers today use this process. **> PAGE 178**

// **TOUCHING AND SEEING**

The Open Library is a web-based project dedicated to capturing digitally the pages of antique books. Every page, in potentially every volume stored in libraries across the world, will be photographed and digitized. An ambitious goal, to say the least.

The hope behind the project is to put these rare books into the virtual hands of readers—those who would not otherwise have access to the actual volumes—with the original typography intact.

The traditional method for photographing a bound book is to open it flat along the **spine** to a **spread**, then shoot the spread from above. The pages face the camera lens at an exactly parallel plane to minimize distortion. But this process can damage frail old books, which have weak spines. Glues have hardened over the decades and so are not as malleable as they once were, and pages are brittle from age and exposure to light, air, and molds.

Technological innovations developed by the Open Library project allow librarians to shoot digital photographs of spreads while verso and recto pages are comfortably positioned at a ninety-degree angle to each other, reducing stress to the spine. A specialized digital camera then photographs each page under uniform lighting. Once every page is captured, the entire book can exist in the digital ether. Rather than typeset the texts for the screen—a task undertaken since 1971 by another altruistic online effort called Project Gutenberg—the Open Library translates the physical pages of library books into pictures of physical pages of library books, and collects the pages into a simulation that behaves not unlike an actual book. A click or swipe "turns" the page, as if we are lifting the corner and turning it ourselves. Current

4.1 *(above and opposite, top)* Opening pages of *Westward Ho!* by Charles Kingsley. Open Library.

4.2 *(opposite)* Opening pages of *Westward Ho!* by Charles Kingsley. Project Gutenberg.

electronic readers often use such verisimilitude. What is unique about the Open Library is that it offers intact covers, endpapers, and pages marked by the stains, wrinkles, and notes each volume has collected over the years. The impression is that of a real old book rather than of an animation that makes virtual pages more book-like.

This should not be a surprising occurrence to those of us accustomed to virtual representation of actual artifacts. And yet, how very curious it is. Real paper book leaves—that is, typography printed on paper with metal type and thick, sticky ink on heavy iron presses—are transformed into data **bits** and transmitted through **pixels** on an RGB screen to be "held" by our eyes. The illusion of a physical book escapes our other senses. We cannot smell the faint odor of mildew. And, although we might pick up visual clues that imply the subtle texture of letters inked onto paper, we cannot feel its heft or measure its volume. Were we turning each page gingerly, we would have a sense of the book's age. On screen, its oldness is merely implied. Material transmutation from physical to virtual and sometimes back again to physical (as with laser-printer output) is not on the average reader's mind. It is, however, an unavoidable and fascinating arena for designers, and has far-reaching implications for typography.

Compare the material cues of typography in the physical volume of *Westward Ho!* (1855) by the novelist Charles Kingsley, captured in pixels by Open Library [4.1], to the same novel typeset by Project Gutenberg for a web browser [4.2]. The latter offers no reference to its tangible incarnation. Both exist on screen. Both accommodate reading. The web-browser version—typeset in a standard typeface (adapted for the screen) and backlit—does not seem to be anything out of the ordinary. Only the language and writing style indicate that this novel is not contemporary. The version from the Open Library, by contrast, is represented in its physical form, in the original classic book typeface, and so embodies aspects of the volume's history as well as the attributes of "bookness." Both versions communicate in their own ways through their different formats, as well as their typography. This goes to show that when typography crosses different media, it can express ideas as much through its material nature as by content, typeface, color, size, and composition.

////////////////// **PRODUCTION AND REPRODUCTION**

Typography as we know it was first produced by inscription. Hand-made letters were painted or inked onto, or carved into, such **surfaces** as papyrus and stone. They were also made by impression. Copies were reproduced from a single master, such as a carved woodblock. Today our hard drives, **software**, screens, and printers produce typography, which is then reproduced by such physical means as printing presses, and by digital means, say the **television** screen.

The roots of the word "typography" lie in the classical Greek for "a blow" (typos) and "writing" (graphē). From the very beginning, then, the process of producing type was physical. Today, however, our digital **media** present us with many choices for producing typography that ends up in print or in the environment, virtual typography that lives only on screen, or variations and hybrids of both physical and virtual type. To appreciate the implications of our options, we should look briefly at four major technological advances leading to our current state of affairs.

THE FOUR TYPESETTING REVOLUTIONS

hand typesetting: metal and wood

The Gutenberg Bible is celebrated as the first complete book to be printed in Europe using **movable type** made of hand-cast metal [4.3]. Before the invention of **typecasting**, apprenticed monks and scribes labored to ink by hand every letter of every word of every page of every chapter of every religious or scholarly text. The Gutenberg Bible's typeface emulates German gothic **calligraphy** of the period, to the extent that the font consists of around three hundred variations of letters, suggesting that the punch-cutters were attempting to replicate as near as possible the hand of the scribe. It is also possible that crude molding techniques account for the variation instead. Despite the inconsistencies in the font, the text still looks more uniform than its calligraphic counterparts. This is not to say that scribes did not do a remarkable job of crafting uniform letters. A hand inking every letter, however, can never be steady enough to avoid slight differences, at least not compared to the demonstrably few variations of these initial metal fonts.

In the centuries following the introduction of moveable type in Europe, scribes copying volumes letter by letter gave way to type composers setting galleys by hand, letter by letter, page after page. As printing spread throughout Europe and the Americas, various societies contributed to the development of typographic forms [4.4]: they built on existing type designs and invented new ones. In the late fifteenth century, the Venetian printer Nicolas Jenson designed a typeface that would significantly alter the trajectory of type design. Individual metal letters were cast from the same mold, so every p and every

4.3 *(above)* Gutenberg Bible, 1450s. British Library, London.

4.4 *(opposite, above)* American Type Founders Company specimen book, 1912.

4.5 *(opposite, center)* The Woman's Journal, January 6, 1912.

4.6 *(opposite, below)* Poster for Bickford's Cough Elixir, 1883.

Galleys
Trays used to gather and organize composed metal type and to carry the composition from the composing area to a letterpress printing bed. The term also refers to paper output (sheets of composed type produced by phototypesetting technology) that was cut and pasted into camera-ready artwork.

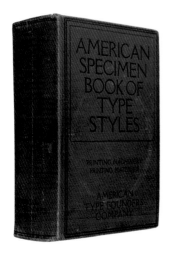

q was identical. Moreover, the letters were designed to work together in any combination. Although Gutenberg and others before Jenson had created some degree of modularity in their metal types, they maintained aspects of writing wherein each letterform was designed to pair with the letters preceding or following it in a line. Jenson's typeface was the first truly uniform and modular set of glyphs.

This means of composing large bodies of text and reproducing print matter in high volume on a letterpress endured through to the late eighteenth century. As the demand for printed material increased across Europe and the Americas during the Enlightenment, type design, printing, and paper-production methods evolved—sometimes toward refinement, sometimes toward efficiency. **Stereotyping**, for instance, duplicated whole **formes** so that the same composition could be printed on a number of presses simultaneously, increasing the number of impressions per hour. The technique, used extensively for newspaper reproduction [4.5], produced a weak replica of metal type hand-set on a **composing stick**, but when it was perfected in 1829 (the same year the American **typewriter** was patented), print quality improved.

Additionally, the **pantograph** router (invented in 1834) accelerated the manufacture of wood types, which were quickly becoming a mainstay for a new era awash in advertising. Wood responded well to carving, too, which inspired a plethora of elaborate letterforms. These and other inventions signaled a sea change for typographic production and the options for creating typographic form.

machine typesetting: hot type

The Industrial Revolution spawned thousands of devices that mechanized manufacturing processes of every sort, including type production. Two late nineteenth-century inventions automated the process of typesetting and increased its speed, which in turn affected type design. The pantographic punch-cutter (1884), coupled with the revolutionary **Merganthaler Linotype** and Lanston Monotype casting machines (1884/86), shifted mass production of metal type from being labor-intensive hand processes to mechanically assisted ones. These **technologies** also expanded the variety and size of typefaces. In addition to typesetting, chromolithographic printing had, by the late nineteenth century, become popular. This process brought hand-etched type, graphics, and image onto one printing plate. The new technology supported the contemporary trend for decorative types and other forms of fanciness [4.6]. Chromolithography evolved into today's printing standard, offset lithography. Hot type continued to be used well into the 1980s, alongside the technologies that emerged in the mid-twentieth century.

phototypesetting: cold type

The first major movement away from the physical nature of letterpress in continuous text occurred as computers began their ascendancy in the 1960s. **Phototypesetting** quickly dominated the graphic industry [4.7, 4.8], sporting names that referred to the new electronic age: Diatype, Compugraphic, PhotoTypositor, Varityper. These machines moved type composition from the metal **chase** to the drafting table. Photographically produced paper galleys, also called "repros," were processed in chemicals similar to those used in wet photography. <u>Production artists</u> cut paragraphs and headlines from the galleys and pasted them into page compositions called "mechanicals" (also called "<u>camera-ready</u>" artwork). **Stat cameras**, another high-contrast photographic process, joined photocomposition machines in freeing type from its wood-and-metal shackles. Letterforms could be stretched, twisted, angled, squeezed, and shadowed to within an inch of their life.

Letterspacing, too, could be altered in minuscule increments and, for the first time in typographic history, could be easily decreased. Glyphs once constrained by physical **side bearings** could now touch and even overlap. Typesetting jargon for specifying type, such as "TBNT" (tight but not touching) and "K1/2U" (kern one half unit), would have been inconceivable before 1960.

Photocomposition methods evolved over forty years and became the professional standard. By the mid-1980s, though, electronic technologies had given way to digital means, suggesting that the former constituted a transitional blip between five hundred years of metal typesetting and the processes employed today.

Production artist
A person skilled at preparing files for print. Today production artists work exclusively in page-production software, but historically they worked with such physical material as paper galleys, masking film, precision pens, and ink.

Camera-ready
A term that refers to former production processes in which prepared artwork was captured on negative film that, in turn, was used to make printing plates. Today the term still refers to digital artwork ready for print production, despite current technologies that bypass camera and film processes.

4.7 *(top)* Photo Lettering catalog, 1950.

4.8 *(above)* Specimen page from a Photo Lettering catalog.

digital typesetting: room-temperature type

The fourth revolution began with desktop publishing (**DTP**), **PostScript** programming language, publishing software, and laser printing. It is likely to carry us into the next five hundred years, providing we are able to continue producing electricity. In the few decades since its arrival, digital production has moved from kilobytes to terabytes, from eight-inch screens to room-sized displays, from chunky **bitmap** fonts to **OpenType**, and from oil-based ink to digital dye printing and **e-ink**. As this chapter reveals, digital technologies replicate nearly any typographic feat that previous technologies accomplished, and much more. Never before have typefaces been so precisely (or so undiscriminatingly) drawn, nor as widely distributed. Digital environments bring photography, typography, graphics, and **vector** forms together in one platform, spawning typographic forms as intricate and as varied as any in history. Digital grids and organizing systems are exact to quarter points and half pixels. And letterforms that originated hundreds of years ago enjoy revivals: Trajan capitals are a case in point.

MULTUM IN PARVO

THE HOT-TO-COLD, STONE-TO-PIXEL LIFE OF TRAJAN

4.9 *(below)* Original Roman inscription displaying the Trajan letterforms.

4.10 *(center) Ex Divina Pulchritudine*, 1926. Eric Gill. *Inscription on Hoptonwood stone.*

4.11 *(bottom)* Forum Title (left) and Record Title (right). *Both these typefaces were originally inspired by letterforms chiseled into stone that Frederic Goudy saw in Rome in 1910. Both typefaces have since been redrawn, extended, and digitized by the type foundry P22.*

Roman square capitals are notably preserved on the Trajan Column, a Roman monument completed in 113 BCE to commemorate victory in war over the Dacians [4.9]. But such classic letterforms have lived many lives since. Following the path of these ancient letterforms from inception to the present day confirms the relationship between the stuff of typography and the technologies that make it. Before and throughout all four revolutions introduced above, reworkings of the classic style have kept pace with technological advances. Roman capitals were carved in stone on the original column, and have been imitated on stately buildings ever since. They have also been hand-lettered, cast in metal, and redrawn for photo- and digital typesetting.

The geographical and chronological span of the Roman Empire ensured that the letterforms would be influential. Their longevity was sealed by the interest in and revival of ancient Greek and Roman cultures during the Renaissance, despite the existence of many other forms. Square capitals were the first to have serifs as we know them today. One theory posits that these letters were first painted with a brush in a way that flared the terminals and apexes, which were then chiseled with metal **tools**. Another theory speculates that the form evolved out of aesthetic preference.

The first modern rendition based on the original Trajan letterforms is credited to the master stone carver and type designer Eric Gill [4.10]. His great respect for their classic proportions and character evolved as he learned to chisel the traditional letters in stone. His rendition is faithful to the original, primarily because he drew tracings from the column itself, then refined them to be chiseled in stone. Later, Frederic Goudy designed Record Title (for the journal *Architectural Record*), based on his study of the carved Trajan column letters. The typeface was drawn to be set by line-casting machines, such as the Merganthaler, and to be printed. Consequently, Goudy introduced greater uniformity across the glyphs [4.11]. Other versions were issued from various digital type foundries in the 1990s, including <u>Goudy Trajan</u> (following Goudy's original drawings, and now available as a webfont), <u>Cresci LP</u>, and <u>Pontif</u>.

A ubiquitous, and perhaps the most respected, version of Trajan today is the only typeface that claims the Trajan name, designed by Carol Twombly for Adobe (the typeface

Goudy Trajan

Jason Castle followed Goudy's early twentieth-century drawings of Trajan to digitize a complete character set in three weights, distributed by Castle Type.

Cresci LP

Garrett Boge based this typeface, distributed by Letter Perfect Foundry from 1996, on an alphabet drawn by Giovan Francesco Cresci, a Renaissance writing master whose guide to penmanship, *Il Perfetto Scrittore*, was published in 1570.

Pontif

Also designed by Boge in 1996, based on the inscriptional lettering of Luca Orfei da Fano, a Vatican scribe who designed inscriptions for Pope Sixtus V during the Baroque period in Rome.

is now included in Apple's system fonts). Compared to the versions by Gill and Goudy, Adobe Trajan is refined in its details and precision, to an extent that only digital technology and careful study of the Trajan column and preceding cuts could allow [4.12]. In an odd twist of fate, the timeless Roman capital has proven a favorite among designers of horror and epic genre movie logotypes. Why, I could not say. The effects that can be added with software—rough textures, glowing halos, ominous shadows—probably contributed. For whatever reason, Trajan has come to be associated with forboding and tragedy.

Each translation reveals cultural forces at work, as well as technological ones. The thin line that distinguishes all of these fonts from each other might relate to the economics of type production.

Goudy, for instance, met the need for additional glyphs by extending the basic square capital set into a more complete font, usable by other designers, which also benefited Goudy's livelihood and reputation. Similarly, foundries will design their own "cut" of a typeface and sell it at a competitive price. Type designers often capitalize on the popularity or limits of an existing typeface by devising a fresh version. For instance, a typeface from Letterhead Fonts, Classic Roman Regular, adds lowercase letters to Trajan-like capitals.

In the last decade, the designer of the mini-font Quadratis dared to capture the essence of Trajan in a bitmap font, with surprising success [4.13]. Another interpretation, Quadratus, uses **anti-aliasing** to its advantage [4.14]. Some typographers might argue that each of these permutations is a bastardization of some authentic Trajan—or that well-meaning designers are assisting in the ruin of the classic letterforms.

Whether or not one takes this position, typeface translations owe something to entrepreneurialism, and to the ready availability of new technologies and materials. As Adobe's font design manager, David Lemon, wrote in an exchange with the type designer John Downer, "Trajan is a typeface, not an inscription. Not only are the two media quite separate, their different functions require differences in design."[1] New uses introduce and inspire new forms in order to remain relevant.

Quadratis
Atomic Fonts released this ingenious minifont, designed by Miguel Hernández, in 2002.

NULLA DIEM SINE LINEA

A QUOTE

ATTRIBUTED TO THE GREEK PAINTER
APELLES

BY GAIUS PLINIUS SECUNDUS
{ 23–79 ANNO DOMINI }

LIBROS NATURALIS HISTORIAE,
NOVICIUM CAMENIS QUIRITIUM
TUORUM OPUS, NATOS APUD
ME PROXIMA FETURA
LICENTIORE EPISTULA NARRARE
CONSTITUI TIBI,
IUCUNDISSIME IMPERATOR

ABCDEF
GHIJKLM
NOPQRS
TUVWXYZ

4.12 *(opposite, above)* Sample of Adobe Trajan.

4.13 *(opposite, center)* Quadratis minifont.

4.14 *(opposite, below)* Quadratus typeface design, 2007. Jarred Eberhardt, WeAreNotYou.

Professional graphic designers sometimes joke that they design only a handful of kinds of artifact. An understatement to say the least. To wit: books and book jackets, posters, broadsheets and one-sheets, periodicals, letterheads, envelopes, forms, cards of every size, mailers, brochures and catalogs, tickets, digital and mobile interfaces, television and **projection** screen graphics, signage, T-shirts and accessories, packaging and labels, awnings, kiosks, construction barriers, billboards, and banners. These formats and platforms by which readers meet content—the means of delivery— bring visual and tactile properties to the typogyroscopic equation. **Opacity, transparency**, roughness, smoothness, light reflection and absorption, weight, and volume all contribute to the reader's experience of content, and therefore to the communication.

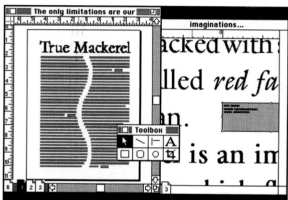

4.15 *The Mackerel Stack, 1989. Kevin Steele, Mackerel. Small and coarse computer screens rendered crude typography in bitmap form. The screens above are from a digital "capabilities brochure," created with an Apple program called Hypercard the year before the invention of the World Wide Web. Such digital information was dispersed by way of "floppy disks," precursors to the CDs we use today. The means of delivery, then, included placing the floppy in a computer drive and launching the disk.*

artifacts, devices, and formats

As readers interact with content, they are influenced by artifacts, devices, and formats, which usually delimit what might be designed, or at least what typography can do when delivered in various media. Let's focus for a moment on LCD screens, television screens, and LED displays—devices by which typography is delivered more and more. While these media have dynamic mutability and internal light going for them, they can also have crude **resolutions** by print standards. For example, current computer **monitor** resolutions are 72 pixels per inch (**PPI**), whereas laser printers can output up to 1,800 dots per inch (**DPI**). Typography rendered in screen technologies was once considered a mere approximation of "real" type; but now it can hold fairly minute detail, enough to convince the human eye. Meanwhile new display devices have inspired wholly new typographic territory. The first computer monitors were so coarse that new typefaces—such as <u>Chicago</u>, a bitmap font— were designed to accommodate fewer available pixels and good readability, as well as minimize bytes [4.15].

All devices have inherent properties that typographers exploit, or for which they must compensate. Letterforms in 100 percent black ink, for instance, when offset-printed on highly <u>calendered</u> **stock**, yield crisp and clear detail, depending upon the precision of the press and the skill of the press operator.

Chicago

A sans-serif font designed by Susan Kare for Apple Computer, used as the primary operating-system interface font for the Apple II screen, and then the Macintosh from 1984 to 1997.

Calendered

The word "calender" is derived from *kylindros*, the Greek for "cylinder." The process of calendering employs heat, as well as friction and pressure between rollers, to produce a slick and often glossy paper surface.

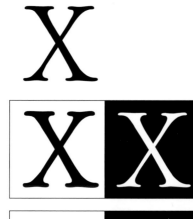

The material nature of viscous pigment laid or pressed onto paper surfaces thickens letterforms (a phenomenon called **ink spread**), if only slightly. The opposite is true of screen devices. The same dark letterforms created by the absence of light on screen will look thinner than their printed counterparts because the light encasing them **flares** around and inside the letter [4.16]. When text is <u>reversed</u> out of black ink, letterforms may lose weight because the ink surrounding them might spread. Screen-based light letterforms set against darkness react, again, in the opposite way. White-light type gains weight because the light that forms it expands.

The device itself can sometimes be as present as the typography it delivers. For those of us accustomed to seeing and reading typography on computer screens and in books, the means of delivery might not seem to influence us that much. If a woman happens to be reading a rather large book while standing at a bus stop, odds are good she is achingly aware of its heft, but not quite conscious of its "book-ness." On such devices as the iPad, the typography replicates qualities of the book, including virtual page edges and behavior that replicates page-turning.

4.16 Ink spread and flare. *Relative to a normal weight (top), print media can introduce ink spread (middle), whereas screen-based media introduce flare (bottom).*

While a reader may be more aware of a device during his initial experience with it, the means of delivery soon fades into the background. Less familiar artifacts tend to have greater presence. The LED Bitman wearable object, an early "shaker device," displayed the time and alphabetic messages input by the wearer. When shaken and rotated, Bitman also turned into a dancing fool. It was housed in a conspicuous plastic device, meaning that users would have been as conscious of the artifact and its format as they would have been of the typography—which was presumably the aim of the manufacturers of such a novelty.

Although the precise qualities and constraints of the means of delivery often escape the reader's awareness, typographers are acutely attuned to them, because the means influence communication. If ever there was a time when designers produced artifacts in just a handful of categories, our perpetual technological innovation and creative imagination ensures that those days are gone for ever [4.17]. Every medium invites specific consideration when we design. Each artifact predetermines certain formats, too—shapes, structures, sizes, and material attributes. The book format, for example, predisposes the designer to choose from within a range of proportions, scales, type sizes, and set-widths to maximize readability

4.17 Interactive book, 2009. David Small and Cesar Sesio, Small Design Firm. *Although the primary device in this work is a large-format, handbound, blank book, a computer and video projector "print" the typography onto the book. The physical pages are embedded with sensors that, when turned, signal to the computer running the video. In addition, sonar sensors allow visitors to disrupt, combine, and manipulate text with their hands.*

4.18 *Bibliotype. Craig Mod. Printed formats are immutable, whereas dynamic formats introduce variability. This aspect changes how and what typographers design. Bibliotype is a rapid prototyping tool that quickly displays long-form texts to help designers gain a sense of how that text would appear on reading tablets. A designer can quickly see the complete text rendered in basic typefaces (serif and sans serif), set in full- or left-justified paragraphs, with and without hyphenation. Additionally, three settings—"bed," "knee," and "breakfast"—anticipate the possible type sizes that a reader might opt for on his or her device.*

in a fixed space (which does not mean that designers do not break with the conventions regularly). Books are a static format. Other static formats are book jackets, posters, periodicals, calling cards, catalogs, tickets, T-shirts, packaging, awnings, windows, walls, and sidewalks.

A host of other formats are dynamic: television and web browsers, of course, but also signage and electronic readers. The digital billboards found on the sidelines of sports fields and arenas present similar considerations for the typographer to static formats, but with the addition of viewing distance, animation, and fast delivery. Browser windows and mobile-device interfaces are very common dynamic formats that allow readers to adjust typeface and size [4.18]. Each format has characteristics peculiar to its physical qualities. And every format intended for any number of contexts and uses demands some awareness of the physical, material, and reading systems that create it.

The most ubiquitous bounding shape for typography is the rectangle, from the smallest postage stamp to the most expansive wall. Imagine, though, that as typography evolved over the centuries, oval formats had been economical and simple to produce. Formats would have evolved quite differently, as would our tools and, ultimately, our typography.

TOOL AND MEDIUM

A celebrated poster announcing a winter lecture at Cranbrook Academy of Art displays the Austrian designer Stefan Sagmeister with words scratched onto his arms, chest, and groin. The means (a pin) and medium (scratches) of this format are not the most practical promotional device. To get his message to the locals the designer would have had to walk around Bloomfield Hills half-naked: not so wise in a Michigan February. Not only that, within a few days the scratches would also have healed, compromising the whole enterprise. To make the announcement functional, Sagmeister employed other tools and media for a more sensible format, one that could be reproduced in multiple, distributable copies. So he used a camera to capture the freshly scratched words inscribed on his body, and a printing press to create a reproduction of the image.

The "four revolutions" discussed in the last section are evidence that the making of typography presumes the use of technologies (the means) in some process that manipulates materials and surfaces (the medium). More specifically, as technologies advance, existing tools and media are perfected, and new ones emerge. The most fundamental typographic tools and media are the oldest, naturally: incisions on skin, of course, but also a writing implement and pigment, a chisel and wood, a stylus and clay—each worked by the hand.

4.19 Hand lettering by Sean Barton, 2010. From the film *The Sign Painter*.

Lettering artists produce type with brush and paint on a surface such as glass or wood [4.19]. Although each painted sign is a one-of-a-kind production, the trained lettering artist (like the scribe) is able to repeat and match letterforms skillfully across any number of windows and doors. Even with such virtuosity, each sign will show variation compared to the others. Because the sign painter is not a machine, his means and media are pliant. He is also a living person predisposed to produce organic variation, or "flaws." This technology inevitably leads to formal differences, however slight. Seemingly minor variances in paint thickness and edge quality add up to a look and feel quite distinguishable from such mechanically produced typography as machine-cut vinyl letters, for instance.

4.20 Edition of the opera *Solimano* by Johann Adolf Hasse, published by the Staatsoper Unter den Linden, Berlin. *The carefully crafted Staatsoper book series strikes a fine balance between the traditions of typographic style and contemporary innovation.*

Typographers draw or construct typography using combinations of tools and media: brush and ink, soft pencils, fingers and paint, scissors and cloth. Current technologies give us hundreds of typefaces drawn and constructed by hand, yet available for reproduction on all kinds of surfaces and in a range of materials [4.20]. Designers first create an alphabet by whatever means, then capture the originals in some way, perhaps with a scanner (which is another sort of camera). They collect the complete alphabet into a digital file, and voilà! Anyone can use what was once a set

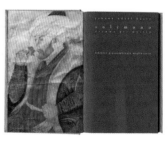

4.21 FFF Tusj typeface design, 2008. Magnus Cederholm.

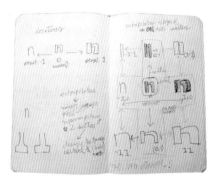

4.22 Page from the sketchbook of the type designer Cyrus Highsmith, 2004. *The drawing on the right maps out interpolations of type weight and width ranges, extrapolating from "neutral" weight and width. Expert thinking is as much an aspect of the craft as expert making.*

of one-of-a-kind letters for their own purposes, and reproduce them at will (providing the users have acquired licensing permission, of course).

Current vector and bitmap software is capable of producing facsimile letterforms that correspond to the characteristics of solid matter, as well as visual effects: sketchy graphite-like marks, photo-like blurs, gelatinous gooeyness. Note that I say "correspond to characteristics." In the hands of skilled typographers and illustrators, software creates very realistic likenesses. The type may look "handmade," yet it has been created in software on the computer. It presents the same visual cues as genuinely handmade typography—but it is not tactile, and nor was it necessarily created by tactile means.

Our electronic means have ushered in "digital handmade" type. This seeming oxymoron promises typographic innovation that will be commensurate with the speed, power, and pure genius of computing. We might begin with words set on screen in a digital typeface—the well-crafted <u>Aachen Bold</u>, say— then set our software tools and processors to bubbling and blurring, extruding and rippling, to render the words in perpetual motion. The letterforms are thus transformed into something never before seen on planet Earth. Taste-wise, some might regret that such things are ever realized, but that is another matter. Odds are good that in thirty or forty years, technological developments will have added yet more possibilities, making our current media seem archaic to us.

Aachen Bold

This heavy Egyptian typeface, designed by Letraset's type director Colin Brignall in 1969, exploited the phototypesetting capabilities of the time with narrow counters and subtle slab serifs.

TYPOGRAPHIC CRAFT

Designers are known to utter two seemingly incongruent axioms: "God is in the detail" and "The devil is in the detail." To paraphrase: the particulars of a work reveal the essence of its character and its beauty, subtly (to the unknowing eye) but still to striking effect. In the same way, the damnable details, if not given their due, can lead to work gone awry. Both sentiments caution us to attend to the minutiae of our craft.

Craft implies "hands-on" making, or what is commonly referred to as craftsmanship. Peter Dormer, a leading voice on craft culture, points out that "handicraft" does not adequately define contemporary craftsmanship. Rather, craft "is knowledge that empowers the maker to take charge of the technology." Typographers and type designers engaged in their specialist activities are in control of their work. They possess what Dormer terms "personal know-how," that is, mastery of tools and technology [4.21, 4.22]. Know-how is simple enough to understand but not easily acquired. Know-how is empirically won knowledge of the "how to" sort. It is knowledge that we call upon again and again as we make things—knowledge that affords greater control and allows us to anticipate the results of our labor. Dormer adds that one not only knows that one knows, but also *feels* that one knows. Such expert knowledge comes only with experience.

The ubiquity and convenience of today's digital technologies challenge the importance of know-how in typographic practice, because they place in the hands of anyone keen enough to read a manual the very same tools that experienced typographers use. Meanwhile, menus of options simplify production. Virtuosity, therefore, no longer seems to be a requirement. Most design and production programs include design templates, complete with predetermined typographic, graphic, and image elements already composed or animated in common formats—all aimed to free users from any choice beyond which one to use. Open a template, replace "<u>lorem ipsum dolor</u>" with real text, and build a presentation, make a movie or a webpage, or print out a full-color magazine. This practice is not craft. It is paint-by-numbers. As Dormer points out, a critical ingredient of craft is "knowledge that can supplement or override that which you have bought as a package." Assembling a work from the kit of parts available in software moves everyone closer to making something, but it does not offer the possibility that everyone will be able to craft something.

<u>Lorem ipsum dolor</u>

Now a standard feature in typography-producing software. The phrase refers to placeholder text used to demonstrate general paragraph color and texture. Such text is sometimes called "greeking," which is odd because the text is Latin—an altered excerpt from a text by Cicero.

Typographic craft requires three active players engaged in an ongoing relationship: the typographer, of course; his tools; and, most importantly, the artifact in the process of becoming. It sounds a little strange to advocate developing a relationship with typography as it takes shape before us. But the craft-conscious typographer responds to his medium—or media, if there is more than one—because he is shaping it so that it can ultimately speak for itself. He is training his work to connect to readers in part by its physical, visual presence. A typographer who merely operates the buttons and menus of his software, blind to the medium as it is brought into service, is merely fiddling with his tools.

Technologies and media earn and lose favor over time, and sometimes they even fall off the radar entirely, only to surface again one day in the future. The last decade has seen hand-set metal and **wood type**, joined by digitally produced **photo-polymer plates**, revived by a new generation of designers and artisans captivated by the properties and processes that only physical letters printed by a letterpress bring. Some devotees seek knowledge from experts who pass on their understanding of this time-honored craft. Others are self-taught novices deliberately exploiting what the master would call "mistakes," sometimes pushing the frontiers of the craft but at other times just making an interesting mess of things.

Photo-lettering, too, is enjoying a small renaissance [4.23]. The foundry House Industries has developed an online typesetting tool that simulates the old phototypesetting process. The company's type designers digitized fonts

4.23 Photo-lettering website, 2011. Andy Cruz, Bondé Prang, Ben Kiel, and Brook Elgie, House Industries.

traced from the original font film, which they acquired from the type house Photo-Lettering, Inc. (familiarly called PLINC). House Industries could have scanned the films into an online reference library, but opted not to because they believed that doing so would have misrepresented the intentions of the original artists. "The films and the lettering they contain were designed to be [type] set by an experienced Photo-Lettering machine operator, not some hack with a Mac and an autotrace program." This decision demonstrates three craft-centered practices: a respect for history; an awareness of the skills and ideas held in that history; and a sensitivity to the construction and visual quality of the final work.

As typographers we should apply our craft skills in service to the artifact, and ultimately to the reader. The computer expands our skills to some degree. For example, most publication programs today allow **hanging quotes**, an option that was not available in earlier versions of the software, which infuriated typographers who knew that hanging quotes are a sign of connoisseurship. Crafting a work can never be automatic, though. Only our discernment—by eye and by touch—creates work of a quality valued by current craft standards. We manifest knowledge of historically refined craft standards, and strive not only to meet but also even to exceed them [4.24, 4.25].

Quality requires time, of course, sometimes more time than designers can be compensated for. But the desire to make a well-considered thing that resonates with readers, and other experts, drives the effort. Whether we create typography with software and a digital printer or with pen and ink, it is our connection to the means and medium that lives and breathes in the final artifact. We fret and delight and noodle and wheedle until the thing we had set out to make materializes, at which point we release it to the world.

4.24 Poster for Bon Iver concert, 2011. Laura Baisden, Hatch Show Print. *This letterpress-printed poster using wood types was produced by the Nashville-based company that created nearly every event poster for the famed Ryman Auditorium throughout the twentieth century.*

4.25 Inscription for Dallas Museum of Art, 1982. John Benson, The John Stevens Shop.

THE MEANS AND THE ENDS

Steel flat-nib pens dragged across paper at a consistent angle create calligraphic marks that correspond to the width and rigidity of the nib, to the consistency of the ink, and to the receiving surface. A super-fat felt-tip marker makes super-fat letterforms. The soft lead and clumsy tip of an unsharpened graphite pencil ensures irregular, imprecise strokes, so is not, perhaps, the best tool with which to draw precise letterforms. The correspondence between the tool, the way it is used, and the resulting form is an equation of sorts. The degree to which the physical nature of a tool engenders form, directly and readily, determines the tool's fitness for the process of making the form, and for the form itself. The form of elegantly penned calligraphy is the result of pen strokes that correspond to the character of the nib. A dull pencil would be an unfit tool to draw a fine script in typography class, unless one's aim is to test the professor's tolerance for imprecision. Entertaining, but ill-advised.

Then again, a tool might be effectively inefficient, yielding fresh and unusual results. The 1960s and 1970s witnessed the unorthodox use of the letterpress in the work of the French designer and author Robert Massin and the Swiss designer Wolfgang Weingart. Weingart famously worked against the physical properties and perpendicularity of metal **sorts** by setting them on handmade arcs to print text on curves. More recently, Marian Bantjes has used sugar to compose five separate designs for text that would have been easily accomplished with other tools. Pushing about crystalline granules obviously complicates the task of producing typography, but expediency could not be farther from the point. The painstaking work that a lesser craftsperson might rush to avoid ended up producing delicate letterforms quite unlike any other.

The fitness of tool to process and form is dramatically evident in Chinese calligraphy [4.26]. On the surface, the tools are visually clear: a brush lays ink onto paper. Yet artists complicate the seemingly straightforward process by applying their judgment and by working toward a particular intention. When wielded by the experienced hand of the calligrapher, brush and ink are capable of more subtle expression than the tools alone might promise. Similarly, typographer know-how instills originality, variation, and subtlety in the work—typographic wonders beyond those that the same means and media would deliver in the hands of a novice.

Early twentieth-century typographers could not have imagined how the media of type design would evolve within a hundred years. Digital cameras, scanners, and animation and image software allow us to manipulate typographic properties beyond those that can be realized in the physical realm. Today not only do we select meaningful typefaces and materials appropriate to our purposes, but we can also readily change their features. As our predecessors did before digital technologies came along, we can typeset the script Natalya, but now the image of Natalya renders instantly. We can then set it at 1,000 pt, and morph it into Natalya Monoline.

Technologies define and expand the possibilities for new forms of typography, and similarly, these forms and processes inspire technological advances. Before computers became ubiquitous, photographic and **film** technologies prompted innovative typographic form in the intertitles of silent films. The first intertitles were motionless, following print-based precedents. Before long the idea of applying filmic properties to text dawned on some director: shoot the typography going in and out of focus! Zoom in! Pan across the text!

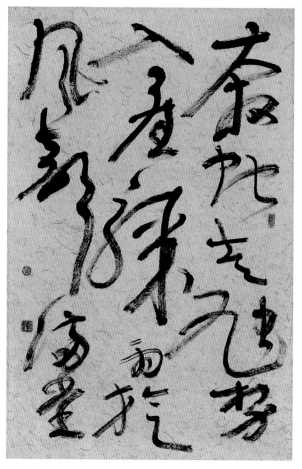

4.26 *Magnificence I*, 2006. Lampo Leong. Ink on rice paper.

Natalya
A round, flourished script with alternate swashes designed by Jeremy Dooley, and published in 2007 through his independent foundry Insigne. The font was later adapted to a monoline script.

Intertitle
A piece of filmed, printed text spliced between action scenes to reveal dialog or other text-based narratives.

Soon a time- and image-based medium precipitated the application of new filmic and animation techniques to typography. And today, words behaving like insects or fire on screen seem perfectly normal.

New technologies frequently inspire imaginative designers to innovate within the new means toward new forms of typography. Even old and less than perfect technologies, placed in the hands of curious designers, can introduce fresh ideas. Christian Schwartz describes how imperfect printing conditions spawned the text version of his typeface family, <u>Houston</u>. Roger Black, who commissioned the work, originally wanted only headline styles designed, but "a misunderstanding and a bad cell phone connection" intervened. A test on press for the headline fonts was scheduled, and Schwartz "threw together" a text version for a test run as well. "Nobody thought it would work," he writes, "but the [*Houston*] *Chronicle*'s horribly over-inked presses turned out to be the perfect environment for [the typeface]. None of the traditional news text faces we were looking at even compared."[2]

Designer ideas and the desire to make something look or behave in a certain way frequently overwhelm the supposed efficiency of means and medium. To quote Eric Gill: "the mind is the arbiter in letterforms, not the tool or the material."[3]

MEDIUM

In the physical world molecules build matter, and humans harness all sorts of matter to manufacture materials: ink, light waves, toner, plastic, tiles. All materials behave according to their physical properties, whether wet, dry, liquid, powdery, oily, rough, slick, flat, or spherical. The matter of typographic elements is printed or scribbled onto surfaces. It is inscribed, <u>embossed,</u> or <u>debossed</u> into surfaces. Sometimes it is even woven. Letterforms can be three-dimensional—forged in steel, die-cut in cloth, molded from plastic, constructed from boxboard, assembled in tiles. Additional letterforms might even be applied onto, inscribed into, or pierced through their surfaces [4.27–4.30].

4.27 *If I Want to Explore a New Direction Professionally, It Is Helpful to Try It Out for Myself First*, 2010. Marian Bantjes.

4.28 *Newsknitter*, 2007. Ebru Kurbak and Mahir M. Yavuz. *The News Knitter converts Internet news feeds, gathered within a twenty-four-hour period, into machine-knitted material.*

Houston

A family of proprietary bracketed serif fonts, commissioned by Roger Black and designed by Christian Schwartz for the redesign of the *Houston Chronicle* implemented in 2003.

Embossed

A three-dimensional image or design pushed very slightly above a substrate, such as paper, by passing the paper through metal "male" and "female" dies.

Debossed

The same process as embossing, except that the three-dimensional image or text is very slightly depressed into a substrate.

We tend to think of paper as a surface without depth, but wood, cloth, or polymer pulp can in fact be measured, if only by a micrometer. And while a photocopy will be nothing more than a photocopy to most, typographers understand it as an amalgam of materials producing a visual effect. The *Oxford American Dictionary* defines **xerography** as "a dry copying process in which black or colored powder adheres to parts of a surface remaining electrically charged after being exposed to light from an image of the document to be copied." Sounds very material:

infinitesimally raised matter, fused to paper. The medium has garnered cultural associations as well—from cheaply produced 'zines, to legal documents, to do-it-yourself promotion.

Because typography requires some light source to be seen, we need to include light as a characteristic of all media. Today, when LEDs, LCDs, and electronic screens are common, it will help to think of this light as a kind of "material."

light on, light within, and light essence

We perceive the properties of material—Plexiglas, rosewood, gold leaf, ink, concrete—relative to the kind of light cast upon it. Moonlight, a reading lamp, or a fluorescent tube allow us to perceive the volume, surface texture, and coloration of whatever material the typography is made of as it absorbs or reflects light waves. Gold-leaf typography, for instance, only appears to be gold when light produces a glint. I call this kind of medium "light-on" because it employs external illumination [4.31]. A medium composed of both physical material and light is a "light-within" medium—neon tubing, say, or an object built from LED lights [4.32].

4.30 Dharma lounge chair, 2008. Nathan Tremblay, Samuel Ho, and Ian Campana, Palette Industries.

4.31 NWB alphabet, 1987. Nicholas Benson, The John Stevens Shop.

Three-dimensional signage is often a combination of light-on and light-within media. The sun sheds light upon it during the day, and, when the sun sets, an internal light source takes over to illuminate from within. The two light sources give definition to the material properties of the typography quite differently, and readers experience the materials accordingly. So, the typographer probably needs to consider how both conditions will affect typeface, scale, and compositional choices.

Light-on and light-within media tend to be static. Typography is stamped onto a roadside sign, for instance, or is backlit to advertise a movie theater. If the type moves, it does so in limited and concrete ways: internally lit letters made of plastic might rotate above a supermarket; neon letters might flash on and off outside the proverbial seedy hotel.

A third category, "light-essence" media, also utilizes intrinsic light—that of a monitor, a television screen, an LED display, or a mobile device. One distinguishing characteristic of light-essence media, as compared to light-on and light-within media, is that the material of typography is light. Another difference is its mutability. Light-essence media perpetually transform the material of light [4.33]. Pixels or LEDs are activated and deactivated by way of signals, and typography is rendered in a variety of states, from sitting still as a stone to disappearing like vapor.

These three categories identify the qualities that give typography its material form, or materiality, whether carved in stone or flying through virtual space. Naturally, the medium affects how readers interpret typographic messages. The next section addresses how the material nature of typography affects communication. But first, a riddle of sorts. If we create typography with software that renders its results on a computer screen, and then we project that typography onto a stone surface, what is the medium? Okay, I'll tell you the answer. It's Typogyroscopic!

4.32 Garage sign in San Francisco.

4.33 *Making Future Magic*, 2010. Campbell Orme, Dentsu London; directed by Timo Arnall and Jack Schulze. *Stills from a short experimental video in which typography is created with light. The design group, Berg, describes its innovative technique: "We use photographic and animation techniques that were developed to draw moving three-dimensional typography and objects with an iPad. In dark environments, we play movies on the surface of the iPad that extrude 3D light forms as they move through the exposure. Multiple exposures with slightly different movies make up the stop-frame animation."*

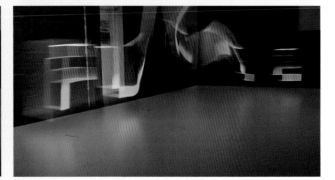

///////////////////////// **MATERIALITY**

MATERIALITY AND MESSAGE

Stone carvers have chiseled letterforms into marble and granite since the beginning of civilization. We associate these works with ceremony, permanence, antiquity, or stateliness, owing to historical use and also to the solidity and solemnity of earthbound rock. The Boston Public Library and the New York Stock Exchange state their venerability in dignified letters incised into imposing facades. The labor, craft, and cost that are evident in the materiality of these letterforms, in the context of commanding architecture, contribute to the message of formality. Many cultures also relate stone carving to monuments and memorials great and small. The 58,267 names inscribed on the Vietnam Veterans Memorial in Washington, D.C., are machine etched, not hand carved [4.34], and headstones lovingly placed in cemeteries are not always grand, yet the connection between honor and letters cut into stone persists.

4.34 The Moving Wall, 1984. John Devitt. *The Moving Wall is a half-sized replica of the Vietnam Veterans Memorial that is permanently installed in Washington, D.C., and was designed by Maya Ying Lin. Some of the permanent memorial's power stems from its materiality. Visitors touch the etched names and make rubbings from them. If the Moving Wall were not as tangible, or were constructed of less permanent materials, it would not carry the same power.*

We "feel" typography through both touch and sight. With closed eyes our fingers report type in three dimensions. A slight impression of type on paper tells us it was probably printed by means of metal type and letterpress. A roughly textured surface might reveal that the type is fashioned in wood. And from the cold slick surface of a volumetric letter that does not budge, we surmise that it is constructed of some heavy metal. Try to touch type on a computer monitor and the most we might feel is fuzzy static and smooth glass.

Our experience fiddling about with all sorts of matter tells us how to interpret typographic form that looks tactile. As a case in point, there is a "**Letterpress**" theme available in some presentation software. Light projected onto a screen that looks like pressed ink on paper? There is no soft paper to press into, nor is there ink to smudge. The point of alluding to classic and classy letterpress printing in a digital environment is to associate the content with social status or literary sophistication. In other words, a user might choose the template to capitalize on the cultural connotations of implied materiality.

4.35 Smith wedding invitation system, 2008. Cleve Smith and Brooke Smith.

Letterpress typography earned its grand reputation by inheritance, though, not by intrinsic worth. Before the turn of the nineteenth century any book or ephemeral printed document was composed in metal and wood type, or **engraved**, and printed on stock, be it newsprint or fine cotton rag paper. For centuries this technology produced almost every magazine and playbill, newspaper and book. Letterpress was simply standard procedure, and, if truth be told, it was not always impressive.

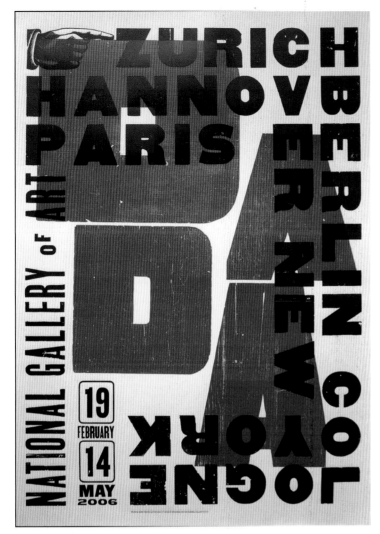

4.36 Poster for Dada exhibition, 2006.
Kevin Bradley, Yee-Haw Industrial Letterpress
and Design Co.

Very fine printing standards also evolved over those same centuries: luxurious books and formal announcements printed on classic laid and vellum papers gave people of financial means the beautiful expression of money well spent. Today, letterpress and engraving reflect their rarefied history. People of every class can purchase some form of letterpress printing today, to announce births and weddings, or any special event [4.35].

When letterpress was ubiquitous, press operators struggled to maintain the integrity of the printed surface while making solid and crisp impressions. Printed paper that showed indentation (caused by metal type pressed too firmly against the paper) was a sign of poor craftsmanship. The ultimate ubiquity of **offset** printing eliminated the problem altogether. Now that letterpress has made a modest comeback for certain artifacts, a more tactile material quality appears to be in demand. Consequently, exaggerated impressions can indicate fine craftsmanship and uniqueness.

A participant in an online forum for typography professionals and aficionados uploaded an image of a poster for an exhibition [4.36]. The typefaces appeared to be nineteenth-century wood types, and the participant wanted help identifying the typefaces. One respondent suggested that the typefaces were probably a digital manipulation of Champion Gothic, a digital typeface family designed in the 1990s based on gothic wood types. Important to note here is that neither the writer nor the respondent had laid their hands on the actual poster.

The creators of the poster chimed in to explain that they had designed the poster with authentic nineteenth-century American wood types from their extensive collection. Additionally, the poster was in fact printed on a letterpress. If manipulation by means of software figured in the design, the task would have been quite an ambitious undertaking. The typefaces look worn and, well, old. Yet the assumption that the poster was a digital simulation of an antique typeface superseded the plausible fact that the piece might be a letterpress print, pressed from wood types. Only in this age of ubiquitous and accessible digital tools would such a misreading be possible. We live in confusing times, as far as materiality is concerned. Readers must construct meaning from both actual and implied materials. Maybe a less exasperating way to think about materiality is to recognize that with our multi-media world comes multi-materialness.

AUTHENTIC TYPOGRAPHY AND THE "ASIF FACTOR"

The materiality of the poster described above is authentic to the tools and process that produced it. Typography might also be designed to look as if it is made of material we find in the physical world. In fact, typographers quite often allude to material found in the world to illustrate and pin down meaning. A classic and quaint example is the word "ice" set in snow-capped letters as if they were freezing. We see these kinds of fanciful treatments [4.37], as well as more restrained ones, in typographic communication everywhere: 3D effects in software applied to letterforms in a two-dimensional space appear volumetric, as if they are made of solid matter; perspective effects make typography look as if it is situated somewhere in space, piercing the picture plane.

4.37 Christmas card, 2010. Jen Montgomery.

This imaginative play with established typographic form might be called regrettable by some, if not downright cheesy. Traditionalist typographers tend to view it as an affront to typographic traditions— what we might call the authenticity of typography. The perception that there is something authentic to be referred back to is rooted in typography's craft-based genesis. Cutting, founding, and setting typefaces were activities with a clear task: to make typography look and function like, well, typography. Typography must not look like logs or lace or pickles. As some would have it, the farther typography strays from its type-like nature, the more affected it is, and therefore the less true it is to the nature of typography.

Frederic Goudy, a self-proclaimed traditionalist, wrote of this authenticity in terms of sincerity: "Quaintness in an old piece of printing may be admired because of its sincerity; to revive it in a piece of modern work is distasteful, hateful even, because of its affectation."[4] Among Goudy's points is that the use of typefaces (and by extension, the design of typography) should resonate with the age one lives in. Reasonable advice. But his exhortation also reveals a value to which many trained typographers subscribe: artificiality (affectation) in typography is unacceptable.

Let's consider our current moment in typographic history, though, when the material of typography is frequently bytes of memory and pixels arranged on a screen. The possibilities for expression and form far exceed what traditional typographic values embrace.

When our current production and processing devices first appeared, information was displayed on a monitor as if it had been typed, a reference to its predecessor, the typewriter. Users entered commands that showed up

4.38 *Vas: An Opera in Flatland* by Steve Tomasula. Design by Stephen Farrell. *The title on the cover of this book's first edition (right) is deeply embossed and physically tangible. The title on the cover of the second edition (left) is a lithographic print of a photograph of an embossed cover. The allusion to material is stronger in the one on the left than the actual materiality of the one on the right.*

4.39 Frames from *The Road Less Traveled*, 2010. Matt Owens. *Materiality is implied in this animation that renders letterforms as if they were made of ribbon. In the past, this treatment might have been accomplished with an airbrush and animation cels, tools that have long facilitated the Asif Factor.*

on-screen in a coarse and clunky typeface—one that Goudy and company would surely have found distasteful, if not unreadable. Yet the typeface was quite authentic to the medium and the moment. Our CPUs and screens render letterforms that are much more refined than those first screen typefaces. And, while some typefaces today resemble those pressed from the metal sorts of old, they are most definitely not the same material thing. Our means have changed extraordinarily since the mid-twentieth century, and our media are far more diverse. Technology has inserted compelling wrinkles into typography's neatly pressed heritage.

Current production software and screen and projection technologies handily facilitate the illusion of, and allusion to, our material world [4.38]. And why should they not? Humans have always communicated graphically using visual references from the physical world, "authentic" typography notwithstanding. I have named this ubiquitous characteristic the Asif Factor. Designers sensitive to its charms (and sometimes utter silliness) employ the Asif Factor for thoughtful and surprising communication, which is as valid a tactic as any other.

REMATERIALIZED TYPE

Eric Gill famously asserted that "letters are things, not pictures of things,"[5] meaning that the abstractness of letterform submits to a logic all its own. Gill's letters possessed historical integrity but were nevertheless subject to the vagaries of mass production. Typographers today sometimes describe the computer as a soulless box that lures type into disrepute; they complain that the means and media formerly reserved for experts have been democratized, for the worse. Under the artless thumb of digital production, some argue, typography's vital physical roots are diminished. If the truth be known, typesetting had lost its material status some fifty years earlier, with the emergence of phototypesetting, when typographic form split into two possible states: physical typesetting, as in metal or wood material composed with blocks of **furniture** for letterpress printing; and an image of physical typesetting, a representation composed on a sheet of photographic paper, then captured on negative film in preparation for offset printing. Phototypesetting, offset lithography, and other reproduction processes dematerialized type long before the digital revolution.

An essay by the graphic designer Loretta Staples chronicles the relationship of typography and the screen from 1984 to 1997, a period when the personal computer and software proliferated. She points out that designers initially translated the on-screen "image of pixellated letterforms" into fonts for print, "a wry visual commentary on the play between page and screen." In the year her essay was published, 2000, innovation in typography had already moved on to "computer-modeled and algorithmically driven" form, as we have seen. She concludes that digital technologies have subsumed typography into the image, which has, certainly by now, leveled the relationship between the two [4.39].[6]

In light of our current tools, does the "fitness" of the tool to the process and form (discussed earlier in this chapter) still hold true? If we typeset a word in a typewriter-like font, and our output is a laser print, does the typography we create correspond to the tools? Absolutely. Computers, monitors, software, scanners, still and video cameras, and digital printing are all perfectly fitted to the form they produce, engineered as they are to create an image of type, in this case typewriter type. As a representation, the literal feel might be alien to the real thing: digitally produced typewriter type cannot capture the feel of ink struck against paper. The outcome does, however, fulfill the promise and capacity of the tools in use. With all due respect to Gill, I believe we can now proclaim that letters are both things and pictures of things [4.40]. This notion of "typographic pictures" is discussed further in Chapter 5.

To recognize the two-pronged materiality of typography produced in our digital age, and often for digital media, is to extract it from its exclusively print-based origins and attach it to the full potential of screen-based form and meaning. Every medium embodies some kind of "materiality," whether produced by cutting or by coding. And the means of producing physical type in different and new materials grow more sophisticated with every new software release and update.

"REAL-DEAL" AND "TOKEN" MATERIALITY

Materiality speaks directly and indirectly to our senses. We might be able to smell inked type, and, in the unusual case of edible letters [4.41], taste it, but touch and sight dominate typographic reception. We do not hear typography either. Instead we hear speech, one of the things that letters signify. As physical beings, we are familiar and quite comfortable receiving such sensory information. We are also inclined to associate information with other experiences, thoughts, and feelings.

One could argue that sumptuously engraved typography printed on creamy paper elevates the heart rate because it looks and feels so sumptuous and, well, creamy. Actually, the relative rarity and expense of fine engraving contributes to its perceived value. Engraved stock certificates assume value in relation to all the other readily available documents marking everyday transactions. Stock certificates are engraved because we associate the means and medium with high-quality production, versus what the average Joe might procure at, say, the local copy shop. Compare the materiality of pre-printed stock-certificate-like paper available in stationery stores. The typography the buyer imprints on it later may refer to all that fine printing signifies, but adding printer toner in all its ordinariness would negate our impression of the certificate as the real deal.

The materiality of type helps to establish authenticity and voice [4.42], reveals levels of craft and artfulness, and assists us in distinguishing the actual from the virtual. For instance, the logotype of a stocks and bonds company in Anchorage, printed in three colors on letterhead, probably convinces Alaskans

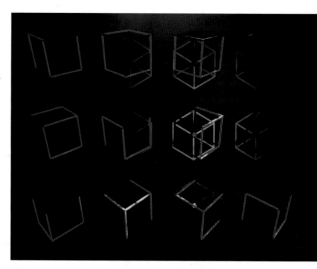

4.40 Exhibition signage for *Now and When: Australian Urbanism* at the Venice Architecture Biennale, 2010. David Pidgeon, Alex Ward, and Dean Homicki, Pidgeon. *Three-dimensional letterforms created by painting the edges of wire-frame cubes in contrasting red. The letters appear when seen from certain perspectives, and dissolve into abstract geometric forms from other perspectives. The typography's material form seems to echo digital form.*

4.41 *Chocogram*, 2007. Anne van Harte. *Photograph of chocolate letters.*

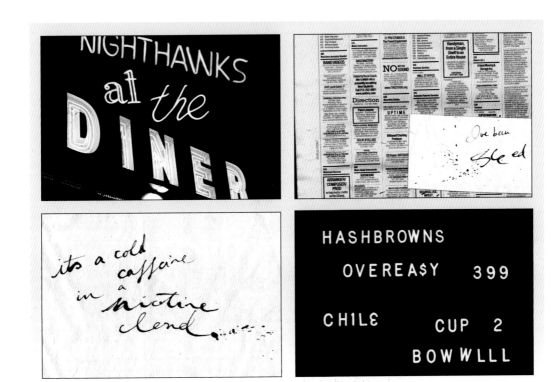

4.42 Frames from *Eggs & Sausage*, 2010. Jackie Lay. *This student video, designed to accompany the Tom Waits song "Nighthawks at the Diner," exploits token materiality to convincing effect. Typography on marquees, newspapers, menu boards, storefront signs, and napkins is drawn and animated. Yet it looks as if it was found on the mean streets of Manhattan.*

that the laser-printed text describing the state of their assets is official and legitimate. The businessman selling stocks and bonds who produces his letterhead from a dot-matrix color printer will not garner the same respect. Each artifact carries cultural connotations that are expressed through its material form.

Suppose the dot-matrix letterhead belongs to a businessman practicing in a place where dot-matrix printers are rare. Whereas someone from a big city might interpret such a letterhead as the product of an unreliable entrepreneur, a reader who hails from the same place of scarce means might perceive it to be official, very much the real deal. Alternately, suppose an Alaskan wild-berry farmer intends to sell homemade berry pies to tourists in Anchorage. Labels made on a dot-matrix printer would probably convince buyers who recognize "do-it-yourself" materials that the pies are made in a home.

Real-deal materiality relies on context to get messages across to readers. Day-glo orange injection-molded plastic spelling "Char" in a loglike typeface sitting on top of a downtown steak restaurant might communicate "we are hip" to fellow city-dwellers because the contemporary material and color are not typical of a rural lifestyle. The restaurateurs are having a bit of fun, with the expectation that their clientele appreciates cheekiness. The same typeface on the masthead of a cheaply printed newsletter called *Log Cabin Monthly* says to its readers "log cabins are our passion but our passion is not exactly lucrative." An avid cabin-lover took the time to have the thing printed; but to a schooled typographer not particularly attached to log cabins, the newsletter still registers as the product of a hobbyist, and possibly as corny or **kitsch**; in other words, the real deal. The presence of actual full-scale logs spelling "Big Lodge" at an entrance says to visitors "authentic rustic retreat." The real deal.

What if an image of the actual lodge entrance sign sits on the masthead of the lodge's website? The sign takes on token materiality by embodying the visual and sometimes behavioral attributes it enjoys in the physical world.

Typography in the digital realm with a form that references some physical state is not synonymous with "fake" or unreal. A fake connotes pretense on the part of the maker, intentional deception. Those of us accustomed to digital media comprehend that when we see the image of logs making letterforms, or when we see those presentation slides on screen looking as if they were printed on a letterpress, we are looking not at the real deal, but at a reference to it.

Token materiality is not physical, but it isn't not physical either. First, it is referring directly to its physical counterpart [4.43]. For instance, word-processing software gives the impression we are typing letters onto paper. Adding three-dimensionality to or animating type can intensify the illusion of physical materiality. Second, the screen and light and pixels that construct the illusion are subject to the same craft and communication concerns that exist in physical formats and devices. Typographers need to know an **aspect ratio** from a hole in the ground; and they need to anticipate what the medium can do. Finally, screen-based media have their own physical properties, which constitute materiality unique from those of others—actual wood pulp does not glow, for example.

Software allows (if not enforces) unprecedented precision—or even, more optimistically, perfection. On the issue of craft, Dormer speculated that in a world of perfection easily achieved, flaws might become special. That was 1997, and today his words sound prophetic. Nearly a decade ago, typographers started working more and more in real deal materiality, perhaps having grown weary of the possibilities of token materiality. A spate of letterforms constructed out of everything from sugar cubes and stitching to mold and duct tape graced posters, magazines, and other printed matter [4.44]. Concurrently, the Asif Factor (introduced earlier in this section) blossomed. New and improved filter effects, processing power, and refined techniques spawned typography made of simulated glass and rubber; of scratches, scrawls, scribbles, and scrubs. Perhaps typographers were, and are, reacting to the perfection and virtuality that proliferated and were exploited in the years following the digital revolution.

By making these distinctions between real and token materiality, and embracing "affectedness" as contemporary authenticity, I am taking the stance that all means and media are acceptable in the service of expression and communication. In the typogyroscopic realm, the question is not whether or not typographic materiality is more or less genuine or legitimate. Rather, the question is what the material message is communicating within given cultural and production contexts.

4.43 (above and opposite) Spreads from American Craft magazine, October/November 2007. Jeanette Abbink and Emily C. M. Anderson, Rational Beauty.

4.44 Promotional material for lecture series "ADC Young Guns Live," 2007. Jonathan Jackson, Jennifer Lew, and Sarah Nelson, WSDIA|WeShouldDoItAll. *The title typography is made with brown fabric, stuffed with cotton. The designers dubbed the typeface "Gotham Stuffed."*

STORY BY
Sabrina Gschwandtner

LETTERING PHOTO BY
M-36

LET 'EM EAT CAKE

"I believe the simple act of making something, anything, with your hands is a quiet political ripple in a world dominated by mass production... and people choosing to make something themselves will turn those small ripples into giant waves."—Faythe Levine

PROMPTS

/// **In an online image-search engine**, search for images evocative of the typesetting revolutions discussed in this chapter: (1) hand typesetting; (2) machine typesetting; (3) phototypesetting; (4) digital typesetting. Select a few images from the results of each search to inspire a short story, brief essay, or poem that imagines the conditions of production. *(See "The Four Typesetting Revolutions," page 164.)*

/// **During the next sporting event** you attend, or watch on television, tally the number and describe the kinds of different artifacts and devices you see that deliver typographic messages: held in the hands of people sitting in the stands; dispersed on concession stands, on the field, and in its environs; worn by fans, players, and officials. *(See "The Means of Delivery," page 169.)*

/// **With a couple of classmates**, select some typefaces from online foundries. Brainstorm together on tools, means, and media that would be fit, and thoroughly unfit, for constructing or drawing those typefaces.

Then, just for fun, try to make the letterforms in the unfit way. *(See "The Means and the Ends," page 175.)*

/// **Locate a sign**, or a cluster of signs, that uses light-on and/or light-within media. Create a "day/night in the life" photo-essay of the sign(s), focusing on the materials and how the text in the signs changes character, however slightly, throughout the day. *(See "Light On, Light Within, and Light Essence," page 178.)*

/// **Build a digital image library** of typography you and your classmates find in the environment, then categorize by material—paint, clay, metal, stone, wood, plastic, glass, fibers and fabric, paper, organic (natural). Caption each image with the connotative qualities that the material brings to the text. *(See "Materiality and Message," page 180.)*

/// **Hold a class competition** where teams try to collect the greatest number of typographic examples that demonstrate the "Asif Factor." *(See "Authentic Typography and the "Asif Factor,"" page 182).*

language

systems 5

Chapter 5 introduces some components of visual language, including hierarchical syntax, visual irony, and simile. A section on consonance and dissonance introduces the ways typographers manipulate meaning through form to particularize messages—whether the typography is readable as text or is readable only as image. The chapter lays out a range of visual styles and how they function rhetorically—that is, the ways in which you will employ style as a tactic to inform, persuade, and engage readers. The concluding section focuses on message systems: how different uses and contexts shift the meaning of visual language over time, and therefore its rhetorical power; and how visual rhetoric is put to use in identity and symbol systems.

primer

ABSTRACT

A quality or characteristic apart from concrete experience. Typographic form can suggest abstract ideas. For example, typographic compositions can be "formal" or "playful" through arrangement alone. Abstraction in design refers to non-representational form that bears no physical resemblance to people, objects, or places. The letters of the alphabet in phonetic languages (such as English), for example, are unlike the pictorial characters in ideographic languages (like Chinese). They are visual abstractions that, when combined, represent sounds in spoken language. **ILL. 01 > PAGE 202**

AMBIGUITY

The ability of typography to express more than one possible meaning or to invite inference beyond the literal meaning of the word. **> PAGE 215**

APPROPRIATION

The act of borrowing form from one context and repurposing it for another. **> PAGE 204**

CLICHÉ

A visual or verbal expression that has lost its meaning through overuse. **ILL. 02 > PAGE 211**

CODIFY

To reduce to a code or an accepted set of principles or rules. Typographic conventions are those formal arrangements that readers expect, such as the hierarchical arrangement of title, author, and publisher on the title page of a book, or the use of serif typefaces to communicate "tradition." **> PAGE 208**

FLOURISH

Any kind of decorative elongation of serifs or strokes, including swashes. Flourishes add expression and calligraphic references to roman and italic variations of a typeface family. In an OpenType font, flourish letterforms can appear as additional glyphs in a typeface, or as their own file. **ILL. 03 > PAGE 219**

GENRE

Any category of form or content that is defined by its style or structure. Documentary is a film genre and signage is a typographic genre, typically defined by a designer's concern for simplicity and legibility. **> PAGE 212**

IRONY

A rhetorical form in which the visual or verbal statement means exactly the opposite of what it says. Setting the words "big idea" in very small type or the *New York Times* in Comic Sans would be ironic. **> PAGE 203**

LIGATURE

A single typographic character combining two or more letters. **ILL. 04 > PAGE 219**

01 : ABSTRACT

FROM THE OFFICE OF

02 : CLICHÉ

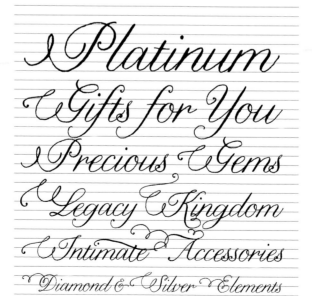

Platinum
Gifts for You
Precious Gems
Legacy Kingdom
Intimate Accessories
Diamond & Silver Elements

03 : FLOURISH

METAPHOR

A figure of speech that draws a comparison or an analogy between two seemingly unlike things that actually have something in common. Through its style or treatment, dynamic typography often refers to things that expand the literal meaning of words. **> PAGE 195**

METONYMY

A figure of speech in which one thing is substituted for another that is related to it through association. In typography, the word "rustic" set in a typeface that looks like logs compares the word to rough wood or the forest, which is a naturalized association. **> PAGE 201**

MIMETIC

Characterized by imitation or mimicry. For example, the page-turning behavior of an e-reader mimics a physical book. Physically, the computer tablet is nothing like a book: text and image are not printed on paper and actions are created by mathematical code. Because the electronic page behaves like a real book, many people are more comfortable with reading in this format than through the typical scrolling behavior of the computer. The French poet Guillaume Apollinaire created typographic compositions that mimicked sensory experience. His "calligramme" of 1918 titled "Il Pleut" ("It's Raining") reflects its topic. **ILL. 05 > PAGE 206**

04 : LIGATURE

05 : MIMETIC

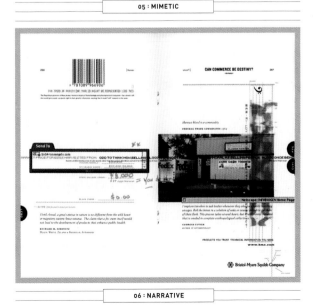

06 : NARRATIVE

NARRATIVE

The telling of a story with a beginning, middle, and end. Typographically, narrative unfolds across time in a book, film, or dynamic medium, and follows a linear structure for the visual sequencing of episodes or events. **ILL. 06 > PAGE 195**

REFERENT

The thing that a word or sign stands for. **> PAGE 203**

REPRESENTATION

Something that expresses or stands for something else that originated in another form. The strokes in letterforms, for example, represent the hand gestures necessary to make the form. A map represents landmass configurations, paths, and destinations, or the physical activities necessary to travel from one place to another. **ILL. 07 > PAGE 214**

RHETORIC

The art of argumentation and discourse. Rhetorical analysis has, since the time of the ancient Greek philosopher Aristotle, looked at the logic of the argument (*logos*); the character of the speaker as revealed by his or her language and reputation (*ethos*); and the emotional appeal (*pathos*). Layout and typographic choices produce similar outcomes: typography can be straightforward and "speak" with authority, or be personal and "shout" with emotion. **> PAGE 204**

SEMANTIC

Refers to the meaning of words or other symbols. Syntax refers to the ordering of words and symbols and pragmatics refers to their context of use. Meaning, therefore, is established by the interplay of these three factors. **> PAGE 196**

SIMILE

A figure of speech used to embellish or refine meaning, in which one thing or idea is compared to another thing or idea. In typography, the choice of a typeface can employ simile: the word "heavy" set in an angular machine-like typeface refines the message to communicate "heavy like a machine." The word set in a plump, round typeface might particularize the word to mean "heavy like a dumpling." **ILL. 08 > PAGE 201**

SYNECDOCHE

A figure of speech in which a part is used to represent the whole or the whole is used to represent a part. The phrase "Madison Avenue," for example, stands for the advertising industry even though it is only the New York street address where some agencies are located. A logo for a delivery company may be a parcel tied with string, even though the company delivers many different kinds of package. **> PAGE 201**

TROPE

Figurative language (see metaphor, metonymy, synecdoche, and irony) that is used as a substitution for or expansion of literal description. Typography, in a literal sense, links a word with its dictionary meaning, but it is also figurative in that specific choices about typeface and arrangement on the page can influence its interpretation. **ILL. 11 > PAGE 201**

07 : REPRESENTATION

08 : SIMILE

09 : VERNACULAR

10 : VERNACULAR

VERNACULAR

The everyday language of a specific population or context. According to twentieth-century modernism the goal of typography was to be the neutral carrier of literal meaning. Following the publication of the architect Robert Venturi's *Complexity and Contradiction in Architecture* (1966) and his *Learning from Las Vegas* (1972), later design questioned the authority of rules-based practices, deriving inspiration from forms found in the common culture instead. Such design asserted the value of style in communicating something about culture and context. Designers were attracted to the vernacular typography produced by people not trained in design. They drew on such work as visual criticism of the highly codified forms of modernism. In some cases, the use of these references reinforced literal messages and suggested a particular context or time. In other instances, vernacular form played the role of decentering literal meaning, of introducing typographic elements or styles from outside typical associations with the intended meaning. Student work at Cranbrook Academy of Art and California Institute of the Arts explored such repurposing of vernacular form; the typography recalls places, times, and cultures other than the literal meaning of the text. **ILLS. 09/10 > PAGE 210**

HYPERBOLE
Overstating to reinforce the importance of the subject.
This sale is *really* big.

BIG SALE

IRONY
Representing the subject in terms opposite to its meaning, often for comic effect. The rhetorical strength of all tropes depends upon reader understanding of subject meaning and the context of use. Reproducing the words "Print is Dead" in print adds to the irony.

PRINT IS DEAD

oh joy.

UNDERSTATEMENT
Representing the subject in terms that are less forceful than the subject merits.

Cancer
claimed over one-and-a-half million
American lives in 2011.
Make a difference in 2014.
Support cancer research.

ALLUSION
Referencing a style to evoke connotations associated with that style.

ART WANTED
WORKS IN ALL MEDIA
Will Be Culled From Every Continent
GLOBAL EXHIBITION
DETAILS & SUBMISSION INFO @
www.globexhib.org

YESTERDAY'S BAGELS

SIMILE
Comparing qualities to something outside the subject to specify a connotation. Letters that look as if they are hewn from rock compare yesterday's bagels to hard stone.

SUNRISE CAMP

METONYMY
Representing the subject by way of things affiliated with the subject. We readily associate campsites with mountain settings, which include trees. Common use of log-like typefaces for campsite graphics further grounds the meaning.

U.S. PRESENCE

SYNECDOCHE
Representing the whole of the subject with an essential part. "U.S." is a linguistic synecdoche: inititials stand in for "United States." The typeface Stencil is a visual synecdoche: it is recognizable as a typeface used to identify U.S. Army property.

///////////////////////////// SAYING AND PLAYING

Diner. The neon letters prefigure a no-frills meal served up quickly and cheaply. The menu tucked behind napkin holders on tables confirms it, as do the names embroidered on the blouses of servers.

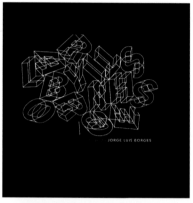

Logotypes and text printed on placemats and condiment labels speak to us, gesturing quietly or excitedly to emote, characterize, justify. The experience is practically theatrical, bursting with expression—even if it is just to identify humble sugar and ketchup.

Letters and words dressed in typography are minor and major players—actors who, under a typographer's direction, enter on cue and perform lines upstage or down, standing or pacing. Words carry visible tones and inflections, conveying deadpan wit or peerless elegance or supercilious arrogance, each interacting with the other while enacting a story.

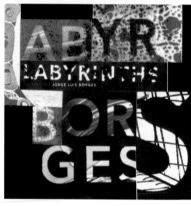

Typographers assign roles and expressions to text to act out simple punchlines or epic musicals. To think of text as vital typographic players with parts to enact, rather than aloof design elements, is to confront a few complications. First there is the likelihood that our actors will initially sit inexpressively like lumps of dumb matter, or run about willy-nilly unsure what to do. That's okay. It's not opening night. Second, a slew of decisions needs to be made before the final performance. When will the players enter and exit? Where will they stand? Will they shout, or speak softly? And how will they be adorned? These and a host of other details can make all the difference between a lackluster and an irresistible production. Third, while the script—the content—guides choices and dictates which letters must be onstage and when, in the end it is up to the typographer to interpret and give form to the words [5.1].

5.1 *(above and opposite, above)* Covers for *Labyrinths* by Jorge Luis Borges, 2007. Anne Jordan, Hypothesis.

5.2 *(below and opposite, below)* Storefront sign in Burlington, VT.

Consider, as an example, a little skit wherein the anagrams "Henry's Diner" and "Nerdy Shrine" serve as the script [5.2]. Dressed in 12 pt Courier Bold and the color red, the words take on one kind of persona. Not a terribly eloquent one, granted. We can alter the quality of the performance, though, which will affect meaning. We assign the actors postures and gestures that register personalities and relationships of finer distinction. We can spotlight certain parts in ways that alter reading order and emphasis. We clothe the content in typefaces and materials that add connotations of fanciness, comfort, seriousness, roughness, and so on. And we can distribute color and adjust weights such that some words become more central to the plot than others, or activate specific associations. Each choice manifests a different interpretation of the very same script.

Recall that letterforms are the parts that typographic actors employ to add nuance, much as rolling eyes would add a touch of irritation to the words "enough with the stage **metaphor** already." To consider solely the whole of words, at the expense of the individual letterforms, is to overlook the crucial role details play in particularizing the larger action. Serifs, weights, and curves wield communicative power in the way that a finger, a minor part in relation to the body, can point resolutely in condemnation or curl flirtatiously. These minutiae are the sort of thing type designers agonize over, and which typographers employ with deliberate intent. Conversely, were we to focus on the parts and their individual behaviors to the exclusion of the whole, we would risk a bunch of unrelated bits twittering and fidgeting with little to show in the way of an interpretable message.

Grids and hierarchy set up positions and cues on our metaphorical stage to deliver more complex, and longer, **narratives**. Organization and pacing establish the scenes for scripts of many parts that require extensive space, and that are drawn out over time. Texts that share formal qualities might speak across compositions and pages, connecting ideas or strengthening overarching themes. Some texts might step forward in the middle of the action, while others withdraw, awaiting attention.

Visualized words exploit the interplay between what is written and the way what is written is "performed." Whether shrieking on a neon sign outside a diner, or speaking a soliloquy, modulated and strategically placed elements set up relationships as stories play out. Okay. Enough. Like a character in the final scene of a Greek tragedy, this metaphor is now, officially, dead.

RHETORICALLY SPEAKING ////////////////////////////////

Choosing the precise word or series of words to express an idea or argue a point is a delicate matter. For instance, back in Chapter 2, I wrote "I love jam" to demonstrate how word sequences—or grammatical syntax—dictate meaning. I will now refine the statement to say "I idolize jam." By choosing "idolize" rather than any number of other options (adore, cherish, prize, and so on), I am attempting to express my thoughts more precisely. I idolize jam, and any person hearing me say that would have to accept my statement as true for lack of evidence to the contrary.

Henry's Diner
Nerdy Shrine

Had I written "jam can be enjoyed only with ham," my statement would rightly be taken as assertion rather than personal expression, and not necessarily accepted as true, unless someone already agrees. If he doesn't agree, or has no opinion on the subject, and if I want to convince him how necessary ham is to jam, I need to stage an argument. I would need to persuade him. For that I would employ rhetorical tactics, decide which words to write and which points to emphasize in what sequence, and determine the style of delivery that would all serve to convince my reader.

Similarly, the play between what is read and what is seen constructs every class of message, from brief declarations, like advertising headlines or blurbs, to longer narratives, such as book chapters or newspapers. Choosing typefaces and sizes, formats and materials, and all manner of other choices layer meaning upon the content to help position the message.

Some texts are pronouncements. One-liners on billboards and signs, or logotypes that declare company names on stationery, succinctly capture one idea or a cluster of simple ideas [5.3]. The words tend to deliver uncomplicated and generalized statements, more along the lines of a cursory remark. Inserting a visual stance—adding expressive visual character—is often key to stabilizing the meaning of such words. The word "turn," for instance, connotes anything from twisting to transformation. Suppose the word is the name of a company. Let's say it is a business selling computer systems that track advertising responses. To fix the connotation of the word, a designer will need to take a **semantic** stance. The letters might be formed from geometric and angled shapes that appear to fold in and out as if made of paper strips. "Turn" now connotes printed advertising, perhaps, or information [5.4].

5.3   Packaging for Smile! cider, 2002. Hålean Schallinger and Jörgen Olofsson, Amore.

As typographic elements multiply, the plot, as it were, thickens. More complicated narratives written by an author or a <u>copywriter</u> argue topics and describe events at greater and varying length. A lot of the rhetorical work, then, is accomplished by the written text. Textbooks and online news journals that deliver instructions and stories deliver the voices of <u>exposition</u> or <u>reportage</u>, to position the content as believable and, of course, to hold the attention of their targeted readers. A typographer will assign formal qualities that both mirror the writer's intentions and fulfill the reader's expectations for such writing. She might choose credible-looking typefaces and a grid structure and hierarchy that are already familiar to readers. Just as the writing sets out to persuade readers of the reliable nature of the content, so does the typography. Visual interpretations are rhetorical in the way they corroborate, expand, and sometimes contradict the meaning of content [5.5]. The tactics are intentional, and learned.

VISUAL SEMANTICS AND SYNTAX

In the attempt to make sense of how human speech and writing function, the study of linguistics has established terms for describing the dynamics of language. It is not uncommon to borrow these principles from linguistics to analyze "visual language." While I intend to do the same, I do so uneasily. The principles, applied to typography, are at best rickety analogies. For lack of an

Copywriter

A professional writer hired to write text (copy) for advertising and promotional material.

Exposition

A written work in the "expository prose" style that aims to explain and analyze a subject with precision and clarity using facts, details, opinions, and examples.

Reportage

A writing style typically employed for news reporting, but the term can refer to any writing that aims to offer objective descriptions of events.

5.4   Logotype design. *Two variations on the word "turn": the first version, a static form, connotes a shifting path; the second version, a dynamic form, connotes rotation and transformation.*

5.5 *Political Climate*, 2010. David Albertson and Paul Torres, Albertson Design. *Magazine illustration.*

5.6 *James Levine: 40 Years*, 2011. Nathan Stock, AdamsMorioka. *Book design for the Metropolitan Opera.*

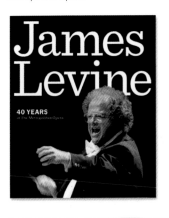

alternative, I will persist because, like speakers and writers, typographers manipulate their specialty language in order to communicate.

The meaning of words, as well as of typographic style, is referred to as semantics, and concerns how people understand and use signs, symbols, and style. The arrangement of words and sentences is syntax, which was introduced in Chapter 2. The relationships among words, and typographic elements, yield meaning because they submit to certain rules of order understood by people who share the language. A third branch of linguistics, pragmatics, describes how people understand (or not) what is being said or written, and does not concern the language of typography. So we will focus on visual semantic and syntactic parallels to verbal language.

semantics and syntax

Designers encode content with visual style and voice—the semantics in typography—and readers decode their connotative properties. As with all things typogyroscopic, sometimes this equation is straightforward, and sometimes it is more complex.

The commemorative book at left illustrates a straightforward example of semantics [5.6]. The cover design pairs an image of the energetic James Levine conducting with an equally assertive title that fills half of the composition. The typeface <u>Clarendon</u>, set in upper- and lowercase letters, takes the semantic stance that Levine, the famous conductor, is grand yet not stuffy, formidable yet accessible. Compare this stance to one inside the book, where a paragraph in which Levine humbly recalls his tenure with the Metropolitan Opera is placed at a respectful distance

Clarendon

Robert Besley designed the original decorative, slab-serif typeface, for which he acquired a patent. The English foundry Thorowgood & Co. first released the typeface in 1845 and it has been perennially popular. The original design has since been imitated, redrawn, digitized, and issued under various names.

from an image of the conductor looking intently at the reader. Here the focus is on Levine, the man. Content and semantics coalesce to represent and embody the position of the work [5.7].

As another example, because a serious newspaper is not a tabloid, a typographer would not style the newspaper to look like one. In order to function as credible journalism, the visual delivery must conform to semantic conventions—in this case, clear but not garish hierarchy, understated typefaces, and so on. Let's say a tabloid publisher wants to alter how readers perceive his stories, so he asks a designer to select typefaces and typographic relationships that resemble the *Chicago Tribune*. First of all, the sensationalistic headlines would prove the tactic a failure, or at best, indicate playful allusion to serious journalism. Unfortunately, too, readers wanting gossip would question the tabloid's commitment to serving it up. Similarly, the *Wall Street Journal* set in Curlz would hardly inspire confidence in its journalistic integrity.

We might be able to conceive of typography that willfully ignores or misapplies culturally understood semantics. For instance, one could design fertilizer packaging to look like laundry detergent. Such discordant typography might be confusing to readers, but because they invariably attempt to construct meaning from the things they encounter, and because this particular artifact appears to be produced by a business or institutional entity, readers will surmise that the typography looks the way it does for some good reason.

The designer of a series of postcard announcements for an art-school event opted to set the words "Open" and "Welcome" in the popular style of retail door signs [5.8]. Coupling this "low-brow" form with terse but vague words might seem an odd choice to express an event at an elite private art school (as compared to applying the style and voice to a retail store). The designer may have decided on boldly staged but ambiguous words to stir the targeted reader's curiosity. Although the message is initially unclear, the secondary text clarifies it. Readers quickly add up the pieces to learn, first, that the event is an open house, which justifies a word like "Open." When readers discover

Curlz

As the name implies, Curlz is a whimsical typeface that sports curly details and bounces up and down on its baseline. Designed by Carl Crossgrove and Steve Matteson, the font was released in 1995 by Monotype and is very popular in desktop publishing.

5.7 Product design, 2008. Jason Schulte, Jill Robertson, Rob Alexander, Will Ecke, Gaelyn Mangrum, and Jeff Bucholtz, Office. *This collection of fictional products is sold in a "pirate supply" store that fronts 826 Valencia, a tutoring center in San Francisco. The design and writing use humor to entertain and persuade, playing on people's knowledge of pirate archetypes. All proceeds benefit 826 Valencia's writing programs, which adds to the rhetorical strength of the design.*

5.8 Advertising postcards for California College of the Arts open studios, 2009. Jon Sueda, Stripe.

that the event is hosted by an art school, they might deduce that the style and voice are elements of a creative and playful pun.

If text is meant to be read and understood, then typographic syntax—the arrangement of the words—must somehow correspond with linguistic syntax. Fairly straightforward, but not as inflexible as it might seem. Typographers modulate this order through visual composition. For instance, thoughtful use of hierarchical relationships allows us to diverge from linguistic syntax. The open house postcards might logically have presented the information in order of standard importance: the event title at the top of the composition in large, clear type, then the date and time, and finally the name of the school. The designer instead used hierarchy to configure a slightly different order. The first-level reading is "Open." The second-level reading is "Open House." And the third and final reading explains where and when the event takes place. The rhetorical stance is celebratory, which is possibly a more persuasive argument than listing the facts.

the semantics and syntax of hierarchy

Previous chapters have discussed hierarchy in a variety of ways: how spatial relationships and human perception set the precedent for interpreting two-dimensional reading orders; how word order affects reading and comprehension; and how pattern and variation within compositions generate hierarchies. Here we focus on hierarchy in relation to semantic and syntactic dynamics.

Consider the textual syntax of a simple book cover: title, author, publishing house [5.9]. We tend to think of book-cover text in precisely this order. The title—say, *A Handlist of Rhetorical Terms*—identifies what the object is (a book), and in this instance describes the content. Since books are all about their content, a prominent title makes sense. The author's name, Richard A. Lanham, follows the title because he wrote the book. The publisher's name is third because University of California Press paid to print and distribute this particular book, and so wants to link it to their other publishing successes right up front. This is not only a semantic but also a syntactical convention. We have seen it hundreds of times: the title placed topmost on the cover; the author placed lower in the composition; the publishing house typeset across the very bottom. First. Second. Third. In emphatically descending order.

Imagine the same three texts typeset each to a line, in one typeface at one size, still in their same order. This basic hierarchy tells of a straight-ahead book to which the content, author, and publisher share equal claim. If we change the visual order without touching the textual order—say we set Lanham's name in the largest size and heaviest weight possible—the visual syntax now begins with the author, which means he is a very important scholar, even though his name is placed after the title [5.10]. Moving the name above the title in such grand terms might indicate that he is a super rock-star scholar, but for the moment we won't add that complication. Let's try shrinking the author back down to size, and scale the title up to fill the upper half of the composition. Now the meaning changes to an author of nominal consequence who has

**A HANDLIST OF
RHETORICAL
TERMS**

Richard A. Lanham

UNIVERSITY PRESS

A HANDLIST OF RHETORICAL TERMS

RICHARD A. LANHAM

UNIVERSITY PRESS

5.9 Hierarchy demonstrated with mocked-up covers for *A Handlist of Rhetorical Terms* by Richard A. Lanham.

incidentally written a book chock-full of enormously useful terms. Next, set the publisher name in a typeface and weight that is much bolder than the treatment of the author's name. What is the publisher saying?

Text placement and word emphasis are just two examples of strategies that affect meaning. A table of contents, for instance, has a set of conventions that signify what it is, semantically and syntactically speaking. Restructuring standard hierarchies can add meaning, or cause it to shift. The contents page for an edition of *The Mechanical Bride* published in 1951 "reads" like an index to a book, owing to the structure and its lack of hierarchical contrast [5.11]. Both treatments are uncommon for contents pages. The tribute volume to the conductor James Levine lists articles under large numbers that represent the decades covered in the book, accentuating time periods through form, and therefore setting up relationships that give prominence to the decades [5.12].

Dynamic type on screen multiplies the syntactical, hierarchical, and therefore semantic possibilities because the variables of time, behavior, and duration complement those of scale, weight, and placement. Not every word needs to be on screen at the same time. It would seem that the linear order of appearance, then, determines hierarchy, presuming each element remains on screen for the same length of time, and behaves similarly. Let's return to *A Handlist of Rhetorical Terms*. The title might enter the screen initially (first level of hierarchy), followed by subsequent text, which comes and goes in the same order that appears on the book cover. In this context, the importance of the title is actually diminished because, by the end of the sequence, the title is the farthest element from a reader's attention.

Time in dynamic media equals distance between elements on the printed page. The longer the interval between the first and last text on screen, the further the first moves down in hierarchy, so the first becomes the last. If the textual order is reversed, beginning with the publisher and ending with the title, then the hierarchy mirrors that of the book cover.

We might also maintain the order and change the duration of each element on screen, or vary the behavior of each. Let's say the author's name swells into view over a five-second span

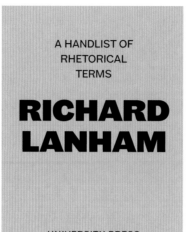

A HANDLIST OF RHETORICAL TERMS

RICHARD LANHAM

UNIVERSITY PRESS

A HANDLIST OF RHETORICAL TERMS
Richard A. Lanham

UNIVERSITY PRESS

Contents

5.10 *(opposite, top)* Hierarchy demonstrated with mocked-up covers for *A Handlist of Rhetorical Terms* by Richard A. Lanham.

5.11 *(opposite, center)* Contents page for *The Mechanical Bride* by Marshall McLuhan, 1951. Ernst Reichl.

5.12 *(opposite, bottom)* Contents page for *James Levine: 40 Years*, 2011. Nathan Stock, AdamsMorioka.

5.13 *(below) Ride*, 2010. Rob Draper. Ink on paper. *This drawing of the word "ride" alludes to the style of decorative letters hand-painted on customized cars. The word ride is sometimes used to refer to one's car. "Nice ride" can mean "nice car." The style connotes "cool" or "custom."*

of time, then is replaced by the title for three seconds, which is in turn replaced by the publisher's logotype. Temporal, hierarchical syntax now communicates that the title and author are important, but not as central as the publisher. The author, Lanham, is not so happy with this arrangement. Instead, the publisher's logotype fades in and stays on screen first; then letters of the title dance in from all sides and settle in proper sequence below the logotype; and finally the author's name drops like a ton of books, obscuring the other two texts. Has the meaning changed? (That's a rhetorical question.)

RHETORICAL TROPES

Spoken and written forms of language are relatively imprecise. In isolation, nouns and verbs are not all that descriptive. The word "ride," for instance, will conjure as many images as there are people who read the word [5.13]. We add adjectives, adverbs, and synonyms to bolster words against the fickle winds of connotation. For instance, if I want to describe the way in which a shopping bag swings, I would not say, "the shopping bag swung from his arm like a shopping bag." I would pinpoint meaning by comparing the bag to something it is like: invoke the qualities of other things to express in more exact terms what I want understood. The statement "the shopping bag swung like an iron pendulum" uses comparison to describe what the swing is like. Now the bag sways portentously, suggesting it probably does not contain new socks, but rather something more menacing.

If spoken and written language is wobbly, then visual typographic language is utterly unstable and fuzzy without the help of modifiers. And so typographers attempt to stabilize and focus messages using **tropes** similar to those that writers employ to particularize written language. Such rhetorical tropes as **synecdoche**, **metonymy**, **simile**, and metaphor originate in writing, but are useful to help us understand the many ways typographic form interacts with content.

synecdoche, metonymy, simile, metaphor

An updated identity for the retailer Saks Fifth Avenue divides the confining square of the store's logotype into sixty-four parts, which are then scrambled and applied to shopping bags as cropped letterforms in various combinations [5.14]. The bag design uses visual synecdoche—a trope in which a single characteristic means, or refers to, the whole kit and caboodle. In this case, parts of the logotype stand in for the full Saks Fifth Avenue logotype. Critical to effective description in using synecdoche is that the part selected to represent the whole be an essential one. For instance, the bag could have been designed as a black square. Although an important aspect of the logotype, it is not, however, as essential to the Saks identity as are the curvaceous script forms in stark black-and-white contrast.

The American Poets Project is a book series that presents "the most significant American poetry, selected and introduced by today's most discerning poets and critics." The book covers join the first letter of each author's surname to form an **abstract** typographic image, resulting in a hybrid monogram [5.15]. The synecdochic use of letterforms rhetorically presents the writers as the most significant feature of the volumes. Authors' full names are also typeset on the covers, so the synecdoche does not completely stand in for the whole, as do the Saks cropped letterforms. In the context of the series (about thirty titles), however, the monograms satisfactorily identify the entire project.

Another book jacket, for *The Druid King*, renders words in sticks from trees [5.16]. Trees or forests happen to be forms of nature the Celtic druids worshiped, so the designer has added a level of specificity to the words by way of metonymy. Metonymy makes associations to things that are affiliated with the subject, but that are not part of the denotative or connotative meanings of the word. The awkward assembly of the letters suggests things cultish or secretive. Try to envision the same words constructed from popsicle sticks. The reader might interpret that the story is about a popsicle vendor who fancies himself as a mystic.

The associative power of metonymy particularizes, amplifies, and sometimes adds to meaning by way of contiguity—the reference is connected to the subject because of some previous association. In this case, druids worshiped trees, so the designer had the idea to render the words in sticks from trees. Simile, by contrast, connects through analogy, locating comparable aspects between the subject and previously unassociated things. Dynamic media employ similes regularly: imagine words bouncing like a ball. Analogy juxtaposes the subject to things that describe like qualities. Were that shopping bag to swing like a popsicle, readers would be confused. Popsicles are icy, drippy, and sweet. None of these characteristics are shared with a swinging bag. Whereas metonymy requires

some adjoining association, simile allows comparison to anything, as long as the selection is based on comprehensible, parallel properties.

Similes present both the subject and the thing it is being compared to. "Mornings are like new buds." In other words, two distinct things (mornings and buds) interact in the same scene. In typography, the textual meaning is one distinct thing, and the letterform meaning is another. The two interact to create visual simile. A logotype set in cloudlike letterforms for a fabric softener called Drift essentially states that the product is like clouds [5.17]. (Comparisons to tumbleweeds would probably not have been rhetorically wise.) Drift set in a more standard typeface, paired with a photograph of clouds, sets up a comparison between the word "drift" and clouds. Here the word provides the context for understanding which aspect of clouds is being compared—the

5.14 *(opposite, left and center)* Identity for Saks Fifth Avenue, 2006. Michael Bierut, Pentagram.

5.15 *(opposite, below)* Book covers for American Poets Project, 2003–7. Chip Kidd and Mark Melnick.

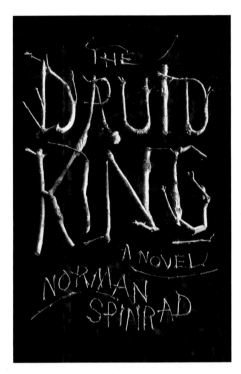

lightness and airiness of clouds versus their whiteness. If the word was "bright," then the whiteness of the cloud would be the dominant comparison.

Metaphors are relatives of similes in that they compare one thing to another. But metaphors do so by replacing denotative words with the comparison. Rather than say "I wake up early every morning," we could use the metaphor "I'm an early bird." A metamorphosis takes place wherein the subject is turned into something else.

In typography, utter replacement is difficult if not impossible to achieve. For instance, if the word "Clouds" replaces the word Drift, the subject of the communication disappears. The marketing director (who paid experts handsomely to come up with a winning name) will just read "Clouds." Not good. The connotation might sufficiently communicate airiness, cleanliness, and freshness—but the valued product name is conspicuously missing. Thinking forward to the buyer, a product named "Clouds" will never be interpreted as a product named "Drift."

Metaphors might occur in dynamic media because the latter are time-based, so a literal metamorphosis from one subject to its comparison is possible. Say Drift floats across the screen in a television spot, and dissolves quickly into footage of slow-moving clouds. For the duration of the sequence, clouds will be associated with the name even though they are not on screen at the same time.

Because metaphors replace the subject, it may be safe to assert that static typography does not employ metaphors. But the use of synecdoche, metonymy, and simile is quite common. Other tropes introduce yet more rhetorical possibilities.

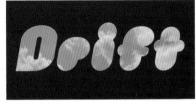

5.16 *(top)* Cover for *The Druid King* by Norman Spinrad, 2003. Stephen Doyle.

5.17 *(above)* Visual similes (top row) and unsuccessful metaphor (bottom row).

more rhetorical tactics

A few other rhetorical tactics, or tropes, are used frequently in typography, namely **irony**, allusion, hyperbole, and understatement. Let's look at each as they are used typographically. Take note that each tactic relies on a reader's knowledge of precedents and contexts, whether tacit or explicit.

Irony is the device that uses words to convey the direct opposite of their apparent meaning. Ironic typography plays the content (the word) against the form of the word to create contradiction or discordance [5.18].

Allusion is a form of metonymy in that it usually refers indirectly to a person, place, or event. Typographic allusions typically refer to a style or format from a previous era, styles established by other designers, and/or physical characteristics of people, places, and things [5.19]. Allusions are not wholesale stylistic copies or renderings. They isolate aspects of the **referent**

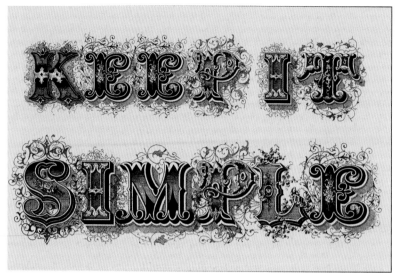

5.18 (*left*) *Simple* (limited-edition print), 2009. Seb Lester.

5.19 (*below*) Kicksology business cards. Carlos Segura.

5.20 (*bottom*) Nellie's Nuggets packaging. Batten Industries.

style to help situate content and particularize its meaning [5.20]. When designers blatantly imitate a style, they may aim to parody or satirize a subject, or may be paying homage to an honored, inimitable predecessor. To steal the style of a particular historical designer flagrantly is **appropriation**, if done with rhetorical purpose (discussed later in this chapter). If not, it's just plagiarism.

Hyperbole is the use of deliberate overstatement or exaggeration for emphasis. Hyperbole in typography tends to be playful, making light of the content, or comic: hugely scaled or overwrought letterforms making dubious claims to epic status. Hyperbole is sometimes deployed to convince a reader of a subject's supposed grandness; if, however, the subject is indeed grand, hyperbolic treatment might be redundant, which would entirely deflate the meaning rather than accentuate it.

Writers or speakers use understatement to downplay the seriousness of a statement. Subtle, minimal, tasteful typography is often called "understated," which is a sort of rhetorical stance, although not exactly "understatement" [5.21]. Consider a small title stamped along the spine of a modestly sized book—say, Jean-Paul Sartre's *Nausea*. The text is set in 16 pt bold sans-serif caps, open letterspaced, and perfectly centered and balanced. Given the gravity of the content, we could interpret this treatment as an understatement; that is, if we did not know the volume is one of the New Classics series from New Directions publishers. In this context the understated type reveals a precedent: the visual **rhetoric** of classic book design, which helps communicate high seriousness. Similarly, tasteful and understated typography for luxury items and couture labels flaunts importance and refinement, which is the opposite of understatement.

The use of tropes greatly expands the range of communication that is possible when textual language meets with the language of typographic form. This relationship is compounded as typographers insert rhetorical stances that mirror and expand upon textual meaning.

CONSONANCE AND DISCORDANCE

Typographers routinely choose styles to match the content at hand. Appropriate typefaces and structures are sympathetic to and confirm the denotations and connotations of the written text [5.22]. For example, the word "modernism" typeset in Helvetica communicates, broadly, "an art and design philosophy characterized by economy of form relative to means and function," owing to its history and earned reputation. The formal connotations bear out those of the concept of modernism by declaring "modernism looks thus." Judging whether or not typography *Works* usually includes the criterion of consonance.

Although a writer's carefully crafted words tend to drive the reader's interpretation of his text, particularly in longer narratives, typography might also be designed discordantly to assist in conveying meaning. "Modernism" drawn in speed-metal letterforms transforms the word into humorous irony, saying something to the effect of "modernism looks thus, and I dare you to

5.21 *(top)* Reusable glass water bottle, 2009. Adam Maclean.

5.22 *(above)* Crosswalk, 2007. Draftfcb Portugal.

5.23 *(below)* *Modernism Backdrop*, 1998. Marieke Stolk, Erwin Brinkers, and Danny Van Den Dungen, Experimental Jetset.

argue otherwise." Or maybe, "modernism rocks" [5.23]. Whatever the case, we might add meaning in contrast to, or in conflict with, what words mean. Whereas consonance mirrors and adds shades of meaning to written words, discordance shifts the meaning of the written words toward additional or other meanings.

We can easily understand why typographers might design in consonance. If words mean something in particular, it stands to reason that the visual form should follow suit. Why on earth would typographers design in discordance, then? Recall that such tropes as simile (the comparison of one thing to an unrelated thing) and irony (stating the opposite of what one means) help to sharpen meaning. On the surface some formal language might appear discordant, yet the discordance is in fact telling a new story. Because typography is a human-constructed language, it enjoys a range of expression similar to written language. Abstract letterforms compel us to make some associations, but tropes add layers to heighten the meaning of the story.

statement. A reader unacquainted with the brand who spots the bag in the hand of someone walking up Fifth Avenue will not be able to decipher the marks. But she will "read" them as an abstract, and ideally a compelling, image. Then, when she arrives at the 49th Street store to see the logotype, she will make the connection, and from then on, every such bag she encounters will communicate "Saks Fifth Avenue."

Context, then, imbues abstract typography with meaning, whether the type is seen or read. The four extremes of expression—abstract, mimetic, readable as text, and unreadable as text—establish the complete territory within which typographers work [5.27]. The gradation of possibilities among these forms makes for lively variations of style, and infinite possibilities for communication.

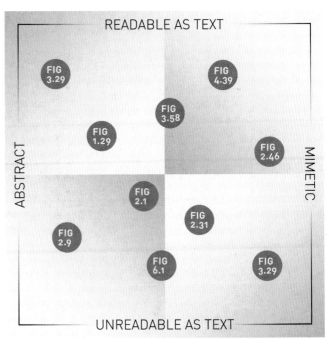

5.27 The full terrain of typographic expression.

///// VISUAL STYLE, RHETORICALLY SPEAKING

REPLICATION AND TRANSFORMATION STYLES

New generations exhume past styles for any number of reasons: novelty, allusion, illusion, reverence. Once historical styles are resurrected and applied anew, their associations shift, and some connotations are lost entirely. Consider two styles, Art Nouveau and Victorian Gothic, which, separated from the complex contexts of their origins and reduced to recognizable, generalized styles, became **codified** by the mid-twentieth century.

When designers apply typographic genres to contemporary work, they are creating what I shall call "replication styles," usually to make some convincing statement about the content. The replication may copy a style exactly, but more typically typographers revise or refine the style somewhat to suit their own, or contemporary, tastes. For instance, the French bakery and brasserie in Manhattan, Balthazar, wanted a visual brand reminiscent of classical Victorian signage. The designer developed the identity to communicate the client's "obsession with authenticity and quality." Balthazar's subsequent success as a luxury retailer led to a third enterprise in wholesale goods, and again the design firm borrowed classical French style from the mid-1800s to give the offshoot brand "a sincere and substantial life of its own." The connotations of this style replication—in the context of a menu that delivers on its promises—help convince readers they are purchasing good food as authentic as a vague original from bygone days. Although the typographers name no specific place, the typography connotes quality baked goods and nineteenth-century charm [5.28].

5.28 Balthazar identity design and storefront signage, 1997. Matteo Bologna, Mucca Design.

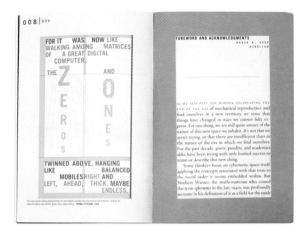

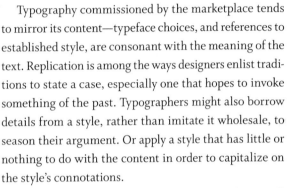

5.29 *101010: Art in Technological Times, 2001. Gail Swanlund. This book's typographic style settles on the side of transformation because it does not derive exclusively from other styles. The work references both vernacular and classical form; it is both bookish and posterish; and each illustrated page seems to follow its own typographic rules that are nonetheless related to the rules set out on other pages.*

Typography commissioned by the marketplace tends to mirror its content—typeface choices, and references to established style, are consonant with the meaning of the text. Replication is among the ways designers enlist traditions to state a case, especially one that hopes to invoke something of the past. Typographers might also borrow details from a style, rather than imitate it wholesale, to season their argument. Or apply a style that has little or nothing to do with the content in order to capitalize on the style's connotations.

By contrast, some typographers create what I call "transformation styles": they innovate within stylistic conventions, or invent wholly new forms relative to accepted style standards. Let's return to the adventures of Art Nouveau and nineteenth-century wood types. Both period styles are themselves historically significant transformation styles. By the mid-twentieth century, however, their qualities were seldom if ever applied by style-conscious designers. If borrowed at all, the styles would have been employed to connote their respective periods of origin. Otherwise, the styles were simply old, of another time. Markedly contemporary typographic approaches would instead speak for the times, in styles that reflected modernism, modern advertising, or modern book production. These styles became the standard in the 1960s and 1970s.

Meanwhile Art Nouveau letterforms and nineteenth-century wood types were bubbling up in pop and subculture arenas, namely in American folk and rock-music ephemera and underground and avant-garde magazines. The re-emergence of such letterforms and wood types may well have been a reaction against "the establishment" and its preferred rhetoric of neutrality, or against decades of advertising kitsch. Whatever the motives, a generation of typographers, designers, and illustrators adopted some aspects of these and other historic styles, reinventing them to serve their own purposes [5.29]. Psychedelia transformed the swooning curves of Art Nouveau typography into mind-bending phantasmagoria. And music culture in the 1970s moved wood types from their practical advertising roots into the visual equivalent of the anthem "sex and drugs and rock 'n' roll."

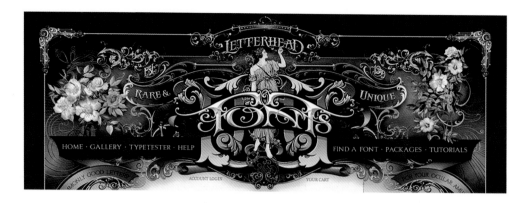

Typographic style that balances replication with transformation, or tends toward the latter, frames content as familiar but not known, surprising but not shocking. Tipping the scale acutely to the side of transformation styles, the reference or source may be as present as a ghost. The rhetorical power of transformation styles depends on their degree of invention, the typography's relative originality in the context of its use.

In recent years new connotative layers have been heaped upon modern, Victorian-era, and Art Nouveau styles alike. Type designers in the early twenty-first century have rediscovered these original styles, many by way of the typographic transformations of the 1970s. Some of these designers replicate the older styles wholesale, some regurgitate a few typefaces, and a rare few reinvigorate the old with new points of view, new form, and sometimes new function [5.30].

Whether replicative or transformative, typographic style is central to cultural expression and communication. Some designers see style as a superfluous layer, subservient to content and, if too self-conscious, outside the scope of serious concern, or even wrong. Whether or not we choose to acknowledge it, any style can be valid and communicative when understood in context.

APPROPRIATION, VERNACULAR, CLICHÉ

The replication and transformation continuum naturally implies imitating, tweaking, reviving, borrowing, and flat-out stealing. A common design strategy is to fit older styles to contemporary contexts that have little, if anything, to do with the historical moment when those styles originated. This kind of appropriation may be motivated by a style's oddity or kitsch factor. Perhaps an old style interacts with contemporary content in a surprising way. Then again, sheer irreverence could be a motive too [5.31].

Since the 1960s, appropriating **vernacular** styles, in particular, has become a common rhetorical tactic. The popular and prolific foundry House Industries was one of the first successful enterprises to draw and digitize typefaces based on "classically relevant lettering" of the 1940s and 1950s, such as popular advertising brush scripts and hot-rod hand-lettered styles [5.32]. These and other "retro" typefaces are typically put to retro purposes, naturally [5.33]. As such,

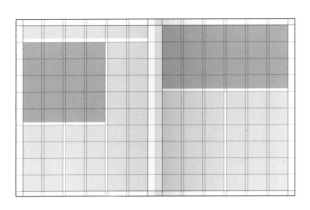
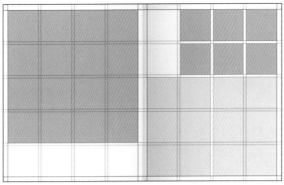

THE TEXT-ORIENTED and **IMAGE-ORIENTED PERIODICAL:** Although these two grid genres share a few governing principles, they differ in one significant way. The former (above left) organizes less prominent images alongside the text, while the latter (above right) unifies larger images and captions. Text-heavy magazine grids not only control hierarchy among headlines, subheads, pull-quotes, captions, and diagrams; they also facilitate last-minute text changes. Image-heavy grid fields tend to be fewer and each cover more area than in text-oriented grids.

CORPORATE COLLATERAL: This kind of grid (right) applies comparable logic to a more extensive system than a series of pages. The grid functions across a wide range of applications by establishing consistent relationships among elements across media and formats, from promotional brochures to information sheets.

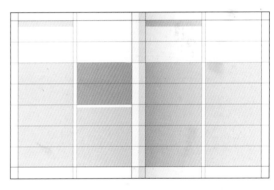

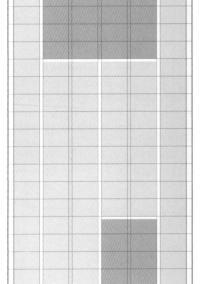

THE NEWSPAPER: This grid (left) relies on columns as well—as few as six and as many as ten or twelve—and the baseline grid plays a critical organizing role. Article lengths tend to be specified by the number of columns and lines they will occupy. Unlike newsletters, newspapers require maximum flexibility to manage multiple kinds of information that change daily or weekly.

THE NEWSLETTER: Taking its cues from the magazine and newspaper grid genres, this grid (right) flows and floats text and images within columnar frames. The typical newsletter template has little regard for such secondary structuring devices as hang lines and baselines because the two or three columns can sufficiently handle short word counts and the occasional photograph or image.

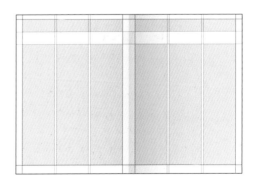

THE WEBSITE: This fairly new grid genre was made possible by Cascading Style Sheets, a system of coding that controls the placement and style of text and images on-screen. When hypertext markup language was introduced in the early 1990s, designers had limited options for placement because basic HTML could position elements only in relation to the upper-leftmost pixel, and to the text line or table with which it shares parameters. Hence the "inverted L" came into being. Readers have come to expect orientation that places universal and sub-navigation menus along the top and left of browser windows.

THE WEBLOG: It stands to reason that the weblog grid should follow a logic similar to that of the website. The proliferation of web-savvy users has helped rapidly to establish this genre. The weblog genre, adapted from the website grid, adds multiple navigational lists to the left and right of the central content. This system is driven less by a grid than by measured pixel standards, for instance consecutive table widths of 200/500/200 pixels or 150/400/150. Doubtless these measures will in time evolve and inspire a grid logic related as much to typographic standards and image presentation as to screen and pixel.

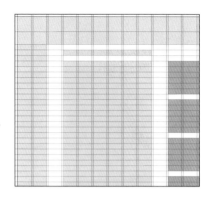

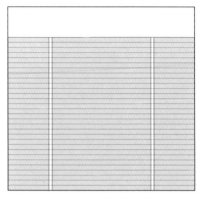

5.36 Online grid genres.

Organizational standards exist for way-finding and environmental signage as well—and for movie posters, invitations, information pamphlets, book jackets, and so on. Just as musical structures prescribe the beats and progressions that go to make up "hip-hop" or "waltz" music, so grid genres anchor the meaning of any content they contain, regardless of the subject. In the end, they emulate rudimentary rules for facilitating sustained reading or navigating reading spaces. Beyond that, these structures can be strictures if not understood for what they are: the stealth conventions of stable, but stock, rhetorical stances. Maximus facillium.

LUCIDITY AND AMBIGUITY

Recall the "crystal goblet" notion that I mentioned in Chapter 2: the proposal that book typography's principal function is transparency. A similar guiding principle for creating typographic messages holds sway among graphic designers: typography should reflect the literal meaning of the content, or, at the very least, not look alien to it [5.37]. This prevailing wisdom implies that content **representation** is always the ideal strategy. So, if we are designing the packaging for fabric softener, the visual claims would include clean or fresh or light or soft, because that's what words like Bounce, Downy, Softy, and CuddleFluff connote; and because that's what fabric-softener packaging tends to communicate. This approach favors lucidity in that the typographic treatment aligns with those of known and understood genres. But what if the manufacturer does not wish to align the product one-to-one with the current genre, or wants to distinguish it from other brands, or to connect with a niche consumer? The designer might then depart from the genre.

5.37 Packaging for Bitch wine, 2005. Jeffery Keedy.

Suppose the typography for packaging a new laundry product is targeted at busy young professionals [5.38]. It might visually represent not only cleanness and freshness, but also hipness and new-techness. The latter two attributes are not common in laundry product packaging that is typically marketed to busy household members. The typography, then, is less lucid because it is in a style that is not generally understood as meaning "laundry product." It is, however, usefully ambiguous.

The term **ambiguity** is often mistaken for vagueness, and therefore the opposite of lucidity. In fact, ambiguity is a rhetorical tactic that functions alongside lucidity to communicate multiple meanings, rather than a single, familiar meaning. A host of products and services that claim environmental friendliness have emerged in the last ten years. To distinguish these "green" products from the existing genres, designers have attached references to contemporary graphic style, or to nature.

Ambiguity expands and deepens content—often adding messages to those that might be present in the text—to convey a range of connotation, including the uniqueness of a product, institution, or publication relative to the competition. Ambiguity can also bring refreshing newness to otherwise predictable clichés.

Both lucidity and ambiguity are useful to clarify and denote complex or layered concepts. Ironic messages, for instance, tend to capitalize on familiar genres (lucid) made less familiar by complicating the relationship between the content and the typography through ambiguity. To understand this further, we need to revisit the connotation and denotation exponents.

5.38 *(top)* Vaska Natural Detergent packaging, 2009. Monica Hernandez, Scott Hickman, and Sarah Labieniec, Tomorrow Partners.

5.39 *(above)* An example of lucidity in logotype design.

MESSAGE SYSTEMS //

By now I hope it is abundantly clear that the simplest typographic decision is the consequence of myriad interrelated influences, fueled by the forces of various systems. Connotation, semantics, and syntax are but a few of the intricacies at work in the tersest logotype [5.39], the most direct poster headline, the briefest bumper sticker. Predicting and harnessing these forces to construct fairly straightforward messages is achievable enough. As content becomes more complex and the desired messages more layered, managing typography within such systems becomes particularly challenging and, commensurately, more fun.

THE CONNOTATION AND DENOTATION EXPONENTS

Language reveals levels of meaning by way of connotation and denotation, concepts introduced in Chapter 1. Take the rise and fall and rise again of Helvetica—the typeface, not the movie (yes, there is a movie). In the decades following its release in 1957 [5.40], Helvetica connoted newness and neutrality, in part because its machine-inspired form appeared to embody rationalist ideals characteristic of the period, compared at least to older fonts that used forms created by the less-than-rational hand of man. International institutions—wanting to promote themselves as progressive but non-threatening—used the über-modern face in identity systems, advertising, and signage. And so Helvetica became synonymous with serious, forward-thinking enterprise. Through usage it came to connote more than

its origins suggested: international trade, reliability, and reasonableness. The face also emerged at a moment when reproduction technologies were gaining speed and extended distribution. Within twenty years Helvetica was being used in nearly every language, and was available to any business. Such ubiquity ensured its diffusion to lowbrow and middlebrow sign manufacturers [5.41], rapid-print shops, and ultimately, desktop publishers. It soon became the obvious flavorless typeface. Eventually, the type family had come to stand for the generic and commonplace. Think of any number of strip malls scattered throughout cities and suburbs from Williamsburg to Walla Walla. Predictably, the typeface lost favor among the forward thinking.

In the mid-1990s a younger generation resuscitated the typeface and re-energized it in fresh applications, though in some cases still referring back to its original usage. The new old typeface suddenly connoted hipness and subculture style [5.42]. No longer generic and flavorless, Helvetica was seen as direct, hyper-understated, representative of an "undesigned" aesthetic, and perhaps even ironic. At least for a while. As these things go, Helvetica became a globe-trotting superstar once again, adopted first by other hipsters, then by mainstream designers and corporate wannabe hipsters, and finally by everybody else wanting to appear stylish.

Today Helvetica is no more reliable or commonplace than scores of other typefaces, yet it has garnered another set of connotations, this time through upmarket retail usage. As of this writing, the typeface connotes simplicity and straightforwardness (trumping neutrality), or friendliness and familiarity, and is therefore still considered "undesigned," or designerly cool. In the article "For Logo Power, Try Helvetica," published in *Business Week* (the masthead of which is a modified Helvetica) in 2007, the journalist Reena Jana observed that major retail corporations have adopted the typeface, including American

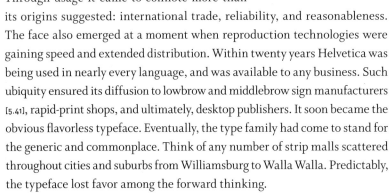

5.40 *(top)* Process notes from the Haas foundry, showing the development of Helvetica.

5.41 *(center)* Post Office sign, 1972.

5.42 *(below)* T-shirt design, 2001. Marieke Stolk, Erwin Brinkers, and Danny Van Den Dungen, Experimental Jetset.

Meet the cast:

ABCD EFGHIJK LMNOP QRSTUV WXYZ

Now see the movie:

Helvetica

A documentary film by Gary Hustwit

5.43 *Meet the Cast*, 2006. Marieke Stolk, Erwin Brinkers, and Danny Van Den Dungen, Experimental Jetset. *Film poster for a documentary about Helvetica.*

5.44 JetBlue logotype, typeset in DIN.

Apparel, the Japanese home-and-office accessory company Muji ("a favorite among design fans around the globe"), and the Japanese avant-garde fashion label Comme des Garçons. She reported that observers believe these usages to be "ironic and subversive, rather than conformist." Christian Larson, the curator of the exhibition "50 Years of Helvetica" mounted in 2008, observed that these design firms "are using Helvetica in a cheeky way . . . aware of major companies' use of the typeface and how the font is allied to the business world." This adds a modern, "snarky" twist, writes Jana, "the graphic design equivalent of a hipster wearing a T-shirt with a pin-striped blazer."[2]

When experts claim that a typeface is perfectly logical, as Matthew Carter and Mike Parker say in the film *Helvetica* [5.43], they are describing its denotative character. Unlike spoken and written words whose denotations arise through use and tacit agreement, typefaces can denote only their formal character and, perhaps, their origins. Helvetica denotes a sans-serif typeface designed by Max Miedinger and Eduard Hoffman for the Haas Foundry, with specific attributes: squared terminals, optically even stroke-widths, uniform counters, and so on. Typeface histories and formal characteristics inspire designers to apply them, but it is the way in which the applications resonate with dominant cultures and subcultures that establishes connotation. In short, cultural use germinates, perpetuates, and sometimes terminates the life of typefaces.

TYPEFACE AS IDENTITY

Typography is an integral player in the visual identities of products, institutions, corporations, and civic and government agencies. The American airline jetBlue Airways bases its image on two primary visual features: the color blue, naturally, and the type family FF DIN [5.44]. Aspiring to be "people-driven," jetBlue claims lower-than-average fares, excellent customer service, and operates under the "core values" of safety, caring, integrity, fun, and passion. This range of qualities and characteristics may seem like a lot for one typeface and color to convey. And so it is. The FF DIN family does offer a no-nonsense and familiar persona, conveyed in part by its similarity to modern, sans-serif typefaces. Compared to more typical typefaces that airlines employed as air travel became ubiquitous, FF DIN looks friendly and trustworthy, particularly when it acts out such phrases as "Let's Go!" and "True Blue."

In the United States, FF DIN has become synonymous with "jetBlue." The visual identity of the company does not rest solely in the typeface, however. The typography also follows rules of application, such as the use of capital letters for certain kinds of message. The degree to which any typeface becomes a defining facet of a graphic identity is proportionate to how extensive is the use, how consistent the application, and how wide the distribution.

FF DIN

German foundry FontFont released the initial family, by the Dutch designer Albert-Jan Pool in 1996. The family has since grown to more than seventy fonts. It is based on DIN 1451, designed in 1936 for use in engineering, transportation, and administration.

Severance
ABCDEFGHIJKLM
NOPQ RSTUVWXYZ
abcdefghijklmnopqrstuvwxyz
„.!?@#$%^&9*()__–"=;:'{}?‹›˜˜
1234567890

Chunk Style
ABCDEFGHIJKLM
NOPQ RSTU VWXYZ
abcdefghijklmnopqrstuvwxyz
„.!?@#$%^&*()__"=;:'{}?<>~`
1234567890

Imagine what a tragedy it would be, though, if such a talented typeface family could play only this one gig. Luckily, while keeping its job at jetBlue, FF DIN can take on any number of other parts, from posters for the New York City Ballet to a bit part in the titles of a romantic comedy (or the headings in this textbook). The typeface can be reapplied in this way because new contexts, content, and configurations obviously create different associations.

Some typefaces are destined for a single, long-running production. One of Ben & Jerry's typefaces, Severance, started out as hand-drawn lettering when the company was a solitary ice-cream store in Burlington, Vermont. As distribution expanded, the letterforms were digitized into a complete <u>proprietary font</u> [5.45, 5.46]. Many companies and publishers elect to commission fonts and families to express the qualities, mission, and content of their enterprise and, more recently, to ensure brand strength. Unilever (the corporation that now owns Ben & Jerry's), Yale University, Nike, Virgin Media, and the Mexico City newspaper *Reforma* are just a few of the organizations that have commissioned type families to distinguish their materials and to accommodate certain typesetting needs. An additional benefit is that some businesses discover that commissioning a proprietary type family is less costly than signing hundreds of individual <u>end-user license agreements</u>.

Once a proprietary typeface is established by the original brand, it is sometimes released and sold to the general public. The Whitney Museum in New York, for instance, commissioned the aptly named <u>Whitney</u> for its signage and print materials. Hoefler/FrereJones extended the family, and released it for public use in 2004. The font has since been assigned to perform in the graphic identity of Delta Airlines, as well as countless other gigs.

Proprietary font or typeface
A type design created for exclusive use by a company or institution, typically commissioned by the end user.

End-user license agreement
Familiarly called "EULA." The legal contract between the manufacturer or designer and the end user of software or a font, detailing how the purchased material may be used and distributed.

Whitney
Designed to be "clear for signage, compact for print," as Hoefler/FrereJones's website states, the family consists of twenty-four alphabetic fonts and twenty-eight numeric and symbol fonts, in several languages.

5.45 *(top)* Severance and Chunky typeface designs. Lyn Severance.

5.46 *(above)* Ben & Jerry's ice cream packaging.

WORDMARKS

While fonts and typography do much of the heavy lifting in identity systems, wordmarks tend to be the more recognizable stars. Designed to be unique in personality and succinct in delivery, these carefully crafted identifiers are almost always present on stationery, websites, packaging, and products, and in advertising [5.47-5.49]. Some globally recognized wordmarks include FedEx,

5.47 Tate logos (wordmarks), 2010.
Wolff Olins.

5.48 Cover for Wright Auctions' *Books on Modernism* catalog, 2005. Rick Valicenti and John Pobojewski, Thirst.

5.49 Sofi handmade soap, 2010. Visual identity by Boris Marčetić and Bratislav Milenković, Popular.

CocaCola, the *Harry Potter* and *Star Wars* film franchises, CNN, eBay, and Disney. Regional examples can be found on sports-team jerseys, automobile fenders, restaurant facades, CD covers, and even government property (think of NASA emblazoned on the side of a spacecraft).

Like symbols and logos, wordmarks represent an entity or enterprise, associating products and services with various explicit or implicit attributes, or attitudes, by way of repeated usage. Wordmarks are compact, as visually distinct as the Apple apple, the Nike swoosh, or the five rings of the Olympic Games. Wordmarks are a subset of symbols, though different in that they are mainly typographic. Designers fit together bundles of letters using distinctive and connotative letterforms joined in **ligatures**, sometimes enhanced with **flourishes** or swashes, or accented with other forms and symbols.

These pithy packages wield communicative power in several ways. First, the designer injects repetition throughout the letterforms to build greater commonality among disparate glyphs. Hence, the alphabetic shapes that make up a name influence formal possibilities. An entity with the name "odopo" offers built-in repetition, whereas "yelloxanitas" asks the designer to deal with a jumble of stems, ascenders, descenders, cross bars, apexes, and counters. Still, wordmark designers can take great liberties with letterforms in the fixed relationship of one or two words; more so than can the type designer creating a complete set of characters, each needing to be readable no matter where it is positioned among others. Also, once a wordmark is established, legibility is less important than quick recognition.

Second, because wordmarks (as true stars) are nearly always on or around the stage—heading up a website or striking a pose on a T-shirt—they gain meaning from all that surrounds them, contexts comprising text or images, products or activities. For instance, if the only element in view is a bold red "ESPN," and if we have had exposure to the Entertainment and Sports Programming Network, we associate the simple mark with a history of related experiences, programming, and personalities.

Understanding what wordmarks are meant to communicate is like learning a new language with a lexicon of one or two words—not terribly difficult. Creating that language for the wordmark of a particular institution is another thing altogether. A typographer's choice of typeface, color, weight, orientation, treatment, and so on prompts connotations and denotations that can reach far beyond those of the institution's obvious business dealings. For instance, graffiti-like forms will gather a host of subculture attitudes and values into the qualities of a sportswear company. Or a manipulated classic roman serif will add historic credibility and elegance to a vintner. No-nonsense block letters identifying a technology company suggest scientific confidence and expertise.

Once the chosen language is established, and readers grasp, share, and build on its meaning, the little yet mighty wordmark carries on its central role as a communicator to global or regional audiences.

GRAPHIC SYMBOLS AS SYSTEMS

I end this chapter with a look at visual languages that are not alphabetic but pictorial, or graphic. Although not typographic per se, graphic symbols as systems are created with similar formal rules that address particular communication needs.

The icons found in many software programs make up such a graphic symbol system. Each visually uniform tool represents a simple message like "pick up a paintbrush here" or "make a box with this." The design of these systems is similar to that of typefaces in that each icon needs to be distinguishable from the next, just as each letter of the alphabet needs a shape that sets it apart from the rest. Yet these icons also communicate that they are of a kind. Common visual attributes indicate that their functions are related. The Universal Symbol Sign system functions to identify places and services in airports, hospitals, and other public places. Whether a symbol points the way to a cash machine, a fire extinguisher, or a place to eat, it communicates in the same visual language as all the symbols within the system so that readers will interpret each as the same kind of identifier.

Whether a person is in Istanbul or Quebec, he will be able to spot the men's bathroom because the featureless silhouette of a figure (sometimes called the popsicle man) stands near the door. Today this language is ubiquitous and therefore understood by people around the globe. Road signs are less universal. Their visual attributes and abstract forms tend to differ from region to region. Still, within a given state or country this system is consistent. Imagine what would happen if every road symbol within a city was different. How would drivers know whether a sign were part of the road system or just a handsome graphic? If every symbol was a different weight, color, and shape, how would drivers distinguish a Stop sign from every other bit of information blaring at them in the environment? The answer is obvious: they wouldn't. Let's hope they're wearing a seat belt.

Some symbol systems represent very private languages, peculiar to a specific activity [5.50]. The system of stripes, arcs, and markers on the tarmac and runways of commercial airports might look like cool super-graphics to the uninitiated, but for pilots and airport personnel, not knowing what they mean would be highly dangerous.

Not all symbol systems are designed to avoid hazard. Design for the Olympic Games, for example, typically includes a symbol system that represents each sporting category—swimming, skiing, volleyball, and so on. This kind of symbol systems functions in concert with the style and voice of the enterprise. The iPhone and iPad revolution has spawned a visual language that has been adopted by every app developer on the planet. That language

5.50 Universal healthcare symbols, 2010. Society for Environmental Graphic Design.

Super-graphics
Large, bold, and high-contrast typographic and graphic elements painted onto walls. The trend emerged in the late 1960s, when the term was coined, and flourished through the 1970s.

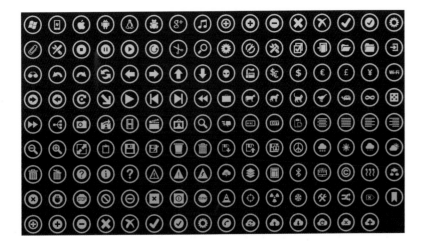

5.51 Screen icons from Windows Phone 7.

enfolds thousands of disparate symbols into one system [5.51]. Each icon communicates to users that the little rounded "glossy" square on their touch screen is, indeed, an app.

PROMPTS

/// **Visit any newsstand** or the periodicals section of a library. Select a few types of periodical (cars, fashion, music, home, science, world affairs) and identify the visual semantics shared among the various periodicals within each genre. In small groups, discuss and list the similarities as they pertain to typography, as well as the different uses of typography in one genre compared to another. *(See "Visual Semantics and Syntax," page 196.)*

/// **Study the delivery of typography** on a few animated web banners. Sketch out the hierarchies and syntax that would be used in each case if the same information were reproduced in print. *(See "The Semantics and Syntax of Hierarchy," page 199.)*

/// **Identify five uses** of simile and five of metonymy in typographic treatments found in restaurant advertising. *(See "Rhetorical Tropes," page 201.)*

/// **Somewhere in the studio** or classroom, set up a large quadrant to map typographic treatments: the word "abstract" on the left side of the area faces "mimetic" on the opposite right; "readable as text" at the top faces "unreadable as text" at the bottom. Pin typography up according to where the work fits best within the four extremes, until the map is full. *(See "Two Extremes—Make That Four," page 206.)*

/// **Typeset an action verb** in a variety of mimetic typefaces and print them out. Position each sheet in a context out in the world and consider whether the typeset verb functions in consonance or dissonance with the context, or is ambiguous. Does the meaning of the text change in each context? How does the presence of the text in that typeface define or direct the meaning of the context? *(See "Consonance and Discordance," page 205, and "Lucidity and Ambiguity," page 214.)*

the disorder

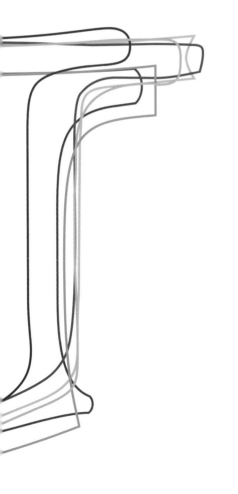

# of things 6

Chapter 6 offers background information about the systems that concern the professional side of the discipline, and the language in which typographers talk among themselves. The section on measuring systems in a variety of media covers traditional measuring schemes, with some historical insight into measurement systems still in use, as well as relational schemes. The chapter also describes the differences between typeface classification and categorization, with introductions to current options for understanding and sorting the variety of typefaces available. Finally, the sections on typographic anatomy, glyph types, and naming conventions serve as references from which to build your typographic vocabulary.

primer

ATA

A point-based typographic measuring system in the United States, sanctioned by the now-disbanded Advertising Typographers Association. There have been several typographic measuring systems used over the last 300 years, each with slightly different values. Efforts to drop the ATA system in favor of metric measurement as a global standard have been slow in gaining support. **> PAGE 230**

BRITISH STANDARD

A section of the British national standards, developed in 1967, that classifies serif typefaces in five categories (Humanist, Geralde, Transitional, Didone, and Slab Serif); classifies sans-serif typefaces in four categories (Grotesque, Neo-Grotesque, Geometric, and Humanist); and includes individual categories for Incised, Script, Blackletter, and Non-Latin. **> PAGE 237**

CHARACTER BOX (EM BOX)

The bounding box that establishes font size in HTML code. The rendered size on screen is determined in relation to the em unit of the specified font, which is a measure borrowed from traditional typesetting. If the font is 10 pixels high, from ascender to descender, the em unit is 10 pixels. **> PAGE 235**

CLASSIFICATION

The categorization of typefaces according to distinguishing characteristics, such as historical origin or formal attributes. **> PAGE 228**

COPYFITTING

The process of fitting text type to a preset area or number of pages by adjusting point size and spacing. **> PAGE 230**

DECORATIVE TYPEFACE

An ornamental typeface characterized by embellishment, and typically used in display sizes. Darius Wells's wood typefaces, such as his Antique Tuscan Outlined (1854), are examples of decorative typefaces. **ILL. 01 > PAGE 237**

DIN

A standard developed by the German national standards institute, the Deutsches Institut für Normung, in 1984 for the specification of type size based on cap-height. The standard includes the recommendation for worldwide adoption of the metric system for digital typography. **> PAGE 232**

01 : DECORATIVE TYPEFACE

02 : EM UNITS

EM AND EN UNITS

Measurements related to the height of the metal body on which a raised letter sits in metal type. The em is equal to the point size; one em of 14 pt type is 14 pt in width. The en is half the size of the em; one en of 14 pt type is 7 pt in width. The measurement is arbitrary in digital type and is determined by the type designer, though the height of capital letters is typically 70% of the em. An em dash (—) is the width of the em and used to indicate a break in the train of thought within a sentence. **ILL. 02 > PAGES 235/246**

INCH

The base spatial measure of United States customary and English imperial units. An inch is one-twelfth of a foot. Officially, typography encounters the inch through the pica system, as a pica is equal to one-sixth of an inch. Though the pica system is perhaps more appropriate due to its integral relationship to the sizing of type and line spacing (leading), inches and fractions of an inch are used widely in the United States as units of measurement in typesetting. **> PAGE 229**

ISO

The International Organization for Standardization, a global consortium of national standards institutes from more than 150 countries. The ISO defines measurement standards for the design and application of typography, as well as paper sizes. In 1975 the ISO adopted DIN 476 paper sizes (first developed in Germany in 1922), which determines the page proportions in publications except in the United States. In the 1990s, the ISO developed standards for printing technology and a uniform character set for electronic messages. **> PAGE 232**

LOCKING UP

The process of assembling all the printing and non-printing elements in place on a letterpress before printing. Lines of type are separated by bars of lead called leading, and surrounded by wood or metal blocks called furniture. These individual components are tightly arranged within a frame, called a chase. Metal turnkeys called quoins are locked and prevent the entire assembly (called a forme) from moving during printing. The forme is attached to the press and printed. **ILL. 03 > PAGE 229**

03 : LOCKING UP

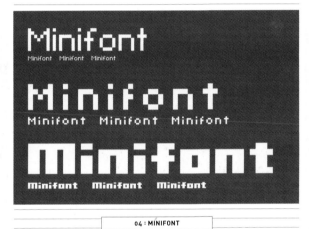

04 : MINIFONT

LINESPACE LESS THAN PT. SIZE

Exquisite Corpses

05 : NEGATIVE SPACING

METRIC SYSTEM

An international system of measurement based on decimals and powers of ten. All spatial units are derived from the meter. The United States is the only industrialized country in the world that does not use the metric system. The DIN system is based on metric measurements. **> PAGE 231**

MINIFONT

A typeface designed for on-screen reading at small sizes. In minifonts, every pixel of character detail corresponds to a pixel on the monitor. Because they are designed pixel by pixel, minifonts do not use anti-aliasing to smooth edges. Minifonts are commonly used for website navigation, software interfaces, and mobile displays. They are sometimes called Flash fonts because they are also used in Flash software. **ILL. 04 > PAGE 234**

NEGATIVE SPACING

The reduction of letterspacing, by kerning or tracking, to a value less than that established by the type designer. Digital fonts have preset spaces between individual letter combinations (kerning pairs) that are represented by "0" in the type specifications of software and that can be adjusted positively or negatively. **ILL. 05 > PAGE 234**

PUNCH-CUTTING

The process of manually cutting characters at a particular point size into one end of a metal shaft to produce a punch. Once finished, the punch is driven into a soft copper or bronze plate to make a matrix. In typecasting, molten metal is poured into the matrix impression to make a sort, a raised metal character. This process guarantees that all versions of the letterform used in printing are identical. **ILL. 06 > PAGE 230**

SET SOLID

Setting lines of type with no additional spacing than what is already accounted for in the design of the font. When the numbers designating point size and line spacing match (for example, 12/12), the type is said to be "set solid." **ILL. 07 > PAGE 232**

TYPE DRAWER

A drawer in which metal sorts for letterpress printing are stored. In letterpress, the term "font" refers to all the characters of a single typeface at one point size. 12 pt Garamond Bold is a font and would be stored in one drawer, 10 pt Garamond Bold in another. Capital letters are stored in one section of the drawer, lowercase letters in another. The typesetter typically removes the drawer and places it on an angled table for composing, with capitals at the top and minuscules at the bottom, hence the designations of uppercase and lowercase. **ILL. 08 > PAGE 230**

06 : PUNCH-CUTTING

LINESPACE EQUALS PT. SIZE

Exquisite Corpses

07 : SET SOLID

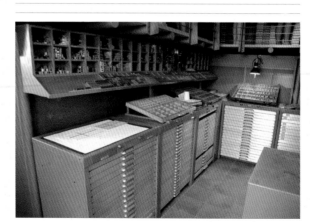

08 : TYPE DRAWER

TYPEFACE ANATOMY

The diagrams opposite are designed to help you identify and describe the parts of a letterform. **ILL. 09 > PAGE 245**

UNIT

The horizontal division of the width of phototypeset letters into uniform increments of the em. Each character is assigned a specific number of units that include the width of the letter and typical spacing to the left and right. Different foundries used different number of units per em (Monotype used 96 units/em, Linotype used 54 units/em). The differences determined how finely letters could be kerned by adding or taking away units. Units are used in digital typography but at a substantially finer increment: PostScript fonts contain 1000 units/em. **> PAGE 230**

THE DISORDER OF THINGS

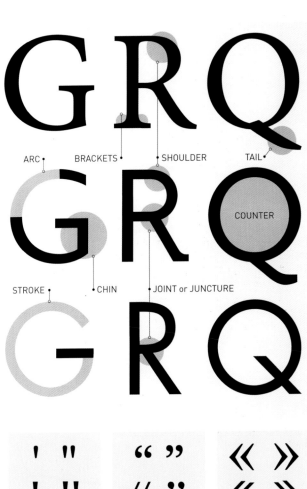

G R Q

ARC · BRACKETS · SHOULDER · TAIL

G R Q

COUNTER

STROKE · CHIN · JOINT or JUNCTURE

G R Q

gaskpitef

LINK · SERIF · BRACKET · STEM or STROKE

BOWL · EAR · SPUR · LEG · TITTLE · FLAG

gaskpitef

DOUBLE STORY · DESCENDER · FINIAL · APERTURE

LOOP TAIL · SINGLE STORY · ASCENDER · EYE

gaskpitef

OPEN TAIL · SPINE · ARM · COUNTER · TERMINAL · CROSSBAR

STROKE · APEX · CROTCH

TVAX

BEAK · VORTEX · CROSSBAR

PRIME MARK

QUOTATION MARK

GUILLEMET

ñ ñ

TILDE

à à

ACUTE ACCENT

æ æ

GRAVE ACCENT

ô ô

CIRCUMFLEX

ö ö

UMLAUT

ž ž

HACEK

ç ç

CEDILLA

ĕ ĕ

BREVE

Å Å

RING

CAPITALS
SMALL CAPITALS
ffl fi fl ff   st ct sþ

CAPITALS
SMALL CAPITALS
ffl fi fl tt   st ct sþ

LIGATURE   DISCRETIONARY LIGATURE

09 : TYPEFACE ANATOMY

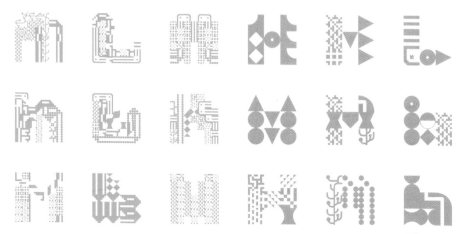

/// **CONTAINING**

You get into a car—say, your older brother's pristine 1982 Honda Civic. The kind of car matters because it dictates how fast you will be able to drive, and how cool (or not) you will feel when driving it. Which side you sit on is predetermined, as are the location and function of the brake and accelerator.

You start the engine and back out straight onto your brother's spotless driveway. Proceeding down the street you drive on one side of the asphalt designated by a painted line, and let the curve of the road and the curb alongside guide you. Already you have been subjected to at least three descriptive systems: the car's construction; its mechanics; and the system of driveways and roads.

Similar descriptive systems in typography influence what is producible, sometimes even what is thinkable. Production systems, for instance— the software and reproduction technologies required to produce and distribute typographic work—influence what you can make, how you work [6.1], and how letterforms behave in any given context. Another descriptive system, typeface **classification**, is one among many systems we call the semantics of the profession. Classification systems lay out terms and categories that professional typographers and type designers use to talk about historical and current type-design activity.

These systems are like gravity in that you cannot see them. They help you stay grounded, but they can also keep you from flying. Unlike gravity, the unseen forces that underpin typographic practice are products of circumstance [6.2]. As such, the systems change continually, owing to technological advances, practical convenience, and commercial viability, among other factors.

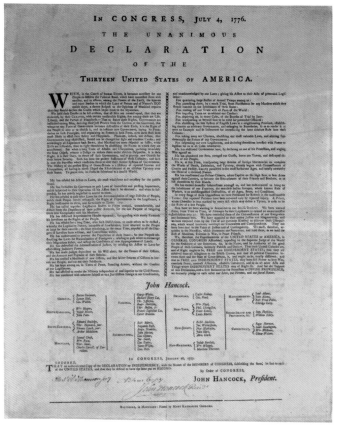

THE DISORDER OF THINGS

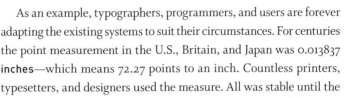

6.1   *(above and opposite, above)* Mobile
Media Lab website design, 2008. Anouk
Pennel and Raphael Daudelin, Feed.
Variants of the letters M and L are designed to
overlay randomly, resulting in hundreds of logo
variations. This degree of variability would have
been impossible before the days of digital production.

6.2   *(opposite, below)* Goddard Broadside, 1777.
This rendition of the Declaration of Independence
is less hastily produced than the Dunlap Broadside
(the first version).

As an example, typographers, programmers, and users are forever adapting the existing systems to suit their circumstances. For centuries the point measurement in the U.S., Britain, and Japan was 0.013837 **inches**—which means 72.27 points to an inch. Countless printers, typesetters, and designers used the measure. All was stable until the personal computer introduced PostScript, and the point changed to 0.013888889 inches to fit an even 72 points into one inch. That change also fitted the standard screen resolution of 72 pixels per inch—a one-to-one ratio of pixels to points. Very tidy. At the time of writing, a remnant of the old system and the new exist side by side in publication software, where "PostScript point" or the "Traditional" point are options when setting up preferences.

Whether working with typography on the computer, on a composing stick, or on a vinyl letter-cutter, typographers follow invisible and sometimes unspoken standards. This chapter looks under the hood, so to speak, to see which descriptive systems are at play in typography, which ones continue to be useful, and which ones are a bit broken.

MEASUREMENT SYSTEMS ////////////

Typographic measuring systems begin with the letterpress, where uniformity is critical because the sorts are physical. The printing process demands that the sorts **lock up** solid on press, one glyph or space packed tightly to another, line following line, all held snugly with furniture formulated to a standardized system. To this end, larger sizes are evenly reducible to smaller sizes. So in the pica and point system, 18 pt = two lines of 9 pt; 24 = two lines of 12 pt; 48 = two lines of 24 pt; 72 = two lines of 36 pt, or six lines of 12 pt, and so on. Such logic served for hundreds of years, and has been adapted to newer technologies because typesetters, designers, and printers understood the system. Even today, some type-production software offers what might seem an odd array of point sizes to choose from: 18, 24, 36, 48, 64, 72, 96. The sizes were standards back in the old days of metal sorts. Today software offers several ways to size typefaces. Visual sliders and scaling tools are the least precise, but enable us to size by eye. Dialog boxes, by contrast, allow us to specify 47.13 points, or 0.655 inches, or 16.62 millimeters, or 47.13 pixels.

SOME WHYS AND WHY NOTS OF TYPE MEASURE

type measures

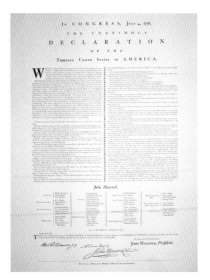

The idea to divide an inch into seventy-two points originates with the Table of Proportions that was proposed in the early eighteenth century by the French typographer Pierre-Simon Fournier Le Jeune. Subsequently, seventy-two equal **units** became the norm for standardizing font sizes. The concept of the inch, though, was not universal. The French Royal inch used by Fournier equaled 27.07 millimeters, or 1.065 American inches. So the Anglo-Saxon point (**ATA**) is very slightly smaller than that of the European Didot system (named after Françoise Ambroise Didot, who refined the Fournier system). The cicero comprises twelve Didot points, or 0.1776 inches. The comparable ATA pica is 0.116 inches shorter, at 0.166044 inches. Fournier's program assigned names to incremental font sizes from 5 pt to 36 pt: *Parisienne* (the smallest, at 5 pt Didot); *Nonpareil*; *Mignon*; *Petit-texte*; *Gaillarde*; *Petit-romain*; *Philosophie*; *Cicero* (12 pt Didot), and so on. Other regions developed similarly peculiar naming systems.

By the nineteenth century, typesetters throughout the printing world offered only a handful of standard sizes, compared to our almost infinite options: 2 through 8 pt was designed for small print, footnotes, equations, captions, and marginalia, and 9 through 14 or 15 pt for body text. The one-point accretion in text sizes allowed for refined **copyfitting**. A choice of 11 instead of 10 pt type would affect text length relative to a fixed line length and page format, and therefore increase the page count and the cost of printing. Larger fonts offered less range: 16 to 28 pt for crossheads and subheads; and 36, 42, 48, 64, 72, and 96 pt for large headlines and titling. The more dramatic jumps ensured visibly distinguishable differences at larger sizes. Fewer fonts at larger sizes also meant more economical use of material and space resources.

A full complement of point sizes from 2 to 96 in metal type would have been impossible to produce or manage in the days of metal sorts [6.3]. The amount of time and resources required would have precluded it. Imagine **punch-cutting** uppercase and lowercase alphabets, including letters with diacritical marks, in every point size. At a speedy four punches a day, a skilled punch-cutter could produce a two hundred-plus character set for each of ninety-one sizes in a little under sixteen years. That's one typeface. Upon completing a single family of four faces he'd be at retirement age, if he survived. Plus, a printer would need **type drawer** space to store and organize every last sort. About 2,160 American cubic feet of type cases. More, if you happened to live in France.

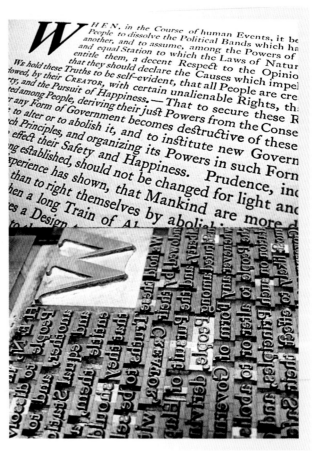

6.3 *Declaration of Independence*, 2009. Mindy Belloff, Intima Press. *A contemporary rendition of the Goddard Broadside is painstakingly true to the original. Refinements in letterpress technology that have been made since the original document was produced in 1777 are evident. The limits imposed by type measure, however, remain.*

Before the eighteenth century, many tiny or massive or sub-point sizes would have been excessively difficult to produce in metal, if not inconceivable. A 3 pt italic, for instance, would have been rare. A punch-cutter or engraver might have been skilled enough to produce the intricate punches, and harder metals might have been alloyed to preserve and transfer their fine detail when cast. Such careful measures would not save the fine work from disfiguring imperfections inflicted by less refined presses, ink, and paper. Didot did introduce a few half-point type sizes at small sizes for reasons that had little to do with quality. He developed them to reconcile two systems: his own with Fournier's. So, within this antique production system, the difference between 17 and 17.25—measures we achieve today with a click—would hardly have justified the effort.

6.4   Nineteenth-century wood type specimens. Hamilton Wood Types.

Massive sizes, such as 576 pt metal type, would have been unthinkable. The sorts would have been expensive to produce, to say nothing of a challenge to lift onto a press bed once composed. The early nineteenth-century demand for bold advertising and large underlined broadsides did, however, inspire a proliferation of wood types [6.4]. Wood is lighter and cheaper than metal, holds sufficient detail for printing at larger scales, and by the late nineteenth century, any size could be produced using a single pattern and a pantograph. (These technologies are discussed in Chapter 4.) The standard sizing of wood types is based on how many "lines" of page height the font occupies. Each line is equal to 1 pica, so 6-line fonts occupy 6 vertical picas (36 pt, or 1 inch); 18 lines, 18 picas (216 pt); and so on. That 576 pt type we mentioned would be 96-line type in wood, or 8 inches. Typographers working with wood types introduced their own system of measurements to serve their particular usage, just as they had done after the invention of metal type.

In the same way that pica and Didot systems supported earlier forms of production and usage, other measuring systems are developing for our contemporary contexts. A current push to adopt the **metric system** worldwide promises to eliminate incongruity and useless precedents for all typographic applications. We can thank the French once again for the metric system, which was devised in the late eighteenth century during the French Revolution, when the National Assembly of France requested the French Academy of Sciences to devise a simple and scientific standard for measures and weights. A unit was first derived from a measure of the Earth's circumference, then larger and smaller units were created by multiplying or dividing the basic unit by 10 and its powers.

Broadside

The largest of the common long, vertical newspaper formats, printed on one side. Also refers to inexpensively produced prints (posters) that have been used since the seventeenth century to distribute information publicly, including political satire, popular ballads, and typeface specimens.

The **DIN** 16507-2 and **ISO** type-measuring systems that dominate Europe today readily convert to the metric system. In Japan, font sizes already fit to "Q"s, one of which is equal to 0.25 millimeters. Despite the fact that the ATA pica is a recognized standard in the international software and font trade, the metric measure appears to be the more robust system. The age-old dream of global standardization could become reality with the metric system, although temporary unease will accompany the transition. Unfortunately for Americans, 72 ATA points equates to an awkward 25.3 millimeters. But if software developers comply, our computers can easily accomplish the conversion.

the type body measure, and beyond

Why do different typefaces of the same point size not always look the same size? Blame the body [6.5]. In the days of metal typesetting, the nominal size of letters was measured by the height of the metal slug that contained the glyph. Point size, then, includes the topmost to the bottom-most parts of characters, accommodating ascenders, uppercase letters, and diacritical marks (whichever is tallest), and descenders. Hairline spaces on top and bottom are added to avoid letters touching when **set solid**. All it takes for metal fonts to be 64 pt is to make sure all the parts are tucked within 64 vertical pt. The baseline, meanline, and capline, though, can sit anywhere inside that measure, limited only by the legibility of each character.

56 POINTS

VERDANA REGULAR

BERNHARD MODERN STD.

ADOBE CASLON REGULAR 43 PT

X-HEIGHT

HELVETICA LIGHT

ITC CASLON 224 STD.

BUREAU GROTESQUE COND. BOOK

Bernhard Modern

Designed in 1937 by
Lucian Bernhard
for American Type
Foundry. The typeface
borrows from
old-style engraver
typefaces that were
popular at the time:
it shares with them
attributes including
small x-heights, tall
ascenders, and
short descenders.

The baseline of Bernhard Modern sits quite low on the body compared to the others shown above. Its x-height-to-cap-height ratio is more pronounced, and the topmost ascender of the l reaches above the uppercase letter, or capline. So, even though the ratio and size look more like 58 pt Caslon Regular, Bernhard registers as 64 pt. Exaggerated ascenders and a baseline positioned low on the body necessitate a rather short descender compared with other typefaces of the same size. According to body-based measure, had the tail of the letter y dropped below the body perimeter, the font would probably be a larger size. Therefore, measuring printed letterforms themselves will not reveal their size.

As computer-aided typesetting was making its ascendancy in the 1960s, designers were already speculating about the problematic body measure within

6.5 Variations in font sizes within type body measures.

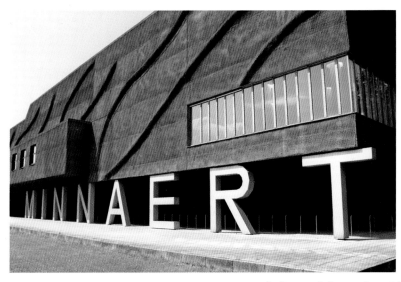

6.6 Minnaert Building, Utrecht University, 1997. Neutelings Riedijk Architecten.

the new technology. Ernest Hoch, an Austrian-British designer, proposed that the nominal size of a typeface be measured (in millimeters) by the height of capital letters, which is more comparable to the visual size than the body point size is. This H-height, as it was named, moves closer to a more objective size description. Séamas Ó Brógáin, the printing officer of the Industrial Development Authority of Ireland, writes that, although the concept was a breakthrough, "it still failed to indicate the true visual size . . . and alienated those who wished to retain mechanical (body) size." In 1983, Ó Brógáin, with Hoch, proposed that the x-height should provide the nominal measure [6.6, 6.7]:

One has only to scan any page of text . . . to see that what constitutes the text is rows of varying character shapes that, in combination, present to the eye a quite uniform pattern . . . created by the x height . . . . Ascenders and descenders, and occasional capital letters, are not sufficient to break this pattern. Here, surely, is the "size" of the type . . . . The concept of a standardised range of sizes is redundant, as digital type can be scaled up or down to any size.[1]

Exactly
Exactly
Exactly
Exactly
Exactly

6.7 X-height as nominal measure.

In the digital realm, a close inspection of typefaces hints at the fact that our pica and Didot systems are breaking down, if not already broken. For instance, the ascenders or descenders of some digital typefaces dip above or below the old point-size body limits (such oddities did exist in metal, but were not common). Additionally, one screen pixel cannot be divided as a point can be. And the Didot measure does not align to the pixel. These measures are also inadequate when applied to large-scale environmental typography: 12 feet is much easier to visualize than 10,368 points.

The common ATA point system is hardly as exact as a slide rule, but then typography is not a science. Typeface engineering, however, requires enough precision to be efficient for production and usage within a variety of technologies [6.8].

MEASURING AND TECHNOLOGY

Typography production software attempts to accommodate all measuring systems in use today, and the consequences can be absurd. In publication software, we can set vertical rulers in points and picas, and horizontal rulers in millimeters and centimeters. WYSIWYG software allows us to scale typefaces (and other elements) by eye, with no measuring required. We can settle on a size of text in relation to screen edges, or other elements, as we scale it. Then we have shortcut keys, which allow us to enlarge or reduce type by points or half-points until it fits our grid. Size is determined, then, in relation to structure. Animation software allows us to scale type over time

"WYSIWYG"

Pronounced "wizziwig." An acronym for "what you see is what you get."

by specifying a beginning and ending point (or pixel) size, say from 12 to 89 pt, over a 2-second duration. On the other hand, we can scale the type to one size and place it in an area on screen (click), then scale it to a larger size and place it in another location (click), and software fills in the incremental size increases between the smallest and largest. Clearly the value and use of nominal measurements are tethered to the technologies we use. Looking back at older technologies will confirm this claim.

Phototypesetting, which I introduced in Chapter 4, produced high-resolution type in sizes ranging from the minuscule to the monumental. A single font on a strip or disk of film could generate sizes from 2 to 72 pt and larger. Stat cameras, a similar photographic technology, reduced and enlarged originals. Designers would specify percentages—anything from 10 percent to 400 percent—to achieve a desired size in picas or inches. Both technologies introduced malleability and, with it, distortion (a characteristic our software readily produces today). This new flexibility rapidly moved measuring from the nice rational system of points and picas to the brink of ridiculousness. Type might be scaled horizontally to 32 percent, and vertically to 239 percent, which created letterforms that were radically alien to those the type designer drew. Letterspacing, word spacing, and line spacing, too, could be manipulated incrementally, by units or percentages. In fact, **negative spacing**, unthinkable in the age of typeset metal, was added to the inventory of nonsensical measures.

Early digital production software offered the same means to manipulate and contort type, nearly beyond measurability. Simultaneously, digital processes initiated the pixel measure in typography. In 1985, Zuzana Licko introduced type families for print, the members of which are identified by their uppercase height in pixels: Eight, Ten, Fifteen, and Nineteen. Ten years and an Internet later, the early web guru Joe Gillespie designed the first "pixel font" to minimize download times when bandwidth was a pathetic 54 kilobits per second (kbs). How exotic to think of font size in terms of data-transfer speed! Gillespie's experiments inspired Flash designers to develop **minifonts**, tiny typefaces designed to occupy as few as five pixels, top to bottom, and very few bytes [6.9]. One professor has taken the concept to the extreme. Ken Perlin, a computer scientist, wanted to design "the smallest screen font that would actually be readable." His Tiny font manages to render the entire Declaration of Independence within 320 × 240 pixels—the size of standard mobile-device screens.

SYSTEM LOGIC

Today we might put our faith in the principle that concrete measures—whether calculated in points, micro-millimeters, bits, or pixels—steady a precarious world. Yet as they submit to scalability in the digital environment, stable ground turns to mush. Luckily, system logic comes to the rescue.

6.8 *(above and opposite)* IDTV brand identity, 2007. Lava. *This identity system is built from a basic square decorated in various ways. Permutations range from signage on the side of a building to rendered images. The system logic is rooted in the square base unit, and is further constrained by a reduced color palette.*

Minifonts can perform amazing feats of (relative) readability in very few pixels.

Minifonts can perform amazing feats of (relative) readability in very few pixels.

Minifonts can perform amazing feats of (relative) readability in very few pixels.

6.9 *(above)* Minifonts.

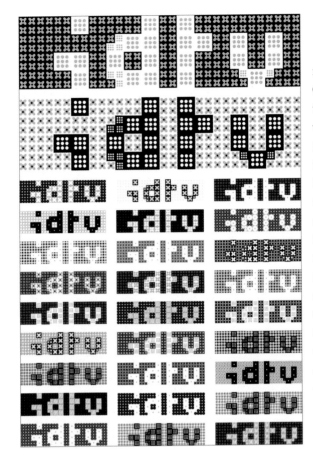

Like print-based body sizes, web-based type size is measured by a **character box**. All similarity ends there. Cascading Style Sheets and XML code specify one of two possibilities for sizing. One is an exact absolute size, which is the nominal size of the character box—16 pixels (px), for example. An increasingly common practice is to specify a relative size of a font. Here, type is measured in either **em** units (1.2 ems is one unit plus two tenths of a unit) or some percentage (say, 76 percent). Relative size specifications render type size on screen in relation to the size of the default font size programmed into the system. So, if a user's preference settings are set at 16 px, then the code that renders a web page on his screen would set the font at 16 px (1 unit), plus two tenths of that unit. The type would be rendered at 19.2 px. If the relative size is set to 76 percent of the default, the web-page code would set the type 24 percent smaller, or 12.16 px. If a reader has set his screen text to default at 18 px, then the code renders the type at 21.6 and 13.68 px, respectively.

Obviously, the collision of the em and the pixel results in some rather complicated math. Web developers use a trick that helps tame the wild decimals. Typical browser software sets text size at 16 px as the default. Because CSS can override the default, a web designer can declare in the code a corresponding font-size value of 62.5 percent. In doing so, she resets the default size to an even 10 pixels (16 × 62.5 percent = 10). Once that parameter is set, she can code font sizes in em units, which scales text to match pixel sizes: 0.9 em = 9 px; 1.5 em = 15 px; 1.8 em = 18 px; and so on. The tactic not only makes for simpler math, but also correlates to the more familiar point-measuring system.

Typographers need to be familiar with the variety and range of measuring systems across media, certainly. But knowing them is only part of our task. To put them to use, we need to understand the systems, and by extension the technologies, within which measures function. Say we select a typeface and set it at 24 points on screen, anticipating its size in print. When we zoom in, what size is it? When we see it reproduced on a website, what is its size? Well, it's relative. Our technologies have rendered the rationality of our measuring systems distinctly relational. As with all digital production, typographic production is moving from nominal to relational measures.

In light of inconsistent standards and the fluidity of our digital tools, the most crucial (and stable) measuring scheme is the base unit. The people who figured out the coding trick described above had a clear understanding of base units, and put them to work. In typogyroscopic terms, ten points or one em might serve as base units in two-dimensional media; in three dimensions, the volume of a brick or a cube might determine the base measure of constructed letterforms; in the fourth dimension, one second might be the base unit from which we build an animation. In principle, any repeatable distance, object, or span of time can be used as a base unit. This unit then becomes the foundation that builds and extends into a measuring system according to the logic of the technology, to the medium, and to project at hand.

The dream of a single, universal system may be impossible to attain. Should one emerge, it will necessarily reflect new technologies, and the dynamic means they afford.

/// CLASSES, NOMENCLATURE, NAME CALLING

If measurement systems seem to be in upheaval, then systems for typeface identification are reaching anarchy. If the truth be known, the naming and categorizing of types has always been unruly. Since the nineteenth century, scholars of typography have worked to devise a lasting terminology that is not rendered obsolete by further typographic advances. Meanwhile, commercial foundries invent terminologies that are not necessarily the same as those of scholars. The two interests develop naming standards to suit different purposes. The scholar attempts to categorize the history of typeface design in order to study its evolution, or to establish a common vocabulary that can be shared with other professionals. The commercial enterprise creates categories that shift with the tides of consumer fancy.

As with any discipline, typography and type design have a specialized language. The names of things have evolved so that typographers, type designers, design scholars, historians, and foundries can talk among themselves. Various "dialects" exist within this specialized language, too. Let's look at a few.

CLASSIFICATION AND CATEGORIZATION

In the beginning, around 1460, when the first European movable types were cut and applied, typefaces evolved in service to the printed book, fulfilling what was seen as type's enduring duty to record and preserve the written word for the precious few who could read. But as other written communication surfaced—printed matter whose job it was to announce, inform, advertise, greet, and direct—type's one noble obligation evolved into a long list of expanding duties, some more honorable than others. Fast forward to the nineteenth-century Industrial Revolution, in which printing presses across continents spewed thousands upon thousands of book pages, plus countless handbills, newspapers, event posters, mail-order catalogs, bills of sale, monthly gazettes, and medicine bottles, all widely distributed for numerous eyes to behold. Add to the endless flow of ephemera and a growing number of storefronts, municipal buildings, the sides of horse-drawn carriages, and railroad cars. Sign painters and wood- and stone-carvers had ample blank surfaces to elaborate on typographic form.

VOX (1954)	BS 2961 (1967)
Humane	Humanist
Gerald	Gerald
Réale	Transitional
Didone	Didone
Mécane	Slab Serif
Linéale	Lineal
–Grotesque	–Grotesque
–Geometric	–Geometric
Incise (Glyphic)	Incised
Scripte	Script
Manuaire	Graphic
	–Blackletter
	–Non-Latin

6.10 The Vox and British Standard classification systems.

In 1921 a French typographer, François Thibodeau, devised a classification system based solely on the characteristics of serifs. Typefaces with triangular serifs fell into the Elzévir category, named after an influential sixteenth-century Dutch printer. Rectangular serifs with brackets fit into Didot, owing to their similarity to eighteenth-century types originating in France. Rectangular serifs the thickness of which equaled the stroke-width were named Egyptiennes. And typefaces without serifs comprised the antiques, a common name for the relatively few sans-serif faces in existence at the time. Curiously, no category recognized the Frakturs, nor the hundreds of **decorative** display faces designed in the nineteenth century, as though an entire era of typographic invention evaporated into the realm of fantasy. True, the typefaces and times tended to favor the phantasmagoric, but still, they did exist in the physical world. We have plenty of proof.

Nonetheless Thibodeau's system attempted to represent the typographic terrain as perceived at the time. And perhaps it was sufficient, but not for long. By 1935 developments of a different sort had eliminated the viability of such systems. A crop of unique typefaces, serif-less and with names like Futura, Kabel (German for "cable"), and Metro, sprang up to celebrate the age of the machine. In a profession that had been dominated by serif typefaces for hundreds of years, the promise (or threat, as some saw it) of an expanding range of modern experimental typefaces would forever alter the typographic landscape.

The twentieth century gave birth to multifarious new letterforms, revived or updated historical ones, and favorites that were extended into comprehensive families. Classification systems were proposed, adopted, revised, or rejected in an attempt to collect the abundance of typefaces into understandable categories. The most enduring system in North America to date finds its roots in the Vox classification system, conceived by another Frenchman, Maximilien Vox, in the 1950s. The system was adopted in England as the **British Standard** in 1967 (after some revision) [6.10], and modified slightly for U.S. standards. The initial Vox system recognizes nine broad categories. The British Standard added blackletter and Non-Latin types, yet other elaborate and non-traditional types from a century before remained banished. The U.S. version remedied the oversight, however slightly, with its decorative and display category [6.11].

These systems held sway throughout the twentieth century. The philosophy "if it ain't broke, don't fix it" may have applied, but it is probable that too few people could find the wherewithal to straighten out a formidable tangle.

OLD STYLE Adobe Jenson	O	en famille
TRANSITIONAL ITC New Baskerville	O	en croute
MODERN Bauer Bodoni	O	en daube
SLAB SERIF Memphis	O	en poste
SANS SERIF ITC Franklin Gothic	O	en masse
NEO-GROTESQUE Univers	O	en garde
HUMANIST Gill Sans	O	en pointe
LATIN Latin CT	**o**	**en suite**
SCRIPT Bickham Script	*O*	*en passant*
BRUSH Mistral	O	*en brosse*
BLACKLETTER Wittenberger Fraktur	O	en prise
NON-LATIN		
DECORATIVE / DISPLAY Cottonwood	O	EN FACE

6.11 American Standard classification system. *These classes do not represent the full range of typefaces in existence. In particular, "Non-Latin" is loosely defined: it enfolds any typeface not based on the Roman alphabet, such as Arabic and kanji glyphs. Latin-based typefaces are classed according to formal differences. On the other hand, non-Latin typefaces are classed according to glyphic difference.*

Futura

The first widely adopted geometric typeface. Futura was designed by Paul Renner and released in 1927 for the Bauer type foundry. Long and even vertical strokes punctuate optically perfect circles and semicircles, suggesting machined precision.

Kabel

Originally designed by German calligrapher Rudolf Koch and released by the Klingspor foundry in 1927. The name of this geometric sans serif refers to the new transatlantic telephone cable.

Metro

William Addison Dwiggins designed this geometric sans-serif typeface for the U.S. foundry Mergenthaler Linotype. It was released in 1930.

The late 1960s and early 1970s introduced a plethora of new photocomposition faces, and specimen books grew fat with hybrids too difficult to classify. Meanwhile "decorative" and "display" typefaces spanned more and more of their pages. In 1969, the designer and educator Rob Roy Kelly published his collection of nineteenth-century wood types [6.12] in the seminal book *American Wood Type, 1828–1900*. Another book, *Nineteenth-Century Ornamented Typefaces* (1938) by the British typography scholar Nicolete Gray, was republished in 1976. Both brought attention and scholarship to bear on the typographic inventions of the previous century. Typefaces which in previous decades had suffered neglect were here presented as having made significant contributions to typographic history. The books raise a question, though, that continues to haunt neat freaks: where to put "Antique, Tulip Ornamental" and "Tuscan Condensed, Light Shade" or "Antique Amalgamation Shaded"? The young classification system was already beginning to show its limits, to say nothing of its predilection for traditional, classical typefaces, despite the irrepressible imagination of foundries and designers responding to the demands of the moment.

The type foundry of the British Monotype Corporation presented thirty-four categories in its specimen book of 1970, in an apparent attempt to include a wider array of typefaces, and to guide buyers through the morass. Some categories echoed the Vox system, but the terms were jumbled—mixing, for instance, such font categories as italic with formal and historical ones like monoline and transitional. (Today, Monotype lists nearly one hundred "classifications" on its website.)

From 1985 to 2000, thousands of digital typefaces reached the market. Bona-fide type designers, alongside amateurs, created digitized typefaces based on traditional fonts, hybrid fonts, and completely new font types. To anyone paying attention, classification had a mess on its hands. The Slovakian type designer Peter Bilak notes that technological progress challenged the relevance of existing systems: "Digital typefaces negated the existing categories, and typefaces were no longer limited to serif and sans serif but also included such styles as 'semi-serif' and 'mixed.' The new typefaces forced the creation of their own categories."[2]

So foundries got creative. In 2000, the respected foundry and font distributor FontShop sorted its range into eight categories: typographic, geometric, amorphous, ironic, historic, intelligent, handwritten, and destructive. A visit to the site in January 2006 found a new set of categories, with staggering numbers of typefaces in each: sans (4,300), serif (4,589), script (3,023), display (8,051), slab (1,274), Pi&Symbols (1,274), blackletter, (400), non-Latin (3,890), OpenType (466), pixel fonts (17), and the commercially attractive

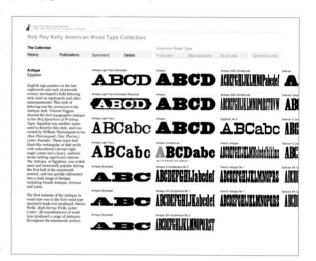

6.12 Rob Roy Kelly American Wood Type Collection website. Design Division, Department of Art and Art History, University of Texas at Austin.

6.13 Font Bureau website showing current categories.

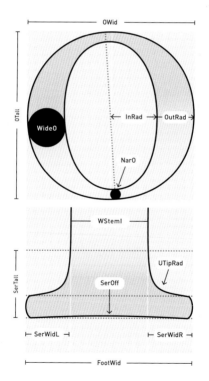

6.14 The Tag Game, 2012. *MyFonts.com's tagging system that identifies font characteristics according to users' votes.*

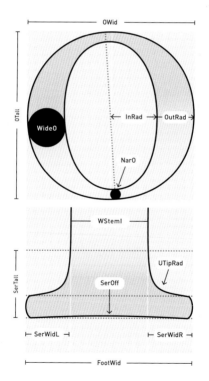

6.15 PANOSE system. *The diagram represents a handful of more than sixty measurements used in this system to determine the attributes of a typeface: OWid = set width; SerWidL = left serif width; OutRad = outside radius in relation to the inside radius (InRad); WideO = widest point of the stroke.*

category, free fonts (no number). Checking in June 2009 revealed that the eleven categories had been narrowed to eight classifications, followed by subcategories including genre, period, application, subclasses, and "special collections called 'FontCases' curated by FontShop experts." In April 2011 the eight categories remained, the FontShop expert evolving into "staff picks" and "award winners."

Classification assists experts and scholars, whereas categories assist sales. Online foundries and font distributors categorize typefaces within familiar classification rubrics, as well as other formulations, suggesting how the typefaces have been or might be used [6.13]. Sometimes they are sorted according to what they connote. One distributor includes: a "hot/cold" category, featuring icy-looking typefaces or ones that appear to be ablaze; "brand names" (complete alphabets designed after famous logotypes); and my favorite, "hard to read." Another distributor sorts by mood or impression, including macabre, fashionable, alien, and corporate. A third distributor sorts its inventory through its own classification system, as well as those of four other popular digital foundries.

A few font distributors attempt categorization using <u>tags</u>, whereby any number of terms might lead to the perfect choice of typeface. Select "fat" from the <u>tag cloud</u> at MyFonts.com, for instance, and brush scripts, geometric sans, novelty, and grotesques join ranks—twenty-six typefaces that would be sorted quite differently were they submitted to traditional classification. Using the mechanics of social networking, MyFonts hosts "The Tag Game," which asks users to agree or disagree with tag descriptors, then tallies the responses [6.14]. While this tactic is uniquely democratic (anyone who registers may play), we can safely conclude that we are some distance from sorting out the sorting issue.

CLASSIFICATION IN CONTEXT

The typographer and type scholar Robert Bringhurst echoes the sentiments of most when he states that type design is not a science but an art, affected by subjective factors and in dialog with society, technology, and history. It is, therefore, in constant flux. Cases in point: the now common "geometric" class would not have existed before Futura, Bauhaus, and Kabel; neither would the class of "modern" types have made sense without the designs of Didot and Bodoni in the eighteenth century.

Bringhurst, along with several other stalwart souls, has posited alternatives to Vox and the like, attempting in the process to allow for future developments. Settling on a single system, though, is fraught with obstacles. By definition, classification captures historical precedents and trends, after the fact. How could anyone have included "digital" as a class in 1954? Additionally, classification systems reflect the subjective priorities of people who develop them, and of those who think similarly about the things being classified. While the practical benefit of understanding and scrutinizing typefaces is obvious to practitioners and scholars, the type designer John Hudson cautions against systems of classification that "cease to be an aid to thinking about a subject."

Tags

A form of metadata. Users assign words or brief phrases to online content, which is used to categorize data and retrieve conceptually related content.

Tag cloud

Also called a "weighted list": a visual representation of user-generated tags that describe website content. The more frequently a tag is applied, the larger or fatter is its visual presence within the cloud. Each tag links to the complete list of data associated with a tag. The concept was introduced in 1995.

The system becomes problematic when it "forces people to think in a particular way or . . . is an esoteric means of excluding outsiders."[3]

The longevity of any classification system is determined by its usefulness to the discipline it serves. Hewlett-Packard, for example, patented the PANOSE typeface-matching system, which was developed to stabilize typography on screen [6.15]. The system uses digits to represent the formal attributes of any font, including "serif tip roundness" and "slant angle." When a font is specified in CSS code, software automatically compares it to available fonts on the computer operating system receiving the data. The PANOSE system determines the closest possible font match, so if the one specified by the browser is not found, another with the highest corresponding attributes is selected in its stead. PANOSE sorts groups of typefaces into distinguishable classes that are useful to designers wanting to manage typography in user-controlled media.

The Type-Expertise Universal Font Classification System, still a work in progress, was developed primarily for commercial contexts, using the Internet's entire font database and the collective intelligence of users. This universal and multicultural system intends to identify classes of every digital typeface available for download, informed by existing classification systems, distributors, type designers, user experience, and application.

On the other hand, an academic context inspired Catherine Dixon to develop what is now known as the Dixon Classification System, which is useful largely for historians and type designers [6.16]. Eight descriptive characteristics of a typeface—its font construction, shape, modeling, terminals, proportion, weight, key characteristics, and decoration—intersect with five "sources," including "decorated," "handwritten," and "nineteenth-century vernacular." The source criterion describes generic influences on the form of the typeface, and identifies larger groups into which existing categories might be placed. Another factor is "pattern," which identifies common, recurrent sources and configurations of formal attributes. Dixon's revolutionary structure is different from previous classification systems in that no typeface is forced into a category that might only barely represent its attributes, nor are any typeface designs omitted. Rather, a typeface is brought to the framework and categorized within a matrix according to how it reflects multiple characteristics. Subsequently, a description of each typeface is built according to the terms of its classification.

Less ambitious but equally thoughtful proposals have set up categories to incorporate the scores of typefaces that have either eluded universally

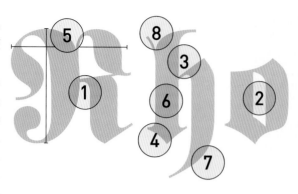

6.16 Dixon classification system. *Inclusion in any given category is based first on formal characteristics. A timeline showing when typefaces surfaced (not shown) helps refine the classification of typefaces according to the degree to which a design is original and/or is based on already existing designs.*

6.17 *Seu Juca: Conserta se Tenis*, 2009. Priscila Farias. *Sample of Seu Juca typeface, inspired by hand-lettered type Farias found in Brazil.*

Dixon: Formal Attributes

1. Construction
2. Shape
3. Modeling
4. Terminals
5. Proportion
6. Weight
7. Key Characteristics
8. Decoration

accepted classification or have simply been considered unworthy of inclusion. The designers and professors Priscila Farias and David Shields, for example, have independently developed rubrics that provide frameworks for studying overlooked typefaces, and for designing new ones.

Farias, a native of Brazil, proposes a typology to distinguish between the many digital typefaces inspired by Brazilian vernacular lettering since the 1990s. She speculates that her five categories—non-specialist, specialist, idiosyncratic, rustic, and urban—may be valid for similar typefaces originating throughout Latin America [6.17], and could "be relevant to the analysis of type design in other parts of the world."[4]

Shields developed a classification system as he catalogued the wood types of Rob Roy Kelly's collection, mentioned earlier, which is archived at

		BODY			TERMINAL				
		INVERSE	LIGHT WEIGHT	CONCAVE	FURCATED	POINTED	WEDGE	BEVELED	ROUNDED
SERIF Roman	FAT FACE								
	OLD STYLE								
Antique	EGYPTIAN	French Antique	Skeleton				Runic		
	CLARENDON	French Clarendon	Ionic				Latin	Grecian	
	TUSCAN			Antique Tuscan	Tuscan	Tuscan		Mansard	
SANS SERIF Gothic	LINEAL								
	ARTICULATED	Gothic Italian							
	TUSCAN	Gothic Tusc. Italian	Gothic Tuscan						

6.18 Shields categorization of Rob Roy Kelly Wood Type collection. *This matrix places only those typefaces included in the collection. As research on the subject advances, however, these categories provide scholars with clear categories within which so-called decorative typefaces can be placed.*

6.19 Periodic Table of typefaces, 2009. Camdon Wilde, Squidspot.com.

the University of Texas, Austin. Kelly had theorized that the vast range of letterforms designed in the nineteenth century evolved from three primary serif styles—roman, antique, and Gothic. Building from this notion, Shields set out a matrix for organizing Kelly's collection in order to analyze and record it [6.18]. What began as a pragmatic means of understanding the 150 archived wood types in the collection evolved into a matrix that not only captures the attributes of each typeface, but also proves a "surprisingly useful tool for generating new forms." By combining characteristics described within the matrix, typographers might "assemble a type with a unique set of attributes."[5]

Whether inspired by professional, commercial, or academic concerns, classification and categorization systems help designers, producers, users, and scholars make sense of the vast and curious range of typographic forms. And, of course, we humans simply have a proclivity for sorting things. The type historian Paul Shaw once published a list of the "Top 100 Types of All

Time," culled from a survey of members of the Type Directors Club. A designer later translated the list into a tongue-in-cheek "Periodic Table of Typefaces" [6.19]. This playful mash-up of the Periodic Table of chemical elements with popular opinion reveals just how creative our ordering systems can be.

MORE FUZZY CATEGORIES

naming types and weights

Another wholly unreliable set of descriptions are font names and weights. We cannot know what the font is like just because we know its name. Jonathan Hoefler observes with some humor the current state of affairs:

Terms restricted to typography often have multiple or even contrary meanings, leading to such delightful oxymorons as Serif Gothic and Times Roman Italic. The terms 'Antique', 'Gothic', and 'Old English' are among typography's most widely used, and entertainingly they are also among its most convoluted: 'Antique' can mean a slab serif (Antique No. 3), a sans serif (Antique Olive), a humanist book face (Zapf Antiqua), or moreover anything which looks old (Caslon Antique); just as 'Gothic' can refer to a sans serif (Franklin Gothic), or a blackletter (Totally Gothic), or occasionally both (Gothic Gothic). 'Old English' is a hornet's nest, best avoided altogether.[6]

An exchange on the typography forum Typophile about the term "Gothic" gives some insight into how some typefaces become labeled. The term describes both sans-serif fonts (Franklin Gothic) and blackletter fonts (Gothic Textura). Uli Stiehl, author of the online essay series "The Font Forging Industry," offers a linguistic explanation. He speculates that when sans serifs were new, early in the nineteenth century, people found metaphorical terms to describe them. Three such words culled from historic or cultural contexts were applied to the then new phenomenon of sans-serif typefaces: Doric, grotesque, and Gothic. "The metaphorical use of the term 'Doric' fell into disuse both in America and in Europe," writes Stiehl. "'Grotesque' became the predominant word in Europe, especially in Britain and Germany . . . [while] 'Gothic' became the predominant word in America." Another contributor to the forum confirmed that "Gothic" was used by early nineteenth-century American type founders, and that it is often misused to classify blackletter typefaces. An alternative, or perhaps simultaneous, explanation is that the new sans-serif typefaces were perceived as "grotesque" by type aficionados and printers. Justin Chodzko, a British lettering artist, adds that the word "Gothic," as applied to hand-drawn blackletter from the Middle Ages, was a disparaging term during the Renaissance, "applied to most, if not all, medieval art and architecture, associating it with the European tribes that had destroyed Rome and the classical civilization the Renaissance was trying to revive." The type designer Nick Shinn suspects that there was "an

Doric
Originally referred to an ancient Greek dialect. When used in design discourse, the term principally refers to the Doric architectural style, characterized by plain and sturdy lines, as compared to the more elaborate Ionic and Corinthian styles.

6.20 Garamond cuts, 2006. Peter Gabor.

GARAMOND SIMONCINI
Hambourgefons

ADOBE GARAMOND
Hambourgefons

GARAMOND MONOTYPE
Hambourgefons

GARAMOND BERTHOLD
Hambourgefons

GARAMOND ITC
Hambourgefons

GARAMOND STEMPEL
Hambourgefons

Flyweight	112 / 50.8
Bantamweight	118 / 53.5
Featherweight	126 / 57.2
Lightweight	135 / 61.2
Welter	147 / 66.7
Middle	160 / 72.6
Heavy	200 / 90.7

6.21 Champion Gothic typeface family, 1990. Jonathan Hoefler.

ITC BERKELEY OLDSTYLE BOOK

Hello. I am a book weight.

ODILE REGULAR

And I am a regular weight.

ITC BERKELEY OLDSTYLE BOLD

I am bold compared to my book weight. However, I am really rather timid.

ODILE SEMIBOLD

I am a semibold. In this company, I look like that bold just above.

ITC BERKELEY OLDSTYLE BLACK

I am a black weight.

FRANKLIN GOTHIC NO. 2

I am a roman, and heavier than all of you.

6.22 Naming weights. *The typefaces within a family are named in relational terms: a semibold, for instance, is named as such in relation to the family's regular and bold.*

element of irony at play, as type founders proudly adopted the name Gothic, by which their clients half-mockingly referred to the new style."[7] To complicate matters, multiple versions of historical typefaces have been designed over the years. Garamond, Bodoni, and Caslon have been revived by type designers and foundries, each interpreting the original differently, often building from a range of historical sources. Each "cut" may have the same or a slightly variant name [6.20]. Current digital versions of Bodoni, for instance, are named ITC Bodoni, Poster Bodoni, Bauer Bodoni, Bodoni Antiqua, Monotype Bodoni, Berthold Bodoni Antiqua, and WTC Our Bodoni. And there are more. All these versions are in fact unique designs, sometimes bearing only a general resemblance to the original, because individual hands, and sometimes profit-oriented motives, brought them into being.

Typefaces are forever being "imitated," or, as Stiehl would have it, blatantly forged. Let's look again at the history of Helvetica. Throughout the 1960s and 1970s, Haas foundry's original Helvetica family was distributed by Linotype, and was in high demand, but this original typeface could be used only in Linotype typesetting machines. The font's popularity prompted other typesetting companies, such as Compugraphic and Alphatype, to design clones that would work within their own proprietary technologies. Under such monikers as Triumvirate, Helios, Megaron, and Newton, typesetting enterprises were able to capitalize on the new geometric sans serif (also called neo-grotesque) rage. Even today, dozens of Helvetica lookalike fonts exist digitally, with Microsoft's <u>Arial</u> among the most widespread.

Multiply the naming of fonts by the naming of weights, and the situation becomes almost comical. Jonathan Hoefler cleverly named his Champion Gothic family members after weight divisions in boxing: because the letterforms borrow from wood types that were frequently used in nineteenth- and twentieth-century boxing broadsides, but more importantly because Hoefler designed the family for use in *Sports Illustrated* headlines, the faces are aptly named Bantamweight, Featherweight, Welter, and so on [6.21]. The range of heaviness, though, is not as appreciable as are the set-widths, which range from super-narrow to very wide. So, while we should enjoy Hoefler's wit, his categories serve his own intentions more than they submit to standard naming conventions, about which he is clearly knowledgeable.

The visual appearance of font weights—ultra thin, thin, light, regular, medium, bold, semibold, extra-bold, ultra-bold, black, extra-black—varies

Arial

Originally named Sonoran Sans Serif, the font was designed by a ten-person team led by Robin Nicholas and Patricia Saunders in 1982. The name changed when Microsoft installed it as a TrueType in their 1992 Windows software. Arial is now a standard sans serif included in most operating systems.

from typeface to typeface. Semibold should refer to a middle version weighing in somewhere between regular and bold. And "black" in typographic language indicates a face blacker than a bold. But if the 14 pt fonts shown on the previous page [6.22] were to be our only reference, we might just as well call bold "sorta-bold" and semibold "almost-black-bold." In this comparison, black would be "not-so-black." Franklin Gothic No. 2? Now there's a nice black—or would that be extra-bold?

The type designer Adrian Frutiger, aware of such inconsistencies, devised a numbering system for his typeface family Univers (one of the first Neo-Grotesques), assigning two defining digits to each of twenty-one weights and widths [6.23]. The scheme was a revolutionary idea when it was released in 1954, and effectively identified this smallish, contained family. Today, though, OpenType and other digital font systems allow for hundreds of weight variations within a given typeface, limited only by the willingness of a type designer to draw them, or the ability of software to generate them. If a new family of fonts extended from 1 to 200, with decimals of sub-weights and postures added along the way, how would it be possible to know the difference between #75.69 and #92.75?

Another number-naming system is applied to the remarkable digital typeface History, which is more of a typeface constructor than a family of fonts. The designer, Peter Bilak, engineered twenty-one sets of independently drawn strokes, serifs, and decorative details to align to an invisible skeleton of roman capitals. Each set occupies a separate "layer" within his web-based software History Remixer, a digital tool Bilak devised that sets text input by a user [6.24]. Activating a layer in the Remixer applies that set of characteristics to the words being set. Deactivating a layer eliminates that set of details. Bilak designed the twenty-one sets to reflect typical typographic forms from history, categorized into four kinds of attribute: bases (strokes), serifs, fills, and ornaments. The twenty-one sets borrow from humanist, Renaissance, transitional, Baroque, script-like, early grotesque, and nineteenth-century vernacular types, as well as contemporary digital ones:

The most interesting things happen when various seemingly incompatible elements are combined. Just try combining pixel letters with Didot-like serifs, or put nineteenth-century slab serifs on top

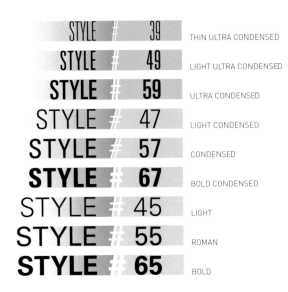

STYLE #	39	THIN ULTRA CONDENSED
STYLE #	49	LIGHT ULTRA CONDENSED
STYLE #	59	ULTRA CONDENSED
STYLE #	47	LIGHT CONDENSED
STYLE #	57	CONDENSED
STYLE #	67	BOLD CONDENSED
STYLE #	45	LIGHT
STYLE #	55	ROMAN
STYLE #	65	BOLD

6.23 Original Univers family numbering system. *The system is theoretically sound, but it is no more practical, nor understandable, than language-based naming systems.*

6.24 *(below and opposite)* History Remixer, 2008–12. Peter Bilak, Jan Šicko, and Ondrej Jób, Typotheque. *The individuation made possible by this software precludes devising a system that would forever stabilize naming systems for typefaces.*

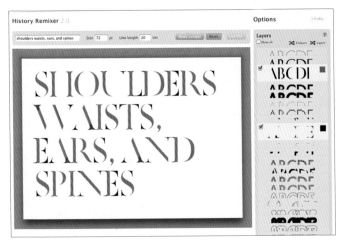

THE DISORDER OF THINGS

of a renaissance construction. While careless use can generate freakish results resembling Frankenstein's monster, more careful experimentation can produce not only amusing, but surprisingly fresh and usable typeface samples.[7]

Assigning numbers rather than names was certainly the most appropriate way to label the components of this innovative system. Additionally, the interface allows a user to select intuitively from options that are shown visually, rather than from a list of names or numbers. The numbers probably serve primarily as identifiers, useful when purchasing individual fonts from the full twenty-one options. Once a typographer makes her choices from the assortment, she might name her combination whatever she chooses, since the next typographer will create something wholly different.

ears, tails, and other typographic arcana

Many letter parts are named after human anatomy—arms and ears, for example. Letterforms can also have shoulders, waists, throats, spines, and eyes. Some letters even have tails—the inspiration here clearly non-human. Many

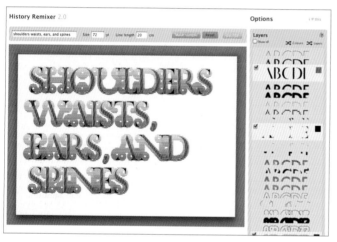

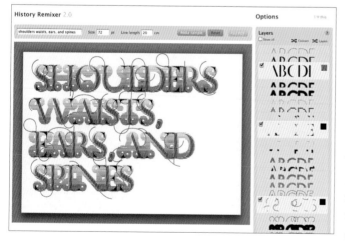

of these metaphors make sense when compared to the parts they describe: the eye of a lowercase e is the space enclosed by the stroke in the top half; the spine of an s is the central curvature; the shoulder of a lowercase n is the curved part at the top of the letter. One would think, then, that the part that looks like a mouth—the opening in the bottom half of a lowercase e, for example—might be called a mouth. But it is called an aperture.

These **typeface anatomy** terms for the Latin alphabet are more stable than font names and weights, although not everyone agrees on which terms are used when. Sometimes a bowl is called a counter. A vertical stroke might be referred to as a stem or a stroke or a bar.

The truth is that many such anatomical terms are less familiar to designers. More than a few earnest and successful practitioners have at some point needed to point to a detail and say "that thing there." This may not be terribly professional, but it is workable as long as the item in question is visible to others who are in on the discussion. Designers use only a handful of terms regularly in daily practice, such as crossbar, aperture, bowl, terminal, serif, ascender, descender, stem, counter, and apex. Knowing even these few separates the expert from the word-processing jockey [6.25].

In addition to the arcana of typographic anatomy, a myriad of glyphs used in other languages calls for some study. A typographer should know the major diacritical terms: the Germanic umlaut, the Central European háček, the cedilla in French and Portuguese (and formerly Spanish), and the tilde in Portuguese and Spanish. One should know that some European and Asian languages use guillemets rather than quotation marks. Many typographers need to know the marks adapted from European languages and put to varying uses in African and Native American languages. Add to all these the ampersand, caret, circumflex, asterisk, dagger, and dozens more—each with a special function.

Then there are the more subtle differences between glyphs, with each modification bearing a name. In Chapter 2 I discussed how using prime marks rather than quotation marks or apostrophes ensures the scorn of experts. Similarly, the em and **en** dashes are very like each other to the undiscerning eye, yet to the experienced typographer they are distinguishable from each other, as they are from hyphens. We typically use an unspaced em dash or a spaced en dash to separate parenthetical phrases within a sentence. The unspaced en dash is used to connect dates and other number spans. The hyphen signals compound words, or connects a word that is split by a line break.

To help those who have not memorized the name of every glyph in every language, type-production software often includes a handy tool that displays glyphs across a matrix, sorted by keyboard location (augmented with the necessary keystroke combinations to access the more obscure ones). Knowing the names of every single glyph and diacritical mark may seem pointless to everyone except the typo-hotshot. Professionalism, though, requires typographers to comprehend the variety of these glyphs and marks at the very least, and to understand that each plays an important role in properly representing language.

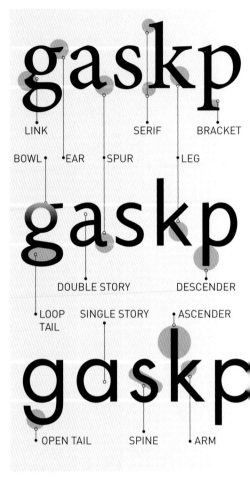

6.25 Typeface anatomy chart (detail). *See the full illustration on page 227.*

See the full illustration on page 227.

PROMPTS

/// **Get to the bottom** of why a typeface is classified as "Old Style," "Transitional," or "Modern." When did these classes of typefaces emerge and who devised them? What typeface innovation spurred the differences? Write a story from the perspective of someone deciding to shift from the precedents. *(See "Classification and Categorization," page 236.)*

/// **Once you understand** the distinctions among the above classes, go to a major font-distributor website and search the three categories. Which typefaces of those listed are consistent with the attributes of the classification? What might be the rationale for naming or tagging a typeface that has only some, or none, of the attributes? *(See "Classification in Context," page 239.)*

/// **Stage a debate** among your classmates wherein one team defends the trueness of one version of a typeface against a team defending another version. Warning: the resulting debate could end up an absurd comedy. *(See "Naming Types and Weights," page 242.)*

THE DISORDER OF THINGS

NOTES

CHAPTER 1: RELATIONAL SYSTEMS

1. Barnard, Malcolm, *Graphic Design as Communication*, London and New York, 2005, p. 68

2. Kepes, György, *Language of Vision*, 1944, repr. New York, 1995, p. 13

3. Heller, Steven, "To the Letter Born," *New York Times* online, April 2, 2008, http://campaignstops.blogs.nytimes.com/2008/04/02/to-the-letter-born/#more-164

4. Hepworth, Katherine, "Yes We Can: Barack Obama, Graphic Design and Liberal Democratic Process," http://www.re-public.gr/en/?p=352

CHAPTER 2: READING SYSTEMS

1. Neruda, Pablo, "Ode to Typography," trans. by Carlos Lozano, *Chicago Review*, 17, no. 1 (1964), pp. 10–20

2. Long, Nick and Susie Long, *S book 3: Interviews with Typographers*, London, 2006, p. 78 (Kitching), p. 101 (Mahoney)

3. Ruder, Emil, *Typographie: A Manual of Design*, Teufen, 1967, p. 6. Weingart quoted from Long, Nick and Susie Long, *S book* 3, p. 157

4. Licko, Zuzana, "Lo-Res," 2001, http://www.emigre.com/EFfeature.php?di=101

5. Shaikh, A. Dawn, "The Effects of Line Length on Reading Online News," *Usability News* 7, no. 2 (2005)

6. Barnard, Malcolm, *Graphic Design and Communication*, p. 24

7. Gillespie, Joe, "Alien Typography," Digital Web Magazine, July 10, 2001, http://www.digital-web.com/articles/alien_typography/

8. http://laikafont.ch/About_eng.html

CHAPTER 3: FORMAL SYSTEMS

1. Warde, Beatrice, "The Crystal Goblet, or Printing Should be Invisible," 1932, repr. in *Looking Closer 3: Classic Writings on Graphic Design*, ed. Michael Bierut et al., New York, 1999, p. 56

2. Gombrich, E. H., *The Sense of Order: A Study in the Psychology of Decorative Art*, London and New York, 1984 (2nd edn), pp. 4–5

3. Dwiggins, W. A., *Layout in Advertising*, 1929, repr. New York, 1948 (rev. edn), pp. 54–55

4. Tschichold, Jan, *The Form of the Book: Essays on the Morality of Good Design*, ed. Robert Bringhurst, trans. H. Hadaler, Vancouver, 1991, repr. 1997, pp. 47, 42

5. Müller-Brockmann, Josef, *Grid Systems in Graphic Design: A Visual Communication Manual for Graphic Designers, Typographers and Three-Dimensional Designers*, Sulgen, 1996, p. 12

CHAPTER 4: MATERIALITY

1. Lemon, David, posting on Type Design discussion list, August 2, 1999, reposted at http://typophile.com/node/36209?page=2, August 22, 2007

2. http://www.christianschwartz.com/houston.shtml

3. Gill, Eric, *An Essay on Typography*, 1931, repr. Boston, 1993, p. 25

4. Goudy, Frederic, *Typologia: Studies in Type Design and Type Making*, 1940, repr. Berkeley, 1978, p. 151

5. Gill, Eric, *Eric Gill: Autobiography*, 1941, repr. Cheshire, CT, 1969, p. 120

6. Staples, Loretta, "Typography and the Screen: A Technical Chronology of Digital Typography, 1984–1997," *Design Issues* 16, 2000, p. 33

CHAPTER 5: LANGUAGE SYSTEMS

1. Tragesser, Matt, Christian Schwartz, and Rudy VanderLans, "The Story of Los Feliz," *Emigre* 61, 2002, republished at http://www.emigre.com/EFfeature.php?di=102

2. Reena, Jana, "For Logo Power, Try Helvetica," *Bloomberg Businessweek*, May 14, 2007, http://www.businessweek.com/innovate/content/may2007/id20070514_464789.htm

CHAPTER 6: THE DISORDER OF THINGS

1. Ó Brógáin, Séamas, "Typographic Measurement: A Critique and a Proposal," *Journal of Institute of Printing* 27

2. Bilak, Peter, "History: Design Concept," http://www.typotheque.com/fonts/history/about/concept

3. Online forum discussion on typeface classification at http://typophile.com/node/9757

4. Farias, Priscila, "Brazilian Vernacular Type," paper presented at ATypI conference, Mexico City, 2009

5. Shields, David, "Unpacking Obscurity: Categorizing 19th C Types," *Design Inquiry*, no date, http://designinquiry.net/failagain/12/test-10/

6. Hoefler, Jonathan, "On Classifying Type," *Emigre* 42, 1997, repr. in *Texts on Type*, eds. Steven Heller and Philip B. Meggs, New York, 2001, p. 204

7. Online forum discussion at http://typophile.com/node/78479

FURTHER READING

Abbink, Jeanette, *3D Typography*, New York, 2010

Albinson, Ian, et al., eds., *Graphic Design: Now in Production*, Minneapolis, 2011

Bain, Peter, and Paul Shaw, eds., *Blackletter: Type and National Identity*, New York, 1998

Baines, Phil, *Type & Typography*, New York, 2005

Barnard, Malcolm, *Graphic Design as Communication*, New York, 2005

Bartram, Alan, *Futurist Typography and the Liberated Text*, New Haven, 2005

Bellantoni, Jeff, and Matt Woolman, *Moving Type: Designing for Time and Space*, Crans-Près-Céligny, 2000

Berry, John D., ed., *Language Culture Type: International Type Design in the Age of Unicode*, New York, 2002

——, ed., *U&lc: Influencing Design & Typography*, West New York, NJ, 2005

Binns, Betty, *Better Type*, New York, 1989

Blackwell, Lewis, *20th-Century Type*, New Haven, 2004

Boutros, Mourad, *Arabic for Designers*, West New York, NJ, 2006

Bringhurst, Robert, *The Elements of Typographic Style*, Point Roberts, WA, 1992

Carter, Sebastian, *Twentieth-Century Type Designers*, Aldershot, 2002

Chappell, Warren, and Robert Bringhurst, *A Short History of the Printed Word*, Vancouver, 1999 (2nd edn)

Cheng, Karen, *Designing Type*, New Haven, 2006

Dodd, Robin, *From Gutenberg to Opentype: An Illustrated History of Type from the Earliest Letterforms to the Latest Digital Fonts*, Vancouver, 2006

Drucker, Johanna, and Emily McVarish, *Graphic Design History: A Critical Guide*, Upper Saddle River, NJ, 2009

Felici, Jim, *The Complete Manual of Typography: A Guide to Setting Perfect Type*, Berkeley, 2012

Garfield, Simon, *Just My Type: A Book about Fonts*, London, 2010

George, Alain, *The Rise of Islamic Calligraphy*, London and Berkeley, 2010

Gerstner, Karl, *Compendium for Literates: A System of Writing*, Cambridge, MA, 1974

Gill, Eric, *An Essay on Typography*, 1931, repr. Boston, 1993

Goudy, Frederic W., *Typologia: Studies in Type Design and Type Making, with Comments on the Invention of Typography, the First Types, Legibility, and Fine Printing*, Berkeley, 1977

Heller, Steven, ed., *The Education of a Typographer*, New York, 2004

——, and Louise Fili, *Stylepedia: A Guide to Graphic Design Mannerisms, Quirks, and Conceits*, San Francisco, 2006

——, and Philip B. Meggs, eds., *Texts on Type: Critical Writings on Typography*, New York, 2001

Hochuli, Jost, *Designing Books: Practice and Theory*, London, 1996

Jaspert, W. Pincus, W. Turner Berry, and A. F. Johnson, *Encyclopaedia of Typefaces*, London, 2008

Jubert, Roxanne, *Typography and Graphic Design: From Antiquity to the Present*, Paris, 2006

Kelly, Rob Roy, *American Wood Type 1828–1900: Notes on the Evolution of Decorated and Large Types*, Saratoga, CA, 2010

Kinross, Robin, *Modern Typography: An Essay in Critical History*, London, 2004

Lawson, Alexander S., *Anatomy of a Typeface*, Boston, 1990

Loxley, Simon, *Type: The Secret History of Letters*, London and New York, 2004

Lupton, Ellen, *Letters from the Avant-Garde: Modern Graphic Design*, New York, 1996

——, ed., *Period Styles: A History of Punctuation*, New York, 1988

Massin, Robert, *Letter and Image*, New York, 1970

McLean, Ruari, ed., *Typographers on Type: An Illustrated Anthology from William Morris to the Present Day*, London, 1995

Mirsky, Lawrence, and Silvana Tropea, *The News Aesthetic*, New York, 1995

Morison, Stanley, *A Tally of Types*, Cambridge, 1973

Müller-Brockmann, Josef, *Grid Systems in Graphic Design: A Visual Communication Manual for Graphic Designers, Typographers and Three-Dimensional Designers (Raster Systeme für die visuelle Gestaltung: ein Handbuch für Grafiker, Typografen und Ausstellungsgestalter)*, Sulgen, 1996

Ogg, Oscar, *The 26 Letters*, New York, 1983

Perfect, Christopher, *Rookledge's International Typefinder: The Essential Handbook of Typeface Recognition and Selection*, New York, 1983

Pohlen, Joep, *Letter Fountain: The Anatomy of Type*, Cologne, 2011

Poynor, Rick, *No More Rules: Graphic Design and Postmodernism*, New Haven, 2003

Robinson, Andrew, *The Story of Writing*, New York, 1995

Rosendorf, Theodore, *The Typographic Desk Reference*, New Castle, DE, 2009

Ruder, Emil, *Typographie: Ein Gestaltungslehrbuch (Typography: A Manual of Design/Typographie: un manuel de création)*, Sulgen, 2001

Smeijers, Fred, *Counterpunch: Making Type in the Sixteenth Century, Designing Typefaces Now*, London, 1996

Swann, Cal, *Language and Typography*, New York, 1991

Tracy, Walter, *Letters of Credit: A View of Type Design*, Boston, 1986

Triggs, Teal, *Type Design: Radical Innovations and Experimentation*, New York, 2003

Tschichold, Jan, *The New Typography: A Handbook for Modern Designers*, Berkeley, 1995

——, *The Form of the Book: Essays on the Morality of Good Book Design*, Point Roberts, WA, 1991

Unger, Gerard, *While You're Reading*, New York, 2007

Vinh, Khoi, *Ordering Disorder: Grid Principles for Web Design*, Berkeley and London, 2011

Walker, Sue, *Typography and Language in Everyday Life: Prescriptions and Practices*, Harlow and New York, 2001

West, Suzanne, *Working with Style: Traditional and Modern Approaches to Layout and Typography*, New York, 1990

PICTURE CREDITS

The authors and publishers are grateful to the individuals and institutions cited in the captions. Additional credits and information are given below.

0.2 Peter Forsberg/Alamy **0.6** Photo Jennifer Farrell, Starshaped Press **0.8** Creative director, art director, producer, animator, and faculty mentor: Brent Barson; writers, designers, and animators: Jessica Blackham, Annalisa Estrada, Meg Gallagher, John Jensen, Regan Fred Johnson, Colin Pinegar, Wynn Burton, Olivia Juarez Knudsen, Casey Lewis, Reeding Roberts, Deven Stephens; editors: Brent Barson, Annalisa Estrada, Reeding Roberts, Meg Gallagher; photographer: Wynn Burton **Primer 1**: 11 © Niklaus Troxler, 13 Blossomy typeface design by Kapitza, 15 © Nico189 (Nicola Laurora), 19 Carol Mullen, 30 Designed by Roger Cook and Don Shanosky, 35 Carol Mullen **1.4** © Turner Entertainment Networks, Inc. A Time Warner Company. All Rights Reserved. **1.5** Photo Tim Magee Photography **1.12** Copyright Guardian News & Media Ltd., 2005 **1.15** Photo Peter Mauss/Esto **1.17** © The Arizona Board of Regents. Reprinted by permission of the University of Arizona Press **1.20** Courtesy FSI Fontshop www.fontfont.com **1.33** Photo Able Parris **1.35** Obama 08 Campaign **1.36** Yale University Beinecke Rare Book and Manuscript Library **1.37** Photo Justin Staple **1.38** Label courtesy Bill Even, nutritionfactsmaker.com **Primer 2**: 07 Mike Abbink, Saffron Brand Consultants, 14 Photo Kiril Kapustin **2.5** Copyright Guardian News & Media Ltd., 2012 **2.16** Copyright intégral Ruedi Baur Paris, photograph Akatre **2.17** Photo Alex Madjitey **2.18** Used by permission. © SIL International **2.21** Photo Tine Harden **2.25** Project design and development by Remon Tijssen, Fluid; art directors, writers, creative directors: Matt Ferrin and Sam Mazur, SS+K; chief creative officer: Marty Cooke, SS+K; developer: Marco Christis, Blixem Med **2.27** Photo Michael Jones; illustrators: Paul Mort, Mark Conahan, Don Rood **2.28, 2.29** Photo Tom Otterness and Diane Bondareff; illustrator: AdamsMorioka, Inc. **2.32** Photo Dan Reynolds **2.36** Photo Alberto Rigau **2.37** © 2009 Juliet Shen. Font licenses owned by the Tulalip Tribes of Washington **2.38** Photo Frank H. Jump, Fading Ad Blog **2.39** Courtesy Marcos Weskamp. http://newsmap.jp **2.40** Photo Ryan Pescatore Frisk **2.42** Courtesy MadeThought **2.43** Courtesy GoogleEarth **2.48** Photos Cameron Wittig **pp. 102–3** © Andrea Tinnes **Primer 3**: 18 Penabico Script typeface design by Iza W and Paulo W, Intellecta Design **3.2** Photo David Lewis Taylor **3.16, 3.19–3.22** Reproduced by permission of Penguin Books Ltd **3.23** Photo Brian Francyzk and Thea Dickman, Wright Auctions **3.25** Photo Jan Middendorp **3.28** Photo Craig Mod **3.38** Courtesy Robin Meek **3.46** Stuart Gregory/Getty Images **3.49** Photo and illustration Tim Kelleher **3.50, 3.52** Copyright Oxford University Press **3.53** Photo Tomas Whitmore **3.55** Photo Studio Rainer Mutsch **3.57** Courtesy Armin Vit, UnderConsideration LLC **Primer 4**: 04 Photo Victoria and Vitalina Lopukhiny, 05 Cari Nakanishi, Miemiko Atelier, 12 Designed by Thomas Couderc, Helmo; includes photographs by Olivier Roller and Tendance Floue, 14 Cari Nakanishi, Miemiko Atelier, 15 Photo Carlos Alejandro, 17 Tobias Battenberg, 22 Ryan Pescatore Frisk and Catelijne van Middelkoop, Strange Attractors Design,

23 Art director: Adam Duplessis, designer: Nancy Harris Rouemy, typographer: Patrick Griffin, 26 Wood type designed by Arthur Larsen, Horton Tank Graphics; photo Shehrzad Maher **4.4** Photo Henning J. Krause **4.5** Reproduced by permission of the Huntington Library, San Marino, California **4.7, 4.8** Photo Carlos Alejandro **4.15** Photo and illustration Kevin Steele **4.17** Photo Justin Manor **4.19** Photo Faythe Levine **4.21** Photo Magnus Cederholm **4.23** Programming: Brook Elgie, Erick van Blokland, Tal Leming **4.24** Courtesy Hatch Show Print, a division of the Country Music Foundation, Inc. **4.26** Photo Lampo Leong **4.28** Photo Mahir M. Yavuz and Ebru Kurbak **4.30** Photo Palette Industries Inc. **4.32** Photo Tiffany Wardle **4.34** Photo Elmo Bass, taken in Indian Trail, NC, 2007 **4.35** Printer and photographer: Studio on Fire; illustrator: Cleve Smith **4.38** *VAS: An Opera in Flatland* © 2002 Steve Tomasula. Art and design © 2002 Stephen Farrell. Reproduced courtesy University of Chicago Press **4.41** Photo Annemieke Spruyt **4.42** Photo and illustration Jackie Lay **4.43** Little But Loud: photos by M-36 (lettering) and Shelley Anderson (still life); Let 'Em Eat Cake: photos Johnny Miller (lettering) and Chris Mottalini (still life) **4.44** Photo Mastromatteo + Steen **Primer 5**: 01 Hans Christian Øren and Christina Magnussen, 03 Nelly Script Flourish typeface design by Font Brothers, 08 Photo Bruce Evans **5.2** Photo Don Shall **5.6** Photos Koichi Miura (cover) and Brigitte Lacombe (spread) **5.7** Writers: Dave Eggers, Lisa Pemrick, Jon Adams, Anna Ura, Dan Weiss, Jennifer Traig; product photographer: Vanessa Chu; studio: visitoffice.com **5.8** Photo and illustration Jon Sueda **5.12** Photo Brigitte Lacombe **5.16** Book cover copyright © 2003 by Alfred A. Knopf, a division of Random House, Inc., from *The Druid King* by Norman Spinrad. Used by permission of Alfred A. Knopf, a division of Random House, Inc. **5.21** Photo Peter Ovesny; illustration Racquel Youtzy **5.22** Draftfcb Portugal, Lisbon, Portugal **5.23** Photo courtesy Experimental Jetset **5.33** Illustration AdamsMorioka **5.37** Lettering by Mr. Keedy **5.38** Product design by Jochen Banks, Studio Banks **5.40** From *Helvetica Forever: Story of a Typeface*, Lars Müller Publishers, 2009 **5.41** Photo Nick DeWolf **5.44** Courtesy JetBlue Airways **5.45** Used by permission from Ben & Jerry's and Lyn Severance **5.46** Used by permission from Ben & Jerry's **5.48** Photo Brian Francyzk and Thea Dickman, Wright Auctions **5.49** Photo Darko Ristić **5.50** 155 symbols designed by students under the supervision of faculty at California Polytechnic State University, University of Cincinnati, Iowa State University, and Kent State University **Primer 6**: 03 Photo Brad Cornelius, 08 Photo Kristian Bjørnard **6.2** Library of Congress, Washington, D.C. **6.4** Image courtesy Bill Moran and Jim Moran, Hamilton Wood Type Museum, Two Rivers, Wisconsin **6.6** Photo Matthijs Borghgraef, Neutelings Riedijk **6.7** Courtesy Harry Parker and Font Bureau, Boston, MA **6.12** Courtesy David Shields, University of Texas at Austin **6.15** Courtesy MyFonts: www.myfonts.com **6.19** Illustration Camdon Wilde **6.20** Illustration Peter Gabor. Originally published in *Le Monde*.

ACKNOWLEDGMENTS

I owe the realization of this book to Meredith Davis, who initiated the series, gave me the opportunity to write the book, and, as a mentor and a model, offered encouragement and guidance. I am grateful, too, for William Temple's support as I committed my concepts to words, and little by little, drafted the chapters. He graciously weathered a sometimes fitful process.

I thank the many talented designers, type designers, artists, and photographers who granted permission to reproduce their work for the benefit of future students. Behind-the-scenes contributors include Master of Graphic Design students at North Carolina State University—Cady Bean Smith, Steve Harjula, Matthew Muñoz, Alberto Rigau, and Michèle Wong—who ably accomplished research and preliminary design. I appreciate their willingness and enthusiasm. Fellow educators, who commented on drafts of the manuscript, offered useful advice: Sibylle Hagmann, Katie Meaney, Silas Munro, Martha Scotford, and William Temple. I appreciate their generosity. I am grateful for my many colleagues and dear friends who never stopped cheering, especially those who listened, corroborated, debated, and promoted the ideas: Caryn Aono, Anne Burdick, Louise Sandhaus, and Gail Swanlund. Other design educators from Europe and the U.S. took time to discuss their perspectives on typography pedagogy: I acknowledge in particular those people who responded to the book's content at the TypeCon conference in Atlanta, Georgia, in 2009; and those who participated in the typography pedagogy workshop at the AIGA National Conference in Phoenix, Arizona, in 2011. Their receptiveness helped to affirm the book's relevance.

This volume would not have been published without the obliging people who assisted in and attended to myriad details: Sally Nicholls, Nate Schulman, and graduate students Matthew Manos and Sarah Needham from the Art Center College of Design helped acquire image permissions; Nida Abdullah and Brian Johnson selflessly assisted with production; and the indefatigable editorial staff at Thames & Hudson's College Publishing division did the yeoman's work of translating my intentions into an accessible textbook. I am truly grateful to all. And finally, I am exceedingly fortunate to be the beneficiary of my family's unwavering support and pride throughout the process.

Typeface families used in the book design: FontFont: FF DIN; The Font Bureau: Whitman.

Typefaces and families used in illustrations: Adobe (from the Adobe Font Library): Aachen Bold, Caslon Pro, Garamond Pro, Jenson Pro, Bauer Bodoni, Bauhaus, Bembo, Bickham Script, Blackoak, Briem Akademi, Briem Script, Calvert, Circus Ornate, Clarendon LT, Cooper Black, Copal, Copperplate Gothic, Courier, Didot, Engravers LT, Fette Fraktur LT, Franklin Gothic, Futura, Giddyup, Gill Sans, Goudy, Helvetica, Helvetica Neue, ITC Avant Garde, ITC Berkeley Oldstyle, ITC Bookman, ITC New Baskerville, ITC Tiffany, Madrone, Magnesium MGV Grime, Minion, Mistral, Monoline Script, Motter Corpus, Rockwell, Snell Roundhand, Stencil, Times New Roman LT, Univers LT, Trajan Pro, Verdana; Berthold: City; Process Type Foundry (Courtesy of Nicole Dotin): Anchor, Bryant, Elena, Fig, Maple, Klavika; The Font Bureau (Courtesy of Harry Parker): Bureau Grotesque; FontFont (Courtesy of FSI FontShop International GmbH): Legato; Hoefler/Frere-Jones: Champion Gothic; House Industries (Courtesy of Rich Roat): House Sampler United Stencil; Kontour (Courtesy of Sibylle Hagmann): Elido (Kontour), Cholla (Emigré), Odile (Village); MyFonts: Banner, Besley Clarendon, Clarendon Heavy, Cooper Swash; Latin CT Not Wide, Latin Wide D, Rodeo Roundup, Woodbadge; P22: LTC Record Title, LTC Forum Title; Underware (Courtesy of Bas Jacobs): Liza Display Pro, Dolly; Independent: C&C Red Alert; Cross Stitch Delicate; Ferox, Frank, Luvbug (Courtesy of Miles Newlyn); Natalya, Natalya Monoline (Courtesy of Jeremy Dooley); Quadratis; Uni 05-54.

INDEX

Page references in *italic* refer to illustrations. Headings in **bold** refer to terms defined in the primers.